FITNESS TO PLEAD

OXFORD MONOGRAPHS ON CRIMINAL LAW AND JUSTICE

Series Editor

ANDREW ASHWORTH CBE QC

Emeritus Vinerian Professor of English Law, All Souls College, Oxford

This series aims to cover all aspects of criminal law and procedure including criminal evidence. The scope of this series is wide, encompassing both practical and theoretical works.

OTHER TITLES IN THIS SERIES

Criminal Justice and Taxation
Peter Alldridge

In Search of Criminal Responsibility
Ideas, Interests, and Institutions
Nicola Lacey

Character in the Criminal Trial
Mike Redmayne

Preventive Justice
Andrew Ashworth and Lucia Zedner

Homicide and the Politics of Law Reform
Jeremy Horder

The Insecurity State
Vulnerable Autonomy and the Right to Security in the Criminal Law
Peter Ramsay

Manifest Madness
Mental Incapacity in the Criminal Law
Arlie Loughnan

The Ethics of Plea Bargaining
Richard L. Lippke

Punishment and Freedom
Alan Brudner

Prosecuting Domestic Violence
A Philosophical Analysis
Michelle Madden Dempsey

Abuse of Process and Judicial Stays of Criminal Proceedings
Andrew L.-T. Choo

A Philosophy of Evidence Law
Justice in the Search for Truth
Hock Lai Ho

The Criminal Justice System and Healthcare
Edited by Charles A. Erin and Suzanne Ost

Rethinking Imprisonment
Richard Lippke

Killing in Self-Defence
Fiona Leverick

Delayed Prosecution for Childhood Sexual Abuse
Penney Lewis

Lying, Cheating, and Stealing
A Moral Theory of White Collar Crime
Stuart P. Green

Defining Crimes
The Special Part of Criminal Law
Edited by Anthony Duff and Stuart P. Green

Criminal Responsibility
Victor Tadros

Proportionate Sentencing
Exploring the Principles
Andrew von Hirsch and Andrew Ashworth

Appraising Strict Liability
Edited by Andrew Simester

Fitness to Plead

International and Comparative Perspectives

Edited by
RONNIE MACKAY
WARREN BROOKBANKS

OXFORD
UNIVERSITY PRESS

OXFORD
UNIVERSITY PRESS

Great Clarendon Street, Oxford, OX2 6DP,
United Kingdom

Oxford University Press is a department of the University of Oxford. It furthers the University's objective of excellence in research, scholarship, and education by publishing worldwide. Oxford is a registered trade mark of Oxford University Press in the UK and in certain other countries

First Edition published in 2018

Impression: 1

Published in the United States of America by Oxford University Press
198 Madison Avenue, New York, NY 10016, United States of America

British Library Cataloguing in Publication Data
Data available

Library of Congress Control Number: 2018930389

ISBN 978–0–19–878847–8

Printed and bound by
CPI Group (UK) Ltd, Croydon, CR0 4YY

For Sally (M) and Glenys (B), whose love and support continues to keep us both fit for purpose.

Foreword

Should we be glad or sorry that so few people are found 'unfit to plead' in a criminal trial? We should certainly be surprised. In England, 7 per cent of people in contact with the criminal justice system have a learning disability; 25 per cent of people in prison have a learning disability; 25 per cent of women and 15 per cent of men in prison reported symptoms indicative of psychosis; and growing numbers of older people are sentenced to imprisonment, in part because of the growing number of prosecutions for historic sex offences.[1] These add up to many thousands of people. Of course, not all people with a learning disability, or psychosis, or the mental frailties of old age are unfit to plead. But it is a fair bet that there are more than the roughly one hundred a year who are found unfit in England and Wales.

Before 1991, when the inevitable result of a finding that the defendant was unfit to plead was indefinite detention for treatment in hospital, reluctance to raise the issue was understandable. Even now, as Rudi Fortson points out from a practitioner's perspective, raising the issue may set in motion a train of events that were not expected or desired. Some defendants may prefer to plead guilty to a lesser charge; others may adamantly deny involvement in the offence rather than raise a mental health issue; or a legal representative may make a tactical decision not to raise it because in his view it is not in the defendant's best interests to do so. An acquittal is obviously preferable to a finding of unfitness, even now. When is counsel bound to follow his client's instructions in the matter?

Quite apart from practical and ethical considerations of this kind, the issue raises profound questions of principle. On the one hand, how can it be fair, and consistent with our notions of dignity and autonomy, to subject a person to the criminal process who is not able to play a proper part in it? On the other hand, unless the matter can be dealt with by diverting an obviously unfit person from the criminal justice system, the public rightly expects that people accused of serious offences, especially of a violent or sexual nature, should be brought to trial and, if guilty, dealt with accordingly.

But what do we mean by being unfit? Should the test be limited to the ability to understand what is going on in a criminal trial—the well-known *Pritchard* test as explained by the trial judge in *R v M (John)*? Or should that be broadened to the test adopted by the European Court of Human Rights, of ability to participate effectively in the criminal process? And should the ability to participate effectively encompass not only understanding but also decision-making capacity? Under the Mental Capacity Act 2005, in England, the test of capacity to make most decisions involves not only the ability to understand the information relevant to making the decision, and to retain it for long enough to do so, but also the ability to use or weigh that information in order to make a choice. This is not the same as saying that the

[1] Prison Reform Trust, *Bromley Briefings Prison Factfile*, Autumn 2017, pp 30, 44, 26.

choice made must be a rational one: rather, that the person must be able to make it. Curiously, the distinction between the capacity to understand what is going on and the capacity to make the decisions necessary to effective participation is not always understood, as is illustrated by the discussion of Jersey law, which has adopted the broader approach. Another relevant distinction, drawn by the Law Commission for England and Wales, is between the capacity to take part in the trial and the capacity to enter a plea of guilty.

Another issue of principle is whether capacity should be judged against the standards of a normal criminal trial, conducted along the adversarial lines traditional in the Anglo-American legal world, or whether it should be judged on the assumption that every effort will be made during the trial to enable the defendant's effective participation in it? Great strides have been made in England in recent years in adapting the trial process to meet the needs of vulnerable witnesses, in a conscious effort to afford them as much protection from the criminal law as everyone else has. But those efforts are only gradually being extended to vulnerable defendants. Yet it might be thought that the best solution to the problem would be to adapt the criminal process so far as possible to accommodate the needs of those with a limited ability to participate effectively. As Professor Dr van Kempen explains, in a civilian legal system such as that in the Netherlands, the inquisitorial process puts more of a burden on the judiciary and less of a burden on the accused and his lawyers. But under the influence of the European Convention on Human Rights (which is directly effective in Dutch law) that process is becoming more adversarial and placing more of a burden on the accused and his lawyers, thus raising a variety of questions about the ability of the accused to play an effective part in it.

In principle, adapting the trial process so that the accused can play as effective a part in it as possible is preferable to finding him unfit to plead and sending him off to a mental hospital for an indefinite period. It is wrong in principle for the State to deprive a person of his liberty because he is accused of having committed a criminal offence without it being determined whether or not he has in fact done so. It is not enough to say that he might have been compulsorily admitted to hospital anyway: in many cases he would not otherwise have been thought suitable for long-term mental hospital admission. It is his alleged criminality which makes him so. But it is unjust to subject him to that if he is not, in fact, a criminal. It is this thought that explains the requirement in English law to have a 'trial of the facts' where a person is found unfit to plead. But as the English chapters in this book make clear, this is not a complete solution. There are many offences in which the factual ingredients are inextricably bound up with the mental processes of the person accused.

There are yet further issues of principle if a person is found unfit and spends time in hospital (or indeed some other place of confinement) before recovering enough to be returned for trial. In what circumstances is it in the interests of justice to do this—or indeed to preserve the possibility of doing this, however remote, as has sometimes been done in international criminal tribunals where there is an understandable reluctance to abandon the possibility of bringing the perpetrator of crimes against humanity to justice no matter how incapacitated he may be.

This book brings together perspectives on these issues from England and Wales, Jersey, Scotland, Canada, New Zealand, Australia, the United States of America, the Netherlands, Italy, and international criminal tribunals from Nuremburg to East Timor. The case histories from the international courts and tribunals are particularly fascinating as they are grouped by mental condition, enabling us to see how the various issues of practice and principle play out in the context of conditions ranging from dementia, Alzheimer's, and amnesia, through psychosis and cancer, to post-traumatic stress disorder. What do we think of people who can understand the trial process, communicate with their lawyers and with the court, and make rational choices, but who genuinely have no memory of the events in question? Their lawyers are put in much the same position as a special advocate in a 'closed material procedure' who has to test the evidence without being able to take his client's instruction on it.

These varied contributions examine the issues in depth and present a variety of solutions. Although the numbers of cases are small, they raise profound questions which can illuminate our thinking about the nature and purpose of our criminal justice systems generally. The authors and the editors are to be congratulated for doing so.

Brenda Hale
Supreme Court of the United Kingdom

General Editor's Preface

This volume presents a truly international study of the foundations, the limitations, and the implications of the requirement of 'fitness to plead'. It is widely accepted that the criminal trial should, in substance, amount to calling the defendant to account for her or his conduct as charged. This calling to account must take place according to the right to a fair trial, and one of the elements of a fair trial is the defendant's ability to understand the criminal proceedings, to make decisions, and to instruct legal representatives. The precise test of competence to stand trial is one of the major issues discussed in the various chapters that follow, but it is certainly not the only issue relating to fitness to plead. A further question concerns the implications of finding that a particular defendant is unfit: is it clear that the court cannot proceed to conviction? What protection should there be for the defendant, who might not have done what has been charged? And what should happen if the mental condition that led to the finding of unfitness changes, with the result that the defendant might no longer lack the competence to stand trial? What protection should there be for the public, if it is found that the defendant acted as charged? Should detention in a mental hospital be inevitable, should it be indeterminate, or should an assessment of proportionality to the offence charged be used to set a limit to any compulsory detention? These and many other questions are analysed by an impressive array of authors. The editors are explicit about their interest in producing improvements to the law on fitness to plead, by exposing the problems and the benefits of the legal regimes of a wide range of national and international jurisdictions. Given the detailed analysis, the publication of this volume is likely to make an important contribution to the cause of law reform in relation to fairness and the criminal process.

Andrew Ashworth

Preface

The impetus for this book came from our collaboration over a number of years on matters relating to the criminal law, particularly defences. This resulted in an ever increasing joint interest in fitness to plead, which we both considered had been somewhat neglected in the legal literature. As a result, we thought it would be useful to submit a book proposal on the topic that adopted a comparative and international approach. This also led to us organizing an international conference on 'Fitness to Stand Trial' held at the Auckland University of Technology in New Zealand in October of 2017. This was a timely and constructive gathering which acted as a forerunner to the book's publication.

The book proposal was accepted by Oxford University Press and we are grateful for the input of the referees, who considered our proposal, and to Professor Andrew Ashworth for his helpful comments on an earlier draft. We are also very grateful to all of the chapter contributors to this volume, who were outstanding in responding to queries and in delivering their chapters on schedule. Finally, we are indebted to Baroness Hale of Richmond, President of the Supreme Court of the United Kingdom, for taking the time to write a splendid foreword to the book. In doing so, Lady Hale expresses surprise 'that so few people are found "unfit to plead" in a criminal trial'. In addition, she closes her foreword with the remark that 'Although the numbers of cases are small, they raise profound questions which can illuminate our thinking about the nature and purpose of our criminal justice systems generally'. In our view, this epitomizes the fundamental nature of unfitness to plead and the problems it presents. Certainly, as far as the law is concerned in many of the jurisdictions discussed in this volume, the unfit to plead are both rarely encountered in practice and are not adequately protected by the criminal process to which they are subjected. In consequence, it is our view that the numbers of those adjudged unfit to plead, together with the protections they are afforded by such a finding, will not be increased unless and until the current law in most jurisdictions is updated and modernized. It is our sincere hope that this book may help to stimulate debate about this complex area of the criminal process and that unfitness to plead may no longer be regarded as a rare finding that is best avoided.

Finally, this book's dedication speaks for itself. Words cannot adequately convey the debt which we owe to our two dedicatees.

RDM
WJB
May 2018

Contents

Table of Cases

AUSTRALIA

CANADA

ITALY

JERSEY

NETHERLANDS

NEW ZEALAND

UNITED KINGDOM

UNITED STATES

COMMITTEE ON THE RIGHTS OF PERSONS WITH DISABILITIES

EUROPEAN COURT OF HUMAN RIGHTS

EXTRAORDINARY CHAMBERS IN THE COURTS OF CAMBODIA

INTERNATIONAL CRIMINAL COURT

INTERNATIONAL CRIMINAL TRIBUNAL FOR RWANDA

INTERNATIONAL CRIMINAL TRIBUNAL FOR THE FORMER YUGOSLAVIA

INTERNATIONAL MILITARY TRIBUNAL

MILITARY TRIBUNAL FOR THE FAR EAST (TOKYO TRIBUNAL)

SPECIAL COURT FOR SIERRA LEONE

SPECIAL PANELS OF THE DILI DISTRICT COURT (EAST TIMOR PANEL)

WAR CRIMES CHAMBER IN THE COURT OF BOSNIA AND HERZEGOVINA

Table of Legislation

ITALY

NETHERLANDS

Statutory Instruments

UNITED STATES

EUROPEAN UNION

Directives

INTERNATIONAL

List of Contributors

Miranda Bevan, Barrister, Doctoral Candidate, London School of Economics, formerly lawyer with responsibility for the unfitness to plead project at the Law Commission for England and Wales, United Kingdom.

Richard J Bonnie, Harrison Foundation Professor of Law and Medicine; Director, Institute of Law, Psychiatry and Public Policy, University of Virginia School of Law, United States of America.

Warren Brookbanks, Professor of Criminal Law and Justice Studies, Director of the Centre for Non-Adversarial Justice at Auckland University of Technology, Auckland, New Zealand.

Alberto Cadoppi, Professor of Criminal Law, University of Parma, Italy.

Mattia Celva, Doctoral Candidate in Legal Sciences, Sector Criminal Law, University of Parma, Italy.

Gerry Ferguson, University of Victoria Distinguished Professor; Faculty of Law, University of Victoria, Victoria, British Columbia, Canada.

Rudi Fortson, QC, Barrister, London; Visiting Professor of Law, Queen Mary University of London, London.

Ian Freckelton, QC, Professorial Fellow in Law and Psychiatry, University of Melbourne, Australia.

Magda Karagiannakis, Barrister, Melbourne; Lecturer, La Trobe University, Melbourne, Australia.

Ronnie Mackay, Professor of Criminal Policy and Mental Health, Leicester De Montfort Law School, De Montfort University, Leicester, United Kingdom.

Gerry Maher, QC, Professor of Criminal Law, School of Law, Edinburgh University, Law Commissioner at the Scottish Law Commission from 2000 to 2008, Edinburgh, United Kingdom.

Stephen J Morse, Ferdinand Wakeman Hubbell Professor Law and Professor of Psychology and Law in Psychiatry, University of Pennsylvania, United States of America.

David Ormerod, QC, Law Commissioner for England and Wales, United Kingdom.

PHPHMC van Kempen, Full Professor of Criminal Law and Criminal Procedure Law, and Dean of the Law School of Radboud University, Nijmegen, The Netherlands.

1

Introduction

Ronnie Mackay and Warren Brookbanks

The law relating to fitness to plead is an increasingly important area in the criminal law of most Western jurisdictions. This is because of both the emerging focus on capacity-based approaches to decision making and domestic and international human rights requirements that the law should treat defendants fairly. While criminalisation may be justified whenever an offender commits a sufficiently serious moral wrong requiring that he or she be called to account, the doctrine of fitness to plead calls this principle into question in the case of a person who lacks the capacity or ability to participate meaningfully in a criminal trial. In such circumstances fairness dictates, either that the person be permanently diverted from the criminal justice system or that their trial be suspended pending the recovery of trial capacity. Thus, the fitness-to-plead rules stand as an exception to notions of public accountability for criminal wrongdoing. However, despite the doctrine's long standing as an aspect of criminal procedure, it has proven complex to apply in practice and has given rise to many varied legislative models and considerable litigation in different jurisdictions. Particularly troublesome is the question of what is to be done with someone who has been found unfit to stand trial. Here the law is required to balance the need to protect those defendants who are unable to participate effectively in their own trial, whether permanently or for a defined period, with the need to protect the public from people who may have caused serious social harm as a result of their antisocial behaviour. The challenge for law reformers, legislators, and judges is to create rules that ensure that everyone who can properly be tried is tried, while seeking to preserve confidence in the fairness of the legal system by ensuring that people who cannot properly engage in the criminal trial process are not forced to endure it. These and related questions are explored in this unique book, the purpose of which is to bring together the work of a number of eminent scholars who are familiar with the law around fitness to stand trial in several, principally common law, jurisdictions. However, a perspective on how the doctrine operates in civil law countries is also offered through an overview of the relevant law in the Netherlands and in Italy. Through an analysis of recent developments in legislation and case law in these different jurisdictions, it is hoped that existing 'soft spots' in the varied legislative models will become apparent, indicating areas where further reform may be justified.

Fitness to Plead: International and Comparative Perspectives. First Edition. Edited by Ronnie Mackay and Warren Brookbanks. Chapter 1 © Ronnie Mackay and Warren Brookbanks 2018. Published 2018 by Oxford University Press.

The Fundamental Basis of Unfitness to Plead

Norval Morris once famously wrote that 'rivers of ink … have been expended on [debating the insanity defense]'.[1] In contrast, the cognate doctrine of unfitness to plead has attracted a mere 'trickle' by way of serious scholarship. What explains this general dearth of scholarship when many more defendants are found unfit to plead than 'not guilty by reason of insanity'?[2] Whatever the reason for the paucity of debate surrounding unfitness to plead, it is clear that the plight of those who are adjudged incompetent to stand trial is every bit as grave as those acquitted on the grounds of insanity, and as such this complex area of criminal law and procedure merits equal consideration. In that connection, it is hoped that this book will help to fill this gap in the literature.

Unfitness to plead presents the criminal law with some fundamental problems. The principle upon which the doctrine is founded is simple enough. It is that those who are unfit to stand trial should not be subject to criminal sanction but protected from the full rigours of the criminal trial process. Although this seems straightforward, it brings with it a degree of tension which is difficult to resolve. First, every citizen who is a litigant in legal proceedings deserves to have his or her case heard in open court and to be given the opportunity to have the case properly litigated. Autonomy interests generally affirm that it is preferable that an offender be able to face his or her accuser in a criminal trial than that they be deprived of that right. But here a clear distinction can be drawn between civil and criminal cases. In the former there are well-developed procedures which permit civil proceedings to be conducted on behalf of a litigant who lacks capacity. This is achieved in English law through the procedures of the Court of Protection and the appointment of a 'litigation friend' to represent him or her.[3] In determining whether a person lacks capacity English Law uses the Mental Capacity Act 2005, which contains detailed provisions dealing with how such determinations should be made. However, this statute only applies to the civil law. So why is there such a difference where in one set of proceedings the litigant can proceed through a 'litigation friend' while in criminal proceedings this is not possible? The answer lies in the fact that a criminal charge represents an allegation that the individual has committed a wrong against society which, if it results in a successful prosecution, entails guilt and punishment stemming from a conviction. These notions make the criminal process fundamentally different from

[1] Norval Morris, 'Psychiatry and the Dangerous Criminal' (1968) 41 S Cal L Rev 514, 516.

[2] eg, in England and Wales around thirty defendants are annually found 'not guilty by reason of insanity' (see RD Mackay, '"Ten More Years of the Insanity Defence"' [2012] Crim LR 946 at 94) compared to around 100 found unfit to plead (see RD Mackay, Appendix A 'Unfitness to Plead—Data on Formal Findings from 2002 to 2014', Law Commission, *Unfitness to Plead, Volume 1: Report*, Law Com No 364 (2016). See https://s3-eu-west-2.amazonaws.com/lawcom-prod-storage-11jsxou24uy7q/uploads/2016/01/apa.pdf.

[3] See Alexander Keene, Peter Bartlett, and Neil Allan, 'Litigation Friends or Foes? Representation of "P" before the Court of Protection' (2016) 24 Med Law Rev 333 for a critical evaluation of the role of the litigation friend.

concepts such as tortious or contractual liability, civil redress and damages which are the hallmark of civil proceedings. In essence, no one can accept that he or she is guilty of a criminal offence except the accused, and if he or she lacks the ability to understand the fundamentals of the criminal trial process, then the proceedings cannot continue. Guilt and punishment can only be attributed to those who are found criminally responsible after a full trial or who accept criminal responsibility by pleading guilty. But should this always require a competent defendant?

Guilt might well be able to be established in a fair and open manner which is sufficient to satisfy the need for reliability in the case of an incompetent defendant. But that is not enough, as there are other important considerations such as maintaining the dignity of the criminal trial process. To try in open court a defendant who is unfit, because of mental impairment or other disability, could be distressing for the defendant and his family (witness the appearance of Lord Greville Janner before the Magistrates' Court, where the High Court ruled that committal proceedings in the Magistrate's Court cannot proceed in the absence of the accused, irrespective of the fact that he suffered from serious dementia[4]), as well as bringing the process into disrepute. However, such an unfortunate spectacle could easily be avoided by trying the unfit accused in his absence which, in exceptional cases, may take place in cases of competent defendants who abscond and voluntarily absent themselves from the trial process.[5] While both fairness and dignity[6] are important considerations, in themselves or taken together, they do not seem to be enough to rule out the possibility of trying an unfit defendant, or rather that steps could be taken to ensure that both fairness and dignity are satisfied in any such case. In which case, it is the principle of 'autonomy' which seems to be vital here, in the sense that a person adjudged unfit to plead is immediately 'barred' from any further participation in the criminal trial process as he is no longer 'eligible' as a competent and capacitated citizen to face criminal charges, unless and until he is later declared fit to stand trial. This then seems to go to the heart of the problem. The criminal law seeks to protect the unfit to plead by placing a 'bar' to his ongoing trial, but in doing so it disadvantages such defendants by removing from them the protections contained in the criminal trial process. In addition, the unfit to plead may find themselves subject to detention in hospital or some other court disposal without having been convicted. This is a particular problem where the predisposing disability is a physical rather than a mental impairment, such as a defendant who is deaf and mute. As a result, some have suggested the abolition of unfitness to plead. A prominent exponent of such an

[4] See https://www.judiciary.gov.uk/wp-content/uploads/2015/08/r-ono-lord-janner-v-westminster-mags-ct-and-cps.pdf. The court emphasised the 'obvious and strong public interest in ensuring those summoned to court attend when required. Equally, there is a compelling public interest in public justice. The Court must not become a place of avoidable spectacle, but it is very important that the route to justice should be public.' However, although this case only relates to committal proceedings as opposed to the trial itself, there remains something deeply unpleasant about subjecting a seriously mentally disturbed defendant to such an experience.

[5] See *R v Jones* [2002] UKHL 5.

[6] For further discussion of the 'values served by the competence requirement', see chapter 9, 'Fitness for Criminal Adjudication: The Emerging Significance of Decisional Competence in the United States'.

approach was Norval Morris, who argued in favour of replacing unfitness to plead with rules of court which would enable trial continuances which, in 'exceptional circumstances', might result in taking 'some unrestorable incompetents to trial',[7] which in turn would result in a criminal conviction. In advocating this approach, it is interesting to note that Morris referred to the work of the Butler Report, which recommended that once found unfit to plead, a 'trial of the facts' should follow 'to the fullest extent possible having regard to the medical condition of the defendant',[8] a proposal which mirrors that of the Law Commission.[9] In doing so, Morris properly draws attention to the fact that US law does not have the hospital order as a sentencing option for convicted defendants and that the use of such orders and other disposal options for the unfit to plead are also unavailable in the United States. But what he fails to concede is that the 'trial of the facts' is not a criminal trial and his reference to the introduction of a range of disposal options for the unfit to plead (other than those acquitted after a 'trial of the facts') as 'sentencing powers'[10] is misconceived, insofar as it equates the 'trial of the facts' with an ordinary criminal trial which can result in a conviction, when this is clearly not so. And this is likely to be why calls for abolition have gone unheeded, for to convict the unfit to plead surely contradicts a fundamental principle of criminal justice, namely that it requires an autonomous, capacitated accused who understands the fundamentals of the trial process and is equipped to make decisions which are instrumental to that process. Granted that the criminal law should not waver from this principle (namely, that we must not prosecute people who cannot effectively participate in the trial process), this itself raises the additional problem of how to establish that the unfit accused is in any way 'accountable'[11] for what he did if he cannot be tried, and if 'accountable', then what powers should be used to deal with the unfit person? While all these issues present the criminal trial process with problems and contradictions, that in itself is, in our view, no reason to favour abolition, but rather to engage in arguing for change and reform of the current law in the hope that a new and fairer way of dealing with the unfit to plead can be achieved. And that is the purpose of this book, for in their respective chapters, the authors confront the problems which unfitness to plead raises in their own jurisdictions, which in turn give readers a unique opportunity to compare and evaluate the way in which these different legal systems have approached such problems. While there are no easy answers to any of these problems, what this book does is to give the views of a range of experts from different jurisdictions who have worked and practiced in this complex area of the criminal law.

An aspect of growing importance has been the impact of both domestic and human rights litigation as a means of protecting and enhancing the rights of the unfit to plead. This topic is discussed in the next section.

[7] Norval Morris, *Madness and the Criminal Law* (University of Chicago Press 1982) 48.
[8] Report of the Committee on Mentally Abnormal Offenders, Cmnd 1 6244 (1975) para 10.24.
[9] See Law Commission, Law Com No 364 (n 2) at ch 5.
[10] Morris, *Madness and the Criminal Law* (n 7) 51.
[11] By 'accountable' we mean that the unfit defendant was the 'author' of the behaviour in question which led to him or her being charged with the alleged offence.

Human Rights Aspects

Recent jurisprudence arising from the European Court of Human Rights (ECtHR) has affirmed the importance of the European Convention on Human Rights (ECHR) in determinations of trial competence. In the case of *Stanford v The United Kingdom*, in the ECtHR the applicant had complained under Art 6 of the ECHR that as he could not hear the proceedings that resulted in his conviction, he did not receive a fair trial. Although the application ultimately failed, the Court noted that Art 6 guarantees the right of an accused to 'participate effectively' in a criminal trial, including not only the right to be present, but to hear and follow the proceedings, rights implicit in the notion of an adversarial proceeding.

In England and Wales a particular human rights problem has arisen in relation to how to construe a 'trial of the facts'[12] hearing under s 4A of the Criminal Procedure (Insanity) Act 1964 for the purposes of Art 6 of the ECHR. The House of Lords held in *H*[13] that the s 4A hearing did not constitute the determination of a criminal charge for the purposes of Art 6. However, the difficulty with such a ruling is that it appears to be incompatible with an accused person's fair trial rights, the presumption of innocence, and right of examination of witnesses under Arts 6(1), 6(2), and 6(3)(d) of the ECHR. The English Law Commission, in addressing this problem, has provisionally recommended that a revised s 4A procedure should involve a hearing as to all the elements of the offence, but would thereafter be qualified by a special verdict. The recommended procedure would be akin to a formal charge and would justify the application of Art 6.[14]

In relation to the rights of defendants with disabilities, in *SC v United Kingdom* the applicant complained that under Art 6 of the ECHR he was denied a fair trial because, by virtue of his age and intellectual disability, he was unable to participate effectively in the proceedings against him. The Court found that the applicant, an eleven-year-old boy with the mental age of a six-year-old, should have been tried in the privacy of a specialist Youth Court with proper sentencing powers. It held that it was clear to any trained observer that the offender was unable to fully comprehend or participate in the trial process and could not adequately give instructions. He was awed by the formalities of the Crown Court, and despite an adapted procedure, his short attention span antagonised the jury. The ECtHR, in upholding the complaint, ruled that the complaint raised serious issues of fact and law under the Convention, the determination of which required an examination of the merits.

While these cases affirm the effective participation test as the appropriate threshold test in determining fitness to stand trial, more recent jurisprudence arising from the Convention of the Rights of Persons with Disabilities (CRPD) has suggested

[12] Discussed in detail in chapters 2 'The Development of Unfitness to Please in English Law', 3 'Unfitness to Plead in England and Wales: A Practitioner's View of a Plea in Evolution', and 4 'Reforming the Law of Unfitness to Plead in England and Wales—A Recent History'.

[13] [2003] UKHL 1, [2003] 1 WLR 411.

[14] Law Commission, *Unfitness to Plead*, CP No 197 (2010) para 6.54.

the need for significant and potentially far-reaching limitations on procedures for determining fitness to stand trial, procedures that may go well beyond any question of effective participation. In *Noble v Australia*,[15] the Committee on the Rights of Persons with Disabilities considered an application under Art 5 of the CRPD that the Mentally Impaired Defendants Act (Western Australia) was discriminatory as it only applied to people with a cognitive impairment, and provided for their indefinite detention without any finding of guilt when they are charged with criminal offences. By contrast, it was argued that people without cognitive impairments are protected from such treatments through the application of the rules of due process and fair trial. The state party argued, on the other hand, that the Act was not discriminatory, but provided for legitimate differential treatment of certain persons with disabilities, subject to safeguards to ensure that it was proportionate to its aims (at para 8.2).

In delivering its decision, the Committee on the Rights of Persons with Disabilities noted that Art 5(1) and (2) of the CRPD requires governments to ensure that all persons are equal before and under the law and entitled, without discrimination, to equal protection and benefit of the law. Discrimination can result from the discriminatory effect of a rule or measure that is not intended to discriminate, but may disproportionately affect persons with disabilities. It found that while the Mentally Impaired Defendant's Act (WA) was intended to address the situation of persons with psychosocial and intellectual impairments found unfit to stand trial on the basis of mental impairments, the legislation allowed a person found unfit to plead to be maintained in custody for an unlimited period of time, on the basis of a presumption that the person is presumed to remain not mentally fit to stand trial until the contrary is found. Meanwhile such a person has no possibility of exercising his or her legal capacity before the courts and, in particular, the possibility of pleading not guilty or testing the evidence against him or her.

The Committee found that the decision that the applicant was unfit to plead because of his intellectual and mental disability resulted in a denial of his right to exercise his legal capacity to plead not guilty and test the evidence against him. In addition, no adequate form of support was provided by the states party to enable him to stand trial and to plead not guilty, despite his clear intention to do so. As a result, the applicant never had the opportunity to have the criminal charges against him determined, and his status as an alleged sexual offender potentially cleared. The Committee concluded that while states parties have a certain margin of appreciation to determine the procedural arrangements to enable persons with disabilities to exercise their legal capacity, the relevant rights of the person concerned must be respected. This did not happen in *Noble* because he had no possibility and was not provided with adequate support or accommodation to exercise his rights to access to justice and a fair trial. In the Committees' view the situation amounted to a violation of the author's rights under Arts 12(2) and (3) and 13(1) of the Convention.

[15] (2016) CRPD C/16/D/7/2012.

What the full implications of this ruling will be for mentally impaired defendants in the context of unfitness-to-plead determinations remains to be seen. We may speculate, however, that viewing mentally impaired defendants as persons with rights equal to those of capacitated persons throws a considerable spanner in the works in the assessment of trial competence and its allied procedures, and may warrant a radical reform of both the conceptualisation of and the process for determining issues of trial competence. As a minimum, and following the recommendations of the Committee in *Noble,* it suggests an ongoing need for legislators and policy makers to consult with persons with disabilities and their representative organisations to ensure compliance with the Principles of the Convention. It also implies a need to ensure that adequate support and accommodation measures are provided to persons with mental and intellectual disabilities to enable them to exercise their legal capacity before the courts whenever necessary.[16] Finally, the decision suggests that a need to ensure appropriate and regular training on the scope of the Convention and its Optional Protocol, including on the exercise of legal capacity by persons with intellectual and mental disabilities, is provided to members of the relevant Review Board, members of the Law Commission and Parliament, to judges and their support staff, and to legal representatives.[17]

Organisation of the Book

What now follows is a brief introduction to each chapter contained in this edited collection.

In chapter 2 'The Development of Unfitness to Plead in English Law', Professor Ronnie Mackay provides an overview of particular problems that have arisen in the application of the fitness rules in England and Wales, through an analysis of recent case law. It includes a discussion of how a new test for unfitness to plead was introduced as a result of litigation in Jersey, the first, and as yet only British jurisdiction to incorporate decisional competence into a test for unfitness to plead.

Chapter 3 'Unfitness to Plead in England and Wales: A Practitioner's View of a Plea in Evolution' is authored by Rudi Fortson, a leading barrister. It discusses the problems encountered by practitioners when called upon to deal with unfitness-to-plead litigation. In doing so, the chapter evaluates the existing legal position together with the reform proposals of the English Law Commission and assesses how the law could be improved for all those who are involved in dealing with the unfit to plead.

Chapter 4 'Reforming the Law of Unfitness to Plead in England and Wales—A Recent History' by Miranda Bevan and Professor David Ormerod contains a detailed discussion of the history of the reform process in England and Wales together with a summary of the recent reform proposals put forward by the Law Commission.

[16] *Noble v Australia* (2016) CRPD/C/16/D/7/2016 at para 9(b)(i) & (ii).

[17] ibid, para 9(b)(iii).

In chapter 5 'Unfitness for Trial in Scots Law', Professor Gerry Maher explains that historically, the focus in Scots law on the defence of insanity was in relation to a plea in bar of trial rather than the substantive defence. However, the law on the definition of the plea in bar and of the procedure fused, and for a long time the doctrine remained undeveloped. This chapter examines recent statutory changes in Scots law; first, the introduction of the procedure of the examination of the facts and the widening of the disposals available to a court where the plea was successful; and secondly, the replacement of the common law test by a statutory test of unfitness for trial, based on the lack of an accused's capacity to participate effectively in the proceedings against him.

In chapter 6 'Unfit to Stand Trial: Canadian Law and Practice', Professor Gerry Ferguson outlines the legal framework for dealing with fitness to plead in Canada. The Canadian law in this area was revised comprehensively in 1992 and there have been no significant amendments since that time. The chapter describes key features of that legal framework and, in the light of legal and psychiatric practices in other countries, considers whether there is a need for further reform of the Canadian law in this area. The key features considered include the criteria for determining fitness to plead, and whether they are consistent with current psychiatric knowledge and practice; postponement of the fitness hearing; whether a jury should continue to decide the issue of fitness injury trial cases; and issues around disposition and review, including the disposition of permanently unfit accused persons.

Professor Warren Brookbanks, in chapter 7 'The Development of Unfitness to Stand Trial in New Zealand', examines the development of fitness to plead in New Zealand. Although the doctrine has been codified in New Zealand since the early twentieth century, subsequent consolidations of relevant legislation have led to refinement of the statutory criteria for determining fitness. The rules themselves essentially mirror the common law test laid down in *R v Pritchard.* However, a new Mental Health Act (Compulsory Assessment & Treatment Act) enacted in 1992 and new legislation governing mentally impaired offenders enacted in 2003 have exposed practical difficulties in the procedures for determining fitness, and have led to an unexpected surge in litigation and resulting case law around these issues. More recently, judicial and doctrinal interest has shifted towards the concept of decisional competence and whether this has a role in New Zealand's fitness jurisprudence. This interest has been largely catalysed by the New Zealand Court of Appeal's decision in *Solicitor-General v Dougherty* [2012] 3 NZLR 586, which rejects decisional competence for purposes of New Zealand law. The implications of these developments are considered in this chapter. The chapter also discusses the implications of recent case law developments which distinguish, for practical purposes, between fitness to plead guilty and fitness to stand trial.

In chapter 8 'Fitness to Stand Trial under Australian Law', Professor Ian Freckelton reviews the statutory and case law in relation to fitness to stand trial in the Australian jurisdictions. The chapter analyses major decisions on the subject in the state Supreme Courts and in the Australian High Court, commencing with the internationally influential formulation of criteria by Smith J in *R v Presser.*[18]

[18] [1958] VR 45.

The chapter considers various decisions relating to the fitness of David Eastman, including both his High Court appeal and the special enquiries convened into his fitness for criminal trial, and including the most recent 2014 judicial review into this issue. The chapter also reviews the consequences of findings of unfitness in the various jurisdictions of Australia and scrutinises proposals for reform in the area. A 2014 report on the subject by the Victorian Law reform commission is also considered.

Chapter 9 'Fitness for Criminal Adjudication: The Emerging Significance of Decisional Competence in American Law' is written by Professor Richard Bonnie. The practice of assessing and adjudicating fitness to plead (or competence to proceed, as it is sometimes called in the United States) developed largely without assistance from the US Supreme Court or other appellate courts for most of the nineteenth and twentieth centuries. However, the need for appellate guidance became evident in the 1980s, especially regarding the significance of conditions that can impair capacity for rational decision making without impairing the defendant's capacity to understand the proceedings and communicate coherently with counsel. In the early 1990s, the author called attention to these emerging issues and pointed the way towards possible solutions. Over the past twenty-five years, some of the governing principles have come into view, but important issues remain unresolved. The chapter summarises the current state of the law in the United States and offers some suggestions for future development.

In chapter 10 'Involuntary Competence in United States Criminal Law', Professor Stephen Morse considers all the stages in the US criminal justice process in which a defendant or prisoner may become incompetent and a potential candidate for involuntary treatment to restore the subject's competence. It surveys the law and offers a normative set of recommendations for when involuntary treatment is justified and recommendations for the disposition of the subject if involuntary treatment is not justified or is unsuccessful.

Chapters 11–13 are devoted to civil and international law implications of the unfitness-to-plead doctrine.

In chapter 11 'The Right to Fair Preliminary Investigation and Trial for Vulnerable Defendants: The Case of the Netherlands', Professor PHPHMC van Kempen considers fitness to plead within the jurisdiction of the Netherlands. Because Dutch criminal procedure is largely based on an inquisitorial model, fitness to plead is not as significant a doctrine in the Netherlands as it is in many common law jurisdictions. Indeed, it barely receives any attention in legal literature or case law in the Netherlands. However, this does not mean that the doctrine is of no practical concern in criminal cases in the Netherlands. Both the Code of Criminal Procedure and criminal procedure case law are concerned with this issue. Moreover, since fitness to plead has much to do with the right to defence and a fair trial, the ECHR (particularly Art 6) is of major importance. The chapter provides an explanation of the ways in which fitness to plead manifests itself in Dutch criminal procedure, and examines the way in which the doctrine is dealt with in case law of the ECtHR. The chapter examines a number of issues, including suspension (stay) of the prosecution as provided for in Art 16 of the Code of Criminal Procedure, the interrogation of defendants who are mentally unfit, and self-representing defendants who waive legal assistance.

Chapter 12 'Competency to Stand Trial in Italy' is authored by Professor Alberto Cadoppi and Mattia Celva. The analysis of competency to stand trial in Italian criminal procedure will be developed in two prongs: first, an analysis of the relevant provisions of the Italian Code of Criminal Procedure (CCP). Pursuant to these provisions, the trial must be suspended in case the defendant is not capable of meaningful participation. The CCP also regulates various aspects connected to this incapacity. In particular, the Code sets forth the grounds on which the suspension must be granted and provides for the means through which the incompetency should be ascertained, if not immediately apparent. The Code also regulates how the suspension is to be declared and how the limited instances in which the process can be continued, when it can be fully resumed, and how to obtain such result. The picture painted by the Code is one of complexity, and many of these provisions have been challenged as unconstitutional in front of the Constitutional Court, with different results. This chapter focuses on such problems, in order to illustrate the approach of the Constitutional Court, as well as examining the solutions proposed by legal scholarship, including the definition of 'incapacity'.

Chapter 13 'Fitness to Stand Trial under International Criminal Law', written by Professor Ian Freckelton and Magda Karagiannakis, commences with a review of the jurisprudence developed by the Nuremberg and Far East tribunals on the fitness to stand trial of persons charged with serious offences after the Second World War. It then moves to look at decisions of the International Tribunal for the former Yugoslavia and that Tribunal's influential decision in relation to Pavle Strugar. The chapter also scrutinises the development of the law in various theatres of international criminal law. In particular, it analyses issues that have been generated in relation to monitoring and evaluating the health of accused persons before the Extraordinary Chambers in the Courts of Cambodia, especially in respect of Leng Thirith, the East Timor Special Court in relation to Joseph Nahak, the International Criminal Court in relation to Laurent Gbagbo, and the Sierra Leone Special Court in relation to Foday Sanhoh. It notes the absence of facilities for housing persons found unfit in some jurisdictions, the difficulties relating to aging defendants in some instances, and the limited guidance provided by the most authoritative decisions in relation to the capacity of persons whose capacity for reason is impaired by reason of injury, illness, or ageing. It raises options for reform of criteria for unfitness under international law and the procedures that might follow an initial determination of unfitness.

The final chapter 14 'Conclusion', written by Professor Mackay and Professor Brookbanks, offers a synthesis of the law around fitness to stand trial drawn from the different jurisdictions surveyed in the book. It seeks to identify common themes and to suggest areas where there is a clear consensus on the need for reform. We hope that this book will serve as a benchmark for the theory and practice of fitness to plead and provide an opportunity for useful reflection and debate on the future direction and development of this important doctrine.

2

The Development of Unfitness to Plead in English Law

Ronnie Mackay

Introduction

English law on unfitness to plead has developed over centuries in a piecemeal fashion and remains one of the few common law jurisdictions where the legal test of fitness to plead is not governed by statute. As a result, the law has been slow to develop and remains enshrined in a test dating back to 1836, namely that of the case of *R v Pritchard*. This chapter gives an account of recent case law on unfitness to plead in English law, together with an analysis of the author's empirical research on the operation of the current doctrine and finally, an evaluation of the law of the island of Jersey, which in rejecting *Pritchard*, has introduced a new test incorporating decisional capacity.

The Doctrine's Development in England and Wales

Section 4 of the Criminal Procedure (Insanity) Act 1964[1] refers to an accused being 'under a disability' such that 'it would constitute a bar to his being tried' rather than 'unfitness to plead', which is merely contained in the marginal note to s 4. However, no matter which term is used to encapsulate the legal doctrine, it is the common law rather than the 1964 Act to which one must turn in order to ascertain the relevant legal test, as English law remains one of the few jurisdictions which has no statutory definition of unfitness to plead.[2]

The common law of England and Wales has long recognised that if an accused person is incapable of understanding or answering the allegations against him then

[1] Substituted by the Criminal Procedure (Insanity and Unfitness to Plead) Act 1991, s 2.

[2] The Law Commission, *Unfitness to Plead, Volume 1: Report*, Law Com No 364 (2016) has recommended a statutory test together with a radical overhaul of the legal framework underpinning unfitness to plead. See chapter 4 'Reforming the Law of Unfitness to Plead in England and Wales: A Recent History'.

Fitness to Plead: International and Comparative Perspectives. First Edition. Edited by Ronnie Mackay and Warren Brookbanks. Chapter 2 © Ronnie Mackay 2018. Published 2018 by Oxford University Press.

an ordinary criminal trial should not take place.[3] For example, in his *Commentaries*, Blackstone stated, 'If a man in his sound memory commits a capital offence, and, before arraignment for it, he becomes mad, he ought not to be arraigned for it, because he is not able to plead to it with that advice and caution that he ought.'[4] Despite some criticism about the way in which the current common law test of unfitness focuses exclusively on intellectual ability rather than the broader notion of 'insanity',[5] there is no doubt that the authoritative definition continues to be that given in *R v Pritchard*.[6] Thus, in *R v M*[7] the Court of Appeal, in adopting the trial judge's direction to the jury, approved the *Pritchard* test, stating:

The original formulation of the appropriate test is that set out in *Pritchard* (1836) 7 C&P 303 where in the case of a deaf-mute it was said at p 304:

> 'There are three points to be inquired into—first, whether the prisoner is mute of malice or not; secondly, whether he can plead to the indictment or not; thirdly, whether he is of sufficient intellect to comprehend the course of proceedings on the trial, so as to make a proper defence—to know that he might challenge any of you to whom he may object—and to comprehend the details of the evidence, which in a case of this nature must constitute a minute investigation. Upon this issue, therefore, if you think that there is no certain mode of communicating the details of the trial to the prisoner, so that he can clearly understand them, and be able properly to make his defence to the charge; you ought to find that he is not of sane mind. It is not enough, that he may have a general capacity of communicating on ordinary matters.'

That passage from the address to the jury by Alderson, B in *Pritchard* has been endorsed subsequently in a number of authorities. In *Podola*[8] that passage was expressly approved by the Court of Criminal Appeal presided over by the Lord Chief Justice, Lord Parker. In that case it was held that a loss of memory would not necessarily render an accused unfit to plead if he was able to do the various things described in *Pritchard*.

In *Robertson*[9] the *Pritchard* test was said to be one which had been confirmed and followed 'over and over again'.

Those authorities clearly establish the law on this topic in this jurisdiction.... Indeed, this Court regards them as admirable directions. They do not set the test of fitness to plead at too low a level.[10]

More recently the Court of Appeal in *R v Walls*[11] again endorsed *Pritchard*, saying: 'The criteria are as the decisions of this court have made clear the firmly established law. The duty of the court is to consider whether the defendant is unfit to plead according to those criteria in the light of all the evidence before it, including the expert psychiatric evidence.'[12]

[3] For an historical discussion, see N Walker, *Crime and Insanity in England*, Vol 1 (Edinburgh University Press 1968) ch 14. For powerful argument that 'fairness' should underpin the legal concept, see J Peay, 'Fitness to Plead and Core Competencies: Problems and Possibilities' LSE Law, Society and Economy Working Papers 2 (2012).

[4] William Blackstone, *Commentaries* (9th edn, 1783) Vol 4, 24.

[5] See D Grubin, 'What Constitutes Fitness to Plead?' [1993] Crim LR 748.

[6] (1836) 7 C & P 303.

[7] [2003] EWCA Crim 3452. Approved in *R v Diamond* [2008] EWCA (Crim) 923 para 43.

[8] [1960] 1 QB 325, [1959] 3 All ER 418.

[9] [1968] 3 All ER 557, [1968] 52 Cr App R 690.

[10] ibid, paras 28–31.

[11] [2011] EWCA Crim 443.

[12] ibid, para 21.

From *Pritchard*, there have developed six basic criteria which must be satisfied where fitness to plead is in issue. These were summarised by the trial judge in *R v M* as follows:

> (1) understanding the charges; (2) deciding whether to plead guilty or not; (3) exercising his right to challenge jurors; (4) instructing solicitors and counsel; (5) following the course of the proceedings; (6) giving evidence in his own defence.[13]

A deficit in just one of these criteria renders a defendant unfit to plead. However, a finding of unfitness to plead in England and Wales does not require the accused to suffer from any form of mental disorder, as it is capable of including some, like *Pritchard*, who are deaf and dumb. Additionally, the fact that the accused suffers from a serious mental disorder will not of itself mean that he cannot understand and follow the trial proceedings, in which case he will be fit to plead. Such is the case even if the accused is unable properly to act in his own best interests during the trial[14] or is found to be suffering from hysterical amnesia, which means that memory is lacking for the events surrounding the offence.[15] Therefore, the fact that the accused has a disability that hinders his defence will not of itself operate as a bar to the trial. Whether it should is a matter of importance as some, including the Law Commission,[16] would argue that, contrary to the view of the Court of Appeal in *R v M*, the current threshold for fitness to plead is set at too low a level. If this is correct, then it seems clear that this fundamental issue, as the Law Commission has confirmed, can only be resolved by legislative reform. In short, the *Pritchard* criteria seem so deeply embedded in English common law that it is unlikely that they will be the subject of any meaningful judicial development. For example, following *R v M*, where the appellant's case on the aspect of the appeal relating to the *Pritchard* test was that the judge misdirected the jury by setting the test too low with the result that it was too easily met, the Court of Appeal in *R v Lederman*[17] followed and applied *Pritchard*. In doing so Patterson J made it clear that 'Concerns about suicidal ideation and mental fragility are not part of the *Pritchard* criteria for consideration of unfitness to plead'.[18] However, by way of contrast, although the decision in *R v Marcantonio*[19] applies *Pritchard*, it does so in the context of the test having been 'reinterpreted by the courts to make it more appropriate for the modern trial process'.[20] Thus, in the course of his judgment, although Lloyd Jones LJ made it clear that the applicable test for fitness to plead in *Pritchard* 'remains the foundation of the current law', he did recognise that this test had been the subject of 'much criticism'—and in doing so drew attention, inter alia, 'to the Law Commission's Report

[13] ibid [20]. These criteria are discussed by Law Commission, Law Com No 364 (n 2) at ch 3.

[14] *R v Robertson* (n 9), 696. See WJ Brookbanks and RD Mackay, 'Decisional Competence and "Best Interests": Establishing the Threshold for Fitness to Stand Trial' (2010) 12 Otago LR 265.

[15] *R v Podola* (n 8). See also *R v M* (n 7).

[16] See Law Commission, Law Com No 364 (n 2).

[17] [2015] EWCA Crim 1308. See also *Moyle v R* [2008], where at [38] Pill LJ states: 'Each case, of course, depends on its own facts but delusions as to the court's powers of sentence, or as to the objectivity of the court, or as to the evil influences which are thought to be present in the proceedings, do not necessarily require a finding that a person is unable to give instructions and to understand the proceedings.'

[18] ibid [52]. [19] [2016] EWCA Crim 14. [20] ibid [4].

on Unfitness to Plead'.[21] He then proceeded to make some interesting remarks about how the test should be applied to the 'modern trial process'.[22] First, he echoed what the Law Commission had recommended, namely that assessment of D's abilities 'should reflect consideration of the actual proceedings'. He put it this way:

> It seems to us, however, that in applying the *Pritchard* criteria the court is required to undertake an assessment of the defendant's capabilities in the context of the particular proceedings. An assessment of whether a defendant has the capacity to participate effectively in legal proceedings should require the court to have regard to what that legal process will involve and what demands it will make on the defendant. It should be addressed not in the abstract but in the context of the particular case. The degree of complexity of different legal proceedings may vary considerably. Thus the court should consider, for example, the nature and complexity of the issues arising in the particular proceedings, the likely duration of the proceedings and the number of parties. There can be no legitimate reason for depriving a defendant of the right to stand trial on the basis that he lacks capacity to participate in some theoretical proceedings when he does not lack capacity to participate in the proceedings which he faces.[23]

It is also noteworthy that Lloyd Jones LJ referred to 'the capacity to participate effectively in legal proceedings', a concept which is integral to the Law Commission's proposal for a new legal test for unfitness to plead.[24]

Secondly, it is of considerable interest that he expresses dissatisfaction with the indivisibility of the current test for unfitness to plead in the sense that if D fails any one of 'the specified competencies' he will be found unfit. The dissatisfaction stems from the fact that:

> the current test does not distinguish between capacity to participate effectively in a trial and capacity to plead guilty. It seems to us that a strong case could be made out for a test which draws such a distinction. There will be cases in which the defendant would be unable to follow proceedings at trial or to give evidence but would not lack the decisional capacity necessary for entering a plea of guilty.[25]

This remark again echoes the recommendation of the Law Commission, which is referred to by Lloyd Jones LJ as follows: 'We note that this issue is addressed by the Law Commission in its recent report on Unfitness to Plead where it recommends the introduction of a second test, one of capacity to plead guilty, for defendants who would otherwise lack the capacity to participate effectively in a trial.'[26] Although the

[21] ibid [6].

[22] See also *R v Janner*, 7 December (2015), where Openshaw J states at page 2: 'Whether the defendant is fit to plead or to be tried depends on whether he is able to understand the charges; whether he can enter an informed plea to those charges; whether he can instruct those acting for him as to his answer to the charges; whether he can understand such advice as is given to him; whether he can properly exercise his right to challenge jurors for cause; whether he can follow and effectively participate in the proceedings (with assistance if necessary); whether he can give evidence on his own behalf (again with assistance if necessary) and whether he can make an informed choice as to whether he should do so and whether any other evidence should be called on his behalf. I have attempted to modify the test as laid down in *R v Pritchard* (1836) 7 C and P 303 ("the Pritchard criteria") in accordance with modern conditions.' Available at: https://www.judiciary.gov.uk/wp-content/uploads/2015/12/R-v-Janner-judgment.pdf.

[23] ibid [7]. [24] Law Commission, Law Com No 364 (n 2) para 3.35. [25] ibid [8].

[26] ibid [9].

court was not required to make a decision on this issue, the judicial recognition of the possibility of separating the capacity to plead guilty from the capacity required to participate effectively in the trial process not only adds considerable weight to the debate as to whether such an approach is desirable, but also gives momentum to the Law Commission's recommendation, which would incorporate important safeguards before any guilty plea was accepted by the court.[27]

Finally, in *R v Orr*[28] the Court of Appeal rejected a ruling by the trial judge which had permitted the trial to proceed where the defendant, although fit to give evidence-in- chief, had become unfit to be cross-examined. Macur LJ made it clear that 'Once the issue of fitness to plead has been raised it must be determined'[29] and in doing so, stated:

> However, we have come to the certain conclusion that the issue of fitness to plead, so called in the Criminal Procedure (Insanity) Act 1964, section 4, but we think more aptly to be identified as 'fitness to participate in the trial process', since 'the supposed disability' can be determined at any stage up to 'verdict of acquittal', cannot be determined by reference to part only of the trial process. The capacity to be cross-examined is part and parcel of the defendant's ability to give evidence in his own defence.[30]

While these cases show that the Court of Appeal is bound by the *Pritchard* criteria, what is significant is the Court's preference for the more modern concept of 'the capacity to participate effectively in legal proceedings' or 'fitness to participate in the trial process', rather than 'fitness to plead', even though neither of these phrases appear in any English statute which deals with 'unfitness to plead'. Rather, as already mentioned, the Court of Appeal is likely to have been influenced by the Law Commission's Report on Unfitness to Plead, which it cites in both cases. While this could demonstrate a judicial shift in attitude towards the need for modernising the law on fitness to plead, it seems likely that this can only be achieved by statute rather than by judicial activism.

Postponing consideration of the issue of fitness to be tried

The 1964 Act maintains the rule that once the issue of fitness to plead is raised it should be determined 'as soon as it arises'.[31] However, in view of the fact that in some cases this could lead to injustice where the accused might be entitled to an acquittal, section 4(2) gives the judge a discretion to postpone consideration of the question of fitness to be tried until any time up to the opening of the case for the defence, provided he is of the opinion that it is expedient to do so and in the interests of the accused.[32] If the prosecution case is clearly weak and is open to challenge,

[27] ibid, para 3.156. [28] [2016] EWCA Crim 889. [29] ibid [29].
[30] ibid [23].
[31] Criminal Procedure (Insanity) Act 1964, s 4 as substituted by the Criminal Procedure (Insanity and Unfitness to Plead) Act 1991 (n 1).
[32] See *R v Norman* [2008] EWCA Crim 1810 at [34ii], where Thomas LJ remarked in a postscript: 'When full information is available, the court will need carefully to consider whether to postpone the issue of trial of fitness to plead under s.4(2), given the consequences that a finding of unfitness has for the defendant.'

then postponement will usually be in the interests of the accused.[33] As such the trial will proceed in the normal manner. Since a finding of unfitness to plead may have serious consequences for the defendant, this approach should be followed if there is a reasonable chance that the prosecution's evidence can be successfully challenged. In addition, if after the prosecution has presented its evidence there is no case to answer, section 4(3) provides that the jury will be directed to acquit the accused and the issue of fitness to plead will not be determined. Conversely, the prosecution case may be so robust and the accused's condition so disabling that postponement would be wholly inexpedient.[34]

Section 4(5) of the 1964 Act provides that where the accused is found unfit to plead 'the trial shall not proceed or further proceed'. Although this provision is retained by s 4A (introduced by the Criminal Procedure (Insanity and Unfitness to Plead) Act 1991) it is also supplemented by the introduction of a new procedure aimed at further protecting those found unfit to plead. This is often known as the 'trial of the facts', described below, and was felt necessary for, as the law originally stood, there was no requirement that the prosecution case against those unfit to plead be tested. In addition, even in those cases where after postponement the prosecution evidence showed a case to answer, the accused might still have a good defence and yet have no opportunity to have it presented. As this was clearly unfair, it was sought to be remedied in the 1991 Act.

The Trial of the Facts

The 'trial of the facts' procedure was introduced by the 1991 Act and is contained in section 4A of the 1964 Act.[35] This procedure applies in all cases where the court has decided that the accused is unfit to plead. In this connection, although s 22 of the Domestic Violence, Crime and Victims Act 2004 now provides that the issue of fitness to plead is no longer to be decided by a jury but rather 'by the court without a jury',[36] this does not alter the need for the 'trial of the facts' to be decided by a jury.

Section 4A makes it clear that once it has been determined that the accused is unfit to plead, the trial must not proceed or further proceed. Instead it requires a jury[37] to examine the evidence both already given and newly adduced to decide

[33] *R v Webb* [1969] 2 QB 278. [34] *R v Burles* [1970] 2 QB 191.

[35] Introduced by s 2 of the 1991 Act. If the accused is unrepresented, then it is the court's duty under s 4A(2) to consider who is the best person to be appointed by the court to put the case for the defence. As to the importance of this responsibility and the burden it places on the court, see *R v Norman* [2008] (n 30) para 34.

[36] This new provision applies only to those arraigned on or after 31 March 2005, as opposed to those committed or sent to the Crown Court. See *R v Hussein* [2005] EWCA Crim 3556 dealing with the confusion arising out of Home Office Circular 24/2005, which at para 6 is wrongly worded and led to the defendant's unfitness hearing being quashed on the grounds that it should have been determined by a judge alone rather than by a jury.

[37] If the fitness issue arises at a time later than arraignment, then the jury which was in the process of trying the accused prior to his being found unfit will determine the trial of the facts (1991 Act, s 4A(5)) as amended by s 22 Domestic Violence, Crime and Victims Act 2004.

whether the unfit accused 'did the act or made the omission charged against him as the offence'. If the jury are so satisfied, then they will make a finding to that effect. However, this 'finding' is not the equivalent of a conviction. On the other hand, if the jury are not so satisfied, then a verdict of acquittal will be returned. The 'trial of the facts' procedure has been the subject of considerable judicial scrutiny both as to essence and to scope, both of which are briefly discussed below.

The essence of the 'trial of the facts'

The problem as to essence has been whether this procedure is one that is criminal in nature, thus bringing it under the protection of Article 6 of the European Convention of Human Rights (ECHR) in relation to the rights of a person accused of a crime. In *R v H*[38] the accused, who was aged thirteen at the time of the alleged offences, was adjudged unfit to plead to two offences of indecent assault. A jury then found that he had done the acts alleged against him in each count, for which he received an absolute discharge. However, the defendant's father was directed to cause him to be registered as a sex offender. The accused appealed against the findings which resulted from the trial of the facts arguing that as this procedure fell within the protection afforded by Art 6 of the ECHR, he had not been afforded this protection since, being unfit to plead, he could not give instructions and participate fully in his defence.

In dismissing the appeal, both the Court of Appeal[39] and the House of Lords concluded that the trial of the facts lacked the essential features of criminal process, as it could not result in conviction or punishment, nor were the notification requirements as to registration as a sex offender to be so regarded, as they were designed to protect the public rather than to punish. Lord Bingham opined:[40]

> It would be highly anomalous if s 4A, introduced by amendment for the protection of those unable through mental unfitness to defend them at trial, were itself to be held incompatible with the convention. It is very much in the interests of such persons that the basic facts relied on against them (shorn of issues concerning intent) should be formally and publicly investigated in open court with counsel appointed to represent the interests of the person accused so far as possible in the circumstances. The position of accused persons would certainly not be improved if s 4A were abrogated.

While it is true that the trial of the facts was introduced partly to protect the unfit to plead, the decision in *R v H* has attracted criticism. In particular, in his application of the three-part test developed by the European Court in *Engel v The Netherlands (No 1)*,[41] Lord Bingham made it clear that as an adverse finding from the trial of the facts could not result in a penalty, then the severity issue raised in the third part of the *Engel* test was irrelevant. However, while his Lordship may have been influenced

[38] [2003] 1 All ER 497. [39] [2002] 1 WLR 824. [40] *R v H* (n 38) 506.

[41] (1976) 1 EHRR 647. The tripartite test provides that in order to determine whether an issue is to be regarded as criminal or civil it is necessary to consider (i) if the proceedings are categorised as criminal under domestic law; (ii) the nature of the offence; and (iii) the severity of the penalty.

by the fact that in the case before him the result was an absolute discharge, his recognition of the fact that 'if an adverse finding leads to the making of a hospital order, there is no bar to a criminal trial if the accused person recovers'[42] fails to reveal that hospital orders are criminal disposals normally meted out after conviction.[43]

Additionally, when imposed with restrictions, the resulting indeterminate detention in hospital seems to qualify as severe. However, Lord Bingham confirms the 'non-punitive nature of the order'[44] for registration as a sex offender. But in doing so he failed to point out that in *Welch v United Kingdom*[45] the court ruled that it 'must remain free to go behind appearances and assess for itself whether a particular measure amounts in substance to a "penalty"'. As part of this assessment it is also clear that severity of outcome is an important factor.

Further, in *R v Chai*[46] the Court of Appeal ruled that the provisions relating to the admissibility of hearsay evidence in a criminal trial applied equally to the trial of the facts. In doing so, it was held that as the purpose of s 4A was to mirror as closely as possible the fact-finding process in a criminal trial, there was thus every reason why the court should not be limited to the common law rules of criminal evidence and that it was not necessary to decide whether s 4A proceedings were 'criminal proceedings' for one purpose but not another.[47]

Despite these problems, the reasoning of the House of Lords in *R v H* was confirmed by the European Court of Human Rights (ECtHR) in *R v Antoine*,[48] where it was again concluded that as the applicant was not under any threat of conviction by virtue of the trial of the facts, such a procedure could not be regarded as involving the determination of a criminal charge. Once more, however, the court ignored the severity point when it remarked that although 'hospital orders may be imposed on defendants in criminal trials and involve loss of liberty, it cannot be argued that such an order is a measure of retribution or deterrence in the sense of the imposition of a sentence of imprisonment'[49] But no one would suggest in criminal proceedings where the defence of insanity is uncontested by the prosecution, that the accused is not protected by Art 6, merely because the disposal options cannot be regarded as penal. Surely, the court should have considered its own decision in *Welch* in order to assess whether a hospital order, particularly one with restrictions, is in 'substance' a penalty. Finally, in *Dewani (No 2)*, although the Divisional Court confirmed that 'Under the law of South Africa and the law of England and Wales a procedure to determine fitness to stand trial does not constitute the determination of a criminal charge and the resulting detention is not punishment',[50] this did not prevent the Court from reaching the conclusion that the unfit defendant could, provided other

[42] [2003] 1 All ER 506. It should also be pointed out that the 1991 Act only permits the Secretary of State to remit for a full trial those who are subject to a hospital order with restrictions (Criminal Procedure (Insanity) Act 1964, see s 5A(4), substituted by The Domestic Violence, Crime and Victims Act 2004, s 24).

[43] Mental Health Act 1983, ss 37 and 41.

[44] *Engel v The Netherlands (No 1)* (n 42).

[45] (1995) 20 EHRR 247.

[46] [2007] EWCA Crim 2647.

[47] See also *R v Creed* [2011] EWCA Crim 144, where it was held that the reasoning in *Chai* relating to hearsay must apply to bad character applications.

[48] Application no 62960/00, decision as to admissibility 13 May 2003.

[49] ibid.

[50] [2014] 1 WLR 3220 [31].

safeguards were in place, be extradited to South Africa as his current state of unfitness to plead did not preclude him from being classed as an accused person for the purposes of the Extradition Act 2003. In short, the prospect of his regaining fitness means that the South African Government's interest in a future prosecution takes precedence over the current civil status of the unfit person. Would it not be better to conclude that extradition should only take place as and when fitness is regained, as the Court does accept that if the unfitness is permanent then the extradition would not be for the purpose of prosecuting that person for a criminal offence, but rather for the purpose of indefinite detention?

The scope of the trial of the facts

The ECtHR in *Antoine* also considered the scope of the trial of the facts and relied on the fact that the case had already been before the House of Lords.[51] The problem, put simply, is whether the s 4A hearing, in requiring a jury to decide whether the unfit defendant 'did the act or made the omission charged against him', requires proof of all the elements of the offence. In *Antoine,* the trial judge, following the decision of the Court of Appeal in *Egan*,[52] directed the jury that both the *actus reus* and the *mens rea* of murder had to be proved in the trial of the facts. In addition, he ruled that the plea of diminished responsibility could not be raised on the hearing under s 4A. In upholding the ruling on diminished responsibility, the House of Lords concluded that as that plea was only available as an alternative to liability for murder, once there was a finding of unfitness the trial could not proceed. This meant that as the unfit defendant was no longer 'liable to be convicted of murder' as required by s 2 of the Homicide Act 1957, the plea was no longer available. With regard to the issue of *mens rea*, the House of Lords ruled that the trial judge had been wrong and that the decision in *Egan* should no longer be followed, as by using the word 'act' and not the word 'offence' in s 4A(2) it was clear that the jury was not to consider the mental ingredients of the offence. According to Lord Hutton:

> The purpose of section 4A, in my opinion is to strike a fair balance between the need to protect a defendant who has, in fact, done nothing wrong and is unfit to plead at his trial and the need to protect the public from a defendant who has committed an injurious act which would constitute a crime if done with the requisite mens rea.... I consider that the section strikes this balance by distinguishing between a person who has not carried out the actus reus of the crime charged against him and a person who has carried out an act (or made an omission) which would constitute a crime if done (or made an omission) with the requisite mens rea....[53]

More recently in the case of *R v B*[54] the problem concerned when an act is to be considered 'injurious' in respect of the offence of voyeurism under s 77 of the Sexual Offences Act 2003. D was a young man of good character who suffered from a

[51] *R v Antoine* [2001] 1 AC 340. [52] [1998] 1 Cr App R 121.
[53] [2001] 1 AC 376–77.
[54] [2012] EWCA Crim 770; see also *R v Wells* [2015] EWCA Crim 2.

learning disability and autistic spectrum disorder. It was alleged that while in a cubicle of a family changing room at a swimming pool, where two young mothers were present with their six-year-old sons, D's head had appeared in the gap below the cubicle and he had looked up at the boys in the adjoining cubicle, one of whom was naked. D was arrested and charged with two counts of voyeurism. He said he was lying on his back in the cubicle because of back pain. D was found unfit to plead in respect of both counts, which alleged that D 'for the purpose of sexual gratification, observed [X or Y as the case might be] doing a private act, knowing that [X or Y] did not consent to being observed for [the appellant's] sexual gratification'.

During the trial of the facts, the judge ruled that all the prosecution needed to prove was that D observed, in the sense of deliberately watching as opposed to incidentally seeing, the relevant boy doing a private act. There was no need to prove that the 'act' was done for the purpose of sexual gratification or that it was done knowing that the victim did not consent to being observed for sexual gratification. Thus, the jury found D to have done the 'act' in question and he was given a two-year supervision order and a Sexual Offences Prevention Order (SOPO). He was also required to register on the Sexual Offenders' Register for five years. The judge's ruling, together with the SOPO and the registration order, were all challenged on appeal.

Doing an act 'for the purpose of sexual gratification' is as clear-cut an example of a mental element as one is likely to find, and it is clear that this is the reason why the judge ruled that this element should be excluded from the jury's consideration in respect of the TOF, as they were 'not concerned to decide whether [D's] motive was or was not a sexual one'.[55] The problem, of course, is that if all the prosecution were required to prove was that D observed the young boys doing a private act, then he would be the subject of a disposal measure and a SOPO when all he had to be seen to do was 'observe' the victims without any need for it to be proved that his purpose was one of sexual gratification. During his judgment Aikens LJ reviewed the authorities and noted how these decisions had each reached a view that a clear-cut distinction between *actus reus* and *mens rea* could not and should not always be maintained for the purposes of a TOF. In short, each offence needs to be the subject of scrutiny to decide which elements should be included and which excluded in TOF proceedings. With regard to the offence of voyeurism for the purposes of s 4A(2), his Lordship opined:

> ... that the link between deliberate observation and the purpose of sexual gratification of the observer is central to the statutory offence of voyeurism. To use Lord Hutton's phrase, it is that purpose which turns the deliberate observation of another doing an intimate act (such as undressing) in private into an 'injurious act'. We have to accept that enquiring into someone's purpose for doing something is to enquire into that person's state of mind when he did the relevant act ... For the offence of voyeurism, these two actions, the one aimed at the outside world and the other going on in the consciousness of the observer, have to go together; the deliberate observation must be done simultaneously with the specific, albeit subjective, purpose of obtaining sexual gratification.[56]

[55] *R v B* (n 54) [16]. [56] ibid [61].

It followed, therefore, that:

in the case of an offence of voyeurism under section 67(1) of the SOA, the relevant 'act … charged as the offence' for the purposes of section 4A(2) is that of deliberate observation of another doing a private act where the observer does so for the specific purpose of the observer obtaining sexual gratification. That omnibus activity is the 'injurious act'. Although the activity has two components, they are indissoluble; together they are the relevant 'act'.[57]

This conclusion, as Aikens LJ points out, is not only consistent with the authorities he had already reviewed, but supported his additional conclusion that (at [63]):

As for the further element in the offence of voyeurism, the observer's knowledge that the person observed does not consent to being observed for the purposes of the observer's sexual gratification, that is not directly linked to the outward component of the 'act'. It refers to the state of mind that the observer must have, but it is not the reason for the observation. Accordingly, for the purposes of section 4A(2), we have concluded that this element of the offence is not a part of the ' act … charged as the offence' and so is not something the jury will be concerned to determine.

While this is undoubtedly the case, the dilemma remains that, although in this case the appeal was allowed both in respect of the TOF finding and the SOPO, it is still the case that the TOF does not fully protect the unfit to plead. If in this case D had indeed observed the victim for the purposes of sexual gratification, believing that the person in question in the adjoining cubicle was his male partner when in fact his partner had already left and a stranger had entered, then D's position becomes more problematical. His mistaken belief in consent will be excluded from the TOF unless, as Lord Hutton made clear in Antoine, there is objective evidence to support the mistake.[58] That could well be the case here, but, if not, D will be the subject of an unfit-to-plead finding when in reality his behaviour would seem to have been no more 'injurious' than the appellant in B.

Perhaps then the compromise the TOF proceedings seek to achieve is simply wrong as it inevitably places the unfit to plead in a less favourable position than their fit counterparts. The reason for this surrounds the nature of s 4A(2), of which the drafting is only partly to blame. An additional and more fundamental problem concerns the very essence, rather than just the scope, of the TOF. The fact that the House of Lords in *H*[59] ruled that the TOF is not a criminal procedure has serious implications. It led Andrew Ashworth to conclude that the TOF 'under s. 4A is sui generis'[60] and Sir John Smith, in his commentary on *Antoine*, to remark: 'No other occasion when the actus reus, standing alone, has been held to have any legal consequences comes to mind.'[61] So it seems best to regard the TOF not only as unique, but also as so unique as to be unacceptable and in need of reform.

However, in following the approach in *Antoine* the ECtHR opined:

While it is true that the section 4A hearing has strong similarities with procedures at a criminal trial, the Court notes that the proceedings were principally concerned with the *actus reus*,

[57] ibid [62]. [58] See below at n 61. [59] [2003] 1 UKHL 1.
[60] [2003] Crim LR 818. [61] ibid 622.

namely whether the applicant had carried out an act or made an omission which would have constituted a crime if done or made with the requisite *mens rea*.[62]

This uncritical acceptance of the limited nature of the trial of the facts is, however, an uncomfortable resolution of the scope of the word 'act' in s 4A(2). In particular, Lord Hutton was clearly concerned about cases where the defendant has an arguable defence of accident, mistake, or self-defence, as 'such defences almost invariably involve some consideration of the mental state of the defendant'. His Lordship sought to resolve this problem in the following manner:

> If there is objective evidence which raises the issue of mistake or accident or self-defence, then the jury should not find that the defendant did the 'act' unless it is satisfied beyond reasonable doubt on all the evidence that the prosecution has negatived that defence.[63] For example... if a woman was charged with theft of a handbag and a witness gave evidence that on sitting down at a table in a restaurant the defendant had placed her own handbag on the floor and, on getting up to leave, picked up the handbag placed beside her by a woman at the next table, it would be open to the jury to acquit.
>
> But what the defence cannot do, in the absence of a witness whose evidence raises the defence, is to suggest that the defendant may have acted under a mistake, or by accident, or in self-defence, and to submit that the jury should acquit unless the prosecution satisfies them that there is no reasonable possibility that that suggestion is correct. [64]

What this passage reveals is the difficulty inherent in achieving the correct balance in the trial of the facts to give sufficient protection to the unfit to plead. The argument accepted by both the House of Lords and the European Court is that this balance is achieved by adopting a procedure which is principally concerned with the *actus reus*, as there is a need to protect the public from those who commit 'injurious acts'.

While there is no doubt that permitting the introduction of defences in the manner described will complicate the trial of the facts, such a compromise seems beyond argument. The question is rather whether it goes far enough, as the act committed in the handbag example given above can hardly be described as 'injurious'. Yet in the absence of objective evidence, in support of her defence of mistake such an unfit accused would be proved to have committed the 'act' of theft and subject to the disposal options under the 1964 Act. Not only that, what is to happen if there is objective evidence supporting the fact that the defendant's mistake was the product of a 'disease of the mind' within the M'Naghten Rules?

In Lord Hutton's view, the defence of insanity should have no role to play in the trial of the facts since if the appellant's submission were correct, 'then *mens rea* could not be proved because of the insanity existing at the time of the alleged offence, and the jury would have to acquit the defendant and he would be released to the danger of the public'.[65] Of course, this danger would not arise if the 1991 Act had expressly

[62] *Antoine v UK* (2003) Fourth Section Decision as to the Admissibility of Application no. 62960/00, 10.

[63] The ECtHR said of this passage that this was 'The only time when *mens rea* might become relevant ...'.

[64] [2001] 1 AC 376–77. For the difficulties over what constitutes objective evidence see *R v Wells* (n 54).

[65] [2001] 1 AC 373.

provided that insanity could be used in the trial of the facts which, as Lord Hutton noted, is the case in Scotland.[66] In addition, the exclusion of insanity in the trial of the facts seems to lead to an ordinary acquittal in cases of 'involuntariness' resulting from insanity in the form of epileptic automatism, which can hardly have been his Lordship's intention.[67]

It is more than likely, therefore, that this type of litigation will continue, leading one to wonder why, if it is appropriate for a jury to consider a defendant's state of mind in some instances relating to *actus reus*,[68] *mens rea* is not permitted as part of this enquiry. In this connection, it is of note that in its Report on Unfitness to Plead, the Law Commission concludes that the TOF procedure in its current form is unsatisfactory. The Commission charts the history of the TOF, which it prefers to describe as 'the section 4A hearing', and is properly critical of its scope and application. In essence, the Commission concludes that the s 4A hearing gives insufficient protection to the unfit defendant as its scope is too narrow and as a procedure it fails to give any protection under Art 6 of the ECHR. Its preferred reform option, which would overturn *Antoine,* is to replace the present s 4A hearing, 'with a procedure whereby the prosecution is obliged to prove that the accused did the act or made the omission charged and that there are no grounds for acquittal'.[69] This mirrors the position in Scotland (see s 55(1) of the Criminal Procedure (Scotland) Act 1995), where the 'examination of the facts' requires the court to be satisfied 'on the balance of probabilities that there are no grounds for acquitting the accused', but with the Commission rejecting the need for the Crown only to discharge the civil rather than the criminal burden of proof. The difficulty, however, relates to cases where the reason for the acquittal is that the accused was legally insane at the time of the offence. In addition, the Commission also wishes to reverse the effect of *H*, but again it is not clear why, if the newly crafted s 4A hearing can, as now, never result in a conviction, this new 'procedure would ... satisfy the "formal accusation" aspect of criminal proceedings',[70] giving it Art 6 protection. Although these matters need careful consideration, the Commission's criticisms of the TOF are well founded and it is surely beyond argument that in its current form the TOF fails to give the unfit to plead the same opportunities to be acquitted as are available to defendants in an ordinary criminal trial. As such, the call for reform is powerful and should not go unheeded.

Regaining Fitness

Section 5A(4) of the Criminal Procedure (Insanity) Act 1964, which was inserted by section 24 of the Domestic Violence, Crime and Victims Act 2004, maintains the position as originally contained in Schedule 1 of the Criminal Procedure (Insanity and Unfitness to Plead) Act 1991. In doing so it provides for a mechanism whereby

66 ibid. Also recommended by the Law Commission at Law Com No 464 (n 2) 164.

67 See RD Mackay and G Kearns 'An Upturn in Unfitness to Plead? Disability in Relation to the Trial under the 1991 Act' [2000] Crim LR 532, 544.

68 As in *R v B* (n 54) discussed above.

69 Law Commission, Law Com No 364 (n 2) para 6.140.

70 ibid, para 6.134.

the Secretary of State,[71] 'if satisfied, after consultation with the treating psychiatrist, that the person can properly be tried, may remit the person for trial, either to the court of trial or to a prison' and that on arrival to such the hospital and the restriction order will cease to have effect.[72]

However, s 5A(4)(b) makes it clear that this only applies where the unfitness-to-plead finding has resulted in the imposition of a hospital order with a restriction order. In addition, this subsection states only that the Secretary of State 'may' remit the person for trial. It is clear that there is no obligation to do so nor, apart from the need to consult the treating psychiatrist referred to above, are there any principles laid down governing the taking of such decisions. It seems, therefore, that all other unfitness-to-plead disposals are in effect final,[73] which means that in practice it is left to the Crown Prosecution Service (CPS) to decide, in any such case where fitness has been regained, whether it is in the public interest to mount a prosecution. In the absence of any formal mechanism similar to that given to the Secretary of State, it seems that the CPS rarely, if ever, mounts such prosecutions.

Matters of Proof

There are several issues relating to proving unfitness to plead that merit consideration.

Raising the issue of unfitness to plead

Section 4(1) of the 1964 Act states that the issue of disability may arise 'at the instance of the defence or otherwise'. Accordingly, although the issue is more than likely to be raised by the defence, it is clear that the prosecution[74] or the judge may also raise the issue. With regard to the latter, if neither party raises the issue, then the judge should do so, assuming he has doubts as to the fitness of the accused.[75] It is worth repeating that no matter who raises the issue of fitness to plead, since the enactment of the Domestic Violence, Crime and Victims Act 2004, fitness is now determined by a court without a jury. In addition, the accused cannot be found unfit to plead unless there is written or oral evidence to that effect by two or more registered medical practitioners, at least one of whom is approved by the Secretary of State as having special experience in the field of mental disorder;[76] if the medical evidence is all to the contrary, then the fitness issue need not be tried.[77] In this context, however, it

[71] This is the Secretary of State for Justice.

[72] See s 5(4) Criminal Procedure (Insanity) Act 1964. This presumably calls for the *Pritchard* test to be considered, in the sense that none of the criteria continue to be satisfied.

[73] For argument to the contrary, see R Fortson, chapter One in B Livings and N Wake (eds), *Mental Condition Defences and the Criminal Justice System* (Cambridge Scholars Publishing 2015) 15.

[74] See *R v Beynon* [1957] 2 All ER 513.

[75] See *R v MacCarthy* [1967] 1 QB 68.

[76] See *Alexander v Isleworth Crown Court* [2009] EWHC 85 (Admin). See also *R v Ghulam* [2009] EWCA Crim 2285, which makes it clear that the requirement for evidence from two medical practitioners only relates to a 'determination' that a defendant was unfit rather than fit to plead.

[77] *R v Borkan* [2004] EWCA 1642.

remains clear that once there is medical evidence which requires that the fitness issue be tried, the decision 'is that of the judge and not that of the doctors ...'.[78] This is made abundantly clear in *R v Walls*, where in the light of the serious consequences which may flow from a finding of unfitness to plead Thomas LJ stated:

> We consider that, save in clear cases, a court must rigorously examine evidence of psychiatrists adduced before them and then subject that evidence to careful analysis against the *Pritchard* criteria as interpreted in *Podola*. Save in cases where the unfitness is clear, the fact that psychiatrists agree is not enough, as this case demonstrates; a court would be failing in its duty to both the public and a defendant if it did not rigorously examine the evidence and reach its own conclusion.[79]

Two important points flow from this remark. The first is that agreement between psychiatrists that a defendant is unfit to plead will not prevent the court from reaching its own conclusion on the issue. Secondly, in order to reach its own conclusion, the court will closely examine the expert evidence against the *Pritchard* criteria and will not be afraid to reject it if it does not consider and apply these criteria. Formerly there may have been a tendency to overly rely on unanimous psychiatric opinion favouring unfitness, whether or not the *Pritchard* criteria were properly applied. But this, it seems, will no longer be acceptable. In future, therefore, it will be important that psychiatric reports on this issue fully address these criteria when forming a view as to a defendant's unfitness to plead. In short, the decision in *Walls* may signal an important shift in the court's attitude towards scrutinising expert evidence about unfitness to plead.

Burden of proof

The position relating to burden of proof seems analogous to the defence of insanity. Accordingly, if the issue of unfitness to plead is raised by the defence, then the onus of proving it rests upon the accused and must be established on a balance of probabilities.[80] If, however, the prosecution raises the issue and it is contested by the defence, then the burden is on the prosecution and must be proved beyond reasonable doubt.[81] It also seems likely that where the issue is raised by the judge and disputed by the defence the onus will again be on the prosecution.[82]

Research indicates that it is the defence which raises the issue of unfitness in most cases.[83] With this is mind, there remains the concern that this means that in most unfitness-to-plead cases the judge need not be sure that the accused can satisfy the test for fitness to plead set out in *Pritchard* so to 'properly and fairly be tried'.[84]

[78] *R v Miller and Miller* [2006] EWCA Crim, para 17. [79] See n 11 para 38.

[80] *R v Podola* (n 8) [196] 1 QB 325; *R v Marcantonio* (n 20) [11].

[81] *R v Robertson* (n 9). [82] See also *R v Chitolie* [2016] EWCA Crim 14 [96].

[83] See RD Mackay et al, 'A Continued Upturn in Unfitness to Plead—More Disability in Relation to the Trial under the 1991 Act' [2007] Crim LR 534.

[84] *R v Borkan* (n 77) para 18.

The disposal of those found unfit to plead

Those found unfit are only subject to the court's disposal powers if there has been a 'trial of the facts' in which the prosecution has proved beyond reasonable doubt that the accused committed the act or made the omission charged.[85]

Prior to the enactment of the Criminal Procedure (Insanity and Unfitness to Plead) Act 1991 all those found unfit to plead received the equivalent of a hospital order with restrictions. This mandatory, indefinite hospitalisation, which was draconian and unnecessary, was replaced by a more flexible disposal regime in the 1991 Act. Initially this regime included a Guardianship Order. However, this option was abolished by the Domestic Violence, Crime and Victims Act 2004,[86] which made a number of other important changes. As the law now stands, those found unfit to plead and to have 'done the act or made the omission charged' may be the subject of one of the following three disposals.

(a) A hospital order (with or without a restriction order)

The original 1991 Act gave the court the power to impose 'an admission order' rather than a hospital order. Such an order did not require compliance with the Mental Health Act 1983,[87] which meant that a person found unfit to plead could be sent to hospital even though he was not mentally ill.

This problem was further exacerbated by the fact that the indefinite and mandatory hospitalisation regime was retained for those found unfit to plead in respect of murder. Because of fears that such a regime did not comply with the ECHR,[88] the 2004 Act now makes it a requirement that there be medical evidence which justifies detention in hospital on grounds of the defendant's mental state, namely a mental disorder within the Mental Health Act 1983, which in turn requires specialist mental health treatment. This applies equally to murder charges. If the conditions for making a hospital order are not met, then neither a restriction order nor a hospital order can be made. Further, the Secretary of State no longer has any role in deciding whether or not such defendants who are found 'not guilty by reason of insanity' are admitted to hospital; this is now a matter for the court based on the relevant medical evidence.[89]

[85] See above.

[86] It is of interest to note that neither Northern Ireland nor Scotland have abolished Guardianship and it is difficult to understand why England and Wales has done so.

[87] See *Narey v HM Customs and Excise* [2005] EWHC 784 (Admin).

[88] See RD Mackay and C Gearty, 'On Being Insane in Jersey: The Case of *A-G v Jason Prior*' [2001] Crim LR 560.

[89] Under the original 1964 Act, the Secretary of State had the power to specify the admitting hospital within a two-month period from the date of the court order. Now the court can require a hospital to admit a person found not guilty by reason of insanity (or unfit to plead). It has no such power in respect of those convicted of an offence, which reflects the fact that the court has the option of a criminal justice disposal following a conviction, but has no such option following a finding of insanity (or unfitness). In addition, admission to hospital must now take place within the twenty-eight-day period specified in s 27(4) of the Mental Health Act 1983, a period which is mandatory, see *R on the application of DB v Nottinghamshire Healthcare NHS Trust* [2008] EWCA Civ 1354.

This alignment of hospital-based disposals with the Mental Health Act 1983 is important as it safeguards those who are not mentally ill, but who are nevertheless found to be legally insane, from unjustified and non-therapeutic hospitalisation. In such cases the court's options are now limited to one of the two remaining forms of disposal.

(b) A supervision order

The supervision order replaces the supervision and treatment order contained in the 1991 Act. The new supervision order differs from the old supervision and treatment order in that although it enables treatment to be given under supervision for physical as well as mental disorders, it cannot include a requirement for a person to receive treatment as an in-patient. It is designed to enable support and treatment to be given to the defendant to prevent recurrence of the problem which led to the offending. There is no sanction for breach of a supervision order designed to provide a framework for treatment which cannot be given without the consent of the supervised person and the nominated supervisor.[90]

However, the fact that admission to a hospital with restrictions in murder charges is no longer mandatory, but rather can only be made if the court has the power to make a hospital order under the Mental Health Act 1983,[91] may well enhance the role of supervision orders. In essence, such orders may become more prevalent as they are now to be used in respect of cases of medical conditions which do not qualify as mental disorders within the Mental Health Act 1983. Thus, the court is not obliged to impose a condition with regard to treatment as was formerly the case with a supervision and treatment order, but may only do so if the required conditions are satisfied. This means that in appropriate cases supervision, rather than treatment, will be all that is permitted as a requirement of such an order. Thus, no matter how serious the alleged offence, even if it results in a murder charge, only a supervision order (or absolute discharge) may be given in such a case.[92] This has led the Court of Appeal to remark:

> A finding that a defendant did the act in question, has the consequence that the court's powers of disposal are limited to a hospital order (where the issues are too well known to need stating), a supervision order for a specified period of no more than two years or an absolute discharge—see s. 5 of the Criminal Procedure (Insanity) 1964. The court's ability either to protect the public or to assist the defendant is severely limited.

It is clear from this that the court has concerns as to whether the current disposals for unfitness to plead are sufficient, in some cases, to protect the public.

[90] See *City and County of Swansea v Swansea Crown Court* [2016] EWHC 1389 (Admin), which makes it clear that if consent is not obtained the order will be quashed.

[91] See s 24 Domestic Violence, Crime and Victims Act 2004, substituting s 5 of the Criminal Procedure (Insanity) Act 1964.

[92] This occurred in the case of Sarwat Malik, who was found 'not guilty by reason of insanity' for a murder charge. Malik was given a supervision order after a judge ruled he had no power to detain him under the Mental Health Act, see http://www.murdermap.co.uk/pages/cases/case.asp?CID=838332255. The same would apply had the case been one of unfitness to plead.

This has led the Law Commission to recommend a tightening up of the disposal regime.[93]

(c) An order for absolute discharge

Section 5(2)(b)(iii) of the 1991 Act as amended by the 2004 Act gives the court the option to make an order for the absolute discharge of the accused. The Home Office Circular's comment on this form of order is brief and is to the effect it might be used 'where the alleged offence was trivial and the accused does not require treatment and supervision in the community'.[94] However, it seems clear that such orders are being given in some cases where the offence could hardly be described as trivial.[95] This is perhaps not a surprise, since if the accused is found to be in need of neither treatment nor supervision, then the only alternative is an absolute discharge.

Empirical Research

My four empirical studies have revealed how the doctrine of unfitness to plead operates in English criminal law. The first such study reported that during the fourteen-year period from 1976 to 1989 there was a total of 302 findings of unfitness to plead (UTP) in England and Wales.[96] The maximum number of such cases in any single year was thirty-nine in 1980, while by the final year of the research this number had fallen to eleven. In assessing the reasons for the fall in the number of unfitness findings, this study echoed the conclusion contained in first empirical study of the insanity defence,[97] namely that the infrequent use of the special verdict could be traced to the inflexible disposal consequences of indefinite hospitalisation originally mandated by the Criminal Procedure (Insanity) Act 1964.

In addition, this early UTP research supported a second criticism of the 1964 Act—the lack of any automatic trial of the facts where unfitness to plead was an issue which, as already discussed, meant that there was little opportunity for the case against the unfit defendant to be investigated. The next two empirical studies examined all findings of UTP during the first five years (1992–96)[98] and second five years (1997–2001)[99] of the new regime under the Criminal Procedure (Insanity and Unfitness to Plead) Act 1991, which introduced flexibility of disposal.

During the first five-year study, there was a total of 123 (average 24.6) findings of UTP in England and Wales compared to 329 (average 65.8) in the 1997–2001 study.

[93] See the Law Com No 364 (n 2) ch 6.

[94] Home Office Circular No 20/2005 para 18.

[95] See Mackay et al, 'A Continued Upturn in Unfitness to Plead—More disability in Relation to the Trial under the 1991 Act' (n 83) 541–43.

[96] RD Mackay, *Mental Condition Defences in the Criminal Law* (Clarendon Press, 1995) 221–24. This updates an earlier study, see RD Mackay, 'The Decline of Disability in Relation to the Trial' [1991] Crim LR 87.

[97] RD Mackay, 'Fact and Fiction about the Insanity Defence' [1990] Crim LR 247.

[98] Mackay and Kearns, 'An Upturn in Unfitness to Plead? Disability in Relation to the Trial under the 1991 Act' (n 67).

[99] Mackay et al, 'A Continued Upturn in Unfitness to Plead—More Disability in Relation to the Trial under the 1991 Act' (n 83).

With regard to diagnostic groups, the picture has altered somewhat. Under the 1964 Act and the first five years of the 1991 Act, schizophrenia was clearly most prevalent, followed by mental impairment. More recently this has changed, with the 1997–2001 study revealing that mental impairment (n = 105) and schizophrenia (n = 104) are almost identical in number.

Overall what was clear was that the number of findings of UTP had continued to rise. The increase from thirty-five findings in 1997 to a peak of eighty in 1999 indicated that the legislative changes contained in the 1991 Act were having an on-going effect. This trend was confirmed in a fourth study of all findings of UTP during the thirteen-year period from 2002–14.[100] This study conducted for the Law Commission[101] confirmed that although hospital-based disposals continued to account for the majority of UTP disposals (60.5 per cent), the judiciary was continuing to make full use of the flexible disposal powers contained in the 1991 Act. In addition, the fact that admission to hospital with restrictions in murder charges is no longer mandatory, but rather can only be made if the court has the power to make a hospital order under the Mental Health Act 1983,[102] removes a further disincentive to use UTP. Overall however, the total number of UTP findings for the five-year period 2007–11 shows a decrease to 488 from 519 in the previous five-year period of 2002–06. It is possible, therefore, that the number of UTP findings may have reached a plateau.[103] If this is so, it lends support to the argument that without meaningful reform of the *Pritchard* test the annual number of UTP findings is unlikely to increase beyond present levels.

The Channel Island of Jersey

The Channel Islands fall into two separate self-governing entities known as bailiwicks. They are the Bailiwick of Guernsey and the Bailiwick of Jersey. Both are British Crown Dependencies, but neither is part of the United Kingdom. Guernsey and Jersey have no laws in common, which is well illustrated by the fact that each has a different test for unfitness to plead. What follows is a brief discussion of the new test for unfitness to plead which has been adopted in Jersey.

Until recently unfitness to plead had received little or no judicial scrutiny in Jersey. This changed in 2003 in the case of *A-G v O'Driscoll*,[104] when the Bailiff (the

[100] RD Mackay, Appendix A 'Unfitness to Plead—Data on Formal Findings from 2002 to 2014', Law Commission, *Unfitness to Plead, Volume 1: Report*, Law Com No 364 (2016). Available at https://s3-eu-west-2.amazonaws.com/lawcom-prod-storage-11jsxou24uy7q/uploads/2016/01/apa.pdf.

[101] ibid. This updates an earlier study for the Law Commission published in RD Mackay, Appendix C 'Unfitness to Plead—Data on Formal Findings from 2002 to 2008', Law Commission, *Unfitness to Plead*, CP No 197 (2010).

[102] See s 24 Domestic Violence, Crime and Victims Act 2004, substituting s 5 of the Criminal Procedure (Insanity) Act 1964. For discussion, see ch 20, s 7(a).

[103] The annual average of UTP findings in the Law Commission study is 100.6 and for the years 2012–14 it is 100.3, showing no change in those subsequent three years.

[104] 2003 JLR 390.

most senior judge in Jersey), Sir Philip Bailhache, ruled that the test for unfitness to plead laid down in England, namely that in *Pritchard,* should not be adopted, but instead a new test should be formulated which would be (a) consonant with the idea of 'effective participation in the criminal process' found in the ECHR; (b) conscious of the developments in medical science since the English test was adopted; and (c) appropriate to the social needs of Jersey. This new test he adopted as part of the law of Jersey is as follows:

> an accused person is so insane as to be unfit to plead to the accusation, or unable to understand the nature of the trial if, as a result of unsoundness of mind or inability to communicate, he or she lacks the capacity to participate effectively in the proceedings.
>
> In determining this issue, the [Court] shall have regard to the ability of the accused—
>
> (a) to understand the nature of the proceedings so as to instruct his lawyer and to make a proper defence;
> (b) to understand the substance of the evidence;
> (c) to give evidence on his own behalf; and
> (d) to make rational decisions in relation to his participation in the proceedings (including whether or not to plead guilty), which reflect true and informed choices on his part.[105]

Paragraph (d) above departs from the narrow approach in *Pritchard* and introduces, the notion of 'decisional capacity'[106] while maintaining a 'foundational concept'[107] which is a clarification and updating of the *Pritchard* criteria in paragraphs (a), (b), and (c). Since then the first case to apply the new unfitness test has come before the Jersey courts, namely that of *Harding.*[108] The court, having considered all the evidence, found the defendant unfit to plead. In his judgment setting out the reason for this finding Commissioner Clyde-Smith stated:

> For the purposes of the *O'Driscoll* test the court has to have regard to the ability of the defendant to make rational decisions in relation to her participation in the proceedings which reflect true and informed choices on her part; 'rational' in this context to be given its ordinary meaning namely based on or in accordance with reason or logic. In this case it was clear from the evidence of both experts that, at any given moment, the defendant had that ability but that, as Dr Dillon said, in the context of multiple snap shots or even a film, her condition, and in particular her changes in emotional state, would impact on her thought processes and ability to make rational decisions.

[105] ibid, para 29. Both the Law Commission of England and Wales, Law Com No 364 (n 2) para 3.120 (2) and the Northern Ireland Law Commission in its Report on Unfitness to Plead NILC 16 (2013) para 2.54 were critical of this test. The former concluded that it would raise further uncertainty, while the latter considered that it would set the bar too high. Both recommend adapting the Mental Capacity Act 2005, but whether this will lead to more certainty or help in setting the bar at an appropriate level is open to question.

[106] See RD Mackay, 'On Being Insane in Jersey Part Three—The Case of *Attorney General v. Neil Liam O'Driscoll*' [2003] Criminal Law Review 291; RD Mackay, 'Unfitness to Plead—Some Observations on the Law Commission's Consultation Paper [2011] Crim LR 433', 436–38.

[107] A term borrowed from Richard Bonnie, see 'The Competence of Criminal Defendants: A Theoretical Reformulation' (1992) 10 Behavioral Sciences and the Law 291.

[108] [2009] JRC198.

> We are concerned not with a snap shot in time but with the capacity of the defendant to participate effectively in her trial i.e. in the whole course of the trial likely to span a number of days. Taking into account the evidence of the experts and all the circumstances of the case as outlined in the joint narrative, the Jurats[109] concluded, on a balance of probabilities, that her impairment by reason of this condition, by which she was severely affected, was sufficiently substantial to render her incapable of participating effectively over the course of her trial.[110]

Clearly the court was persuaded as to the defendant's decisional incapacity and it seems likely that, having regard to the fact that the accused suffered from a personality disorder which impacted primarily on her emotional capacity to make decisions, she would have been adjudged fit to plead applying the *Pritchard* criteria.

The case of *Harding* has now been before the Jersey Court of Appeal. In his judgment, the President of the Court, Sumption, JA, made the following remark:

> Sir Philip considered that this test differed from the English law test; mainly it seems in requiring that the accused should have been capable of making rational decisions in relation to his participation in the proceedings. For our part, we are satisfied that the test which he stated in *O'Driscoll* is correct, *but we do not regard it as any different in principle from that which has been held to apply in England.* We make this point because issues may arise in future cases in Jersey, on which it may be desirable to refer to the much more substantial body of English authority. This process serves the interests of legal certainty. We are reluctant to inhibit it by encouraging the notion that Jersey law on this question exists in a distinct juridical compartment from the corresponding law of England.[111]

Everyone to date, including the Law Commission in its work on unfitness to plead, has opined that the two tests are radically different. Indeed, the Law Commission's entire discussion about a new test is premised on that basis. So, it is remarkable that the President should have reached this view without any real discussion of how it can be justified, apart from the weak notion that it is better to keep the law of both jurisdictions in tandem. Granted there is a more substantial body of English authority on unfitness to plead, but this body of law has repeatedly confirmed the narrowness of the *Pritchard* test and it is difficult to conclude that it comes anywhere close to encompassing 'decisional capacity'.[112]

Conclusion

This chapter has given an account of the law on unfitness to plead in England and Wales and the Island of Jersey. Many argue that there is a pressing need for reform within this area of the law. This is the clear view of the Law Commission,[113] which recommends, inter alia, that the test for fitness to stand trial needs radical change, as

[109] Jurats are elected to serve in the Royal Court of Jersey and decide questions of fact, including unfitness to plead.

[110] [2009] JRC 198 paras 38 and 39.

[111] [2010] JLR 239 para 5, emphasis added.

[112] See C Fogarty and R Mackay, 'On Being Insane in Jersey: Observations *Obiter* and the Road to Perdition' [2012] JGLR 58–62.

[113] Law Commission, Law Com No 364 (n 2).

the *Pritchard* criteria set the fitness threshold at too low a level. This in turn is likely to result in many potentially unfit defendants being subjected inappropriately to the rigours of a full criminal trial.[114] In this connection, it is worth repeating that the Island of Jersey has introduced a new test for unfitness to plead which specifically includes 'decisional capacity'. It is to be hoped that the law of England and Wales will follow suit and introduce a new statutory test[115] which will more fully protect such vulnerable defendants by ensuring that their 'effective participation' in the trial process requires not only foundational but also decisional capacity.

[114] See Peay, 'Fitness to Plead and Core Competencies' (n 3) for detailed discussion.
[115] See the Draft Legislation in Law Commission, Law Com No 364, Vol 2 (n 2).

3

Unfitness to Plead in England and Wales

A Practitioner's View of a Plea in Evolution

*Rudi Fortson**

Introduction

In 2008, the Law Commission for England and Wales expressed its intention to examine the law relating to 'unfitness to plead'[1] along with the defences of insanity and automatism.[2] This it has done,[3] together with its work (albeit in a civil law context) in relation to mental capacity and the deprivation of liberty.[4] As the Commission has pointed out, defendants charged with a criminal offence may be unfit to plead or to stand trial for a variety of reasons, 'including difficulties resulting from mental illness (longstanding or temporary), learning disability, developmental disorder or delay, a communication impairment or some other cause or combination of causes'.[5] Fitness to plead may also be relevant in the context of extradition proceedings (*consider Bobbe v Poland*).[6]

Two issues fall to be considered: (a) how might those defendants who are unfit be accurately identified; and (b) what steps should be taken by legal practitioners and by the courts of criminal jurisdiction to cater for the interests of vulnerable

* Barrister, 25 Bedford Row, London, and Visiting Professor of Law, Queen Mary College.

1 Law Commission, Tenth Programme of Law Reform, Law Com No 311 (2008).

2 Law Commission, *Unfitness to Plead: Summary*, Law Com No 364 (2016), para 1.1.

3 The material prepared and published by the Law Commission in relation to 'unfitness to plead' is considerable and available online: http://www.lawcom.gov.uk/project/unfitness-to-plead/.

The Law Commission published a Consultation Paper, CP No 197 (2010): http://www.lawcom.gov.uk/wp-content/uploads/2015/06/cp197_Unfitness_to_Plead_web.pdf; an 'Issues Paper' (May 2014); and Responses to the Issues Paper (2014).

The Commission published its *Unfitness to Plead, Volume 1: Report*, Law Com No 364 (2016): http://www.lawcom.gov.uk/wp-content/uploads/2016/01/lc364_unfitness_vol-1.pdf; and 'Draft Legislation': *Unfitness to Plead, Volume 2: Report*, Law Com No 364 (2016) https://s3-eu-west-2.amazonaws.com/lawcom-prod-storage-11jsxou24uy7q/uploads/2016/01/lc364_unfitness_vol-2.pdf.

See, also, Law Commission, 'Criminal Liability: Insanity and Automatism', Discussion Paper, 23 July 2013.

4 Law Commission, 'Mental Capacity and Deprivation of Liberty', Law Com No 372 (2017).

5 Law Commission, Law Com No 364 (n 2), para 1.1.

6 [2017] EWHC 3161 (Admin).

Fitness to Plead: International and Comparative Perspectives. First Edition. Edited by Ronnie Mackay and Warren Brookbanks. Chapter 3 © Rudi Fortson 2018. Published 2018 by Oxford University Press.

defendants, victims, and society, and to maintain the integrity of the legal process as one that is fair and just? The Law Commission has published a draft Bill that would, if enacted, give effect to its principal recommendations for reform.[7] The Government has yet to decide which (if any) of the Commission's recommendations it will accept and implement.[8] However, the law has not stood still. As this chapter seeks to demonstrate, by a combination of statutory intervention, judicial action,[9] and invaluable contributions from experts and various organisations,[10] legal rules and practices relating to vulnerable defendants (and victims) have been modified and continue to be honed. The purpose of this chapter is to provide insight into the current law and practices in relation to each of those issues, and to note areas where there has been improvement and where there is room for more.

Overview of the Current Law

There is little doubt that in recent years there has been a significant increase in the number of cases where the issue of 'unfitness to plead' is raised.[11] However, the expressions 'unfitness to plead', 'unfit to stand trial', and 'fitness to stand trial', are often used loosely by legal practitioners such that each expression is not necessarily indicative that a given practitioner has in mind all the determinations that might be made applying *R v Pritchard* and the CP(I)A 1964.[12]

The practitioner's purpose in raising a defendant's lack of fitness to plead or to stand trial may be to:

(i) invite the prosecution to offer no evidence; or

(ii) request that the trial should be adjourned until such time as the defendant recovers;[13] or

(iii) apply for special measures (eg, that the defendant be permitted to give evidence with the assistance of an intermediary); or

[7] Law Commission, *Criminal Procedure (Lack of Capacity) Bill I*: Volume 2, Law Com No 364 (n 3).

[8] Seehttp://data.parliament.uk/DepositedPapers/Files/DEP2016-0605/Mike_Penning_Government_interim_response_on_Unfitness_to_Plead.pdf.

[9] See, eg, the 'Equal Treatment Bench Book' (2013); Judiciary of England and Wales, (https://www.judiciary.gov.uk/wp-content/uploads/2013/11/equal-treatment-bench-book-2013-with-2015-amendment.pdf), and 'Report of the Vulnerable Witnesses & Children Working Group', February 2015.

[10] See, eg, the matters raised in J Jacobson with J Talbot, *Vulnerable Defendants in the Criminal Courts: A Review of Provision for Adults and Children* (Prison Reform Trust 2009).

[11] This was the understanding of the Court of Appeal in *R v Walls* [2011] EWCA Crim 443.

[12] The Criminal Procedure (Insanity) Act 1964. Section 4 and s 4A were substituted by the Criminal Procedure (Insanity and Unfitness to Plead) Act 1991, and amended by the Domestic Violence, Crime and Victims Act 2004.

[13] The Law Commission recommended that an adjournment to allow the defendant to regain capacity for trial where this is a realistic prospect (or to proceed to the 'alternative finding procedure') should not exceed twelve months: Law Commission, *Unfitness to Plead, Volume 1*, Law Com No 364 (n 3) para 4.97.

(iv) ask for a ruling that the trial judge will not give an adverse inference direction to the jury (eg, consider *R v H*[14]); or

(v) seek a ruling that certain evidence ought to be excluded.

In *Rashid*,[15] R was convicted of offences under s 5 of the Terrorism Act 2006. The application to appeal concerned R's capacity to understand questions put to him during the police interview, questions at trial, and his understanding of the trial process. The issue of whether or to what extent R was mentally vulnerable or impaired was disputed. The Court rejected the argument that the interview should have been excluded. The trial judge had not erred in ruling that an intermediary was only required while R was giving his evidence. R did not have a learning disorder or a learning disability within the terms of the mental health legislation. It was neither unfair nor irregular to put him on trial in the usual way.

Applications for proceedings to be stayed as an abuse of process on the grounds of a defendant's 'unfitness' are not unknown but they are unlikely to succeed. In *R v H*,[16] the trial judge rejected an application to stay criminal proceedings on grounds that H was not 'fit to plead',[17] and that there had been delay and material had been lost. In *R v M, H, and Kerr*[18] (not cited in *R v H*),[19] the Court of Appeal remarked that a 'defendant's disability, or matters related to it, cannot ... in themselves found a successful abuse application', adding that this 'would avoid the whole point of ss 4 and 4A':

> An abuse application ... must be founded on matters independent of the defendant's disability, such as oppressive behaviour of the Crown or agencies of the State, or circumstances or conduct which would deprive the defendant of a fair trial e.g. destruction of vital records during a long period of delay, or an earlier assurance that he would not be prosecuted.

It is doubtful that the Court was saying that unfitness falling short of 'disability'[20] (applying the *Pritchard* test) could never be relevant to an abuse application. In *TP, R v West London Youth Court and others*[21]—a case that concerned proceedings in the Youth Court—the Court said:

> The first port of call is not to prevent the court from hearing the case but to grapple with the difficulties. A trial should not be abandoned before all practical steps to overcome the difficulties have been exhausted. It is also ... an important point that the judge who is hearing the trial has a continuing jurisdiction to stay proceedings for abuse of process. Thus, if it becomes apparent during the course of the hearing that the claimant is unable effectively to participate, the judge can stay the proceedings at that point.

[14] [2015] EWCA Crim 782.
[15] [2017] EWCA Crim 2.
[16] [2015] EWCA Crim 782.
[17] See judgment [5]. In *R v H*, the trial judge applied the test in *R v M (John)* [2003] EWCA Crim 3452.
[18] [2001] EWCA Crim 2024 [37]. Affirmed on appeal to the House of Lords, [2003] 1 WLR 411.
[19] *M, H, and Kerr* was cited in *Scorgie* [2003] EWCA Crim 1097.
[20] Which is the word that appears in s 4 and s 4A of the CP(I)A 1964.
[21] [2005] EWHC 2583 (Admin) [18], per Scott Baker LJ.

Given the array of measures and options open to a court when a vulnerable defendant is on trial, some caution is needed before concluding that 'viewed in light of the high numbers of prisoners with mental disorders' the low numbers found to be unfit 'suggest that, as currently formulated, unfitness to plead is not genuinely functioning as a protection for vulnerable defendants'.[22] It is lamentable if there are persons with learning difficulties or who are mentally ill, whose cases ought to have attracted a disposal other than imprisonment. However, the situation may not simply be a consequence of the current rules relating to unfitness to plead but may also stem from current sentencing principles, options for case disposal, deficiencies in the penal system, and—perhaps—that the threshold is set too high before a defendant can be found to lack capacity for a plea to be taken or for trial. As for the latter point, the Court remarked in *R v Marcantonio*,[23] that it is 'in the interests of all concerned that the criminal process should proceed in the normal way where this is possible *without injustice to the defendant*' (emphasis added), noting that 'special measures' may assist an accused at trial.[24] By contrast, a finding that a defendant is 'unfit to plead' is not a soft alternative. It was held by the House of Lords in *R v H*[25] that the s 4A procedure did not, as a matter of domestic law, involve the determination of a 'criminal charge' and the defendant was not 'charged with a criminal offence' within Art 6 of the European Convention on Human Rights (ECHR); and that in any event, the procedure, if properly conducted, was fair and compatible with the rights of the defendant. The effect of a finding of unfitness is that the customary trial process ends and thus the trial judge must not continue with the trial to verdict (other than in respect of an acquittal), even if the unfitness arose at the moment that the defendant was about to be cross-examined.[26] To ensure that 'a weak prosecution case may be examined and if appropriate dismissed', the court can postpone consideration of the question at any time up to and including the close of the prosecution's case.[27]

Upon a finding of unfitness, a jury (which may be the original trial jury) *must* proceed to answer the question whether or not the defendant did the 'act' or made the 'omission' that is a necessary element of the offence charged against him or her.[28] If the answer is in the affirmative, the finding does *not* constitute a conviction[29] and the defendant does not fall to be sentenced, but three disposals are open to the court, namely, an absolute discharge, a supervision order for a specified period of no more than two years, or a hospital order (with or without a restriction order).[30] There

[22] See A Loughnan, 'Between Fairness and 'Dangerousness': Reforming the Law on Unfitness to Plead' [2016] Crim L R 451, 451, and 457.

[23] [2016] EWCA Crim 14; [2016] 2 Cr App R 9.

[24] Consider, in this context, *R v Hamberger* [2017] EWCA Crim 273.

[25] [2003] 1 WLR 411.

[26] *R v Orr* [2016] EWCA Crim 889; and note CP(I)A 1964 (as amended), which applies 'where on the trial of a person the question arises (at the instance of the defence or otherwise) whether the accused is under a disability, that is to say, under any disability such that apart from this Act it would constitute a bar to his being tried'.

[27] CP(I)A 1964, s 4(2).

[28] That is to say, to proceed under CP(I)A 1964, s 4A.

[29] See *R v Chinegwundoh* [2015] 1 WLR 2818; *M (Edward)* [2001] EWCA Crim 2024; and *O'Donnell* [1996] 1 Cr App R 286.

[30] See CP(I)A 1964, s 5.

is a right of appeal against the making of a hospital order or a supervision order.[31] There is also a right of appeal to the Court of Appeal against a 'finding of disability'[32] with powers of disposal given to that Court.[33] Surprisingly, if the Court allows the appeal against that finding, it has no power to remit the case for a s 4A hearing: see *Norman*;[34] and *McKenzie*.[35] In such cases, the Court of Appeal can only direct an acquittal.

A defendant who had been judged unfit to plead, and made subject to a hospital order with a restriction order[36] may be remitted by the Secretary of State, for trial.[37] It is not clear whether there is a wider power to resume the trial of an unfit defendant who has recovered.[38] The Law Commission recommended that a wider power should exist (subject to restrictions) where, under its proposed 'alternative finding procedure', the jury found proved a 'specified violent or sexual offence' or it returned a special verdict in respect of a charge of murder:[39] and that a resumed trial is in the interests of justice. This author has suggested in other writings[40] that there is a principled argument for a wider power, partly because it is in the interests of justice that final judgment be reached if practicable, and partly because from the days of Hale,[41] there were circumstances in which a judge 'in discretion may discharge the jury of [an insane person], and remit him to gaol to be tried after the recovery of his understanding'.

The Legal Test for Unfitness to Plead

Evolution of the legal test

The legal rules relating to unfitness to plead do not appear in a single statutory code,[42] but have largely developed at common law and originated from the principle (commendable insofar as it went) that certain persons of genuine 'non-sane memory', or who were insane or in a state of 'phrenzy', should not receive judgment

[31] See the Criminal Appeal Act 1968, ss 16A and 16B.

[32] Criminal Appeal Act 1968, s 15.

[33] Criminal Appeal Act 1968, s 16.

[34] [2009] 1 Cr App R 13.

[35] [2011] EWCA Crim 1550; and the commentary [2011] Crim LR 884.

[36] That is to say, under CP(I)A, s 5(2)(a).

[37] The power is exercisable only after consultation with 'the responsible clinician': CP(I)A 1964, s 5A(4).

[38] R Fortson QC, 'Reforming Unfitness to Plead for Adults in the Crown Court: A Practitioner's Perspective' in B Livings, A Reed, and N Wake (eds), *Mental Condition Defences and the Criminal Justice System: Perspectives from Law and Medicine*, (Cambridge Scholars Publishing 2015) 15–17.

[39] Law Commission, *Unfitness to Plead, Volume 1*, Law Com No 364 (n 3) para 9.55.

[40] Fortson QC, 'Reforming Unfitness to Plead for Adults in the Crown Court: A Practitioner's Perspective' (n 38) 15–17.

[41] Hale, Sir Matthew, *Historia Placitorum Coronæ*, Volume 1 (*The History of the Pleas of the Crown*) (London 1736) 35; repr Classical English Law Texts (Professional Publishing 1971).

[42] Statutory procedural rules have been enacted by the Criminal Procedure (Insanity) Act 1964, as amended by the Criminal Procedure (Insanity and Unfitness to Plead) Act 1991 ('trial of the facts'), with further reforms enacted under the Domestic Violence, Crime and Victims Act 2004.

and should be spared execution because they 'cannot advisedly plead to the indictment' or because, if they were of sound memory, they 'might allege somewhat in stay of judgment or execution'.[43]

R v Pritchard, decided in 1836, continues to be the cornerstone of existing rules pertaining to unfitness to plead.[44]

There are three points to be inquired into:—First, whether the prisoner is mute of malice or not; secondly, whether he can plead to the indictment or not; thirdly, whether he is of sufficient intellect to comprehend the course of proceedings on the trial, so as to make a proper defence—to know that he might challenge any of you to whom he may object—and to comprehend the details of the evidence, which in a case of this nature must constitute a minute investigation. Upon this issue, therefore, if you think that there is no certain mode of communicating the details of the trial to the prisoner, so that he can clearly understand them, and be able properly to make his defence to the charge; you ought to find that he is not of sane mind. It is not enough, that he may have a general capacity of communicating on ordinary matters.

Pritchard was followed in *Berry* (1876)[45] when Kelly CB said:

Further, I believe it to have been the law from the earliest times, that if it is found at the trial of a prisoner that he cannot understand the proceedings, the judge ought to discharge the jury and put an end to the trial, or order a verdict of not guilty.

More recently, the courts have elaborated on the *Pritchard* test—particularly in the cases of *M (John)*[46] and *Marcantonio*[47]—to give it greater relevance in the context of a modern English criminal trial. The decisions of *M (John)* and *Marcantonio* are discussed in this chapter.

The Pritchard *test: does it require recalibration?*

In its Consultation Paper, the Law Commission stated that the law should be 'consistent with modern psychiatric thinking and with the modern trial process'.[48] Interestingly, CP(I)A, ss 4 and 4A, merely speak of an accused being 'under a disability'—an expression that has not been defined by Parliament and thus its meaning is currently a matter for the courts. Accordingly, the potential exists for the courts to modify or to elaborate on the test for unfitness, subject to maintaining an acceptable degree of legal certainty, clarity, and coherence. The *Pritchard* test was explained in 2003 in *M (John)*[49] to mean that the defendant will be unfit to plead if any one or more of the following was beyond his 'capability':

(1) Understanding the charge(s).
(2) Deciding whether to plead guilty or not.
(3) Exercising his or her right to challenge jurors.

[43] See Hale, *Historia Placitorum Coronæ* (n 41) 35.
[44] (1836) 7 C & P 303.
[45] (1876) 1 QBD 447.
[46] [2003] EWCA Crim 3452, [2003] All ER (D) 199.
[47] [2016] 2 Cr App R 9.
[48] Law Commission, CP No 197 (n 3) para 1.15.
[49] [2003] EWCA Crim 3452.

(4) Instructing solicitors and/or advocates.
(5) Following the course of the proceedings.
(6) Giving evidence in his or her defence.

Notwithstanding the decision in *M (John)*, the Consultation Paper[50] was highly critical of the application of the *Pritchard* criteria by the courts, particularly in cases of murder, such as *Moyle*[51] and *Diamond*,[52] stating that they make 'a mockery of what we know to be the concept of participation' and that 'the participation . . . is ultimately a sham in which legal professionals and the courts are forced to collude'.[53] Those striking statements were not repeated in the Commission's commendable Report.[54]

The usual criticisms made of the *Pritchard* test are (among others) that:

(i) It focuses on the intellectual abilities of the defendant, 'rather than on disorders of mood and other aspects of mental illness which might interfere with the defendant's ability to make decisions and to engage in a rational way with the proceedings'.[55]
(ii) The test for fitness in criminal proceedings, and the test for capacity in civil proceedings differs (see the Mental Capacity Act 2005).
(iii) The expression 'lack of capacity' (as used by the Law Commission) more accurately represents what is in issue than the expression 'unfitness to plead'.[56]
(iv) A specific procedure for determining unfitness to plead in the Magistrates' Court is absent.[57]
(v) Insufficient protection is afforded to persons with learning difficulties and cases of developmental immaturity.

Although certain comments made in *Marcantonio* (2016)[58] might be regarded as supporting the criticism that the *Pritchard* test is a measure of the defendant's cognitive skills,[59] the better view (it is submitted) is that the Court was responding to psychiatric evidence that focussed on those skills. Importantly, the Court explicated the *Pritchard* test in terms that bear a close resemblance to several recommendations made by the Commission in its Report and draft Bill:[60]

> An assessment of whether a defendant has the capacity to participate effectively in legal proceedings should require the court to have regard to what that legal process will involve and

[50] Law Commission, CP No 197 (n 3). [51] [2008] EWCA Crim 3059.
[52] [2008] EWCA Crim 923. [53] Law Commission, CP No 197 (n 3) para 2.86.
[54] Law Commission, *Unfitness to Plead, Volume 1*, Law Com No 364 (n 3).
[55] Law Commission, *Unfitness to Plead, Volume 1*, Law Com No 364 (n 3) para 3.16; and see Loughnan, 'Between Fairness and "Dangerousness": Reforming the Law on Unfitness to Plead' (n 21) 455.
[56] Note that the word 'capacity' was used in *Pritchard*—albeit in a particular context.
[57] For a useful discussion of legal principles relating to persons with mental incapacity or disorder or who are otherwise vulnerable, see K Gledhill, 'Ability to Participate in Criminal Proceedings' in C Wells, 'Abuse of Process' (3rd edn, OUP 2017) ch 10.
[58] [2016] 2 Cr App R 9. [59] [2016] EWCA Crim 14; [2016] 2 Cr App R 9 [50].
[60] Law Commission, *Unfitness to Plead, Volume 2*, Law Com No 364 (n 3).

what demands it will make on the defendant. It should be addressed not in the abstract but in the context of the particular case. The degree of complexity of different legal proceedings may vary considerably. Thus the court should consider, for example, the nature and complexity of the issues arising in the particular proceedings, the likely duration of the proceedings and the number of parties.

... It is in the interests of all concerned that the criminal process should proceed in the normal way where this is possible without injustice to the defendant.... such an approach is essential, given the emphasis which is now placed on the necessity of considering the special measures that may assist an accused at trial. (See, for example, *Walls*.[61]) The effectiveness of such measures can only be assessed in the context of the particular proceedings.[62]

A number of points emerge from the above statement:

1) The Court speaks in terms of a defendant's 'capacity' to participate in the trial and not merely in terms of a defendant's 'understanding' or his cognitive, intellectual, ability.
2) The test is expressed as the capacity to 'participate effectively in legal proceedings'. This is an element of the Commission's recommended legal test.
3) Although the current legal test of fitness to plead is 'expressed as a single, indivisible test which must be met in its entirety',[63] the Court's approach involves taking a disaggregated approach insofar as the nature, complexity, and context of 'different legal proceedings' are material considerations. This mirrors the Law Commission's recommendation that assessment of the defendant's abilities should reflect 'consideration of the actual proceedings'.[64]

With regard to a defendant's capacity for plea and for trial, the Law Commission recommended that a defendant should have the 'abilities' listed in its draft Bill in respect of which his 'decision-making capacity' would be an element in the court's determination of whether the defendant is fit to plead or to be tried.[65] That element would reflect the Mental Capacity Act 2005 criteria,[66] namely (a) an ability to understand information relevant to the decision; (b) an ability to retain that information; (c) an ability to use and to weigh the information when making the decision; and (d) an ability to communicate the decision.[67]

Three points are made about the proposed decision-making capacity element.

1) The MCA 2005 and the draft Bill describe a person's 'lack of capacity' in different ways. The draft Bill is concerned with the sufficiency of the defendant's *relevant abilities to participate effectively* in the proceedings of the offence charged, whereas under the MCA 2005, a person lacks capacity if he is 'unable

[61] [2011] EWCA Crim 443; [2011] 2 Cr App R 6. [62] Per Lord Justice Lloyd Jones [7].
[63] *R v Marcantonio* [2016] EWCA Crim 14 [8].
[64] Law Commission, *Unfitness to Plead, Volume 1*, Law Com No 364 (n 2) para 3.53.
[65] ibid, para 3.108. [66] ibid, para 3.120.
[67] See cl 3(5) of the Commission's draft Bill: *Unfitness to Plead, Volume 2*, Law Com No 364 (n 3); and see the Mental Capacity Act 2005, s 3.

to make a [relevant] decision for himself' by reason of 'an impairment of or a disturbance in the functioning of, the mind or brain'. No such medical condition is required under the Commission's proposals—nor should it be (it is submitted). Tests and concepts that are apt in a civil law context are not always appropriate in the context of criminal proceedings.

2) There is no reason why the Commission's decision-making criteria could not be accommodated within the *Pritchard* test. For example, in *Marcantonio*, the Court considered M's ability to 'retain information'.[68]
3) In its Consultation Paper, the Law Commission contemplated the application of a psychiatric test when assessing decision-making capacity in accordance with the legal test,[69] but no workable definition of the psychiatric test then existed, and the Commission's Report does not provide one.

The Requisite 'Abilities'/'Capabilities' of the Defendant

By cl 1(2) and cl 3 of the Commission's draft Bill the defendant may not be tried for the offence charged if his or her 'relevant abilities' are not 'taken together, sufficient to enable the defendant to participate effectively in the proceedings on the offence or offences charged'. Clause 3(4), which lists the 'relevant abilities', enlarges the number of 'capabilities' referred to in *M (John)*. However, the *M (John)* criteria—discussed below—do not constitute a closed list. As the Court remarked, 'to include additional tests, even if unnecessary, can scarcely lower the standard of the test to be met when the judge had said that a failure to be able to do any one of the six things would suffice to render the appellant unfit to stand trial'.[70]

(1) Ability to understand the charge

In *M (John)*, the trial judge gave directions to the jury of the matters about which a defendant must have an acceptable level of understanding in respect of the offence or offences charged. Those directions were not recited in the judgment of the Court of Appeal, but the Law Commission recommended that the defendant must understand what the charge means, its nature, and have an understanding of the evidence on which the prosecution rely.[71] It is submitted that these abilities can be accommodated within the current test (if they are not already).

Although not expressly stated in *M (John)*, it is arguable that the defendant should have an understanding of the seriousness of the charge, and of the nature and effect of the penalty or penalties that may be imposed on him in the event of conviction (including asset recovery proceedings). Such a requirement would accord with the decision of the European Court of Human Rights (ECtHR) where it was said that

[68] [2016] 2 Cr App R 9 [58].
[69] Law Commission, Law Com CP No 197 (n 3) para 5.16.
[70] Judgment [27].
[71] Law Commission, *Unfitness to Plead, Volume 1*, Law Com No 364 (n 3) para 3.85.

'effective participation' in the context of Art 6§3(c) of the ECHR (the importance of the right to legal representation) presupposes:[72]

> ... that the accused has a broad understanding of the nature of the trial process and of what is at stake for him or her, including the significance of any penalty which may be imposed. It means that he or she, if necessary with the assistance of, for example, an interpreter, lawyer, social worker or friend, should be able to understand the general thrust of what is said in court. The defendant should be able to follow what is said by the prosecution witnesses and, if represented, to explain to his own lawyers his version of events, point out any statements with which he disagrees and make them aware of any facts which should be put forward in his defence ....

It would be ideal if a defendant were able to understand the 'normative dimension to the trial'[73] and 'the moral dimensions of the law and of his own actions'.[74] But, neither statement forms part of the law of England and Wales, nor are they part of Strasbourg human rights jurisprudence. This is hardly surprising: a requirement along those lines would result in a defendant who had an amoral perspective of his alleged offending conduct, being regarded as unfit to be tried.

(2) Ability to decide whether to plead guilty or not guilty

The Law Commission recommended that:[75]

> ... the test of capacity to plead guilty should incorporate a requirement that the defendant has sufficient relevant abilities in relation to his or her understanding of the charge, the evidence adduced in relation to it, what it means to plead guilty and the consequences of doing so. The relevant abilities should also include the defendant's ability to give instructions, follow the remainder of the proceedings and to make the decisions required of him or her in connection with the decision to plead guilty (see draft Bill clause 6(4) and clause 35(4) (magistrates' proceedings)).

The above recommendation can be accommodated within the existing *Pritchard* test, noting that there is a clear overlap between a defendant's capacity to understand the charge (ability (1)) and his capacity to plead guilty.

In its Report, the Law Commission also proposed that a defendant's capacity to plead guilty should be separated from his or her capacity to participate effectively in a trial.[76] The question of whether this is desirable or supportable has attracted markedly different answers.[77]

The problem is exemplified by the facts in *Erskine* where E, on charges of murder, was adamant that he was not involved in, or responsible for, any of the killings. When E appeared at trial, there was unequivocal contemporaneous evidence (not placed before the jury) that his mental responsibility for his actions at the time of the killings was substantially impaired. On appeal, and in the light of further

[72] *SC v UK* (2005) 40 EHRR 10 (App No 60958/00) [29].

[73] RA Duff, 'Fitness to Plead and Fair Trials: Part 1: A Challenge' [1994] Crim LR 419.

[74] RA Duff, *Trials and Punishment* (CUP 1986) 120. Professor Duff clearly recognises that these statements represent ideals rather than the actual position: [1994] Crim LR 419.

[75] Law Commission, *Unfitness to Plead, Volume 1*, Law Com No 364 (n 3) para 3.156.

[76] ibid, para 3.154.

[77] ibid, paras 3.138–155.

unequivocal psychiatric evidence to the same effect, the Crown conceded that (unless the 'not guilty' pleas at the trial resulted from 'tactical pleading'[78] rather than mental disorder),[79] a plea to manslaughter on the basis of diminished responsibility might well have been accepted if offered at trial. On the issue of fitness to plead, and recalling events some twenty years later, the trial lawyers described E as 'a very strange man, capable of saying and doing strange things', but he was also capable of giving 'coherent instructions'. An eminent psychiatrist instructed on appeal stated that 'if a defendant is deluded about matters directly related to his choice of plea, it might reasonably be argued that he is disabled as regards fitness to plead' and that '... the appellant's choice as to how to plead was substantially determined by a symptom of his illness ... and that belief inhibited him, in a fundamental way from pleading "diminished responsibility", given that such a plea requires admission to the killings.'[80]

The case of *Erskine* highlights a number of related issues where tension can exist between them. Personal autonomy is an important consideration:

> ... a defendant is not to be deemed unfit to plead merely because he will not accept what appears to be eminently sensible advice from his legal advisers. It is therefore for him, not his legal advisers or the court, to decide at the time of the trial whether to advance a plea of guilty to manslaughter on the grounds of diminished responsibility.[81]

There will certainly be cases where a defendant would prefer to plead guilty and whose pleas may be accepted if the defendant was found to have capacity to make that decision. But, whether it would be in the defendant's best interest to do so depends on the facts and circumstances of a given case. For example, a defendant may decide to plead guilty to an offence of 'money-laundering', but he may lack capacity to adequately appreciate that protracted and complicated confiscation proceedings may follow, or he may not fully understand the issues that must be addressed in the event that such proceedings are initiated. For the reasons given by Professor Eastman in *Erskine*, the nature of a defendant's mental illness may be such that he is disabled from making decisions with regards to pleas, or even whether he is fit to plead.

In response to the Law Commission's Consultation Paper,[82] the Law Reform Committee of the Bar Council and the Criminal Bar Association Working Group expressed the tentative view that a separation of defendant's capacity to plead guilty, from his or her capacity to participate effectively in a trial, would be undesirable and *might* be open to abuse by some defendants who mount a plea of unfitness to plead in the hope that, for example, (a) a full trial might be avoided; or (b) the defendant can avoid giving evidence; or (c) the defendant can avoid adverse inference directions (eg, failure to answer questions in a police interview[83]). That view was written

[78] Consider *Latus* [2006] EWCA Crim 3187.
[79] [2009] EWCA Crim 1425 [125].
[80] Professor Eastman, [2009] EWCA Crim 1425 [119–20].
[81] *R v Erskine* [2009] EWCA Crim 1425 [88].
[82] Law Commission, CP No 197 (n 3).
[83] See, eg, *R v Ahmed* [2014] EWCA Crim 2647 [6].

on the assumption that the question of capacity to plead guilty would be determined at the same hearing as the question of lack of capacity for trial.[84] Whether there is much (if any) incentive for a defendant to plead guilty having heard a ruling that he lacks capacity and who perceives (rightly or mistakenly) that the prospects of avoiding (or delaying) conviction have improved is, of course, speculative.

However, clinical respondents advanced various reasons to the Law Commission in favour of separating capacity to plead guilty and capacity for trial:[85]

(1) Therapeutic: if a defendant can enter a guilty plea he or she can 'get on with treatment' without the worry of fitness procedures and the prospect of proceedings being resumed on recovery (Charles de Lacy).

(2) Victim and witness advantage: if a defendant can plead this is better for victims and witnesses.

(3) Human rights arguments: allowing a fit enough defendant to plead guilty preserves his or her autonomy.

(4) Clinically apt: several respondents observe that a defendant may be unfit for a trial, but may not lack decisional capacity (Dr Tim Rogers, Charles de Lacy).

In *Marcantonio*,[86] the Court of Appeal saw merit in a test that draws a distinction between capacity to participate effectively in a trial and capacity to plead guilty:

> 8.... There will be cases in which the defendant would be unable to follow proceedings at trial or to give evidence but would not lack the decisional capacity necessary for entering a plea of guilty. We would question the desirability of denying such a defendant the option of pleading guilty.

Part of the reasoning of the Court appears to be that a determination that a defendant is unfit to stand *trial* is pointless because, if the trial went ahead normally, he would plead guilty to the charge anyway. The Court makes the point that the issues in the case are 'defined by the defence'. As the Court clearly recognised, this point of view depends upon the defendant's plea being 'a *sound* basis for a *safe* conviction' (emphasis added).[87] But it also depends on whether the nature and extent of the defendant's mental condition has (or may have) disabled him from defining his defence, making admissions, or to 'define the instructions which he will give which will form the basis of the cross-examination on his behalf'.[88]

The Law Commission proposed in its Report that the separate test of capacity to plead guilty would be applied only in cases where:

(i) the defendant has been found to lack the capacity to participate effectively in a trial;

[84] The Law Commission has recommended that both issues should be determined at the same hearing: Law Commission, *Unfitness to Plead, Volume 1*, Law Com No 364 (n 3) para 3.153.
[85] ibid, para 3.143.
[86] [2016] EWCA Crim 14; [2016] 2 Cr App R 9.
[87] [2016] EWCA Crim 14; [2016] 2 Cr App R 9 [8].
[88] [2016] EWCA Crim 14; [2016] 2 Cr App R 9 [8].

(ii) two suitably qualified experts have specifically addressed in oral or written evidence the defendant's capacity to plead guilty, notwithstanding the defendant's lack of capacity to participate effectively in a trial; and
(iii) the defence apply, immediately following a determination of lack of capacity for trial, for the court to determine whether the defendant has the capacity to plead guilty.[89]

Those measures alone would not ensure that a guilty plea is a 'sound basis for a safe conviction' and thus it is submitted that the courts and practitioners would need to remain vigilant in that regard.

(3) Ability to challenge jurors

This is unlikely to be a significant consideration in the majority of cases given the limited circumstances that now exist for challenging jurors. It is therefore unsurprising that the Law Commission has recommend that the ability to exercise the defendant's right to challenge a juror should not be a specified factor in the test.[90]

(4) Ability to instruct solicitors and counsel

In *M (John)*, the trial judge gave the jury directions (approved by the Court of Appeal) that it was sufficient for the defence to persuade it on the balance of probabilities that instructing his solicitors and counsel was beyond the defendant's capabilities. As to what that entailed, he said:[91]

> This means that the defendant must be able to convey intelligibly to his lawyers the case which he wishes them to advance on his behalf and the matters which he wishes them to put forward in his defence. It involves being able (a) to understand the lawyers' questions, (b) to apply his mind to answering them, and (c) to convey intelligibly to the lawyers the answers which he wishes to give. It is not necessary that his instructions should be plausible or believable or reliable, nor is it necessary that he should be able to see that they are implausible, or unbelievable or unreliable. [Many defendants put forward cases and explanations which are implausible, unbelievable, or unreliable.] The whole purpose of the trial process is to determine what parts of the evidence are reliable and what parts are not. That is what the jury are there for.

The bracketed sentence is more than is needed but, in every other respect, the directions are clear and appropriate (it is submitted).

(5) Ability to follow the course of the proceedings

In *M (John)* the trial judge directed the jury in the following terms (again with the approval of the Court of Appeal):[92]

> [Follow the course of the proceedings] means that the defendant must be able (a) to understand what is said by the witness and by counsel in their speeches to the jury and (b) to communicate intelligibly to his lawyers any comment which he may wish to make on anything

[89] Law Commission, *Unfitness to Plead, Volume 1*, Law Com No 364 (n 3) paras 3.154–156; and see the draft Bill cl 5 and cl 34 (magistrates' proceedings).
[90] Law Commission, *Unfitness to Plead, Volume 1*, Law Com No 364 (n 3) para 3.90.
[91] [2003] EWCA Crim 3452 [21]. [92] ibid [22].

that is said by the witnesses or counsel. Few defendants will be able to remember at the end of a court session all the points that may have occurred to them about what has been said during that session.… There is also no reason why the defendant's solicitor's representative should not be permitted to sit beside him in court to help with the note taking process.

It is difficult to fault this formulation. The Law Commission preferred to remove the reference to the 'course' of the proceedings because that word might be taken to indicate 'a general understanding of the progress of the case rather than an ability, with assistance, to engage with what is actually said in court'.[93] Even if a defendant cannot understand all the points being taken on his behalf, the defendant should at least be able to understand their intended purpose (eg, to exclude evidence).

In *M (John)*, the trial judge referred to the defendant's ability to understand what was said by 'the witness'. The Law Commission favoured a formulation that does not focus on *prosecution* witnesses[94] because 'in order to be able to participate effectively the accused will need to be able to follow, with assistance, other aspects of proceedings apart from the evidence of prosecution witnesses, for example when co-defendants give evidence'. These are reasonable points but it should be noted that neither the Court of Appeal in *M (John)* nor the trial judge in that case, confined this ability/capability to prosecution witnesses.

The judge saw no reason why the defendant solicitor's representative should not be permitted to sit behind the accused 'to help with the notetaking process'. The position has changed since this was said in 2002, given that the presence of a solicitor's representative in a court to assist counsel is now all too rare. Provision should perhaps be made (if not already in existence) to empower a judge to direct state funding for a solicitors' representative to be present in an appropriate case where the defendant is acting under a disability.

(6) Ability to give evidence in his own defence

As for the defendant giving evidence in his own defence, the trial judge said in *M (John)*:[95]

This means that the defendant must be able (a) to understand the questions he is asked in the witness box, (b) to apply his mind to answering them, and (c) to convey intelligibly to the jury the answers which he wishes to give. It is not necessary that his answers should be plausible or believable or reliable. Nor is it necessary that he should be able to see that they are implausible or unbelievable or unreliable. Many defendants and other witnesses give evidence which is either in whole or in parts implausible, unbelievable or unreliable. The whole purpose of the trial process is to determine what parts of the evidence are reliable and what parts are not.… Nor is it necessary that the defendant should be able to remember all or any of the matters which give rise to the charges against him. He is entitled to say that he has no recollection of those events, or indeed of anything that happened during the relevant period.

The Law Commission has described this factor as 'of fundamental importance'.[96] The judge drew a distinction between a defendant's ability to convey answers

[93] Law Commission, *Unfitness to Plead, Volume 1*, Law Com No 364 (n 3) para 3.103.
[94] ibid, para 3.103.
[95] [2003] EWCA Crim 3452 [24].
[96] Law Commission, *Unfitness to Plead, Volume 1*, Law Com No 364 (n 3) para 3.105.

intelligibly and the plausibility or reliability of those answers. With appropriate assistance, young persons and those lacking in maturity may be capable of understanding questions and giving answers capable of being understood. Thus, in *Rashid*,[97] the Court of Appeal (citing *R (OP) v MJ*)[98] remarked that some defendants require 'general support, reassurance and calm interpretation of unfolding events', while others will require 'skilled support' (eg, with the assistance of an intermediary).[99]

Further factors?

The Law Commission has recommended that when a court is determining an issue of unfitness, it should be able to consider 'any other ability that appears to the court to be relevant in the particular case'.[100] Furthermore, the Courts cannot disregard the UN Convention on the Rights of Persons with Disabilities.

Under Scots law, s 53F(2)(b) of the Criminal Procedure (Scotland) Act 1995,[101] empowers the court to have regard to 'any other factor which the court considers relevant'. It is submitted that the provision requires the judge to exercise *judgment* rather than vesting him or her with an unbridled discretion that might result in inconsistent outcomes.

Section 53F(2) of the 1995 Act specifies a set of abilities/criteria that differs in some respects from that discussed in *M (John)*, but the task of the court is (it is submitted) not to slavishly follow a particular list but to identify the criteria that are germane to the case in hand:

(2) In determining whether a person is unfit for trial the court is to have regard to—
  (a) the ability of the person to—
    (i) understand the nature of the charge,
    (ii) understand the requirement to tender a plea to the charge and the effect of such a plea,
    (iii) understand the purpose of, and follow the course of, the trial,
    (iv) understand the evidence that may be given against the person,
    (v) instruct and otherwise communicate with the person's legal representative, and
  (b) any other factor which the court considers relevant.

(3) The court is not to find that a person is unfit for trial by reason only of the person being unable to recall whether the event which forms the basis of the charge occurred in the manner described in the charge.[102]

97 [2017] EWCA Crim 2. 98 [2014] EWHC 1944 (Admin).

99 At the time of writing (February 2018), s 33 BA of the Youth Justice and Criminal Evidence Act 1999 (examination of accused through an intermediary) was not in force. The position is currently governed by the common law (as discussed in *Rashid*).

100 Law Commission, *Unfitness to Plead, Volume 1*, Law Com No 364 (n 3) para 3.70, and see the Law Commission's draft Bill, cls 3(4) and 32(4) (magistrates' proceedings).

101 Inserted into the Criminal Procedure (Scotland) Act 1995 by s 170 of the Criminal Justice and Licensing (Scotland) Act 2010.

102 Consider *R v Podola* [1960] 1 QB 325.

Whether a diagnosable medical condition is needed

In Scotland, the test for unfitness for trial includes a requirement that the defendant's incapacity is due to a 'mental or physical condition': s 53F(1), CP(S)A 1995.[103] In *Murphy*, the Appeal Court of the High Court of Justiciary pointed out that there is no stipulation as to the nature of the evidence upon which the court may be satisfied as to unfitness, but that it was difficult to envisage circumstances in which the court would make a decision of a mental unfitness without the evidence of a psychiatrist, psychologist, or other appropriate medical professional.[104] By contrast, the *Pritchard* test does not require evidence of a 'mental or physical condition', and the Law Commission was 'squarely of the view' that a diagnostic threshold should not be a determinative requirement for a finding of lack of capacity for effective participation.[105] The test to be applied is that the defendant has the ability/capability to participate effectively in the criminal trial. In this context, 'unfitness', as Arlie Loughan points out, is not a medical condition, and thus a diagnostic threshold or test for unfitness to be tried, is not on point.[106]

Who may raise the issue of unfitness?

The issue of a defendant's capacity for trial or plea may be raised by the prosecution or by the defence, or by the court 'on its own initiative'.[107] It was said in *Erskine* that there is a 'judicial responsibility to oversee the process so that if there is any question of the defendant's fitness to plead, the judge can raise it directly with his legal advisers'.[108] That question may arise at an early stage (eg, during a police interview) or during the course of court proceedings. The Law Commission has recommended that, in those circumstances, the courts should have the power to order an investigation into a defendant's capacity to plead or for trial.[109] The Commission has recommended that differing standards of proof should be set out in statute for establishing capacity, depending on whether it is the defence, the prosecution, or the court, that raises it:[110]

(1) Where the defence raise the issue of lack of capacity, they should bear the burden of establishing lack of capacity on a balance of probabilities.
(2) Where the prosecution raise the issue of lack of capacity, they should bear the burden of establishing lack of capacity beyond reasonable doubt.

[103] Section 53F (1) of the CP(S)A 1995 provides: 'A person is unfit for trial if it is established on the balance of probabilities that the person is incapable, by reason of a mental or physical condition, of participating effectively in a trial.'
[104] [2016] Scot HC HCJAC 118 [61].
[105] Law Commission, *Unfitness to Plead, Volume 1*, Law Com No 364 (n 3) para 3.127.
[106] Loughnan, Between Fairness and 'Dangerousness': Reforming the Law on Unfitness to Plead (n 21) 455, 459.
[107] See rule 25.10 of the Criminal Procedure Rules 2017; and note CP(I)A 1964, s 4(1).
[108] [2009] EWCA Crim 1425 [89].
[109] Law Commission, *Unfitness to Plead, Volume 1*, Law Com No 364 (n 3) para 4.16.
[110] ibid, para 4.24, and see the Commission's draft Bill cls 2(2) and 31(2) (magistrates' proceedings).

(3) Where the court determines the issue of capacity of its own motion, the prosecution should bear the burden of establishing lack of capacity on behalf of the court, but the standard of proof should be the balance of probabilities.

Dilemmas facing lawyers acting for persons who may be unfit to plead

Once the issue of a defendant's capacity for trial or for plea becomes apparent, a train of events may be set in motion which the parties had not anticipated, or even desired. On the one hand, a failure to observe that a defendant lacked capacity *might* result in the trial being declared irregular and any conviction rendered 'unsafe'. On the other hand, there may be cases where a *defendant* would prefer not to raise the issue of unfitness (eg, he may wish to plead guilty to a lesser charge (which the prosecutor then instructed at trial is ready to accept) as an alternative to the charge pleaded on the indictment. A defendant may adamantly deny involvement in the offence (eg, murder) rather than raising a defence that is based on medical grounds (eg, diminished responsibility: consider *Erskine*[111]). Although a legal representative would wish to respect the personal autonomy and wishes of the defendant, this might not always be possible.

There will also be cases where, for various reasons, the legal representative is of the opinion that it would not be in the defendant's best interests to pursue a plea of unfitness. Such professional decisions (sometimes described as 'tactical' or 'strategic' decisions) have risks associated with them. In the Scottish case of *McEwan v HM Advocate*,[112] the Court remarked that the decision as to how the defendant's case is to be presented is a matter for counsel's discretion: '[h]e is not subject to orders from the client in this respect. In that area an appeal will succeed only if it can be shown that counsel took decisions which no reasonable counsel could have taken.' But, as the Court in *Murphy v HM Advocate*[113] pointed out, it may not always be easy to draw the dividing line between 'cases of tactical and strategic decisions within the area of professional discretion, and those which fall outwith it'. This is because the issue of fitness for trial goes to the heart of a person's capacity and their ability to participate in an effective way in their trial. In *Murphy*, M was convicted of sexual offences. M suffered from a combination of Alzheimer's and vascular dementia. By the date of the appeal he met the test for unfitness for trial (applying Scots law principles). It was not disputed that by the date of sentence (a short time after the trial) M was incapable of comprehending the sentencing procedure because of his dementia. The High Court of Justiciary was satisfied that it was more probable than not that, at the time of trial, M was not fit to stand trial. His appeal against conviction was upheld. The Court found it 'a little surprising' that, having been made aware of the diagnosis of Alzheimer's and dementia, and advised that it was advisable to obtain a report from a forensic psychiatrist, none of the lawyers obtained such a report. The Court recognised that the circumstances in which legal advisers may be required to

[111] [2009] EWCA Crim 1425.
[112] 2010 JC 95 [22].
[113] [2016] HCAJAC 118 [61].

consider the question of the fitness for trial (mental or physical) of their client 'are many and various':

> 62.... An individual may present somewhat strangely, without being considered unfit for trial. Whether the situation is such as to require investigation, especially in the absence of a medical or psychiatric history, may involve questions of judgement. It is not unknown for legal advisors to be absolutely convinced of their client's mental unfitness only to obtain an expert opinion that he is perfectly fit for trial, although perhaps this occurred more commonly when the only test was one of insanity. Equally, it may be clear that the client has a psychiatric condition which renders him unfit, and where the need to obtain an expert report confirming the fact is obvious. In the latter situation, it may be that obtaining a report is indeed the only reasonable step to take. However, the nature of the decisions which may require to be made, and the variety of circumstances, persuades us that the situation is one which calls for the exercise of professional judgement.

Accordingly, a tactical decision made by the defendant's legal representative not to investigate the nature and extent of the condition from which the defendant was suspected or known to be suffering, or not to pursue a plea of unfitness to plead, may fall outwith the permissible margins of professional discretion. In *Murphy*, the Court did not rule out the possibility that a failure by a legal practitioner to take appropriate action *might* constitute defective representation:

> 60.... The issue ... is whether in light of the information known at the time the failure to obtain an expert report upon which a proper medical assessment of the appellant's fitness for trial might have been made amounted to defective representation, preventing such an assessment, and constituting a miscarriage of justice.

Accordingly, the Court advised that 'where any question of mental fitness arises it may be prudent for advisers to obtain a medical report rather than rely on their own personal assessment'.

The Section 4A CP(I)A 1964 Hearing

Where a defendant is found to be unfit to plead, a 'trial of the facts' under s 4A is held to determine whether in respect of the count or counts being tried, the defendant 'did the act or made the omission charged against him'.[114] The issue is a matter for a jury.

Section 4A(1) and (2) provides:

> (1) This section applies where in accordance with section 4(5) above it is determined by a [court] that the accused is under a disability.
> (2) The trial shall not proceed or further proceed but it shall be determined by a jury–
>
> (a) on the evidence (if any) already given in the trial; and
> (b) on such evidence as may be adduced or further adduced by the prosecution, or adduced by a person appointed by the court under this section to put the case for

[114] CP(I)A 1964, s 4A(2).

the defence, whether they are satisfied, as respects the count or each of the counts on which the accused was to be or was being tried, that he did the act or made the omission charged against him as the offence.

A hearing pursuant to s 4A of the Act is not a criminal trial to determine the guilt or otherwise of an accused person. Its purpose (as explained by Lord Hutton in *Antoine*[115]) is to strike 'a fair balance' between the need to protect the unfit defendant and the need to protect the public from him if he has 'committed an injurious act which would constitute a crime if done with the requisite *mens rea*'.[116]

The s 4A procedure (described as the 'alternative finding procedure' by the Law Commission) differs markedly from a normal trial and thus s 4A is exposed to justified criticisms,[117] including:

(i) s 4A gives no discretion to a judge to decline to hold such a hearing and to divert the unfit defendant away from the criminal justice system;
(ii) the inquiry is into acts and not fault (*mens rea*);
(iii) the determination must be by jury in all cases;
(iv) a determination under s 4A (and s 4) does not involve a determination of a criminal charge, within the meaning of Art 6 of the ECHR;
(v) the court *must* appoint a representative to put the case for the defence,[118]

'but the defendant himself will not give evidence and *ex hypothesi*, his ability to give instructions or the ability to obtain an account from the defendant is limited. Depriving the defendant of these very significant rights is a very serious step.'[119]

The duty is personal to the court of trial and it need not be the same person who conducts the case up to that point: see *Norman*;[120] and *R v B(M)*.[121] The reasoning is that the responsibility placed on the court-appointed person is quite different from the responsibility placed on an advocate where he or she can take instructions from a client (*Norman*).

Proof that the defendant did the act/omission

In English law, offences are analysed in terms of the elements that constitute the *actus reus* (offending act) and *mens rea* (guilty mind). The former can be broken down to its external elements, namely, conduct, circumstances, and results. Not every offence contains all of those elements and, although analysing an offence in this way is often useful, it is not invariably so. In *R v B(M)*,[122] the Court of Appeal

[115] [2001] 1 AC 340; noting *R v H, M and Kerr* [2003] 1 WLR 411; and see *R v Wells* [2015] EWCA Crim 2 to like effect.

[116] [2001] 1 AC 340, 375G.

[117] Fortson QC, 'Reforming Unfitness to Plead for Adults in the Crown Court: A Practitioner's Perspective' (n 38) 15–17.

[118] CP(I)A 1964, s 4A(2)(b). This step had not been taken in *R v B(M)* [2013] 1 WLR 499 when it should have been.

[119] *R v Walls* (n 11) [37(i)], per Thomas LJ, as he then was.

[120] [2009] 1 Cr App R 192.

[121] [2013] 1 WLR 499.

[122] ibid.

preferred not to employ that type of analysis when deciding what the relevant 'act' was for the purposes of s 4A(2), CP(I)A 1964 where the offence was one of 'voyeurism' contrary to s 67(1) of the Sexual Offences Act 2003.[123]

Given that the focus of the enquiry is on whether or not the defendant did the 'act' necessary for the commission of the offence, the mental element is usually regarded as irrelevant notwithstanding that it is this element that often contextualises and characterises the defendant's actions as a criminal offence. Thus, in *R v B(M)*, the defendant's knowledge that the person observed did not consent to being observed for sexual gratification was not an element of the 'act' for the purposes of s 4A(2), CP(I)A 1964. Again, in *R v Grant*,[124] the defences of lack of intent and provocation were not available to the defendant on a charge of murder. By contrast, in *R (Young) v Central Criminal Court*[125] (concerning an offence charged under s 47(1) of the Financial Services Act 1986), the intention of the defendant (not in relation to dishonesty, or in relation to the purpose of making the representations) but as one of the facts represented to the alleged victims of his activity, was part of the *actus reus*.[126]

Cases where the defendant has caused harm, but which was due to mistake, accident, or self-defence, are likely to involve a consideration of the mental state of the defendant. In *Antoine*, Lord Hutton gave the example of self-defence where the issue is 'what the defendant honestly and instinctively thought was necessary' (see *Palmer v R*[127]). In respect of such defences, the approach of the courts (following *Antoine*) is for the jury, on a s 4A hearing, to see if there is 'objective evidence' that raises such matters and, if there is, the jury must only find that the defendant did the act if the jury is sure that the prosecution has negated the defence (see *Jagnieszko*,[128] where the issue was self-defence). 'Objective evidence' is (broadly stated) cogent evidence (other than self-serving assertions made by the defendant), for example, eyewitness accounts, CCTV, mobile telephone cell-site analysis, and scene-of-crime forensic evidence. In *Jagnieszko*,[129] the Court of Appeal left open the question of whether a defendant's interview could qualify as admissible 'objective' evidence.

However, *partial* defences to murder (that reduce the offence to manslaughter), namely, diminished responsibility and loss of self-control (formerly called 'provocation') cannot be advanced at a s 4A hearing: see *Antoine*, and *Grant*.[130] The reasons are largely procedural, namely that if the jury accepted the partial defence and convicted the defendant of manslaughter, but the defendant recovered, the power of the Secretary of State to remit his case for trial under para 4 of Sch 1 to the Criminal Procedure (Insanity and Unfitness to Plead) Act 1991 would be frustrated: he could not be tried for murder following his earlier acquittal by the jury.[131] This is one of

[123] Section 67(1) of the Sexual Offences Act 2003 provides: 'Voyeurism: (1) A person commits an offence if—(a) for the purpose of obtaining sexual gratification, he observes another person doing a private act, and (b) he knows that the other person does not consent to being observed for his sexual gratification.'

[124] [2002] Q B 1030.

[125] [2002] 2 Cr App R 178.

[126] See the useful commentary to that case by the late Professor Sir John Smith QC; [2002] Crim L R 588.

[127] [1971] AC 814.

[128] [2008] EWCA Crim 3065.

[129] ibid.

[130] [2002] QB 1030.

[131] [2001] 1 AC 340, [368A/B].

two main reasons why the Law Commission concluded that the partial defences ought not to be available under its proposed 'alternative finding procedure'[132]). The second reason is that the written 'route to verdict' for the jury would, potentially, be very complicated and the jury would have to engage in careful analysis of complex medical evidence.[133] The Commission did not regard the defendant who cannot participate effectively in a trial, and who is debarred from running a partial defence to murder, as being truly disadvantaged in comparison with the defendant who can participate effectively.[134] The former, said the Commission, is not at risk of conviction for murder, and if he remains unable to participate effectively he will never be tried for the allegation. If the defendant does recover, and trial proceedings are resumed, he will have the opportunity to establish the partial defence at that stage.

It should be noted that the 'bad character' provisions of the Criminal Justice Act 2003 (see *Creed*),[135] and the hearsay provisions of the 2003 Act (see *Chal*),[136] apply to s 4A hearings. Defects in the content and form of the indictment will not necessarily result in a finding against the defendant under s 4A being rendered unsafe: *R v D(A)*[137] (contrast *McKenzie* where the *actus reus* of indecent assault on a woman could not be established by an indecent assault on a man).[138]

Expert Testimony

A determination of unfitness to plead almost always involves the admission of expert opinion, typically furnished by psychiatrist or psychologist, and sometimes by other healthcare professionals. Occasionally such opinion may be supplemented by representations made by advocates or, for example, police officers who had observed the defendant. Sworn evidence from experts is often received by the court when determining unfitness to plead but, in practice, the courts are prepared to receive relevant information in less formal ways (eg, letters and written reports). It is essential that experts meet the requirements of the Criminal Procedure Rules and the Criminal Practice Direction concerning the duties and obligations of experts in the preparation of their reports and when testifying.

The expertise and opinions of experts will be likely to be subjected to scrutiny:[139]

> 38.... save in clear cases, a court must rigorously examine evidence of psychiatrists adduced before them and then subject that evidence to careful analysis against the *Pritchard* criteria as interpreted in *Podola*.[140] Save in cases where the unfitness is clear, the fact that psychiatrists agree is not enough.... a court would be failing in its duty to both the public and a defendant if it did not rigorously examine the evidence and reach its own conclusion.[141]

132 Law Commission, *Unfitness to Plead, Volume 1*, Law Com No 364 (n 3) para 1.72.
133 ibid, paras 5.116–5.118. 134 ibid, para 5.119.
135 [2011] EWCA Crim 144; and see the case comment at [2011] Crim LR 644.
136 [2008] 1 Cr App R 18. 137 [2016] 4 WLR 122. 138 [2011] 1 WLR 2807.
139 *R v Walls* (n 11) [38] per Thomas LJ (as he then was).
140 [1959] 3 WLR 718.
141 *Walls* [2011] EWCA Crim 443 (per Thomas LJ, as he then was).

If a judge or jury rejects unchallenged expert opinion, there must be some rational basis for doing so (see *Golds*,[142] approving *Brennan*[143]).

Conclusion

Despite criticisms, the legal rules and court practices relating to vulnerable witnesses and defendants constitutes an improving picture. However, there are many important aspects pertaining to a defendant's unfitness to plead or to stand trial that have not been addressed in this chapter but which are the subject of recommendations made by the Law Commission. Of crucial importance is its recommendation that a statutory framework for determining a defendant's capacity to participate effectively, comparable to that which it recommended for the Crown Court, should be created in the summary jurisdiction.[144] Other recommendations include electing an alternative finding procedure without a jury,[145] alternative disposals in cases where a defendant lacks capacity,[146] provisions for the redetermination of capacity,[147] powers to resume a prosecution in prescribed circumstances,[148] the reinstitution of fresh proceedings (on the defendant's application) where an alleged matter was proved against the defendant (or where a special verdict was returned),[149] and reforms in respect of rights of appeal from Crown Courts and Magistrates' Courts.[150]

Some of the Commission's recommendations do not require statutory measures. For example, it would be possible for the Criminal Practice Directions or Criminal Procedure Rules to be amended to require the court or the parties to make use of such liaison and diversion services as are available at court to provide an initial assessment of the defendant (with consent) concerning his or her capacity.[151] As for legal training (which the profession takes seriously) cases such as *Murphy v HM Advocate*[152] (discussed above) provide salutary lessons. It is reasonable (it is submitted) to require members of the judiciary engaged in criminal proceedings in the Crown and magistrates' courts (and all legal representatives appearing in such proceedings) to receive relevant training to assist them in understanding and identifying participation, communication difficulties experienced by vulnerable defendants, and the available mechanisms by which the defendant's effective participation can be facilitated.[153]

That said, the tidiest and most satisfactory reform would be for Parliament to give legislative effect to the Commission's draft *Criminal Procedure (Lack of Capacity) Bill.*

[142] [2016] UKSC 61. [143] [2015] 1 WLR 2060.
[144] Law Commission, *Unfitness to Plead, Volume 1*, Law Com No 364 (n 3) ch 7.
[145] Law Commission, *Unfitness to Plead, Volume 2*, Law Com No 364 (n 3) draft Bill, cl 12.
[146] Law Commission, *Unfitness to Plead, Volume 1*, Law Com No 364 (n 3) ch 6, and see paras 10.49–10.56.
[147] Law Commission, *Unfitness to Plead, Volume 2*, Law Com No 364 (n 3) draft Bill, cl 8.
[148] Law Commission, *Unfitness to Plead, Volume 1*, Law Com No 364 (n 3) ch 9.
[149] Law Commission, *Unfitness to Plead, Volume 2*, Law Com No 364 (n 3) draft Bill, cls 16 and 17.
[150] Law Commission, *Unfitness to Plead, Volume 2*, Law Com No 364 (n 3) ch 8.
[151] ibid, para 10.34. [152] [2016] HCA JAC 118 [61].
[153] Law Commission, *Unfitness to Plead, Volume 1*, Law Com No 364 (n 3) para 10.1.

4

Reforming the Law of Unfitness to Plead in England and Wales

A Recent History

*Miranda Bevan and David Ormerod**

Introduction

In recent years the criminal justice system has faced significant challenges in rendering the trial process suitable for participants whom, it is becoming increasingly obvious, are unable to participate effectively. Much of the attention has been on the impact on witnesses and complainants, but where a defendant's participation difficulties mean that he or she cannot fairly be tried the problems are especially acute. The current unfitness to plead procedure is one important part of that broader problem.

It is no exaggeration to say that there has been a revolution in the treatment of vulnerable witnesses, led in part by the former Lord Chief Justice, Lord Judge.[1] There have been continued legislative developments from successive Governments to accommodate vulnerable witnesses, from sections 16–30 of the Youth Justice and Criminal Evidence Act 1999 to more recent proposals to extend the use of pre-recorded cross-examination.[2] In contrast, the treatment of vulnerable defendants seems to lag far behind, despite a welcome increase in awareness of the problems which many defendants face.[3] Vulnerable defendants continue to experience

* We would like to thank Kat Shields for her excellent research assistance.

[1] See The Rt Hon. The Lord Judge, Lord Chief Justice of England and Wales (2011) 'Vulnerable Witnesses in the Administration of Criminal Justice', 17th Australian Institute of Judicial Administration, available at: https://www.judiciary.gov.uk/wp-content/uploads/JCO/Documents/Speeches/lcj-speech-vulnerable-witnesses-in-admin-of-criminal-justice-29092011.pdf. See also, *inter alia*, the decisions in *Barker* [2010] EWCA Crim 4; *Lubemba* [2014] EWCA Crim 2064.

[2] See https://www.gov.uk/government/news/courts-reform-gives-stronger-protection-for-victims-and-witnesses.

[3] See, eg, J. Jacobson et al, *Inside Crown Court, Personal Experiences and Questions of Legitimacy* (Policy Press 2016). See also J. Jacobson et al, 'Effective Participation or Passive Acceptance: How can Defendants Participate more Effectively in the Court Process?' http://www.icpr.org.uk/media/37859/HLWP_9_2014.pdf.

Fitness to Plead: International and Comparative Perspectives. First Edition. Edited by Ronnie Mackay and Warren Brookbanks.Chapter 4 © Miranda Bevan and David Ormerod 2018. Published 2018 by Oxford University Press.

unequal access to special measures,[4] particularly in respect of the assistance of an intermediary at trial.[5]

However, for those who may be unable to participate effectively in their trial, even with all available assistance, the position is even more concerning. The legal test for identifying defendants who are 'unfit to plead' in England and Wales is outdated and unduly restrictive. The statutory framework which sets out the processes to be adopted in such cases is extremely limited, and where alternative procedures do exist they are inflexible and arguably liable to give rise to unfairness. Finally, the disposals which may be available to the court at the conclusion of these alternative procedures give rise in some cases to legitimate public protection concerns.

This chapter opens with a consideration of the particular challenges which arise in respect of defendants who are unable to participate effectively in trial. Against that background, it then charts briefly the development of the law relating to unfitness to plead in England and Wales, and early attempts to reform the legal test and procedures. The chapter then addresses in more detail the recent work of the Law Commission in exploring the problems presented by the current framework, and in recommending far-reaching reforms.

The Challenges Arising in Respect of Defendants who are Unable to Participate Effectively in Trial

In analysing the development of unfitness-to-plead procedures in England and Wales, and the limited reforms achieved to date, it is essential to understand the particular challenges that defendants with significant participation difficulties present for the criminal justice system. There is undoubtedly a difficult balance to be struck when seeking to accommodate vulnerable defendants: their rights must be respected, but at the same time the law needs to protect the interests of those affected by specific offending and provide suitable protection for the public more generally. Defendants with the most significant participation difficulties may face allegations of serious offences which raise substantial concerns about reoffending and potential dangerousness.

The accurate and timely identification of defendants who are unable to participate effectively in trial is central to meeting these challenges, but also presents significant difficulties. Participation problems can arise from a wide range of conditions, including mental health difficulties, physical disability or ill-health, learning disability, and developmental disorders, or a combination of such issues. The position is further complicated by the fact that conditions giving rise to significant

[4] Law Commission, *Unfitness to Plead, Volume 1: Report*, Law Com No 364 (2016), paras 2.18–2.20.

[5] Statutory provision for the assistance of an intermediary for a defendant whilst giving evidence at trial (s 104 Coroners and Justice Act 2009, inserting ss 33BA and 33BB into the Youth Justice and Criminal Evidence Act 1999) has yet to be brought into force. Scope for the provision of an intermediary using the judge's inherent powers has been reduced recently by changes to the Criminal Practice Directions I General Matters 3F.11 [2015] EWCA Crim 1567, as amended April, October, and November 2016 and February and April 2017.

participation difficulties may also be undiagnosed, liable to fluctuation (particularly in defendants experiencing psychosis or mood disorders), or may be manipulated by malingering defendants.

Even where unfitness to plead is appropriately identified, there remains the difficulty of providing a fair examination of the facts of the alleged offence. This is essential to give the defendant the opportunity to be acquitted, and to identify those individuals upon whom a protective disposal can safely be imposed. The final major difficulty lies in ensuring a disposal of the case which is appropriate both for the unfit defendant who is found to have done the act or made the omission in relation to the offence charged, and for the complainants and the wider public. The disposals available to the courts in these circumstances cannot be punitive, since there has been no crime proved. They must be designed to provide appropriate treatment and support for the defendant and to protect the public.

Development of the Current Framework and Attempts at Reform in England and Wales

Identifying unfit defendants: the legal test

The current legal test for determining a defendant's fitness to plead in England and Wales is based on two cases decided in the 1830s—*Dyson*[6] and *Pritchard*[7]—in an era when psychiatry was in its infancy and expert evidence was not a feature of criminal proceedings. In both *Pritchard* and *Dyson*, the defendant's intellectual ability was considered key to their fitness to plead. Alderson B set out the legal test as follows in *Pritchard*:

> There are three points to be enquired into: First, whether the prisoner is mute of malice or not; secondly, whether he can plead to the indictment or not; thirdly, whether he is of sufficient intellect to comprehend the course of proceedings on the trial, so as to make a proper defence—to know that he might challenge any of you [jurors] to whom he may object—and to comprehend the details of the evidence.[8]

The case of *Davies*[9] added a further requirement that the defendant had to be able to instruct his or her legal advisor.

Reiterations and reformulations of the *Pritchard* test in subsequent cases, all maintain a narrow focus on defendants' cognitive abilities. A defendant who is unable to act in his own best interests may be found fit to plead because, as Lord Parker CJ observed in *Robertson*,[10] if a defendant 'appears to have had a complete understanding of the legal proceedings and all that is involved and, … suffers from delusions which at any moment might interfere with a proper action on his part, that is not a matter which should deprive him of his right to be tried'.[11] The perception that the

[6] (1831) 7 C & P 305, 173 ER 135. [7] (1836) 7 C & P 303. [8] ibid, 304.
[9] (1853) Car & Kir 328. [10] [1968] 1 WLR 1767. [11] ibid, 1773.

defendant is better off with a full trial, and all its protections, was in part dictated by the fact that at that time the only available disposal was mandatory hospitalisation.

In a comprehensive review of the legal framework for addressing mentally disordered offenders, the 1975 Butler Report[12] recognised the difficulties created by this prescriptive yet misguided test for fitness to plead. The report recommended a reformulation of the legal test so as to require a defendant to be able to: understand the course of proceedings at the trial so as to make a proper defence; understand the substance of the evidence; give adequate instructions to his legal advisers; and plead with understanding to the indictment.[13] The revised test would also have removed the requirement of the ability to challenge a juror. However, these recommendations have never been implemented.

As has been the case with adjustments for vulnerable witnesses, much of the pressure for reform of this area, as well as changes to the legal test in modern cases insofar as possible, has come from the courts. The case of *M (John)*[14] slightly expanded the *Pritchard* test, to bring it more into line with modern trial processes, albeit whilst being forced to retain its other, outdated criteria. The Court of Appeal described as 'admirable'[15] a set of jury directions which stated that a defendant may be found unfit if any one or more of the following are beyond his capability: (1) understanding the charges; (2) deciding whether to plead guilty or not; (3) exercising his right to challenge jurors; (4) instructing solicitors and counsel; (5) following the course of the proceedings; (6) giving evidence in his own defence.[16]

However, even with modern refinements to the test, there remains no statutory confirmation of the legal test for fitness to plead. Nor is there a statutory framework outlining even a basic articulation of the factors which should be considered by the court where the issue of unfitness is raised. In short, beyond the common law test, little legal guidance exists.[17]

The procedure for those found unfit to plead

The procedures for an individual who has been found to be unfit to plead have been similarly slow to develop and have seen very limited reform. Our starting point is once again the nineteenth-century cases.

In both *Dyson* and *Pritchard* the defendants were deaf-mute, and did not suffer from mental disorders. However, both judgments held that unfit defendants should be considered insane upon arraignment. Although there was no statutory definition of insanity, section 2 of the Criminal Lunatics Act 1800 stipulated that an insane defendant was liable to be detained indefinitely.[18] There was no possibility of a hearing of the facts of the case, and an unfit defendant was subject to detention without proof that he or she had in fact committed the offence charged.[19]

12 Report of the Committee on Mentally Abnormal Offenders, Cmnd 6244 (1975) .
13 ibid, para 10.3.
14 [2003] EWCA Crim 3452, [2003] All ER (D) 199.
15 ibid [31].
16 ibid [20].
17 Law Commission, *Unfitness to Plead, A Consultation Paper*, CP No 197 (2010), para 2.51.
18 D Grubin, 'What Constitutes Fitness to Plead?' (1993) Crim LR 748, 749.
19 Law Commission, CP No 197 (n 17) para 2.14.

Procedural uncertainties continued to plague unfitness to plead hearings well into the last century. It was not until 1960 that the law settled such fundamental questions as the burden and standard of proof when the defence raised the issue of unfitness.[20] These and other procedural uncertainties, including whether there was a right of appeal from unfitness to plead hearings,[21] in part prompted the Home Secretary to ask in 1963 whether the Criminal Lunatics Act 1800 should be reviewed. The Criminal Law Revision Committee (CLRC) subsequently made recommendations which were incorporated into the Criminal Procedure (Insanity) Act 1964 ('the 1964 Act').[22]

Section 4 of the 1964 Act introduced a formal procedure for a finding of unfitness to plead by a jury. Under s 4 an unfit defendant would be found to be 'under a disability' such that it would constitute a 'bar to his being tried'. The 1964 Act also created a statutory right of appeal against such a finding. However, the Act did not allow for a hearing of the facts of the offence charged after a defendant had been found unfit to plead. There was no opportunity to test the allegation and no opportunity for an acquittal. Nor did the Act allow for a more flexible range of disposals: s 5 stated that a defendant found to be 'under a disability' was subject to mandatory and indefinite hospitalisation.[23]

The procedural shortcomings and mandatory disposal for those found unfit to plead were reviewed in the Butler Report.[24] The report's recommendations in this regard were only partially implemented in the Criminal Procedure (Insanity and Unfitness to Plead) Act 1991 ('the 1991 Act').[25] Amongst those recommendations that were enacted, was the mandatory hearing of the facts of the case, to be considered by the jury, once a defendant is found to be unfit to plead. This was inserted as s 4A of the 1964 Act. The s 4A hearing allowed, for the first time, an unfit defendant to be subsequently acquitted where there was insufficient evidence that he or she had done the act or made the omission with which they had been charged.

Although the 1991 Act improved matters significantly, the s 4A hearing was limited to a 'trial of the facts', considering only the 'external elements' of the relevant offence. This was contrary to the Butler Report's recommendations. The attempt to divide the external element (to be proved) and fault element (irrelevant) of a criminal offence is entirely artificial in theory and in practice and yet the House of Lords in *Antoine* upheld that approach.[26] *Antoine* makes only certain defences available

[20] *Podola* [1960] 1 QB 325, [1959] 3 WLR 718. The case held that where the defence raise the issue of the defendant's fitness to plead, the burden of proof lies on the defence; it is discharged if the court is satisfied on the balance of probabilities that the defendant is unfit to plead.

[21] *Podola* (ibid) clarified this question: there is a right of appeal.

[22] Criminal Law Revision Committee Third Report: Criminal Procedure (Insanity), Cmnd 2149 (1963).

[23] Although subsections 4(2) and 4(3) provided a mechanism to avoid a s 5 disposal. If there was insufficient evidence upon which a properly directed jury could convict the defendant, the jury would instead be directed to acquit the defendant at the close of the prosecution case.

[24] Report of the Committee on Mentally Abnormal Offenders, Cmnd 6244 (1975).

[25] For further discussion of the report's recommendations and those which were left unimplemented, see Law Commission, CP No 197 (n 17) paras 2.15–2.24.

[26] *Antoine* [2000] UKHL 20, [2001] 1 AC 340.

in limited circumstances, where 'there is objective evidence which raises the issue of mistake or accident or self-defence'.[27] Their Lordships did not, however, stipulate which kinds of objective evidence would suffice.[28] In addition, in allegations of murder, the unfit defendant is restricted from relying on partial defences to murder, such as diminished responsibility and what is now loss of control.[29] As discussed below, this blunt and sometimes arbitrary division can leave unfit defendants unable to test the core element of the alleged offence.

The introduction of the 'trial of the facts' has given rise to interesting questions in relation to compliance with the European Convention on Human Rights (ECHR). *H*[30] held that the trial of the facts is not a determination of a criminal charge within the meaning of Art 6, as it results in neither a conviction nor a punishment and 'lacks the essential features of criminal process'.[31] However, other domestic cases have held that trials of the facts are 'criminal proceedings' within the meaning of the Criminal Justice Act 2003. The defendant lacks the full Art 6 protections, but hearsay[32] and bad character evidence[33] are admissible nonetheless.

A further change in 2004 removed the role of the jury in the determination of whether a defendant is unfit to plead.[34] A similar recommendation, albeit more limited, was first made by the Butler Report. Lord Justice Auld's Review of the Criminal Courts of England and Wales in 2001 called for the judge to determine the issue of unfitness to plead. Auld stated that 'in the majority of cases the jury's role on the issue of unfitness to plead is little more than a formality because there is usually no dispute between the prosecution and the defence'.[35] Section 4(5) of the 1964 Act now states that the determination of a defendant's unfitness to plead is for the court. As such, a determination may only be made on the written or oral evidence of two registered medical practitioners.[36] Rendering this a decision for the court and not the jury removed significant pressures on time and court resources without compromising safeguards for the defendant.

Disposals

More progress has at least been made with reforming the disposals available for unfit individuals. The 1991 Act, and later the Domestic Violence, Crime and Victims

[27] ibid, 376.

[28] No substantial clarification of that has been achieved since. See *Wells* [2015] EWCA Crim 2, [2015] 1 WLR 499.

[29] See *Grant* [2001] EWCA Crim 2611, [2002] QB 1030, in which the defences of lack of intent and provocation were deemed to relate to the fault element for murder and therefore were not for the jury's consideration during the s 4A hearing.

[30] [2003] UKHL 1. [31] ibid [18]. [32] *Chal* [2007] EWCA Crim 2647.

[33] *Creed* [2011] EWCA Crim 144.

[34] Section 22 Domestic Violence, Crime and Victims Act 2004 ('the 2004 Act').

[35] RE Auld, *Review of the Criminal Courts of England and Wales* (TSO 2001) ch 5, para 213. A debate in the House of Commons before the passage of the 2004 Act includes a speech from Vera Baird QC MP, who stated that in 90% of cases where unfitness to plead was an issue, there was no dispute between the prosecution and defence. See *Hansard* (HC), 27 October 2004, vol 425, col 1525.

[36] Section 4(6) Criminal Procedure (Insanity) Act 1964 ('the 1964 Act'). At least one of these practitioners must be 'duly approved' as having special experience in the diagnosis or treatment of mental disorder as defined by s 8(2) of the 1964 Act and s 12 of the Mental Health Act 1983 ('the MHA 1983').

Act 2004 ('the 2004 Act'), allowed for more flexibility in relation to disposals where an unfit defendant is found to have done the act or made the omission in respect of the offence charged. Sections 5 and 5A of the 1964 Act currently allow the court to make a hospital order with or without a restriction order,[37] a supervision order, or an order for the defendant's absolute discharge. The power of the court to make a guardianship order, introduced in 1991, was removed in 2004. Section 5(4) of the 1964 Act gives 'hospital order' the same meaning as that in s 37 of the Mental Health Act 1983 ('the MHA 1983'). The court must be satisfied, on the written or oral evidence of two registered medical practitioners,[38] that the defendant is suffering from a mental disorder of a nature or degree which makes it appropriate for him or her to be detained in a hospital for medical treatment, that such treatment is available, and that a hospital order is the most suitable disposal.[39] The 'objective medical evidence' that must be presented before a hospital order may be made has ensured that, since the 2004 Act, the disposals available to the courts have complied with Art 5 of the ECHR.[40]

Unfitness to plead in the summary jurisdiction

The unfitness-to-plead framework discussed above is only applicable in the Crown Court; alternative, more limited procedures exist in magistrates' and youth courts by virtue of s 37(3) of the MHA 1983.[41] The available statutory arrangements are limited to those with a mental disorder (under the terms of the MHA 1983) and the provisions are problematic as a result of procedural uncertainties and the lack of suitable disposals.

Early reform: conclusions

The development of the unfitness-to-plead framework in England and Wales has been incremental, reactive, and limited only to that which was regarded as necessary. This may be unsurprising considering the challenges presented by unfit defendants which were outlined at the start of this chapter. However, piecemeal changes to relevant legislation since the 1960s, rather than any holistic reassessment of the law, has rendered the position for unfit defendants yet more unsatisfactory. This is because the resulting legal framework governing unfitness to plead, a mixture of common law and statute, is unusually complex and inaccessible. Not surprisingly, unfitness to plead can be an unfamiliar area of law, even to seasoned practitioners, resulting in

[37] See s 41 MHA 1983.

[38] One of whom must be approved under s 12 MHA 1983 as having special experience in the diagnosis or treatment of mental disorder.

[39] Section 37(2) MHA 1983.

[40] See Art 5(1)(e) of the ECHR, and *Winterwerp v Netherlands* (1979) 2 EHRR 387 (App No 6301/73) [39].

[41] Supplemented by a power to adjourn for medical reports under s 11(1) of the Powers of the Criminal Courts (Sentencing) Act 2000.

the current test being applied and fulfilled only rarely: approximately 100 individuals are found to be unfit to plead each year in England and Wales.[42]

The Law Commission's Consultation Paper: A Case for Reform

The Law Commission's consultation paper on unfitness to plead ('CP 197') was published in October 2010. The project ran partly in tandem with work on insanity and automatism, in order to address a number of concerns with the existing legal framework surrounding vulnerable defendants.

CP 197 addressed many long-standing concerns with the law on unfitness to plead identified above, including the difficulties posed by the *Pritchard* test, concerns relating to the s 4A hearing and appeals against a finding at such a hearing, the inflexible procedures facing those unfit defendants who recover, and the lack of unfitness-to-plead provisions in the magistrates' and youth courts.

Problems with the *Pritchard* test

An outdated test

As outlined above, recent reformulations of the common law test, particularly in *M (John)*, have sought to bring the nineteenth-century *Pritchard* test into line with twenty-first-century trial processes. However, the continuing misalignment of the core criteria of the test with modern trial processes, and with advances in psychiatry and psychology, have meant that the test is applied inconsistently by clinicians[43] and courts[44] alike.

The Law Commission explored recent criticisms of the test, focusing on its high threshold for findings of unfitness: a study by Dr Tim Rogers and others claimed that the numbers of people found to be unfit to plead are 'startlingly low', considering that ten per cent of men on remand had shown signs of psychotic illness in the previous year.[45] It was then estimated that approximately four per cent of the male prison population was so severely mentally ill that they should instead be in a psychiatric hospital.[46] In CP 197 the Commission noted that representatives faced procedural difficulties around obtaining the required evidence to raise the issue of unfitness to plead; many do not raise the issue at all. It was felt that screening defendants in advance of anticipated trials could tackle these problems, and could also prevent unfit defendants from 'slipping through the net'.

[42] RD Mackay, 'Unfitness to Plead—Data on Formal Findings from 2002 to 2014', available at: http://www.lawcom.gov.uk/wp-content/uploads/2016/01/apa.pdf.

[43] RD Mackay et al, 'A Continued Upturn in Unfitness to Plead—More Disability in Relation to the Trial under the 1991 Act' [2007] Crim LR 530, 536.

[44] See, eg, *Wells* (n 28) [1], which omits reference to the giving of evidence.

[45] TP Rogers et al, 'Reformulating the Law on Fitness to Plead: A Qualitative Study' (2009) 20(6) Journal of Forensic Psychiatry and Psychology 815, 816 citing Singleton et al (1998).

[46] Law Commission, CP No 197 (n 17) para 2.62 and the Prison Reform Trust, *Troubled Inside* (n 46).

Undue focus on cognitive deficiencies

The Law Commission also explored further concerns that the *Pritchard test* focused unduly on cognitive deficiencies. Serious conditions which could affect a defendant's ability to participate in a trial, particularly mood disorders and delusional conditions, often do not satisfy the *Pritchard* criteria. CP 197 highlighted a number of particularly concerning recent cases which illustrate the injustice which can result from the court's focus in *Pritchard* on the defendant's understanding, rather than their capacity.[47]

In *Erskine*,[48] for example, the appellant had been charged with seven counts of murder and one count of attempted murder. At the time of his trial, his mental disorder would have rendered him able to plead to manslaughter by way of diminished responsibility. However, he instructed his representatives that he was not involved in the killings and was convicted. He contended, on an application for leave to appeal out of time, that his schizophrenia and psychopathic disorder had substantially diminished his responsibility, and prevented him from running the available partial defence at his trial. Granting the application and allowing the appeal, the Court of Appeal stated that 'as a result of reduced mental acuity, not amounting to unfitness to plead, but part and parcel of his illness, the decision not to advance the defence was irremediably flawed'.[49]

Another case demonstrating the repercussions of the current failure to take decision-making capacity into account is *Murray*.[50] The appellant insisted on pleading guilty to murder owing to the overwhelming guilt she felt at having killed her daughter. She suffered from paranoid schizophrenia, but refused to run a defence of diminished responsibility. The Court of Appeal substituted her murder conviction for one of manslaughter on the grounds of diminished responsibility. CP 197 noted that 'the system [demanded by the *Pritchard* test] does not have any regard for the process by which a defendant comes to the decision to plead guilty.'[51] Toulson LJ stated in his judgment that *Murray* 'illustrates in acute form the problems of the potential mismatch between the legal test and psychiatric understanding in these matters'.[52] Similar patterns in *Moyle*[53] and *Diamond*,[54] where defendants suffering from paranoid schizophrenia refused to avail themselves of the partial defence of diminished responsibility, further illustrate the unfairness which results from prioritising cognitive understanding over true decision-making capacity.

These cases stand in stark contrast to the approach demanded in the civil courts, where the Mental Capacity Act 2005 requires an examination of the relevant person's decision-making capacity. Section 3(1) states that a person is unable to make a decision if he or she is unable to understand the information relevant to the decision, retain that information, use or weigh it as part of the process of making the decision, or communicate the decision. Conversely, a defendant in criminal proceedings will

47 For a fuller discussion of these cases, see Law Commission, CP No 197 (n 17) paras 2.75–2.87.
48 [2009] EWCA Crim 1425.
49 ibid [95].
50 [2008] EWCA Crim 1792.
51 Law Commission, CP No 197 (n 17) para 2.81.
52 [2008] EWCA Crim 1792 [6].
53 [2008] EWCA Crim 3059.
54 [2008] EWCA Crim 923.

be found fit to plead even where 'mental disorder might have affected his ability correctly to appraise, believe, weigh up and validly use information relating to the legal proceedings'.[55]

Alignment with ECHR jurisprudence

A final concern in relation to the *Pritchard* test is its unclear alignment with the requirements for 'effective participation', demanded by Art 6 jurisprudence.[56] *SC v United Kingdom* sets out these requirements as follows:

> '[E]ffective participation' ... presupposes that the accused has a broad understanding of the nature of the trial process and of what is at stake for him or her, including the significance of any penalty which may be imposed. It means that he or she, if necessary with the assistance of, for example, an interpreter, lawyer, social worker or friend, should be able to understand the general thrust of what is said in court. The defendant should be able to follow what is said by the prosecution witnesses and, if represented, to explain to his own lawyers his version of events, point out any statements with which he disagrees and make them aware of any facts which should be put forward in his defence.[57]

The *Pritchard* criteria arguably do not encompass the assertion of the court in *SC* that a defendant should be able to maintain a level of active involvement in his or her trial, and be able to make some decisions during the course of a trial.[58]

Concerns in respect of the Section 4A hearing

In CP 197 the Law Commission also identified a number of problems with the hearing under s 4A of the 1964 Act.[59] The problems flow predominantly from the tension between the need to allow the unfit defendant a fair hearing as to the facts of the alleged offence and the need to protect the public from an unfit defendant who may be dangerous.

The principal difficulty was identified as arising from the requirement, following *Antoine*,[60] for the criminal offence to be split into the external elements, to be proved by the prosecution at the s 4A hearing, and the fault (internal) elements, which would be outside the jury's consideration. As the Law Commission identified, this can be problematic, since the lawfulness or unlawfulness of a defendant's act in respect of some offences depends on his or her state of mind. The challenge lies in ensuring that the identified conduct elements, to be proved by the prosecution, capture the 'injurious act' identified by the offence.

[55] *Moyle* [2008] EWCA Crim 3059 [27].
[56] See, eg, *Stanford v UK* App No 16757/90, *T v United Kingdom* App No 24724/94, and *V v United Kingdom* App No 24888/94, 16 December 1999.
[57] (2005) 40 EHRR 10 (App No 60958/00) [29].
[58] Law Commission, Law Com No 364 (n 4) para 3.21.
[59] Law Commission, CP No 197 (n 17) paras 6.11–6.41.
[60] *Antoine* (n 26).

As Sir Brian Leveson P observed in the recent case of *Wells and others*,[61] there is 'no bright line' between the external and fault elements of some offences, requiring in those cases an 'offence-specific' consideration of the ingredients that the prosecution must prove. The Law Commission raised concerns in CP 197 about the uncertainty and inconsistency that this was liable to give rise to,[62] and this has been borne out in subsequent decisions.

By way of example, the Court of Appeal concluded in *Young*,[63] a case concerning the dishonest concealment of a material fact,[64] that the appellant's purpose in the concealment, and his dishonesty, fell within the fault elements of the offence, and were therefore not required to be proved by the prosecution. However, the Court found that the conduct elements of the offence, of which the jury had to be satisfied, included not only whether the appellant had concealed the material fact in question, but also his intention in so doing. By contrast, in the later case of *B(M)*[65] in which the Court of Appeal considered the offence of voyeurism,[66] the Court concluded that the appellant's purpose, to obtain sexual gratification in observing the private act of another, was to be included in the conduct elements of the offence, whilst the appellant's knowledge that the person observed did not consent was part of the fault element, and so outside the jury's consideration.

The Law Commission also identified difficulties arising from the requirement, articulated in *Antoine*,[67] that common defences such as self-defence, mistake, and accident may only be left to the jury where there is 'objective evidence' which raises the issue. The Law Commission argued that ignoring altogether the defendant's state of mind at the time of the alleged offence was liable to place an unfit defendant at a significant disadvantage compared with a 'fit' defendant.[68] CP 197 identified that this requirement works in a particularly unsatisfactory way in cases of secondary and inchoate liability, where so much turns on the fault elements of the offence.[69]

Inflexible and inadequate procedures for trial on recovery

The Law Commission also highlighted difficulties which had arisen as a result of the inflexibility of the provisions for remitting a recovered accused for trial (s 5A(4) of the 1964 Act).[70] CP 197 focused on the fact that the Secretary of State's decision to remit a recovered accused for trial could not be reversed if the defendant again became unfit to plead before the trial process was completed. In those circumstances, the court was required to engage in a costly and unnecessary repetition

[61] *Wells* (n 28), [2015] 1 WLR 2797 [12].
[62] Law Commission, CP No 197 (n 17) paras 6.24 ff.
[63] [2002] EWHC 548 (Admin), [2002] 2 Cr App R 12.
[64] Now an offence under the Financial Services Act 2012, s 89.
[65] [2012] EWCA Crim 770, [2013] 1 WLR 499 [515]– [516], and case comment by Ronnie Mackay, *R v B* [2013] 1 Crim LR 90.
[66] Contrary to the Sexual Offences Act 2003, s 67(1).
[67] *Antoine* (n 26) 376.
[68] Law Commission, CP No 197 (n 17) paras 6.30 ff. Subsequent case law has continued to illustrate these difficulties, see, eg, *Wells* (n 28).
[69] Law Commission, CP No 197 (n 17) paras 6.36 ff.
[70] ibid, paras 7.14 ff.

of the s 4 and s 4A processes.[71] In addition, the Law Commission was concerned that there was no right on the part of a recovered, but previously unfit, individual to request remission for trial.

A gap in the Court of Appeal's powers

Further to this, the Law Commission reviewed the powers of the Court of Appeal in respect of unfit individuals.[72] There were particular concerns that the Court of Appeal has no power to remit a case back to the Crown Court for a rehearing under s 4A of the 1964 Act, where appeal has been allowed against a finding at such a hearing. The Court can only enter an acquittal.[73] The Law Commission considered this gap in the Court of Appeal's powers to be potentially problematic.[74]

No application of the unfitness to plead framework in the magistrates' and youth courts

CP 197 also identified numerous problems with the lack of unfitness-to-plead provisions in the magistrates' and youth courts.[75] The Law Commission considered that the statutory provisions for imposing a hospital order (or guardianship order) without convicting the defendant (MHA 1983, s 37(3)),[76] were inadequate in a number of respects.

First, it is not clear what will trigger an investigation into the defendant's capacity to participate in trial. There is no common law test or procedure which is applicable to determine a summary defendant's 'unfitness'. This leads to uncertainty for the defendant as to whether the hearing of the evidence is to consider guilt, or to consider whether the defendant 'has done the act or made the omission', as required to be established under MHA 1983, s 37(3).[77]

Secondly, the range of disposals is too limited. A hospital order or guardianship order will not be a suitable disposal in many cases. This limitation was considered to lead to a further difficulty, that where neither disposal is appropriate, full trial is likely to proceed.[78] The alternative of imposing a stay of the proceedings was considered to be undesirable, because of the discretionary and exceptional nature of that remedy, and the inability of the court in such circumstances to put in place treatment for the defendant or protection for the public.

[71] Section 4 and 4A of the 1964 Act. See, eg, case of *R (Julie Ferris) v DPP* [2004] EWHC 1221 (Admin).

[72] Law Commission, CP No 197 (n 17) paras 7.45 ff.

[73] Criminal Appeal Act 1968, s 16(4).

[74] See the case of *Norman* [2008] EWCA Crim 1810, [2009] 1 Cr App R 13.

[75] Law Commission, CP No 197 (n 17) ch 8.

[76] Under MHA 1983, s 37(3). Operating in conjunction with a power adjourn to obtain a medical report, Powers of the Criminal Courts (Sentencing) Act 2000, s 11(1).

[77] MHA 1983, s 37(3).

[78] Law Commission, CP No 197 (n 17) paras 8.26 ff.

Finally, the Law Commission identified additional difficulties arising in respect of cases in the youth court,[79] particularly in relation to problems of developmental immaturity and the issues surrounding the low minimum age of criminal responsibility.

CP 197: the Law Commission's Consultation Paper

The approach taken

CP 197 made fourteen provisional proposals focused largely on replacing the current *Pritchard* test, and making significant reforms to the current 'trial of the facts' procedure under s 4A of the 1964 Act.

With regard to the replacement of the *Pritchard* test, CP 197 proposed a new legal test of decision-making capacity, which would take into account all of the requirements for meaningful participation in criminal proceedings. The new legal test was to be accompanied by a defined psychiatric test, which would be developed to assess a defendant's decision-making capacity.

The provisional proposals also called for the replacement of the current s 4A hearing with a procedure which would allow the jury to return a verdict that the accused did the act or made the omission charged, and that there are no grounds for an acquittal. This new approach would have required the prosecution to prove all elements of the offence charged.

Finally, CP 197 proposed a two-stage process for acquitted defendants, with the second stage—the further hearing—to be undertaken after an acquittal only at the judge's discretion. The purpose of the further hearing would be to allow a jury to determine whether or not the defendant was acquitted because of a mental disorder existing at the time of the offence. This potential 'special verdict' would be determined by the jury on such evidence as had been heard, or on any further evidence called.

In addition to the provisional proposals, a number of questions were posed in CP 197. In particular, consultees' opinions were sought on whether the proposal for a new test of decision-making capacity should apply equally to proceedings in the magistrates' and youth courts. If an accused was found to lack decision-making capacity for proceedings which would otherwise have been triable summarily, CP 197 asked consultees whether a mandatory fact-finding procedure should follow. Consultees were also asked whether this fact-finding procedure should be limited to consideration of the external elements of the offence charged, or whether it should mirror the proposals for a reformed s 4A procedure in the Crown Court.

[79] ibid, paras 8.38 ff.

Responses to the Consultation Paper

CP 197 was well received and garnered fifty-five responses from a range of stakeholders, including the judiciary and legal practitioners, psychiatrists, psychologists, and criminal justice practitioners, as well as academics, non-governmental organisations, and special- interest groups.[80]

There were a number of areas on which there was general agreement. In particular respondents on the whole agreed that the *Pritchard* test is not adequate, especially for young defendants. There was a general feeling from consultees that an individual should only be found unfit to plead if he or she could not participate effectively in the proceedings, including being able to make the decisions required of him or her.[81] This assessment, it was felt, should take into account any assistance available to the individual, by way of special measures or other adjustment.[82] However, the detailed content of the proposed test remained an area of disagreement, with varied views being expressed.

Respondents were clear that the test should continue to be a legal one, to be applied by the judge, rather than a psychiatric or psychological test. There was also support for extending the category of relevant experts to include registered psychologists. However there was no agreement on whether there should be a defined, standardised psychiatric test to accompany the legal test.[83]

There was also little consensus over the Law Commission's favoured approach to the fault element in the s 4A hearing, and the proposal for a two-stage procedure for arriving at the findings, including the availability of a special verdict.[84] Although not an area of focus in CP 197, respondents also raised concerns about the adequacy of disposals, particularly for young defendants.[85]

In relation to the summary jurisdiction there was strong support for the proposal that the same test and procedures should apply in the Crown Court and the magistrates' courts. Respondents also considered it very important to develop a test and procedure to be applied in the youth court.[86]

Respondents also endorsed reform of the processes for returning recovered defendants to court for trial, and were in favour of extending the Court of Appeal's powers in respect of remission for rehearing under s 5A of the 1964 Act.[87]

Finally, respondents agreed with the Law Commission's observations that there was a lack of knowledge on the part of some legal and medical practitioners about the law and the procedures to address unfitness to plead.[88]

[80] See Law Commission, *Unfitness to Plead, Analysis of Responses* (2013) ('AR').
[81] AR, paras 1.7–1.37.
[82] AR, paras 1.100–1.128.
[83] AR, paras 1.163–1.194.
[84] AR, paras 1.195–1.231.
[85] AR, paras 1.324–1.334.
[86] AR, paras 1.275–1.323.
[87] AR, paras 1.232–1.263, 1.353.
[88] AR, paras 1.337–1.339.

Changes in the Criminal Justice System Following Publication of CP 197

Following publication of CP 197 in October 2010, the Law Commission's work on unfitness to plead was delayed by the need for the Commission to turn its attention to other projects. By the time work began again on the unfitness-to-plead project in the summer of 2013, there had been a number of significant shifts in the criminal justice landscape.

Changing approach to vulnerable defendants

One advantage of this shift in time frame was that the intervening three years had seen some advancement in the adjustment of the trial process to facilitate the participation of vulnerable individuals.[89] As identified above, provisions remained unequal, with witnesses continuing to enjoy greater support, in terms of the range and availability of measures guaranteed by statute.[90] However, the position of vulnerable defendants was being more frequently considered by the courts, and there had been a rise in the use of intermediaries to support defendants with significant participation difficulties, following the judgment in *C v Sevenoaks Magistrates*.[91]

At the same time, the Government continued to express its commitment to implementing a national model for liaison and diversion services for individuals with mental health difficulties and learning disability within the criminal justice system, a key recommendation in the Bradley Report.[92] In January 2014 the Government announced a further £25 million spending on such services, with a view to rolling out the scheme nationwide in 2017. If implemented in accordance with the proposed operating model,[93] it was felt that the scheme offered the possibility of a significant improvement in the frequency, accuracy, and speed with which defendants with participation difficulties might be identified and effectively supported.

[89] See, eg, Criminal Practice Directions I General Matters 3D 'Vulnerable People in the Courts' and 3G 'Vulnerable Defendants' [2013] EWCA Crim 1631, [2013] 1 WLR 3164.

[90] L Hoyano, 'Coroners and Justice Act 2009—Special Measures Directions Take Two: Entrenching Unequal Access to Justice?' [2010] Crim LR 345 and J Talbot, 'Fair Access to Justice? Support for Vulnerable Defendants in the Criminal Courts. A Prison Reform Trust Briefing Paper' (2012), available at: http://www.prisonreformtrust.org.uk/portals/0/documents/fairaccesstojustice.pdf.

[91] *C v Sevenoaks Magistrates' Court* [2009] EWHC 3088 (Admin). See also *R(AS) v Great Yarmouth Youth Court* [2011] EWHC 2059 (Admin).

[92] Department of Health, The Bradley Report: Lord Bradley's Review of People with Mental Health Problems or Learning Disabilities in the Criminal Justice System (2009), available at: http://webarchive.nationalarchives.gov.uk/20130107105354/http://www.dh.gov.uk/prod_consum_dh/groups/dh_digitalassets/documents/digitalasset/dh_098698.pdf.

[93] See NHS England's Operating Model for Liaison and Diversion Services across England (September 2013), available at: https://www.england.nhs.uk/wp-content/uploads/2014/04/ld-op-mod-1314.pdf.

Cuts and the reduction in the criminal justice budget

However, these positive changes were tempered by significant budget reductions for the Ministry of Justice, the effects of which were at that time being felt across all parts of the system. A reduction of the Ministry of Justice's projected settlement of approximately one-third by 2015–16[94] promised very careful scrutiny of any proposals which bore a cost implication.

A Further Consultation Process: Broad and Far-reaching

These changes to the criminal justice landscape indicated that a full review of the proposals in CP 197 would be worthwhile. In addition, perhaps unsurprisingly given the complexity of this area of law, the responses received in respect of CP 197 presented a range of often conflicting views, posed numerous further questions and identified some fresh areas for reform.

It was decided that a further consultation process would be beneficial, to hone the provisional proposals in light of the responses and the recent changes to the criminal justice system.

The Law Commission produced an issues paper in May 2014, with the intention of developing the provisional proposals set out in CP 197, and to investigate with stakeholders some of the newer issues. This was accompanied by a symposium on unfitness to plead, held at the School of Law, University of Leeds in June 2014. The day was attended by over 100 experts in the area of unfitness to plead, including members of the judiciary, legal practitioners, academics, psychiatrists and psychologists, specialist nurses, intermediaries, and representatives from non-governmental organisations and government departments.

As the work progressed, the Law Commission continued to discuss the provisional reform proposals, as they developed, with stakeholders and interested organisations, and to present emerging findings at academic conferences. There were, in addition, several larger meetings with groups of judges (at Snaresbrook Crown Court and the Central Criminal Court) and with senior prosecutors.

In something of a change from the usual consultation process, the Law Commission also spoke directly with stakeholder groups as part of this second consultation process. This included meeting with family members of the victims of homicide in cases involving unfitness to plead issues,[95] and a half-day session with a group of young people with autism spectrum conditions.[96] The commitment to building a genuine understanding of the procedures in practice also led the Law Commission to undertake its own data gathering in respect of the frequency with which unfitness to plead was being raised, and the use of intermediaries in such cases.

[94] HM Treasury, *Spending Round 2013*, available at: https://www.gov.uk/government/publications/spending-round-2013-documents.

[95] Kindly arranged by Victim Support.

[96] Kindly arranged by Autism West Midlands and Dr Marie Tidball, then a doctoral candidate at Wadham College, Oxford.

The numerous consultation initiatives meant that as 2014 moved into 2015 there was a feeling of growing consensus around the central proposals that were emerging. As these proposals began to take shape there was also the opportunity to test the emerging recommendations with policy makers within government, the Crown Prosecution Service, and Local Authorities.

Unfitness to Plead Report: Law Commission No 364

This second consultation process culminated in a final report, published by the Law Commission on 13 January 2016.[97] The report recommends comprehensive reform to all areas of the unfitness-to-plead framework.

Full trial wherever fairly achievable

The guiding principle, endorsed throughout the consultation processes, and lying at the heart of the recommendations, is that undergoing a normal criminal trial is the optimum process for an individual facing an allegation in the criminal courts. The full trial process engages, to the benefit of all involved, the fair trial guarantees afforded by Art 6 of the ECHR.[98] Full trial enables rigorous scrutiny of all elements of the offence, and any defence advanced. At its conclusion, the court has at its disposal the broadest range of outcomes, in terms of sentences and other orders.

The clear position of the Law Commission is that the defendant should only be removed from that full trial process as a last resort, and with great caution. Only where the defendant cannot fairly undergo the process, because he or she lacks the capacity to participate effectively in the proceedings, should alternative procedures be adopted. There was consensus amongst consultees that there should be few individuals for whom prosecution was in the public interest, but who could not be enabled by trial adjustments and special measures to participate effectively in trial.

Facilitating full trial through trial adjustments

As discussed, although progress has been made in trial adjustments for vulnerable defendants, there remains an inequity in the treatment of defendants and witnesses. The Law Commission made a number of recommendations aimed at ensuring that vulnerable defendants are afforded the trial adjustments they require in order to be able to participate effectively in trial.[99]

To improve the initial identification of those defendants in need of assistance, the Law Commission recommended that all members of the judiciary, and all legal practitioners, working in the criminal courts should be required to receive training in

[97] Law Commission, Law Com No 364 (n 4).

[98] Under Art 6 of the Convention for the Protection of Human Rights and Fundamental Freedoms (entered into force on 3 September 1953) ('ECHR').

[99] See Law Commission, Law Com No 364 (n 4) ch 2.

understanding and identifying communication and participation difficulties. It was proposed that the training should also focus on raising awareness of the mechanisms available to adjust the trial process to facilitate a defendant's effective participation.

In respect of trial adjustments themselves, the Law Commission made three further recommendations. First was a recommendation to introduce a statutory entitlement for a defendant to have assistance from an intermediary for as much of the proceedings as necessary for him or her to have a fair trial.[100] Secondly, the Law Commission recommended that a registration scheme for defendant intermediaries, supported by a Code of Practice, be put in place to provide quality assurance and cost regulation. Thirdly, the Law Commission proposed that the eligibility criteria for defendants to use live-link should be brought into line with the criteria for witnesses.

Accurate and efficient identification of defendants who cannot participate effectively in their trial

A critical element of a reformed framework was felt to be the accurate and efficient identification of those few defendants who lack the capacity to participate effectively in trial.

A Statutory Test of Capacity for Effective Participation in Trial, Explicitly Incorporating Decision-making Capacity

The Law Commission recommends in the report, with strong support from consultees, a statutory legal test which prioritises effective participation and explicitly incorporates decision-making capacity.[101] The proposed test provides a non-exhaustive list of relevant abilities, modelled on the criteria in *M (John)*,[102] but informed by the corresponding observations in *SC*.[103] The relevant abilities include express reference to the ability to make the core decisions required of a defendant at trial, namely how to plead, whether to give evidence and, where it arises, whether to elect Crown Court trial. These relevant abilities, taken together, must be sufficient to enable the accused to participate effectively in the proceedings.[104] This test would be applied in the context of the particular proceedings faced by the defendant and taking into account any assistance available to him or her. The Law Commission did not recommend that there be a requirement for the defendant to be suffering from a mental disorder or any other diagnosed condition.[105]

[100] This recommendation envisages amendment to, and the bringing into force of, the entitlement to an intermediary for the giving of evidence only (Youth Justice and Criminal Evidence Act 1999 ('YJCEA') s 33BA. See full discussion in Law Commission, Law Com No 364 (n 4) paras 2.31–2.69.

[101] See Law Commission, Law Com No 364 (n 4) ch 3.

[102] *M (John)* (n 14).

[103] *SC v United Kingdom* (2005) 40 EHRR 10 (App No 60958/00) [29].

[104] See Law Commission, *Unfitness to Plead, Volume 2: Draft Legislation*, Law Com No 364 (2016) cl 3.

[105] Law Commission, Law Com No 364 (n 4) paras 3.122 ff. See for an alternative view, Helen Howard, 'Lack of Capacity: Reforming the Law on Unfitness to Plead' (2016) J Crim L 80(6), 428.

A Test of Capacity to Plead Guilty

During the second consultation process, it became apparent that there was significant support for a separate test of capacity to plead guilty. Clinicians in particular identified a distinction between fitness to enter a plea, and fitness to 'be tried'. They explained that it is not uncommon for an individual to lack the capacity to follow lengthy court proceedings, or give evidence, but to be able to understand the charges, the evidence against them, and the ramifications of pleading guilty. With broad support across stakeholder groups, the final recommendations therefore also included a separate test of capacity to plead guilty. This test would be applied only to those who have been found to lack capacity for trial, on application by the defendant and with expert evidence supportive of that capacity.[106] The advantages of a separate test have been considered with approval, albeit *obiter dicta*, in the subsequent case of *Marcantonio and Chitolie*.[107]

Reducing Delays in the Identification of the Issue

Respondents expressed widespread concerns that cases involving unfitness-to-plead issues are marked by considerable delays, both in respect of the raising of the issue and in the obtaining and serving of expert reports. The Law Commission's recommendations seek to improve that position by, amongst other measures, proposing amendment of the Criminal Procedure Rules (Crim PR) to require the parties and the court to keep the defendant's ability to participate under review, and provisions to encourage the instruction of joint experts where appropriate.[108]

Given the range of conditions which might give rise to unfitness to plead, at present delay often arises because a report from a psychologist is required, but that report must currently be obtained in addition to reports from two registered medical practitioners.[109] The Law Commission's recommendations propose that one of the two statutorily required expert reports should be able to be prepared by a registered psychologist.

Finally, in order to prevent the situation arising where a defendant is found to lack capacity for trial, only to recover that capacity during the course of the proceedings, the recommendations also include a requirement that the court consider adjourning the determination of the issue of capacity, where experts assert that there is a real prospect that the defendant might achieve capacity within a reasonable period.[110]

[106] See Law Commission, Law Com No 364 (n 4) paras 3.138–3.157.
[107] *Marcantonio and Chitolie* [2016] EWCA Crim 14 [8].
[108] See Law Commission, Law Com No 364 (n 4) ch 4.
[109] CP(I)A 1964, s 4(6).
[110] See Law Commission, Law Com No 364 (n 4) paras 4.82–4.97.

Fair procedures for scrutinising the allegation

There was a strong feeling amongst consultees that it is objectionable to deprive an unfit defendant of opportunities for acquittal that are enjoyed by all other defendants. There was, as a result, resounding support from respondents for a recommendation that the prosecution be required to prove all elements of the offence. This was proposed not to establish culpability, or the degree of it, but rather simply to enable a defendant who lacks capacity for trial to enjoy the same opportunities for acquittal as any other defendant.

The Crown Prosecution Service (CPS), who had originally opposed such a change, subsequently recognised the support from other stakeholders. Following detailed consideration of difficult case examples, the CPS concluded that whilst in general the burden on the prosecution would be greater than at the current s 4A hearing, it would not be significantly greater than at full trial, and, on balance, the proposal was workable and appropriate.[111]

Introducing the requirement for the prosecution to prove all elements of the offence raises the further issue of ensuring adequate public protection in respect of any defendants who lack capacity, but would otherwise be liable to a special verdict of not guilty by reason of insanity were they to have undergone full trial.[112] To address that issue the Law Commission recommended that a special verdict (equivalent to an insanity verdict) should be available at the reformed s 4A hearing (referred to in the report and draft Bill as the 'alternative finding procedure'). So the options open to the jury would be: an acquittal; a finding that the allegation is proved against the defendant; or a special verdict (where relevant).[113]

Partial defences to murder would not, however, be available under the recommendations. This is primarily because their purpose, in protecting a defendant from a mandatory life sentence, is not engaged for defendants who are shielded in the alternative finding procedure from a triggering conviction for murder. This recommendation needs to be considered in the context of the recommendation that the mandatory restriction order in cases of murder (CP(I)A, s 5(3)) be lifted (see below).[114]

An invitation to consultees in the Issues Paper to consider whether the s 4A hearing should be heard before a judge alone[115] led to starkly contrasting responses. That proposal was not pursued in the final report, although recommendation is made to allow a defendant to elect for the alternative finding procedure to be heard before a judge alone. This is recommended as likely to be beneficial for some defendants, particularly in consideration of the reduced formality of such a hearing and the provision of reasons by the judge in arriving at the verdict.

[111] See Law Commission, Law Com No 364 (n 4) paras 5.62–5.85.

[112] Under Criminal Procedure (Insanity and Unfitness to Plead) Act 1991, s 1(1). *M'Naghten's Case* (1843) 10 Ci & Fin 20, 8 ER 718.

[113] See Law Commission, Law Com No 364 (n 4) paras 5.87–5.107.

[114] See Law Commission, Law Com No 364 (n 4) paras 5.108–5.122, 6.104–6.110.

[115] Law Commission, *Unfitness to Plead, An Issues Paper* (2014) paras 5.57–5.60 ff.

Diversion out of the criminal justice system where appropriate

However reformed, the s 4A hearing exists to identify individuals upon whom a protective disposal should safely be imposed, and to give the defendant the opportunity to be acquitted. Where acquittal is not anticipated, and no such disposal is indicated, the Law Commission considered it important for the judge to be able to review carefully whether it is necessary for the proceedings to continue, or whether diversion out of the criminal justice system instead is desirable. No such discretion is currently available, giving rise to witnesses and defendants being required to undergo s 4A hearings for no substantive purpose in some cases.

The proposal to introduce such a discretion was widely approved by consultees, although not unanimously so. Assimilating concerns raised by those respondents, the final recommendation made in the report grants the judge discretion to decline to proceed with the alternative finding procedure, applying an interests of justice test.[116] In cases involving allegations of serious sexual offending, for example, the judge would be extremely unlikely to decline to proceed, particularly having heard the views of the complainants.

Effective and robust community disposals

Responses in the second consultation process revealed a number of issues with the current disposal regime. These focused on the supervision order. Legal practitioners and judges expressed concern that, with changes to the structure of probation services in England and Wales, and reducing budgets, it was becoming difficult to identify a supervising officer (from a probation provider or local authority) willing to agree to perform the role.[117] In addition, concerns were raised about the effectiveness of supervision orders, and the lack of recourse where compliance was an issue. Consultees stressed the importance of a disposal which represents a suitable and effective alternative to hospitalisation.

The Law Commission's recommendations[118] address both those areas of concern. The Law Commission proposed that the supervision order be made the sole responsibility of the local authority who would have a statutory duty to provide a supervising officer. In addition, it recommended that there be a specific supervision requirement as part of each order, that there be scope to add further constructive requirements to meet the defendant's needs, and that the maximum term of the order be extended to three years.

Addressing the question of recourse for non-compliance was, the Law Commission felt, amongst the most difficult issues encountered in the project. This question goes to the heart of the tension between fair treatment for some of the most vulnerable defendants and the need to protect the public from those same individuals, who may also be amongst the most dangerous encountered by the courts. The Law

[116] Law Commission, Law Com No 364 (n 4) paras 5.43–5.61.
[117] As is required, CP(I)A 1964, sch 1A, para 2(2)(a).
[118] Law Commission, Law Com No 364 (n 4) ch 6.

Commission concluded that it is appropriate to recommend that a review function be available as part of a supervision order, and that there be a procedure to address breach and, where appropriate, impose sanctions. Such a course would only be available where the defendant has sufficient capacity to engage in breach proceedings, and sanctions would be engaged in a stepped process.[119]

No changes were recommended to the availability of hospital or restriction orders under s 5 of the 1964 Act, with the exception of a recommendation to lift the mandatory requirement for a restriction order to be imposed in cases of murder (s 5(3) of the 1964 Act) where the conditions for hospitalisation are met (under the Mental Health Act (MHA) 1983, s 37(2)).[120] There were concerns that this provision may tend to result in arbitrary and discriminatory outcomes, since it is applicable only to those suffering a treatable mental disorder.[121]

Finally, the Law Commission recommended that there be a power to impose a restraining order following a finding that an allegation is proved against an unfit individual.[122] This addresses the anomalous absence of such a power, revealed in the case of *Chinegwundoh*.[123]

Introducing statutory procedures to address lack of capacity to participate effectively in the magistrates' and youth courts

Perhaps the most urgent calls for reform were raised in respect of the arrangements for addressing participation difficulties in the summary courts, particularly the youth court. Consultees provided numerous striking examples of problems arising from the narrow scope of the current statutory provisions, the procedural confusions that result, and the inadequacy of the available disposals, especially for defendants with participation difficulties in the youth courts.

At the heart of the Law Commission's recommendations in this area lies the principle that vulnerable defendants in the summary jurisdiction should be provided comparable protections and disposal options to those afforded to defendants being tried in the Crown Court. The recommendations therefore argue for the introduction of a statutory scheme to address participation issues in the summary jurisdiction which reflects that proposed for the Crown Court. The scheme advanced in the report, and set out in the draft Bill, is inevitably adjusted to correspond with the particular procedural framework and the reduced disposal regime of the summary courts. For example, capacity cases are to be reserved to district judges and there are adjustments to the framework made to address election for Crown Court trial in the adult magistrates' court.[124]

However, the core provisions of the proposed statutory scheme for the summary jurisdiction are broadly comparable to those recommended for the Crown Court.

[119] ibid, paras 6.74–6.100.
[120] ibid, paras 6.104–6.110.
[121] As defined by the MHA 1983, s 1.
[122] See Law Commission, Law Com No 364 (n 4) paras 6.111–6.113.
[123] [2015] EWCA Crim 109, [2015] 1 WLR 2818.
[124] See Law Commission, Law Com No 364 (n 4) paras 7.85 ff and 7.93 ff, respectively.

In making those recommendations, the Law Commission was mindful that summary cases would often involve less serious allegations, and be dealt with in a shorter timeframe than would ordinarily allow for procedures of the sort recommended. However, it was felt that, in those few cases where capacity procedures are engaged in summary proceedings, it would not be appropriate to reduce the protections for a vulnerable defendant who is to be removed from the full trial process.

In respect of introducing participation procedures in the youth court, the Law Commission agreed with those consultees who stressed that young defendants may present with participation difficulties arising for very different reasons than those experienced by adults, including developmental immaturity. There were calls for a different test and procedure in the youth court for this reason, and also because of the specialist nature of youth court proceedings. However, the Law Commission concluded that this was not necessary, first, because the proposed test for capacity for trial is specifically tailored to take account the nature of the proceedings and the assistance available; secondly, because the test for effective participation is not focused on diagnosis, but is a legal test which draws heavily on criteria framed in respect of child defendants, informed as it is by the case of *SC*, and related authorities.

However, the challenge of identifying participation difficulties in young defendants, and ensuring that they are addressed, remains. To that end, the Law Commission recommended that all defendants under the age of fourteen should be screened for participation difficulties when appearing in the youth court for the first time.[125] In addition, training for all professionals engaged in proceedings involving young defendants, in the Crown or youth court, was recommended to facilitate the identification of such difficulties.

Updating the Court of Appeal's powers

The recommendations include a proposal to close the gap in the Court of Appeal's powers by creating the power to order a rehearing of the alternative finding procedure, where a finding arising from such a hearing has been quashed.[126]

Clarification and extension of procedures for the defendant who recovers capacity for trial

Recommendations, in respect of resuming trial proceedings against individuals who have recovered capacity, focus in particular on widening the scope of this function, as well as clarifying and streamlining the processes. The current limitation of resumption to cases where a live restriction order is still in place was considered discriminatory and too narrow in its focus. The Law Commission recommended that a prosecution right to apply to resume proceedings against a recovered defendant

[125] ibid, paras 7.108–7.131.

[126] ibid, paras 8.20 ff.

be extended to all cases where a specified violent or sexual offence has been proved against the individual (or a special verdict returned in respect of an allegation of murder), although the resumption of proceedings would require leave from the judge applying an 'interests-of-justice' test.[127] Some stakeholders have, however, questioned whether this may inhibit the recovery of a defendant who has been found to have done the act for fear of having to stand trial.

Concerns about the inability of a recovered individual to request resumption of trial proceedings are also addressed. The Law Commission recommended that such an individual should be able to apply to court for the prosecution to be resumed against them, whatever the original allegation charged. Again, the judge would apply an interests-of-justice test in considering the application, taking into account particular factors, including the views and availability of witnesses and any delay on the part of the recovered individual in making the application.[128]

A draft Bill

Given the focus in the reform recommendations on introducing a clear statutory scheme and test, it was essential that the recommendations be accompanied by a draft Bill. Instructions to Parliamentary Counsel stressed the importance of a straightforward, simply expressed Bill. The resulting 70 clause Criminal Procedure (Lack of Capacity) Bill[129] might not readily be described in those terms. However, the drafting process cast light on why previous reforms have not sought to enlarge the statutory elements of the unfitness-to-plead framework. Not only is there the challenge of crystallising in statute the 'sui generis' nature of the alternative processes in such a way as to be compatible with other criminal procedure legislation in both Crown and summary courts, but there is also the requirement to articulate procedures which enable the courts to respond to fluctuating conditions throughout the process, as well as introducing the facility to divert a defendant out of the system, to postpone proceedings or resume them on recovery.

Alongside the statutory changes, many of the recommendations are framed, where possible, in terms of amendments to the Crim PR and the Criminal Practice Directions[130] (Crim PD). Reviewed regularly, and without calling on significant Parliamentary time, the Crim PR and the Crim PD have become an important mechanism for achieving swift changes to criminal procedure.[131]

[127] ibid, paras 9.17 ff. [128] ibid, paras 9.66 ff.

[129] Law Commission, *Unfitness to Plead, Volume 2: Draft Legislation* (n 104).

[130] Criminal Practice Directions 2015 [2015] EWCA Crim 1567 as amended April, October, and November 2016 and February and April 2017.

[131] The Rt Hon. The Lord Thomas of Cwmgiedd, 'The Criminal Procedure Rules: 10 years on' [2015] 6 Crim LR 395.

The Government's Response and Prospects for Implementation

The Government issued an Interim Response to the Law Commission's report on 30 June 2016.[132] Whilst it welcomed the 'balanced and thorough consideration of how to ensure that defendants who lack capacity to participate in trial are dealt with appropriately in the criminal courts', the Interim Response stated that the on-going court reforms rendered implementation of the Law Commission's recommendations unlikely in the near future.

June 2016 also saw the EU referendum result and a subsequent change of Government. The political climate which has followed the Brexit vote has been more constrained, and the Governmental timetable for legislation has created different priorities.

Developments since Publication: Changing Approaches

Since publication of the report, cases involving issues of unfitness to plead have continued to illustrate some of the difficulties identified during the reform project. These include uncertainty as to the scope of the *Pritchard* test and lack of clarity over the procedures to be followed under the 1964 Act,[133] as well as difficulties arising in respect of the consent requirement within a supervision order.[134] The inadequacies of the current framework are likely to be placed under ever more strain as practitioners develop an increasing awareness of the participation difficulties for their clients. In addition, these problems are also exacerbated by the high numbers of much older defendants, many with communication and memory difficulties, on trial for historic allegations.

Now that the scale of the problem is being appreciated, it seems that there are new obstacles to reform. The perceived cost of overhauling the law is now a contributing factor to the reluctance to reform. Cost considerations have perhaps been a driver in the only substantive change in this area which has, arguably, been contrary to the direction proposed in the recommendations. In April 2016, the section of the Crim PD which addresses the granting of intermediaries to assist defendants at trial was reworded to stress that the use of the judge's inherent powers to grant an intermediary for a defendant will be 'rarely exercised' (3F.12) and the grant of such assistance for the whole of trial (rather than for giving evidence alone) would be 'extremely rare' (3F.13).[135]

[132] Available at: http://www.lawcom.gov.uk/wp-content/uploads/2016/07/Mike_Penning_Government_interim_response_on_Unfitness_to_Plead-1.pdf.

[133] See *Orr* [2016] EWCA Crim 889. See also *Hamberger* [2017] EWCA Crim 273.

[134] *City and County of Swansea v Swansea Crown Court* [2016] EWHC 1389 (Admin).

[135] Crim PD I General Matters I General Matters 3F.11 (n 5).

However, given the links between criminal justice and mental health that are becoming ever more clearly established, it is short-sighted to deny an investment in reforming the law of unfitness to plead. The unsatisfactory nature of the current law is leading to the imprisonment of high numbers of people with mental health difficulties;[136] this is costing the state far more in the longer term than the proposed reforms would be likely to cost.

Yet, as with previous reform initiatives in this area, inertia on the part of the government can be contrasted with a more forward-looking approach taken by the courts. In some unfitness-to-plead cases the Court of Appeal has started to reflect the language of the recommendations, particularly in the framing of the *Pritchard* test as focusing on a defendant's 'capacity to participate effectively' in trial.[137]

136 Prison Reform Trust, *Troubled Inside* (n 46).
137 See, eg, *Marcantonio* (n 107) [7]. See also *Orr* (n 133) [23].

5

Unfitness for Trial in Scots Law

*Gerry Maher**

Introduction

The nature and name of the plea

Under the current law of Scotland there is a defence known as unfitness for trial. Scots law has long recognised a defence or plea that, given the mental or physical characteristics of an accused person, it would be inappropriate to subject the accused to a criminal trial. This plea is one of a more general category of defences in Scots law known as pleas in bar of trial. Following Robinson's classifications of criminal law defences, these pleas have been described as non-exculpatory defences, which arise where, despite the possible existence of proof of an accused's guilt, there are specific reasons why the state should be prevented from bringing the accused to trial.[1]

In respect of this particular plea in bar of trial, Chalmers and Leverick have identified a number of rationales, including minimising the risk of wrongful conviction and protecting the moral dignity of the criminal process.[2]

At common law the plea was known as insanity in bar of trial. But it has also been referred to as unfitness to plead, presumably as an unconscious borrowing from English law, though English law had played virtually no role in the development of Scots law.[3] Furthermore, the Scottish plea has always focussed on the trial process as a whole rather than the particular stage of pleading,[4] and statutory

* Professor of Criminal Law, University of Edinburgh.

[1] James Chalmers and Fiona Leverick, *Criminal Defences and Pleas in Bar of Trial* (W Green & Son Ltd 2006) 12–14, founding on PH Robinson, *Criminal Law Defenses* (West Publishing Co 1984).

[2] Chalmers and Leverick, *Criminal Defences and Pleas in Bar of Trial* (n 1) 287–88.

[3] Virtually no English cases have been cited in Scottish decisions. In *HM Advocate v Wilson* 1942 JC 75 reference was made in argument to English decisions of unfitness to plead but these related to a specific point about the condition of deaf-mutism.

[4] In its *Report on Insanity and Diminished Responsibility*, Scot Law Com No 195 (2004) para 4.9, n 10, the Scottish Law Commission noted that pleading to an indictment had a crucial importance in the development of English criminal law, as refusal to plead had the consequence that a trial could not proceed (referring to N Walker, *Crime and Insanity in England, Volume 1: The Historical Perspective* (Edinburgh 1968) 220).

Fitness to Plead: International and Comparative Perspectives. First Edition. Edited by Ronnie Mackay and Warren Brookbanks. Chapter 5 © Gerry Maher 2018. Published 2018 by Oxford University Press.

provisions have for a long time referred to a person being insane so that their trial cannot proceed.[5]

In *Bain v Smith*[6] it had been recorded in the court minutes of procedure that the court had found the accused 'unfit to plead' in terms of the relevant statute and had made an order committing the accused to the State Hospital (a maximum-security hospital). It was argued that as the statute contained the expression 'insane so that the trial cannot proceed', the failure to use this terminology invalidated the making of the hospital order. The Appeal Court rejected this argument, holding that, as the phrase used in the minutes specifically referred to the statute, this was a finding of insanity in bar of trial.

Frequency

There is very little by way of data on how frequently the plea is resorted to.

A passage in the standard practitioner text on criminal procedure,[7] in referring to the report of the Thomson Committee (published in 1975) as '25 years ago', states that pleas of unfitness to plead by reason of insanity were more frequent then than they are nowadays, but no source is given for this proposition.

A research project did examine the provisions of the Criminal Procedure (Scotland) Act 1995 relating to insanity as a plea in bar of trial and as a substantive defence over a two-year period between 1996 and 1998.[8] During the period the researchers became aware of fifty-two cases. Thirty-seven of these cases involved the plea in bar, twelve the insanity defence, and in a further three the plea in bar and the defence were both raised. Of the thirty-seven cases involving only the plea in bar, the accused was found insane in bar of trial in twenty-nine, and after the resulting examinations of facts, the facts were established in twenty-two of these cases. Of the three cases involving both the plea and the defence, the accused in all cases was found to be both insane in bar of trial and at the time of the offence.

Current law on unfitness for trial

There are three main strands to the law on unfitness for trial: first, the test or criteria to be applied in establishing the plea; secondly the procedure to be used in proving and determining the plea; and thirdly the modes of disposal available once a plea has been proved.

[5] Criminal Procedure (Scotland) Act 1995, s 54(1) as originally enacted. The Lunacy (Scotland) Act 1857, s 87 refers to 'where any person charged under any indictment or criminal libel shall be found insane, so that such person cannot be tried upon such an indictment'.

[6] 1980 SLT (Notes) 69.

[7] RW Renton and HH Brown, *Criminal Procedure* (6th edn, W Green & Son Ltd 1996, with updating supplements), para 26-06.

[8] M Burman and C Connelly, *Mentally Disordered Offenders and Criminal Proceedings* (The Scottish Office 1999). The research report is summarised in Scottish Law Commission, Scot Law Com No 195 (n 4) paras 1.18–1.19.

The law on the last two of these issue stems from the Criminal Justice (Scotland) Act 1995 and the test for the plea is to be found in the Criminal Justice and Licensing (Scotland) Act 2010. The relevant provisions of these Acts are to be found in the Criminal Procedure (Scotland) Act 1995, which sets out a statutory code on criminal procedure.

Development of the Plea

There is very little case law of the development of the plea of insanity in bar of trial but there is useful discussion in the writings of the two major writers on Scots criminal law, David Hume in the eighteenth century and the contemporary writer, Sir Gerald Gordon.

Early discussion of the plea was characterised by several factors which have continued through to more modern times: first, a tendency to group consideration of the plea with that of insanity as a substantive defence (whilst recognising their different functions and rationales), and secondly greater focus on the possibly unjust outcomes rather than formulation of the test or definition of the plea. For example, Hume considers the 'miserable defence' of idiocy or insanity with a detailed survey of the definition of insanity as a defence, as well the effects of the acquittal where the defence is sustained.[9] In a long footnote at the end of his discussion he refers to the case of *HM Advocate v Jean Campbell or Bruce* (1817; a charge of murdering her three-year-old child), which he said was the first case in Scotland that addressed the question 'whether a person born deaf and dumb, is an object of trial and punishment'. Evidence had been obtained by the Crown that the accused knew right from wrong, was aware that punishment was a consequence of guilt, and could properly conduct herself in the ordinary affairs of life. Furthermore, there was evidence that, with the help of an interpreter, she could communicate her thoughts, fully understood the charge against her, and could provide an innocent explanation of her child's death.[10]

There have been some case-law developments since Hume that are worth noting. In *HM Advocate v Brown*,[11] there were references to an accused being incapable of pleading, which was noted as being the first step in a person being put on trial. The court noted that the procedure to be used was either for the court to hold a preliminary inquiry as to the accused's mental state before calling on him to plead or letting the accused plead and leaving to the jury the issue of whether he was capable of pleading. In this case the second course was followed. In this situation three possible issues were to be considered by the jury once all the evidence had been led.[12] The first was whether the accused was currently insane. If they held that to be the case, no other issues needed to dealt with. But if the accused was not currently insane the

[9] D Hume, *Commentaries on the Law of Scotland Respecting Crimes* (4th edn, Bell & Bradfute 1844), 37–45.

[10] ibid 45. At the trial she was found not guilty.

[11] 1907 SC(J) 67, 73.

[12] ibid 74–75.

jury had to consider whether he had committed the crime. If the answer to that was no, then that was the end of the matter. But if the jury found that the accused had committed the crime, then a third question arose as to whether he was insane at the time of doing so.

Two aspects of this procedure should be noted. The first is that two different aspects of insanity were being presented to the jury, with the possible consequence of the different tests being confused. The accused pleaded not guilty and the case proceeded to a trial before a jury. In his charge to the jury the trial judge mentioned the accused's medical condition (epilepsy) as going both to insanity in bar of trial[13] and to insanity as a defence.[14]

Secondly, the question whether the accused had committed the acts constituting the crime charged could arise only if the accused was not found to be insane in bar of trial, but there was no procedure for considering this issue where there was such a finding.[15]

In *HM Advocate v Wilson*,[16] where the accused was a deaf-mute and also described by medical witnesses as not of normal intellect, the court accepted that a person could be insane for the purpose of the plea in bar of trial even though he did not suffer from mental alienation. In this case, although the trial judge had made preliminary inquiries (on his own initiative) as to the state of the accused's health, no plea in bar had been raised and defence counsel requested that the case proceed before a jury rather than the issue of insanity in bar of trial be decided by a judge. The court accepted this submission on the basis that fuller evidence on the issue might be led at a trial than was presented to the judge as part of his preliminary inquiry. Although it is not made explicit in the report of the case, the jury held that the accused was not insane and found him not guilty.

Similar to Hume's account, Gerald Gordon, in his magisterial work on substantive Scots criminal law, added a section on insanity in bar of trial to his discussion of insanity as a defence.[17] He noted that although the plea was procedural in nature, it was worth discussing because most cases of insanity were dealt with by the plea, a characteristic which explained the lack of development of the defence in Scots law. His discussion deals first with the test for the plea, which he refers to as fitness to plead. He states the general principle as being that 'everyone is entitled to a fair trial'. In the case of unfitness based on insanity, he notes that the usual practice is for the courts simply to accept the evidence of medical experts but that in rare cases the matter is left for the jury to decide. He also considers cases where the plea is not

[13] In referring to the accused's medical history the question for the jury was whether 'it can be said that he is in a position to do what a sane man could do—that is to say, to be certain that in telling his counsel what he did he is really able to tell the true story of his life and action', ibid 77.

[14] The jury was reminded of evidence that a 'minor attack' of epilepsy 'robs the patient of the full control of his faculties, and yet leaves him in many ways free to act, not, I think, automatically, but as of set purpose, while yet a purpose which is not controlled by a rational and sane will', ibid.

[15] In his memoirs Lord Macmillan, who was junior counsel for the accused in this case, noted the problems which could follow in this situation (*A Man of Law's Tale* (Macmillan 1952) 109–10).

[16] 1942 SC 75.

[17] GH Gordon, *The Criminal Law of Scotland* (1st edn, W Green & Son Ltd 1967) 330–32.

based on insanity, as with amnesia of what occurred at the time of offence (which the courts have rejected as a basis for the plea) and the physical condition of deaf-mutism (which could found the plea where the accused had no means—such as an interpreter—of communication during a trial process).

The second broad issue is the effect of a finding of unfitness. A legal effect is that the plea in bar of trial does not, in Scottish terminology, 'thole the assize'; that is, it does not act as *res judicata* to prevent a later trial if the condition underlying the plea is cured or otherwise disappears.[18] But his main focus is on the treatment of persons who have been found unfit to plead. At the time of writing his book, the usual effect was the making of a court order for the accused to be detained in the State Hospital, release from which could be made only by order of the Secretary of State. Gordon noted two fundamental problems with this scenario. The first was that the plea applied to 'insanity' in bar of trial, but where it was based on a physical condition, the effect was that the accused was deemed to be insane and was subject to compulsory measures under mental health legislation, a situation he described as 'highly artificial if not indeed ludicrous'. The second was that an accused could be subject to such an order without there being any proof that he committed the criminal acts he was charged with.[19]

He concluded his discussion with two brief proposals for change: first, different forms of detention for persons whose condition was not insanity but which might lead to repetition of dangerous behaviour; and, secondly, a requirement for the Crown to set a prima facie case against the accused before he could be detained in a hospital.

Accordingly, by the time of Gordon's book Scots law had developed on certain aspects of both the nature of the test for the plea in bar and the consequences of the plea being established. It was also accepted that there were serious deficiencies with the law. But Gordon was to play a key role in bringing change and modernisation to this topic, for he was a member of a departmental committee which made a wide-ranging review of Scots criminal procedure.[20]

The Thomson Committee picked up many of the points made by Gordon in his book.

In terms of the formulation of the test for the plea in bar it noted that the criterion of distinguishing between right and wrong, which was mentioned by Hume, had disappeared and the key issue was whether the accused could properly instruct his

[18] The leading case is *HM Advocate v Bickerstaff* 1926 JC 65, where a plea in bar on a charge of murder was upheld. The accused was committed to a hospital from which he was later released on the ground that he had recovered. He was then served with a fresh indictment for the same offence as originally charged. No objection was taken that this was incompetent. In *HM Advocate v Ward*, it was expressly noted by the judge that where the accused was not acquitted after an examination of facts the Crown may still re-indict the accused if he later recovers (High Court of Justiciary, 27 February 2015, unreported; available at: http://www.scotland-judiciary.org.uk/9/1395/Determination-following-examination-of-facts-in-Her-Majestys-Advocate-v-Paul-Francis-Ward).

[19] Gordon, *The Criminal Law of Scotland* (n 17) 331.

[20] Scottish Home and Health Department and Crown Office, *Criminal Procedure in Scotland (Second Report)*, Report by the Committee appointed by the Secretary of State for Scotland and the Lord Advocate (Chairman: The Honourable Lord Thomson). Cmnd 6218 (1975) ch 52.

defence.[21] This is of interest as separating out the plea in bar from the defence. The Committee suggested a test for the plea as:[22]

> Is the accused incapable by reason of mental disorder (including deficiency) of understanding the substance of the charge and the proceedings and of communicating adequately with his legal advisors?

The Committee noted that the advice given to them by psychiatrists was that the effect of such a test would be that only persons with severe mental disorder would be found unfit for trial.

As for procedural issues, the Committee noted objections to any change on the basis that the present approach worked well in practice, and in particular it was only in very rare cases that a person committed as a consequence of the plea complained that he had not committed the act charged. It was also the general practice of the Crown not to raise criminal proceedings in the absence of sufficiency of evidence, which in Scots law tended to mean corroboration of the Crown case.

The Committee was unimpressed with these arguments and took a principled objection to there being any possibility that someone could be made subject to compulsory detention under mental health law where there had been no proof that he had committed the acts charged against him.[23]

The Committee set out a detailed recommendation on the new procedure for determining the factual basis of the charge against the accused. The first question was whether the accused's condition meets the test for the plea in bar of trial. If it does, there would follow a limited type of inquiry, rather than a full trial, to establish the facts. The procedure envisaged for this inquiry was that the Crown would lead evidence. It would be a matter of judgment for the defence on how they would test the Crown case, for example cross-examination of the Crown evidence or leading defence evidence. But the defence would not be allowed to make any concession in respect of evidence. The judge (sitting without a jury) would make findings of fact established 'to his satisfaction', but the Committee did not specify which standard of proof was to apply. How the judge would then deal with these findings was not made entirely clear.

The Committee took the view that in most cases a person who was insane in bar of trial would probably have been insane at the time of the relevant offence. This view is not explored or explained, but the conclusion drawn is that the new procedure for determining the facts should allow for the consideration of any question of insanity as a defence. Where the facts showed that the accused committed the criminal act, the judge would then go on to consider whether the accused was insane at the time of the act, a procedure which would call for consideration of further evidence. Whether or not the defence applied, the court would order the detention of the accused in an appropriate hospital.

[21] ibid, para 52.13. [22] ibid. [23] ibid, para 52.14.

If the findings of fact indicated that the accused did not commit the act, the judge would order the release of the accused or a remit to a hospital for assessment for possible detention under the non-criminal provisions of the mental health legislation.

So, by the mid-1970s problems (with some proffered solutions) had been identified with the three core elements of the plea in bar of trial, namely the test for the plea, the procedure in establishing it, and the disposal consequences of the plea being upheld.

There was little development since the time of the Thomson Report until the legislative intervention by the Criminal Procedure (Scotland) Act 1995, but there have been some subsequent reported decisions.

In *Stewart v HM Advocate*,[24] a case decided after the introduction of the new procedure for determining the plea in bar, the trial judge considered psychiatric evidence at a preliminary diet in respect of an accused who was mentally handicapped, had a low intelligence, and had a short concentration span. The judge accepted that there might be problems in the accused's understanding of the nature of the presentation of evidence in a trial, but following the decision in *HM Advocate v Wilson*,[25] the accused was able to instruct his counsel and to follow the proceedings against him and therefore was not insane in bar of trial.

The case is interesting as involving the test for the plea in bar of trial. A submission was made for the accused that as the range of disposal options following a finding of insanity in bar of trial had been broadened by the 1995 Act, a wider interpretation of what constituted insanity for this purpose should be adopted, but the trial judge pointed out that a change to the disposal regime carried no implication for the separate issue of the basis of the plea. A further submission was made by the Crown that the test for insanity in bar of trial was the same as that for the defence, and as the accused in this case had no alienation of reason (a key element of the then defence of insanity), it followed that there could be no finding that he was insane in bar of trial. The trial judge held that this submission was without foundation and pointed out that there were authorities going back to Hume to the effect that the tests for the plea in bar and the defence were different.

In *McLachlan v Brown*,[26] a plea in bar of trial was lodged on the basis that the accused had a mental impairment, which the defence claimed was a different plea from insanity in bar of trial. However, the judge held that the term 'insanity' in this context extended beyond mental illness and included mental impairment and handicap.[27]

[24] 1997 JC 183. [25] 1942 JC 75. [26] 1997 JC 222.

[27] The purpose of the defence submission was that under the then provisions of the 1995 Act evidence concerning insanity in bar of trial had to be given by two medical practitioners but in this case the evidence about mental impairment had been given by a psychologist who was not a medical practitioner. This anomalous provision about evidence was removed by the 2010 Act.

Procedure in Dealing with the Plea of Unfitness for Trial

Determining the plea

The decision whether an accused person falls within the scope of the plea in bar of trial is made by the court, which takes place during a preliminary hearing before a trial has started. Where the issue of unfitness is raised during a trial itself, proceedings are stopped to determine that issue, but here again the question is a matter for the judge, and does not involve a jury. It is not a barrier to deciding the issue of unfitness, either before or during a trial, that the question of the accused's unfitness has been considered earlier and the accused at that stage was found not to be unfit. A finding that an accused is unfit for trial must be raised before a trial has concluded by a verdict being returned. In *Murphy v HM Advocate*,[28] the accused was found guilty of rape, but during the pre-sentencing process doubts arose about his mental fitness to understand that process. The question then arose whether the accused had been fit to stand trial. The appeal court heard evidence from psychiatric experts and concluded that it was more probable than not that the accused had been unfit for his earlier trial, and the conviction was quashed.[29]

Where the possibility of the accused being unfit for trial has been raised but requires further investigation, the case can be adjourned to allow for examination of the accused's mental or physical condition.

The hearing on unfitness may proceed in the absence of the accused if it is not practicable or appropriate for him to be present, but this step must be agreed to by the accused or those acting on his behalf.[30]

The exact evidence relevant to the issue of fitness is variable, but in almost all cases the court would require evidence from an appropriate medical expert.[31]

Various medical conditions have been identified as potentially relevant to fitness for trial. Appropriate psychiatric conditions include dementia and other chronic organic conditions, delirium, schizophrenia and related psychoses, severe affective disorders such as mania and depression, and learning disability.[32]

Where a judge makes a finding that the accused is unfit for trial he must state the reasons for so finding.[33]

In *HM Advocate v Ward*,[34] an accused on a murder charge was found unfit for trial. The court noted that a possible consequence of such a finding was that the Crown could end proceedings altogether. This outcome would be appropriate where the accused had not been charged with a serious offence, but this was unlikely in the

[28] 2017 SLT 143.

[29] The Court commented on the duties of defence lawyers where an issue of fitness for trial might arise. It was a matter for professional judgment whether the circumstances of a case required consideration of the issue but if they did, legal advisers should obtain a medical report rather than rely on their own personal judgment.

[30] 1995 Act, s 54(5).

[31] *Murphy v HM Advocate* 2017 SLT 143 para [57].

[32] R Darjee and L Robinson, 'Psychiatric Defences' in Lindsay Thomson and Joanna Cherry (eds), *Mental Health and Scots Law in Practice* (2nd edn, W Green & Son Ltd 2014) ch 10, 323–24.

[33] 1995 Act, s 54(1).

[34] See n 18.

present case, given the nature of the charge. If it was possible that accused's condition was likely to improve, the Crown could discontinue proceedings for the time being and re-indict the accused when he became fit to stand trial. However if, as in this case, the accused was unlikely to become fit for trial, that option would leave various parties (accused and members of the deceased's family) in a state of limbo for an indefinite period.

Accordingly, in most cases a finding of unfitness for trial results in the trial diet being discharged and a hearing for an examination of facts is ordered. The accused may then be remanded in custody or released on bail. In addition, if the accused has a mental disorder for which (a) medical treatment would have an effect; and (b) if no medical treatment were provided, there would be a significant risk to his or anyone else's safety or to his health or welfare, the court may make a temporary compulsion order for his detention in a specified hospital.[35]

The effect of the order is that the accused is detained in a hospital until the conclusion of the examination of facts.

Table 5.1 shows the use of temporary compulsion orders over the period 2010–2016:

Table 5.1 Number of Temporary Compulsion Orders

Order type	2010/11	2011/12	2012/13	2013/14	2014/15	2015/16
Temporary compulsion order	13	12	17	7	20	19

Source: Mental Welfare Commission for Scotland, *Mental Health Act Monitoring 2015–16* (2016) 27, Table 6.2.

Examination of facts

The examination of facts proceeds as nearly as possible on the basis of the same powers of the court and the rules of evidence and procedure as used in a criminal trial,[36] which presumably means that corroboration is required to prove the prosecution case. The examination should be held immediately following the finding of unfitness for trial. As with the proceedings for determining unfitness, the examination of facts may take place in the absence of the accused if it appears to the court that it is not practicable or appropriate for him to be present and no objection had been made by or on behalf of the accused.[37]

[35] 1995 Act, s 54(1)(c), (2A), (2B). Medical treatment is defined by s 329(1) of the Mental Health (Care and Treatment) (Scotland) Act 2003, as including—(a) nursing; (b) care; (c) psychological intervention; (d) habilitation (including education, and training in work, social, and independent living skills); and (e) rehabilitation (read in accordance with (d)). An order can only be made on the evidence of two medical practitioners that the accused suffers from the relevant type of mental disorder and a suitable hospital is available.

[36] 1995 Act, s 55(5). Special provision is made where an accused person is not legally represented. The court must appoint a lawyer to represent his interests at the examination of facts (1995 Act, s 56(3)).

[37] 1995 Act, s 55(5).

After hearing evidence, the court must acquit the accused of the charge against him unless two issues have been established.[38] First, the court must be satisfied beyond reasonable doubt that the accused did the act or made the omission constituting the offence with which he has been charged. Secondly, it must be satisfied on the balance of probabilities that there are no grounds for acquitting the accused. Where the court is satisfied on both of these issues, it makes a finding to that effect, but where it is not so satisfied it acquits the accused.[39]

There has been little guidance in the case law on the meaning of these provisions. One interpretation is that the Act is drawing a distinction between the conduct and mental elements of the offence with which the accused is charged, and it is only the former that has to be established beyond reasonable doubt. The absence (or presence) of *mens rea* would be a matter for consideration on the second issue, the lack of a defence which would lead to an acquittal. However, in some cases it is difficult to establish the conduct element without examining an aspect of the accused's mental state. An example is the offence of sexual exposure, which is defined as exposing one's genitals to another person with the purpose of either obtaining sexual gratification or of humiliating, distressing, or alarming that person.[40] It is a better reading of the 1995 Act provisions to hold that such a purpose is something which the court has to find proved beyond reasonable doubt, rather than its absence found on the balance of probabilities.

A further, and more significant, difficulty with this interpretation is that it seems unprincipled to hold that the absence of a defence which would lead to the accused's acquittal should only be established on the balance of probabilities, rather than beyond reasonable doubt.[41] The latter is the standard of proof used in many instances where a defence is an issue at a trial.

This criticism suggests an alternative way of interpreting the provisions in question, although this second approach is less easy to reconcile with the language of the statute. On this view, the Act is replicating the rules on burdens of proof in criminal trials. The first issue identified by the Act requires the prosecution to prove beyond reasonable doubt all of the essential prerequisites of proof of the accused's guilt, which would include disproving any defence which the accused has made an issue for determination. This situation would arise where an accused has satisfied an evidential burden by adducing enough evidence to require that the defence is to be considered. The second issue, of the court being satisfied on a balance of probabilities that there are no grounds for acquitting the accused, arises only where the accused has a legal burden of proving a defence.

This interpretation has been suggested in relation to the common law defence of insanity, and its more recent statutory replacement,[42] and in *HM Advocate v Ward*,[43] the judge in an examination of facts accepted it would also apply to the plea of

[38] 1995 Act, s 55(1). [39] 1995 Act, s 55(2), (3).

[40] Sexual Offences (Scotland) Act 2009, s 8.

[41] This criticism has been made by RD Mackay and WJ Brookbanks, 'Protecting the Unfit to Plead: A Comparative Analysis of the "Trial of Facts"' 2005 Jur Rev 173, 183–84.

[42] Renton and Brown, *Criminal Procedure* (n 7) para 26-11. [43] See n 18.

diminished responsibility. However, the same position would apply to any defence where the accused has a legal burden of proof. It follows that where an examination of facts involves a statutory reverse burden, the court will have to determine whether the burden on the accused is a legal or evidential one.[44]

The reference to acts (or omissions) constituting the offence and to acquittal in these provisions gives rise to a further problem. The focus of the examination of facts is on the crime charged on the indictment or complaint, but it is not clear whether an accused can be found guilty on an alternative charge. Consider s 50 of the Sexual Offences (Scotland) Act 2009, which allows for a wide range of alternative verdicts for offences under that Act (eg, common law assault as an alternative to rape). The procedure in s 50 of the 2009 Act refers to a 'trial' in which the jury finds that the accused committed the alternative offence rather than that charged against him, but the question arises as to whether an examination of facts is a trial for this purpose. As noted above, s 55(6) of the 1995 Act states that for an examination of facts, rules of evidence and procedure as well as the 'powers of the court' shall as far as possible be those applicable to a trial, which suggests that findings in relation to alternative verdicts are possible in an examination of facts.[45] So, if an accused is charged with rape, the court in an examination of facts could find that the accused did the act constituting a common law assault. But the issue here is whether this finding involves an 'acquittal' on the charge of rape.

The possibility of a finding of an alternative charge is an important factor in relation to the partial defences of provocation and diminished responsibility in cases of murder. The Scottish Law Commission argued that the common law defence of diminished responsibility would not be considered during an examination of facts because the defence would not be a ground for acquitting the accused.[46] However, it has been argued that this partial defence does result in an acquittal, or at least an implied acquittal, on the charge of murder.[47] But it would be absurd to hold that if the court in an examination of facts finds that there is the basis for the plea of diminished responsibility, it must acquit the accused of murder tout court, without examining the issue of culpable homicide. In any case, the argument about acquittal in cases of partial defences does not accurately capture Scottish legal practice in recording verdicts. Where a partial defence has been established, the verdict which is recorded is guilty of culpable homicide, but there is no verdict of not guilty in respect of the charge of murder. The similar approach is taken with alternative verdicts. So, in the example noted above, the recorded verdict would be that of guilty of assault, but there would be no acquittal recorded in respect of the charge of rape.

If, following an examination of facts, the court does not acquit the accused, this still allows the Crown to re-indict if the accused does later recover. If the accused is

[44] On this issue Scots law has tended to follow the influential decisions of the House of Lords in *R v Lambert* [2002] 2 AC 545 and *Sheldrake v DPP* [2005] 1 AC 264. See *Glancy v HM Advocate* 2012 SCCR 52 and *Urquhart v HM Advocate* 2016 JC 93.

[45] Chalmers and Leverick, *Criminal Defences and Pleas in Bar of Trial* (n 1) 298, advance this interpretation of s 55(6) but with some hesitation.

[46] Scottish Law Commission, Scot Law Com No 195 (n 4) para 4.3, n 5.

[47] Chalmers and Leverick, *Criminal Defences and Pleas in Bar of Trial* (n 1) 297.

acquitted, then criminal proceedings against him come to an end, but he may still be subject to a mental health disposal under civil law.

Special provision is made where the court in an examination of facts finds that the ground for acquitting the accused is that at the time of the conduct he was not criminally responsible in terms of s 51A of the 1995 Act.[48] In these circumstances, the court must state that the acquittal is by reason of that defence.[49]

Appeals

An accused may appeal against a finding that the accused is unfit for trial or the refusal of the court to make such a finding. An appeal can also be made against a finding that the accused committed the act charged or that there were no grounds for acquitting him (including the defence that the accused lacked criminal responsibility—the equivalent of the former insanity defence).[50] The appeal is made to the High Court of Justiciary sitting as a court of appeal where the accused had been charged on indictment, which includes cases where the proceedings were to be tried in the sheriff court. Where the charge was to be tried in summary proceedings, the appropriate appeal court is the Sheriff Appeal Court.

In disposing of an appeal, the appeal court has the power to affirm the decision made in determining unfitness or at the examination of facts, or it can make any other finding or order which the court could have made. Further, the appeal court can remit the case back to that court with directions to be followed.[51]

An appeal can also be made by the prosecution to the same appeal courts, but only on a point of law.[52] The appeal can be made against a finding that the accused is unfit for trial or an acquittal based on a finding that the accused did not commit the act charged against him or that there was a ground for acquitting (including a finding of the special defence that the accused lacked criminal responsibility).

The powers of the appeal court in disposing of the appeal are broadly the same as those for an appeal by an accused.

The Test for the Plea

The developments in the Criminal Justice (Scotland) Act 1995 dealt with procedures for establishing that an accused committed the acts at the basis of the charge against him and of the disposal consequences if the relevant facts were found. However, the substantive test of what constituted insanity as a plea in bar remained governed by the common law. Reform did come about as a result of a law reform project by the Scottish Law Commission on wider aspects of mental disorder and the criminal

[48] This defence is the statutory replacement for the common law defence of insanity, introduced by the Criminal Justice and Licensing (Scotland) Act 2010.

[49] 1995 Act, s 55(4).

[50] 1995 Act, s 62.

[51] 1995 Act, s 62(6)(c).

[52] 1995 Act, s 63.

law.[53] Although it had long been recognised that the law on insanity (both as a defence and as a plea in bar of trial) and diminished responsibility were in need of modernisation and reform, this project was not part of any of the Commission's programmes of law reform. Rather, the Commission considered these topics as result of a reference from the Scottish Executive (now the Scottish Government). The spur for the reference was a report on civil aspects of mental health law.[54] The Committee which had carried out that review had received evidence from professional witnesses who reported that they had been encountering problems in using the tests for insanity and diminished responsibility. However, as issues of criminal law were beyond the remit of the Committee it recommended that the Scottish Law Commission should examine this area of the law.

It is fair to say that the focus of the Commission's project was insanity as a defence rather than as a plea in bar of trial.[55] The responses to the Commission's consultation paper almost uniformly accepted the proposals in relation to the plea in bar. What is more, the final recommendations were fully implemented by statute but with only a brief consideration of these provisions during the Parliamentary process.[56] Accordingly the Scottish Law Commission's considerations offer a good basis for a full description and interpretation of the current law.[57]

Name of the plea

At common law the plea was known as insanity in bar of trial. As part of its general strategy the Commission wished to get rid of the term 'insanity' in the criminal law as being pejorative and stigmatising in nature. As regards the plea in bar of trial there was a further objection that some of the conditions which the plea covered were physical in nature. As a replacement, the Commission had considered both 'incapacity' and 'disability' but each of these had meanings fixed in other areas of law. It saw advantages in adopting the term 'unfitness', which is widely used in legal systems based on English law, but saw the reference to pleading as too narrow and instead recommended the name as 'unfitness for trial'.

[53] Scottish Law Commission, Scot Law Com No 195 (n 4). The Report followed on from an earlier consultation paper (Scottish Law Commission, Discussion Paper on Insanity and Diminished Responsibility, Discussion Paper No 122 (2003). The Commission stressed the importance of looking at the law in other jurisdictions and consulted a panel of internationally renowned academic specialists from England and Wales, Ireland, New Zealand, and the United States.

[54] New Directions: Report on the Review of the Mental Health (Scotland) Act 1984 (2001). Chairman Rt Hon Bruce Millan (SE/2001/56).

[55] By the time the project had started the law on diminished responsibility had been significantly developed by the decision in *Galbraith v HM Advocate* 2002 JC 1. The Commission's recommendations were that the law on diminished responsibility should be put on a statutory basis largely on the lines set out in *Galbraith*, subject to one major change to allow the defence to be based on the condition of psychopathic personality disorder.

[56] Criminal Justice and Licensing (Scotland) Act 2010, which added a new section, section 53F, to the Criminal Procedure (Scotland) Act 1995.

[57] Scottish Law Commission, Scot Law Com No 195 (n 4) Part 4 and paras 5.54–5.65.

Nature of the test

As a result of the Commission's recommendations the test is now to be found in s 53 F(1) of the Criminal Procedure (Scotland) Act 1995, which provides that a person is unfit for trial if he or she is incapable, by reason of a mental or physical condition, of participating effectively in a trial. Subsection (2) sets out a list of factors concerning the abilities of the accused which are to be considered in determining whether he or she is unfit for trial in this sense. These are the ability of a person to:

- (i) understand the nature of the charge;
- (ii) understand the requirement to tender a plea to the charge and the effect of such a plea;
- (iii) understand the purpose of, and follow the course of, a trial;
- (iv) understand the evidence that may be given against the person;
- (v) instruct and otherwise communicate adequately with his or her legal representative.

It is clear that these particular competences are not exhaustive of matters which a court may consider, as the subsection further provides that the court shall also have regard to any other factor which it considers relevant.

The Commission saw the focus on competences of the accused in respect of the trial as developing the approach of the common law. At an earlier stage the test for the plea in bar of trial had used aspects of the test for the defence of insanity, especially the factor of knowing right from wrong. However, by the beginning of the twentieth century the law had developed to stressing aspects of understanding and engaging in the trial process. In *HM Advocate v Brown*,[58] the jury were directed that the plea:

> means insanity which prevents a man from doing what a truly sane man would do and is entitled to do—maintain in sober sanity his plea of innocence, and instruct those who defend him as a truly sane man would do.

A fuller account on the same lines was the jury direction used in *HM Advocate v Wilson*:[59]

> Now, what exactly is meant by saying that a man is unfit to plead? The ordinary and common case, of course, is the case of a man who suffers from insanity, that is to say, from mental alienation of some kind which prevents him from giving the instructions which a sane man would give for his defence, or from following the evidence as a sane man would follow it, and instructing his counsel as the case goes along upon any point that arises. Now, no medical man says, and no medical man has ever said, that this accused is insane in that sense. His reason is not alienated, but he may be insane [sc in bar of trial] . . . although his reason is not alienated, if his condition be such that he is unable either from mental defect or physical defect, or a combination of these, to tell his counsel what his defence is and instruct him so that he can appear and defend him; or if, again, his condition of mind and body is such that

[58] 1907 SC(J) 67, 77.

[59] See n 3, 79. The accused in this case was a deaf-mute.

he does not understand the proceedings which are going on when he is brought into Court upon his trial, and he cannot intelligibly follow what it is all about.

The Scottish Law Commission saw advantages in maintaining this approach of defining the plea in terms of the skills of an accused person arising from his or her involvement in a criminal trial.[60] Moreover, the Commission argued that the statutory formulation of the plea should in addition set out the general rationale of the plea in bar of trial. Such a rationale had been recognised in earlier Scottish cases,[61] which suggested that someone was fit for a trial provided that he or she could both understand and participate in a trial in some meaningful way. The Commission noted ways in which this broader rationale had been expressed in other legal systems, such as the notion of adjudicative competence formulated by the Supreme Court in the United States.[62] Likewise English law had referred to the ability of the accused to 'understand and reply rationally to the indictment'.[63] A further example is the stress in New Zealand law on the 'adequate' nature of an accused's understanding of the trial and its possible consequences, and of his ability to communicate with his lawyers for the purposes of conducting a defence.[64]

These formulations do not differ from each other in substance. Moreover, the Commission had examined the case law of the European Court of Human Rights (ECtHR) on this issue, especially the cases of *Stanford v United Kingdom*[65] and *T and V v United Kingdom*.[66] The Commission saw advantages in Scots law explicitly adopting the general rationale derived from that jurisprudence, which it identified as that of effective participation in the criminal process.[67]

The inclusion of physical factors

The common law recognised that the plea in bar of trial might apply to persons with a physical condition, as opposed to a mental condition, which precluded their ability to use or perform any of the skills which constituted the test for plea.[68] One

[60] The formulation of the ability factors in the 1995 Act was based directly on that in the Commission's final Report but differed in one respect from the original drafting in the consultation paper. Instead of the ability to understand the evidence given against the accused, the earlier formulation was the ability to understand the substantial effect of such evidence.

[61] *HM Advocate v Russell* 1946 JC 37, Lord Justice Clerk Cooper 46: 'A plea in bar of trial, as distinguished from a plea or special defence in exculpation, or in mitigation of the gravity of a charge, is a claim that the accused is not a fit object for trial—at least in the meantime.'

[62] *Dusky v United States* 362 US 402, 406 (1960): 'the test must be whether [the defendant] has sufficient present ability to consult with his lawyer with a reasonable degree of rational understanding—and whether he has a rational as well as a factual understanding of the proceedings against him'. See Richard J Bonnie, 'The Competence of Criminal Defendants: Beyond *Dusky* and *Drope*' (1993) 47 University of Miami Law Review 539.

[63] *R v Friend* [1997] 1 WLR 1433, 1441.

[64] Criminal Procedure (Mentally Impaired Persons) Act 2003, s 4.

[65] Series A282-A.

[66] (2000) 30 EHHR 121.

[67] The validity of an Act of the Scottish Parliament requires that its provisions comply with the ECHR (Scotland Act 1998, s 29(2)(d)). The general principle of effective participation has been used to describe unfitness to plead in Jersey (*Attorney General v O'Driscoll* [2003] JLR 390 (Royal Court of Jersey (Samedi Division) 9 July 2003)).

[68] In the leading case *HM Advocate v Wilson* (n 3), the accused as a deaf-mute.

objection to this extension of the plea was the absurdity involved in labelling such a person as insane, but that issue no longer arises once the plea is given a different name. Indeed, s 53F of the 1995 Act expressly refers to someone being incapable of effective participation in a trial by reason of a mental or physical condition. In many cases involving an accused with a physical disability adaptations can be made to the physical lay-out of the court to allow the accused to better follow the proceedings. Where someone cannot understand the language used in court because of a physical condition, the services of an interpreter should be provided.[69]

The inclusion of a lack of ability to participate because of a physical condition had previously led to the objectionable outcome that the accused in this situation was liable to be treated in the same way as someone with a mental disorder, which could lead to unlimited detention in the State Hospital. In the present law, any disposal following on from the plea in bar is governed by the mental disorder provisions of the1995 Act. For a person with a physical condition the disposal would almost always be that the court would make no order, but there remains the problem that the accused would still be considered as someone subject to a disposal under criminal mental health law.

Excluded conditions

At common law the plea in bar of trial could not be based on the fact that at the trial the accused was suffering from amnesia about the actings at the basis of the charge against him or her.[70] The court was clear in stressing that the reason for this rule was that this condition did not deprive the accused of the ability to understand or participate in the proceedings. Matters would be different where the accused suffered memory problems during the trial which could interfere with the exercise of the required abilities.

The current law, as recommended by the Scottish Law Commission, expressly embodies a similar exclusion from the scope of the plea.[71] This seems odd, as the condition of amnesia about the facts charged is not an exception to the rule set out in the test for the plea. The test would not, in any case, apply to the condition. It may be that the provision on amnesia was added from an abundance of caution arising from the abolition of the common law on insanity in bar of trial.[72]

It is worthwhile returning to one of the general elements of the test. It is not enough that a person is incapable of participating effectively in a trial; rather that lack of capability must be by reason of a mental or physical condition. This requirement was important for the Commission in explaining that the test they were recommending

[69] Providing an interpreter for a deaf-mute was used in the old case of *Jean Campbell*, discussed by Hume, I (n 9) 45.

[70] *HM Advocate v Russell* (n 61); *Hughes v HM Advocate* 2002 JC 23.

[71] 1995 Act, s 53F(3): 'The court is not to find that a person is unfit for trial by reason only of the person being unable to recall whether the event which forms the basis of the charge occurred in the manner described in the charge.'

[72] Criminal Justice and Licensing (Scotland) Act 2010, s 171(c), which provides that any rule of law providing for insanity in bar of trial ceases to have effect.

was not over-inclusive. The Commission was dealing with the objection that there were many reasons why people facing a trial could not fully understand the nature of the proceedings, as with someone with a poor education or a deprived social background. Even the presence of a lawyer might not help if the explanations given to an accused were not communicated in a way that the accused could follow.

The Commission argued that the requirement of a mental or physical condition as the cause of the failure to participate effectively would rule out the application of the plea in bar in these situations. Indeed, the Commission stated that there would have to be a clinically recognised condition at the basis of the plea. But the Commission did not recommend, nor is it now the law in the 1995 Act, that the accused had to have a mental or physical *disorder*, so it is difficult to see why the plea is said to be restricted to medical conditions.

Consider the case where someone with deaf-mutism has problems in following trial proceedings and in communicating with his or her lawyer. It is accepted practice that in this situation an interpreter should assist the accused. But there are other situations where an accused cannot speak the language of a trial. Indeed, Art 6(3)(e) of the European Convention on Human Rights (ECHR) provides the right to a person charged with a criminal offence to have the free assistance of an interpreter if he cannot understand or speak the language used in court. In the curious case of *Mikhailitchenko v Normand*,[73] the accused, a Ukrainian whose language was Russian, was a professional footballer who played for a Scottish club, and was described in court as having little or no understanding of the English language. An interpreter was provided at the trial who spoke Bulgarian but not Russian. The appeal court later found that these proceedings were unfair. Now this case did not involve a plea in bar of trial, but if the problems of language and lack of an interpreter had been raised prior to the start of the trial, then the trial could not have proceeded. Perhaps what would be involved here was some other plea in bar of trial,[74] but nonetheless the re-description of the plea as not being based on insanity may have unwittingly widened the scope of the plea beyond what the Commission had envisaged.

Burden and standard of proof

At common law, there was little authority on the issues of burden and standard of proof in relation to insanity in bar of trial, but it seemed that the plea could be raised by the accused, by the Crown, and by the court itself.[75] In its consultation paper the Commission had suggested that these matters should be dealt with in the same way as the defence of insanity. The Commission had proposed that in relation to the defence the accused should bear an evidential burden to make the defence an issue and thereafter the Crown should have a legal burden to disprove it beyond

[73] 1993 SLT 1138.

[74] Recognised pleas in bar include oppression through prejudicial publicity or abuse of process, but as currently understood these pleas would not extend to language problems. For discussion of pleas in bar of trial, see Chalmers and Leverick, *Criminal Defences and Pleas in Bar of Trial* (n 1) chs14–19.

[75] Scottish Law Commission, Scot Law Com No 195 (n 4) paras 5.54–5.59.

reasonable doubt.[76] A similar proposal was made for the plea in bar of trial, namely that the ultimate burden would be on the Crown to establish an accused's fitness for trial beyond reasonable doubt.

In response to the points raised during consultation the Commission changed its mind in respect of both the substantive defence and the plea in bar. Unlike the defence, the plea in bar concerned the appropriateness of the entire proceedings, and accordingly the burden of raising and proving the plea should not rest with any one party. Accordingly, the Commission recommended that there should be no change to the common law position, and where the issue of fitness for trial was raised by either party or by the court, the matter would be decided on the basis of all evidence before the court.

As regards the requisite standard of proof, the common law position was probably that insanity in bar or trial had to be proved on the balance of probabilities, even if the issue had been raised by the Crown. The Commission noted that Scots law recognised only two standards of proof, beyond reasonable doubt and on the balance of probabilities. As the issue of the plea in bar did not in itself involve proof of guilt, it recommended that the lower standard of proof should apply to the statutory plea. Section 53F expressly states that the issue of unfitness for trial has to be established on the balance of probabilities, but makes no provision about the burden of proof, presumably on the basis that the common law rule on this matter survives the abolition of the common law plea.

Disposal of Cases after the Examination of Facts

Where an accused has been found unfit for trial and has not been acquitted after an examination of facts, or has been acquitted on the ground of being not criminally responsible, he may be subject to any of the following orders as the court thinks fit:[77]

(1) a compulsion order authorising the detention of the person in a hospital;
(2) a compulsion order and a restriction order;
(3) an interim compulsion order;
(4) a guardianship order;
(5) a supervision and treatment order;
(6) no order.

[76] Under s 52(1) of the 1995 Act the Crown is under a duty to bring before the court any evidence it may have as to the accused's mental condition where it appears that the accused may be suffering from a mental disorder. This provision was not amended by the 2010 Act.

[77] 1995 Act, s 57(2). For a detailed discussion of these disposals, see R Darjee and G Skilling, 'Legislation for Mentally Disordered Offenders' in Lindsay Thomson and Joanna Cherry (eds) *Mental Health and Scots Law in Practice* (2nd edn, W Green & Son 2014), ch 11.

It should be noted that these are the same types of disposal applicable in the case of someone acquitted at a trial by reason on lack of criminal responsibility based on mental disorder at the time of the offence.

General criteria: ECHR compliance

The use of at least some of these disposals is subject to the requirements of the ECtHR. Article 5(1) provides for a general right to liberty and security of a person and states that no one 'shall be deprived of his liberty save in the following cases and in accordance with a procedure prescribed by law'. One of the specified cases is in paragraph (e) of that article, which provides for 'the lawful detention of persons for the prevention of the spreading of infectious diseases, of persons of unsound mind, alcoholics or drug addicts or vagrants'.

In the leading decision of the ECHR on this provision, *Winterwerp v The Netherlands*,[78] the Court noted that the 'lawful detention' of such persons required that 'no one may be confined as "a person of unsound mind" in the absence of medical evidence establishing that his mental state is such as to justify his compulsory hospitalisation'.[79]

Accordingly, to be ECHR compliant, a disposal of a case where someone has been found unfit to plead but not acquitted after an examination of facts (or has been acquitted on the basis of the mental disorder defence) three pre-conditions must be satisfied: (a) there must be a mental condition at the time of making the disposal; (b) the mental condition must be established by medical evidence; and (c) the mental condition requires compulsory detention, including detention in a hospital.

Compulsion order

A compulsion order may be used where the offence which the accused was found to have committed is punishable by imprisonment but not one for which the sentence is fixed by law (ie, murder).[80] The appropriate medical criteria are that:

- the offender has a mental disorder;
- medical treatment which would be likely to prevent the mental disorder from worsening, or to alleviate any of the symptoms of effects of the disorder, is available;
- if no such treatment were provided there would be a significant risk to (a) the health, safety or welfare of the person in question,[81] or (b) the safety of any other person;
- the making of the order in respect of the person in question is necessary.

[78] (1979) 2 EHRR 387. [79] ibid, para 39. [80] 1995 Act, s 57A.

[81] In the context of disposals, the 1995 Act use the term 'offender'. In this chapter that has been replaced by the phrase 'person in question' or 'person' (see 1995 Act, s 57(4)).

These criteria require medical evidence from two medical practitioners, one of whom is an approved medical practitioner.[82] Both practitioners must agree that the person suffers from the same category of mental disorder and should also provide details of the compulsory measures which are to be set out in the order.

The compulsory measures may be carried out on the person in question in the community, in which case the order will require the person to reside at a specified place and attend for treatment and other services, and to allow access by mental health and other medical officers.

If compulsory powers in the community are not appropriate, the order may require detention in a specified hospital, but the treatment must be such that could only be provided in a hospital and there is a bed available within seven days of the making of the order.[83]

Before making a compulsion order the court must have regard to any alternative way of dealing with the person.

A compulsion order lasts for six months. After the initial period, it may be renewed for a further six months and thereafter can be renewed annually.

Compulsion order with a restriction order

A restriction order is an additional element of a compulsion order, which has the effect that the person may be detained in hospital without limit of time.[84] An order may be made if it appears to the court that it is necessary for the protection of the public from serious harm. In making the order the court must have regard to (a) the nature of the offence which the person was charged with; (b) the antecedents of the person; and (c) the risk that as result of his mental disorder he would commit offences if set at large. The mental disorder should play a substantial part in determining this risk.

Before making the restriction order the court must be presented with oral evidence on this issue from the approved medical practitioner whose evidence was taken into account in respect of the accompanying compulsion order.

The person is detained in hospital until he or she is conditionally or absolutely discharged by the direction of the Mental Health Tribunal for Scotland.[85]

The suspension of detention or transfer of the person to another hospital must be approved by the Scottish Ministers.[86]

Interim compulsion order

These orders are used where the person in question has been found to have committed an offence which is punishable by imprisonment but not where such a sentence

[82] That is, a medical practitioner who has been approved under s 22 of the Mental Health (Care and Treatment) (Scotland) 2003 Act as having special experience in the diagnosis and treatment of mental disorder. An approved medical practitioner will often be a consultant psychiatrist.

[83] In practice, the vast majority of compulsion orders are hospital rather than community based (see Tables 5.1–5.3).

[84] 1995 Act, ss 57A(7) 59. [85] 2003 Act, s 193. [86] 2003 Act, ss 224, 218.

is fixed by law (ie, murder).[87] Their purpose is to allow for more information about the person's mental health to be obtained where, because of a significant risk of harm to that person's own health, safety, or welfare or to the safety of other people, there is the possibility that the court will make a compulsion order with an added restriction order. They have been described as allowing for 'a thorough, prolonged inpatient assessment of serious offenders with mental disorder'.[88]

The order can be made on the basis of written or oral evidence from two registered medical practitioners (one of whom must be an approved medical practitioner) that medical treatment is available which would prevent the person's mental disorder worsening or would alleviate the symptoms or effects of the disorder. The person is ordered to be detained in a hospital for up to twelve weeks, which can be extended for further periods of twelve weeks up to a total of one year.

The order comes to end when the court makes a final mental health or penal disposal.

Guardianship order

A guardianship order is appropriate where a person has lost the capacity to make decisions by reason of a mental disorder.

Where the person in question has been found to have committed an offence which is punishable by imprisonment but not where such a sentence is fixed by law (ie, murder), the court may place his or her personal welfare under the guardianship of a local authority (or someone else approved by the local authority).[89]

Before making an order, the court must be satisfied that there are no other means under the 1995 Act which would be sufficient to safeguard or promote the person's interest in his own welfare. There must also be evidence from two medical practitioners (one being an approved medical practitioner) that the person in question is incapable of making decisions about or acting to safeguard or promote his interests in his property, financial affairs, or personal welfare.

A further requirement is that the person in question had earlier been interviewed and assessed by a mental health officer who has given an opinion on the general appropriateness of an order.

Supervision and treatment order

This type of order places the person in question under the supervision of a social worker, requiring the person to comply with instructions given by the social worker and to submit to treatment by a medical practitioner with a view to improving his mental condition.[90] Treatment may include being a non-resident patient at any

[87] 1995 Act, s 53.

[88] Darjee and Skilling, 'Legislation for Mentally Disordered Offenders' (n 77) 364.

[89] 1995 Act, ss 58–58A. Guardianship orders are governed generally by the Adults with Incapacity (Scotland) Act 2000, ss 57–61.

[90] 1995 Act, s 57(2)(d); Sch 4.

place or institution specified in the order, but an order cannot require the person to be a resident patient in a hospital. An order cannot be made where the person does not have a mental condition. An order can be made for any period up to three years.

To make this order the court must be satisfied that, having regard to all the circumstances of the case, this would be the most suitable means of dealing with the person. The court must also be satisfied that the person's mental condition requires and may be susceptible to treatment but that it would not warrant the making of a compulsion order (with or without a restriction order), nor a guardianship order. The evidence on these mental condition issues must be given by two or more approved medical practitioners.

The court has power to amend an order on the basis of a medical report indicating that (a) the treatment should continue beyond the period of the order; (b) the person needs different treatment; (c) the person is not susceptible to treatment; or (d) the person does not require further treatment.

The order may be revoked where it appears to the court, in light of circumstances since the making of the order, that it would be in the interests of the health or welfare of person, to revoke it.

Use of disposals

Table 5.2 shows the use of these various orders over the period 2010–2016. However, these figures are combined totals for person acquitted by reason of the mental disorder defence as well as those found unfit for trial and not acquitted after an examination of facts.

Table 5.2 Use of Disposal Orders over the Period 2010–2016

Order type	2010/11	2011/12	2012/13	2013/14	2014/15	2015/16
Compulsion order	8	8	11	15	21	24
Compulsion order—community	1	0	0	1	0	0
Compulsion order with restriction order	0	4	4	8	7	3
Guardianship	0	1	0	0	0	1
Supervision and treatment order	0	0	0	0	1	0

Source: Mental Welfare Commission for Scotland, *Mental Health Act Monitoring 2015–16* (2016) 27, Table 6.3.

There are also figures available for interim compulsion orders, but these deal with orders applying not only to persons unfit for trial or acquitted on the non-responsibility ground but also to anyone convicted of an offence where no issue of unfitness or mental disorder arose at the trial (see Table 5.3).

Table 5.3 Interim Compulsion Orders 2010–2016

Order type	2010/11	2011/12	2012/13	2013/14	2014/15	2015/16
Interim compulsion order	17	18	26	31	21	24

Source: Mental Welfare Commission for Scotland, *Mental Health Act Monitoring 2015–16* (2016) 27, Table 6.4.

Conclusion

The defence of unfitness for trial in contemporary Scots law reflects a lengthy development of the legal system's aim of ensuring that criminal trials should not proceed against anyone whose mental or physical condition makes it inappropriate for them to be subjected to such a process. Initially the common law plea of 'insanity in bar of trial' was not clearly distinguished from the idea of insanity as a substantive defence. Although the common law was unclear in certain key respects, it came to be recognised that the plea involved three different but related elements, namely the test or definition of the plea, the procedures to be used in determining the existence of the plea in a particular case, and the proper ways of dealing with people who had been found to be unfit for trial.

Partly because of the relatively small number of cases where insanity in bar of trial was in issue, the common law remained undeveloped, yet at the same time this was not a topic on which the Scottish courts were prepared to look at other jurisdictions for guidance, and critical discussion was mainly the preserve of academic commentators and law reform bodies. Reform eventually arrived by way of statutory changes in 1995 and 2010.

These changes established the procedural arrangements for dealing with the plea, by a two-stage process which involved determining whether an accused was insane in bar of trial and if he was found to be so, a new procedure of an examination of facts to inquire whether or not the accused would have been acquitted if a trial had been held.

A further set of changes concerned the disposal options to be used where an accused who was insane in bar of trial would not have been acquitted at a trial. These new disposals were focussed on providing the correct medical treatment for the accused's current condition and removed the objectionable outcome of the previous law whereby an accused in this situation was automatically committed to a mental hospital.

The final piece of reform resulted from the wide-ranging recommendations of the Scottish Law Commission on the test for the plea, not the least of which was removing the term 'insanity' from the name of newly defined test for a defence of unfitness for trial.

One point of major significance about these reforms was the extent to which Scots law was now willing to consider the law and practice in other legal systems, and as the law in Scotland on unfitness for trial continues to develop it will continue to benefit by maintaining this comparative outlook.

6

Unfit to Stand Trial

Canadian Law and Practice

Gerry Ferguson *

Introduction

The expression 'unfit to stand trial', which is the term used in the Canadian *Criminal Code*,[1] is somewhat imprecise. The law of fitness is concerned with more than 'fitness at trial'; it applies at all stages of the criminal process from first appearance to sentencing.[2] Despite its under-inclusiveness, I will use that expression in this chapter for convenience and familiarity.

This chapter provides a brief review of the origins of the doctrine of unfit to stand trial in Canada, as well as its major legislative revision in 1992,[3] and the inadequacy of that revision and its subsequent judicial interpretation. The chapter also sets out a brief analysis of the characteristics of those found unfit and the legal procedures for assessing, trying the issue, and making dispositions and subsequent reviews for those found unfit. While these procedures are, for the most part, fair and in accordance with principles of procedural justice, the disposition and subsequent review

* Distinguished Professor, Faculty of Law, University of Victoria. The author gratefully acknowledges the excellent assistance of Ashley McDonald, Dmytro Galagan, and Sarah Chaster in the research and writing of this chapter.

[1] RSC 1985, c C-46, ss 672.22–672.32.

[2] Fitness to stand trial provisions in the *Criminal Code* do not apply to appeals. An appeal can proceed even if the accused person is unfit to stand trial, provided that the accused is treated fairly: *R v Ta* [2002] OJ No 1453 (CA). The issue of an offender's fitness to be sentenced arises infrequently. Nonetheless, a sentencing hearing is considered by Canadian courts to be part of the trial process and thus the offender has a right to be physically and mentally present. See *R v Lowry* [1974] SCR 195 (SCC). The same proposition can be found in the House of Lords decision in *R v Lawrence?* [1993] AC 699 (HL) 708. Both these cases are cited by Clayton Ruby et al, *Sentencing* (8th edn, LexisNexis Canada 2012) 95. In *R v Sabourin* (2009), File No 03-G30181 (Ont SCJ), the accused pleaded guilty and subsequently claimed he was unfit at his sentencing hearing. His claim was dismissed on the basis that he was malingering. The requirement for fitness at the time of sentencing was referred to in Hale and applied in *R v Dyson* (1831) 7 Car & P 305, 173 ER 135, and subsequently repeated in *R v Leys* (1910) 17 CCC 198 (Ont CA). See now *R v Balliram* (2003) 173 CCC (3d) 547 (Ont SCJ) 563; *R v Jaser* 2015 ONSC 4729; and *R v Morrison* 2016 SKQB 259.

[3] An Act to amend the *Criminal Code* (mental disorder) and to make consequential amendments to other Acts, SC 1991, c 43.

provisions do not yet adequately resolve the problem of capping the maximum length of time a person can be held as 'unfit'.

The Origins of the Fitness Doctrine in Canada

The early common law origins of the doctrine of fitness to stand trial are rooted in the old common law trial procedures and *peine forte et dure*; these roots have been described elsewhere.[4] By the eighteenth and nineteenth centuries, based on commonly quoted passages from Hale[5] and Blackstone,[6] courts became more focussed on the accused's ability to comprehend and thereby participate in his or her trial. In the nineteenth century, the English decision in *R v Pritchard*[7] was treated as one of the leading authorities on the test for unfit to stand trial. The directions to the jury in *Pritchard* make it clear that the standard of fitness required the accused to be able (a) to plead to the charge; (b) to understand the course of the proceedings; (c) to understand the details of the evidence; (d) to challenge a juror; and (e) to communicate his defence to the judge and jury personally (or through counsel).[8] Pritchard, a deaf-mute with limited abilities to communicate, was found unfit to stand trial. The *Pritchard* test is still the operative test in England.[9]

While there are few, if any, *reported* cases in Canada on the test for fitness to stand trial prior to 1892, there is no doubt that those statements from Hale, Blackstone, and *Pritchard* would have been accepted as the governing Canadian law. When Canada enacted its first *Criminal Code* in 1892,[10] it included two sections on fitness to stand trial. Section 737(1), which applied only to indictable offences, gave a court the power to order a trial on 'whether the accused is or is not then on account of insanity capable of conducting his defence'.[11] Section 737(2) stated that the issue of fitness shall be tried by a jury and if the jury's verdict was that the accused was unfit on account of insanity, the court was required to order the accused 'to be kept in custody till the pleasure of the Lieutenant-Governor of the province shall be known'. And s 740 indicated that where a person was found unfit to stand trial (or insane at

[4] Warren Brookbanks, *Competencies of Trial: Fitness to Plead in New Zealand* (LexisNexis NZ Limited 2011) 13–20.

[5] Sir Matthew Hale, *Historia Placitorum Coronæ*, Volume 1 (*The History of the Pleas of the Crown*) (London 1736) 34–35; repr Classical English Law Texts (Professional Publishing 1971). as cited by Brookbanks, *Competencies of Trial* (n 4) 20.

[6] William Blackstone, *Commentaries on the Laws of England*, Volume 4 (Harper 1850) 24.

[7] (1836) 7 C&P 303, 173 ER 135. *Pritchard* is discussed in greater detail in chs 2 'The Development of Unfitness to Plead in English Law', 3 'Unfitness to Plead in England and Wales: A Practitioner's View of a Plea in Evolution' and 4 'Reforming the Law of Unfitness to Plead in England and Wales—A Recent History'.

[8] In felony trials, the accused was not entitled until the mid-1800s to be represented by counsel except to argue points of law, so the accused's ability to defend himself was all the more important. It should also be noted that an accused was not entitled to be sworn as a witness for the defence until 1893 in Canada.

[9] Ronnie Mackay, chapter 2 above at page 12.

[10] 55–56 Victoria, c 29.

[11] See *Criminal Code* 1892, s 737 and *Criminal Code*, s 542 as it stood in January 1992.

the time of the offence), 'the Lieutenant-Governor may make an order for the safe custody of the person ... in such place and in such manner as to him seems fit'. The above sections were, to say the least, quite threadbare, yet they set the basic legislative framework for fitness for the next 100 years.[12] All details and gaps in these sections were left to be filled by common law.

Studies by the Law Reform Commission of Canada in the mid-1970s[13] and the Department of Justice in the mid-1980s[14] eventually led to the coming into force in February 1992 of an entirely new Part XX.I of the *Criminal Code*, containing ninety legislative provisions which in a clear, organised, and reasonably comprehensive way dealt with mental disorder in the criminal law process from start to finish.[15] Amongst other matters, Part XX.I introduced more modern language (eg, the word 'insanity' was replaced by the expression 'mental disorder'; the word 'natural imbecility' was abolished); the authority, criteria, and limitations for mental health assessments and reports were specified; an accused's self-incriminating statements made during an assessment were not admissible at trial to convict the accused; detailed provisions were added on fitness to stand trial, including its definition, when it may be raised or postponed, the procedures for its determination, the consequences and dispositions depending on whether the court's finding is fit or unfit, as well as the role of the courts and Review Board in cases where the accused is held to be unfit. The composition, powers, and duties of Review Boards in respect to unfit accused persons are spelt out, as well as clear provisions on the appeal process for unfit persons. Twenty-five years after its enactment, the 1992 mental disorder provisions remain largely the same.[16]

The Canadian Test for Unfit to Stand Trial

Fitness Prior to 1992

The legislative test for fitness remained the same from 1892 to 1992. As noted, it provided that an accused would be unfit if 'on account of insanity' the accused was not 'capable of conducting his defence'. The word 'insanity' was not defined but Canadian courts agreed that it should be given a broad and liberal interpretation

[12] Over the following 100 years, only a few modest changes were made to this legislative framework, eg, the legislative provisions were amended (a) to apply to summary conviction, as well as indictable trials; (b) a judge, rather than a jury, was authorised to determine fitness in all criminal proceedings except jury trials; and (c) the judge was given the power to postpone a fitness hearing until the end of the Crown's case to ensure that the accused was not subjected to the consequences of a finding of unfitness when the Crown did not have sufficient evidence to convict the accused of the crime charged.

[13] See, eg, Law Reform Commission of Canada, The Criminal Process and Mental Disorder, Working Paper 14 (1975) and A Report to Parliament on Mental Disorder in the Criminal Process (1976).

[14] The federal Department of Justice project is briefly described in Edwin A Tollefson and Bernard Starkman, *Mental Disorder in Criminal Proceedings* (Carswell 1993) 1–12.

[15] An Act to amend the *Criminal Code* (mental disorder) and to make consequential amendments to other Acts, SC 1991, c 43.

[16] There have, however, been a few modest legislative amendments to them in 2005 and 2014, and one significant amendment allowing judges to grant a permanent judicial stay to accused persons held in custody as unfit for long periods of time discussed under the section 'Maximum Length of Time an Unfit Accused can be Held as Unfit'.

and was certainly not restricted to its meaning in respect to the insanity defence.[17] Likewise the expression 'capable of conducting his defence' was not defined in the *Criminal Code*. However, Canadian courts continued to give that expression a *Pritchard*-like meaning.[18] In later years, the most commonly cited description for the fitness test was set out in *R v Roberts* as follows:

> It is prerequisite to any criminal trial that the accused be capable of conducting his defence. Subject only to disruptive conduct on his part, he must be physically, intellectually, linguistically and communicatively present and able to partake to the best of his natural ability in his full answer and defence to the charge against him....[19]

The Court of Appeal specifically approved of the judge's instruction to the jury which stated in part (my emphasis):

> *Would he understand the evidence that is given by the various witnesses so that he can confer with his counsel and give instructions?*
>
> *Does he have the mental capacity to instruct his counsel, on the evidence that is led, properly, so that he can make full answer and defence?*
>
> *Would his counsel be able to get a factual and truthful account of his testimony, or anyone else's testimony, in the event that counsel should advise and the accused should decide that evidence should be called by the defence?*
>
> *Is he able to understand advice given by his counsel and reach a decision as to whether evidence should be called in his defence?* And here you will bear in mind again that although counsel may advise him he makes the decision; *and if he is not fit then he might make decisions to call evidence which would harm his case rather than assist him*, that is, if he is unfit.[20]

The above highlighted passages from the trial judge's instruction strongly suggest that fitness must include a capacity to consider these matters *analytically and rationally*. This type of *Roberts* instruction was routinely applied by judges for many years.[21]

The most difficult aspect of the fitness test in practice was the extent to which a person suffering from delusions was capable of conducting his defence. In other words, did the accused's inability to perceive reality in respect to one or more issues

[17] *R v Smith* (1936) 65 CCC 231 (Sask CA); *R v Woltucky* (1952) 103 CCC 43 (Sask CA) 46–47.

[18] In *R v Kierstead* (1918) 33 CCC 288 (NBKB) the trial judge instructed the jury that the issue for them was whether the accused is 'now, on account of insanity, unfit to take his trial; is his mind so diseased that he cannot instruct counsel intelligently or converse with them or something of that kind, and [thus] unfit to take his trial'; eg, in *R v Woltucky* (n 17) the court cited with approval the English decision *R v Lee Kun* (1916) 11 Cr App R 293 (CCA), which stated that 'the presence of the accused means not merely that he must be physically in attendance, but also that he must be capable of understanding the nature of the proceedings'. See also *R v Gorecki* (1976) 14 OR (2d) 212 (CA) [20] and *R v Hughes* (1978) 43 CCC (2d) 97 (Alta SC).

[19] (1975) 24 CCC (2d) 539 (BCCA) [12], application for leave to appeal dismissed (1975) 24 CCC (2d) 539. *Roberts* was subsequently applied in several other decisions. See, eg, *R v Budic* (1977) 35 CCC (2d) 272 (Alta CA); *R v Steele* (1991) 63 CCC (3d) 149 (QCCA) [62]; and *R v Brigham* (1992) 79 CCC (3d) 365 (QCCA) [52].

[20] *Roberts* (n 19) [7]. *Roberts* involved a relatively easy decision on the fitness issue. While he had been found unfit at previous proceedings, all the evidence at the time of his murder trial pointed to the fact that he clearly met the tests for fitness.

[21] See Gerry Ferguson and John Bouck, *Canadian Criminal Jury Instructions* (Continuing Legal Education Society of British Columbia 1987) 8.28.

interfere with the accused's ability to provide full answer and defence to the charges? *R v Gibbons* (1946),[22] *R v Woltucky* (1952),[23] and *R v Hubach* (1966)[24] were cases in which the accused persons' offences arose out of their delusions of persecution. In each case the courts held that the accused was unfit because he would not be able to accurately describe or testify to the motivations or reasons behind his actions. On the other hand, in *R v Budic* (1977),[25] the Court held that the accused's delusion that his doctor (whom he killed) was conspiring to kill him may be relevant to the insanity defence but did not render the accused unfit because in the circumstances of this case the accused otherwise demonstrated that he was able to give a lucid account of the crime and his actions. And in *R v Gorecki* (1976),[26] there was evidence that the accused was deeply depressed and suicidal at the time of the murder. However, the fact that the accused steadfastly refused to allow his counsel to raise the defence of insanity did not render the accused unfit in circumstances where the accused otherwise clearly demonstrated that he was able to rationally participate in his defence. It should be noted, however, that neither *Budic* nor *Gorecki* suggested that fitness to stand trial merely required a bare minimal cognitive understanding, rather than a rational analytical understanding of the charge, the evidence, and the accused's options in responding to the charge.

R v Steele (1991)[27] was the last appellate decision on the meaning of fitness prior to the 1992 amendments. The accused was charged with a bizarre and brutal murder. He insisted on representing himself at trial. Both the evidence and some of his conduct at the trial strongly suggested that the accused may not be fit. The trial judge refused to hold a fitness hearing. The accused was convicted and subsequently appealed. The Court of Appeal held that the trial judge erred in not holding a fitness hearing and therefore the Court ordered a new trial where fitness could be raised. Justice Fish, writing for the unanimous Court, emphasised that the ability to engage in rational analysis is a necessary component of the fitness test,[28] while at the same time acknowledging that:

> ... the law is helpless to protect an accused against his own bad judgment. On the other hand, I do not understand *McIlvride and R. v. Gorecki (No. 1)* (1976), 14 O.R. (2d) 212, 32 C.C.C. (2d) 129 (C.A.) to preclude a finding of unfitness where, by reason of serious mental illness, the accused is incapable of acting in her or his own best interests. That issue should be left for another day.[29]

Fitness after 1992

The 1992 mental disorder amendments deleted the expression 'on account of insanity' and substituted instead the expression 'on account of mental disorder'. The

22 (1946) 86 CCC 20 (Ont CA).
23 (1952) 103 CCC 43 (Sask CA).
24 [1966] 4 CCC 114 (Alta CA).
25 (1977) 35 CCC (2d) 272 (Alta CA).
26 (1976) 14 OR 212 (Ont CA).
27 *R v Steele* (n 19).
28 ibid [97]. In describing the fitness test, Fish J stated that the accused must be able to communicate and 'converse with counsel rationally [and] make critical decisions on counsel's advice'.
29 ibid [96].

expression from the previous legislation 'unable to conduct a defence' was retained in the 1992 amendments but it was legislatively defined for the first time. Section 2 of the *Criminal Code* stated (my emphasis):

'unfit to stand trial' means *unable on account of mental disorder to conduct a defence* at any stage of the proceedings before a verdict is rendered or to instruct counsel to do so, *and, in particular, unable on account of mental disorder to*
(a) understand the nature or object of the proceedings,
(b) understand the possible consequences of the proceedings, or
(c) communicate with counsel.

This definition[30] is a truncated version of the five criteria in the *Pritchard* test. Unfortunately, this definition is not, on its face, a sufficiently comprehensive test,[31] and the subsequent judicial interpretation of it has rendered it even more inadequate. *R v Taylor*[32] was the first appellate decision to interpret this new definition. With inadequate analysis of the previous fitness cases, the Court of Appeal concluded that fitness under s 2 only required a 'limited cognitive capacity' and not an 'analytical or rational capacity'. This was an entirely new label which had not been used in previous fitness cases. This label was adopted by the Court to indicate that it was a lower threshold than that of 'analytical capacity'.

The trial judge had found that Taylor, a lawyer representing himself, was unfit on the basis that although he could clearly understand the nature and object of the trial and its consequences, his delusions were so pervasive and irrational that he could not rationally communicate with counsel or perceive his own best interests. In reversing the trial judge's decision, the Court of Appeal described its 'limited cognitive capacity' test in the following words (my emphasis):

Under the 'limited cognitive capacity' test …, the presence of delusions do not vitiate the accused's fitness to stand trial unless the delusion distorts the accused's *rudimentary understanding* of the judicial process.… under this test, a court's assessment of an accused's ability to conduct a defence and to communicate and instruct counsel is limited to an inquiry into whether an accused can recount to his/her counsel the necessary facts relating to the offence in such a way that counsel can then properly present a defence. It is not relevant to the fitness determination to consider whether the accused and counsel have an amicable and trusting relationship, whether the accused has been cooperating with counsel, or whether the accused *ultimately makes decisions* that are in his/her best interests.[33]

[30] This definition is very similar to what the Law Reform Commission of Canada recommended in 1976.

[31] First, the test equates 'the capacity to conduct a defence' with the 'ability to communicate with counsel'. It does not contemplate and therefore ask whether the accused has the capacity to proceed to trial *without* counsel. Secondly, the definition gives no direction on the nature or level of understanding that the accused must have in respect to the proceedings, the evidence, and the consequences of the proceedings. Thirdly, the definition fails to list a number of specific mental abilities that are essential to effectively 'conducting one's defence'. See, eg, the discussion between notes 45 and 48. Fourthly, the test deals with 'fitness before a verdict' and therefore does not apply to fitness at sentencing. Fifthly, the fitness provisions are restricted to unfitness due to mental disorder and therefore do not cover classic cases such as a deaf-mute who has no mental disorder but cannot communicate with counsel or the court.

[32] (1992) 77 CCC (3d) 551 (Ont CA). For a discussion of the implications of *Taylor*, see Joan Barrett and Riun Shandler, *Mental Disorder in Canadian Criminal Law* (looseleaf edn, Thomson 2016) ch 2.

[33] ibid [44].

The Court suggested that the 'limited cognitive capacity' test struck the proper balance between two competing objectives:

The 'limited cognitive capacity' test strikes an effective balance between the objectives of the fitness rules and the constitutional right of the accused to choose his own defence and to have a trial within a reasonable time.

In asking the court to require that the accused be able to act in his own best interests, the respondent is asking this court to adopt the higher threshold 'analytic capacity' test for determining the accused's fitness to stand trial.[34]

The Court's 'limited cognitive capacity' test was immediately criticised.[35] Schneider and Bloom stated:

... the *Taylor* decision has so narrowed the fitness standard that it is out of keeping with the realities of mental illness and the true impact of mental disorder on an accused's ability to assume the role of the accused.[36]

However, the *Taylor* decision received an unfortunate boost, soon after, by the Supreme Court of Canada in *R v Whittle*.[37] The Supreme Court used the expression 'limited cognitive capacity' in describing the degree of mental competence required by an accused before that accused can lawfully waive his or her right to counsel. While waiving the right to counsel is an entirely different context, *Whittle* is nonetheless accepted as the Supreme Court's endorsement of the 'limited cognitive capacity' test in fitness hearings. For example, in *R v Morrissey*[38] the Ontario Court of Appeal stated that the limited cognitive capacity test has been 'accepted across the country' and has been 'adopted by the Supreme Court of Canada in *R. v. Whittle*'. The Court in *Morrissey* also noted that 'the threshold [for fitness] is not high'.[39]

R v Jobb[40] is a good example of just how low the Canadian fitness test can be. The Court described the accused's mental and social capacities as follows:

The respondent is 22 years old. He suffers from fetal alcohol spectrum disorder, attention deficit disorder and substance abuse/dependence disorder. He has been diagnosed as mildly mentally retarded. One assessment puts him at grade seven level for reading single words and spelling (a level above the level predicted by his overall IQ) and at grade three to four level in arithmetic. He has deficits in both visual and verbal memory that are greater than one would predict on the basis of his IQ alone. He is easily led. He is considered incapable of handling

[34] ibid [52]–[53].

[35] Hugh Harradence, 'Re-applying the Standard of Fitness to Stand Trial' (2012–13) 59 Crim LQ 511, 529.

[36] Richard D Schneider and Hy Bloom, '*R. v. Taylor*: A Decision not in the Best Interest of some Mentally Ill Accused' (1995–96) 38 Crim LQ 183, 186.

[37] [1994] 2 SCR 914 (SCC).

[38] (2007) 227 CCC (3d) 1 (Ont CA) [27].

[39] ibid. It could be argued that the Court in *Morrissey* gave the *Taylor* test a bit more life when the Court stated: 'Meaningful presence and meaningful participation at the trial, therefore, are the touchstones of the inquiry into fitness' (ibid [36]). However, this statement on meaningful participation has been of limited value because *Morrissey* was not a case involving cognitive impairment, but rather a case involving amnesia in respect to the offence.

[40] (2008) 239 CCC (3d) 24 (Sask CA), also discussed in Harradence, 'Re-applying the Standard of Fitness to stand Trial' (n 35) 533–34.

the responsibilities that would enable him to live independently and it is considered he will always need a protected living environment and sheltered employment.[41]

Notwithstanding these intellectual and cognitive deficits, the Court reversed the trial judge's finding of unfit to stand trial. In applying the *Taylor* 'limited cognitive capacity' test, the Court noted:

That Mr. Jobb be able to participate in his defence in 'a meaningful way or assist his counsel during the course of a trial' is not, with respect, an accurate application of the limited cognitive capacity test, which requires only that he be able to recount the facts of the offences with which he is charged to his counsel.[42]

The fact that the accused's attention deficit disorder would make it very unlikely that he would or could follow the evidence at trial seems to have been given little importance.[43]

There is the occasional liberal interpretation of *Taylor* such as that by Trotter J in *R v Adam*.[44] However, without any recent studies or data on the many unreported cases where fitness to stand trial has been raised, it is hard to know whether lower court judges are actually applying *Taylor* strictly or are simply purporting to follow *Taylor*, but actually using a wider test. Canada is clearly in need of a comprehensive study, like those undertaken recently in England[45] and the states of Victoria[46] and New South Wales[47] in Australia. Indeed, a recommendation for further study of the fitness test in Canada was made to Parliament fifteen years ago by its Standing Committee on Human Rights, but no such study has been carried out.[48] Such a study is definitely needed and it should examine what test Canadian lower court judges are actually using, what extra-legal factors seem to affect the fitness decision (discussed below), and what the options are for a new fitness test. An analysis of what would constitute the best fitness test should include an examination of (a) the objectives of the fitness doctrine; (b) whether a 'rational capacity' or a 'limited cognitive

[41] ibid [4]. [42] ibid [43].

[43] For a somewhat similar case where the accused was also found fit in spite of an inability to follow the evidence at trial due to an attention deficit disorder, see *R v M (RC)* 2011 SKPC 61. But cf *R v Sewap* (2008) 341 Sask R 31 (PC). For a strong critique of the narrowness of the *Taylor* test, see Schneider J, who is a well-known author on mental disorder and a key judicial player in Toronto's Mental Health Court, in *R v Xu* [2007] OJ No 5796 (Ont CJ) [9], cited in Harradence, 'Re-applying the Standard of Fitness to Stand Trial' (n 35) 536–37. See also Richard D Schneider et al, *Mental Health Courts Decriminalizing the Mentally Ill* (Irwin Law 2007) 145.

[44] 2013 ONSC 373.

[45] Law Commission, *Unfitness to Plead*, CP No 197 (2010) and Law Commission, *Unfitness to Plead*, Law Com No 364 (2016). The Commission has recommended replacing the *Pritchard* cognitive capacity test with two separate decision-making tests: 'capacity to participate effectively in a trial' and 'capacity to plead guilty', with relevant abilities set out for each test and a general description of what 'a relevant ability' entails.

[46] Victorian Law Reform Commission, *Review of the Crimes (Mental Impairment and Unfitness to be Tried) Act 1997* (2014), available at: http://www.lawreform.vic.gov.au/sites/default/files/Review_of_the_Crimes_Mental_Impairment_and_Unfitness_to_be_Tried_Act_0.pdf.

[47] New South Wales Law Reform Commission, *People with Cognitive and Mental Health Impairments in the Criminal Justice System: Criminal Responsibility and Consequences*, Report No 38 (2013).

[48] Standing Committee on Justice and Human Rights, *Review of the Mental Disorder Provisions of the Criminal Code*, Report No 14 (2002).

capacity' test best meets those objectives; (c) the difference between *capacity to make* and *actually making* rational choices; (d) the possible adoption of a functional, contextual fitness test; and (e) the desirability of a decision-making test such as that proposed by the English Law Commission in 2016.[49]

Such a study also needs to pay special attention to setting criteria for fitness in respect to certain groups such as (a) persons who have significant intellectual impairment due to fetal alcohol spectrum disorder, autism, and attention deficit disorder; or (b) persons with paranoid schizophrenia who refuse to be represented by counsel on the basis of their belief that counsel are part of a state conspiracy against them.

Characteristics of Persons Found Unfit

Review Boards

Most of the data on unfit accused comes from Review Boards which were legislatively created in the 1992 amendments. These Review Boards were a new and markedly improved approach to addressing mentally ill persons in the criminal justice system.[50] Section 672.38 of the *Criminal Code* requires each province to establish a Review Board. Review Boards have jurisdiction over accused persons found unfit to stand trial until they are found fit by a court or a stay of proceedings is granted by the prosecutor or the court.[51] The power and procedures for these Boards are specified in the *Criminal Code* and include crucial procedural protections which were previously lacking for mentally disordered accused.[52]

Review Boards normally sit in panels of three and are typically composed of a lawyer, a psychiatrist, and a community member such as a social worker.[53] Subject to some limitations, hearings are open to the public, are inquisitorial rather than adversarial,[54] and operate somewhat more informally than courts. Their decisions are recorded, must be supported by reasons, and can be appealed directly to the Court of Appeal.[55] Overall, Review Boards are crucial to the integrity and fairness of the fitness-to-stand trial regime. They bring significant, diverse, and necessary expertise to the issue.[56]

[49] Law Commission, Law Com No 364 (n 45).

[50] For more on this point, see Harradence, 'Re-applying the Standard of Fitness to Stand Trial' (n 35) 548–54.

[51] Lyle D Hillaby, 'Mental Disorder Prosecutions Overview', Continuing Legal Education seminar, Criminal Law and Mental Health Issues, Vancouver, 24 May 2008, 1.1.12.

[52] Harradence, 'Re-applying the Standard of Fitness to Stand Trial' (n 35) 549.

[53] Diane J Nielsen, 'A Primer for Defence Counsel at Review Board Hearings', Continuing Legal Education seminar, Criminal Law and Mental Health Issues, Vancouver, 24 May 2008, 1.3.2.

[54] Harradence, 'Re-applying the Standard of Fitness to Stand Trial' (n 35) 551.

[55] Hillaby, 'Mental Disorder Prosecutions Overview' (n 51) 1.1.12–13. Review Boards are courts of competent jurisdiction for the purposes of determining whether a patient's *Charter* rights have been violated and issuing a remedy if they have been. See *R v Conway* 2010 SCC 22, [2010] 1 SCR.

[56] Harradence, 'Re-applying the Standard of Fitness to Stand Trial' (n 35) 553.

Characteristics of Unfit Accused

National statistics on the characteristics of unfit accused are not collected. The data and statistics that are available are sporadic and outdated. Latimer and Lawrence have conducted the most extensive study to date. They randomly selected samples of cases processed through Review Boards between 1992 and 2004. Their sample covers five of ten provinces and two of three territories (representing approximately eighty per cent of Canada's total population).[57]

Gender

During their twelve-year review, Latimer and Lawrence discovered that eighty-three per cent of those admitted to Review Boards were male and seventeen per cent were female, which percentages are similar to the gender make-up of all adult offenders.[58] However, Anne Crocker et al found in their study (a) that a significantly higher portion of women than men were assessed as unfit to stand trial *by the examining psychiatrist*;[59] and (b) that *courts* also decided that a higher proportion of women than men were unfit.[60] Using a regression analysis, Crocker et al were able to identify four variables that they assert reliably predict fitness status: gender, age, index offence, and signs of psychosis.[61] Specifically, they concluded:

> Women are twice as likely as men to be recommended UST [unfit to stand trial]; individuals 45 years of age and over are 2.6 times more likely than individuals between the ages of 19 and 29 to be recommended UST; those charged with a violent offence are five times more likely than those who were charged exclusively with nonviolent offences to be recommended UST; and individuals who displayed at least one sign of psychosis during their assessments are approximately 14 times more likely than individuals without such symptoms to be recommended UST by the examining clinician.[62]

Crocker et al suggest that women are more likely to be found UST than men due to chivalrous or paternalistic views of women in fitness assessments.[63] In other words, women are viewed as needing protection from the potentially difficult situation of a criminal trial and harsh prison environment.[64]

Age

Latimer and Lawrence revealed that unfit accused (median age of thirty-seven years) were older than the average person in the criminal justice system and slightly older than persons found Not Criminally Responsible on Account of Mental Disorder

[57] Jeff Latimer and Austin Lawrence, *The Review Board Systems in Canada: An Overview of Results from the Mentally Disordered Accused Data Collection Study* (Canada Department of Justice 2006) 5–7.
[58] ibid 14.
[59] Anne G Crocker et al, 'Gender and Fitness to Stand Trial: A 5-Year Review of Remands in Quebec' (2002) 25 Intl J of L and Psychiatry 69, 70, and 75. The study was conducted in the province of Quebec between 1992 and 1997.
[60] ibid 75. [61] ibid 77. [62] ibid 77–78. [63] ibid 80. [64] ibid.

(NCRMD).[65] Only four per cent were under the age of eighteen; another fifty-four per cent were between the ages of eighteen and forty; and forty-two per cent were aged forty-one or older.[66]

Aboriginal status

Latimer and Lawrence's study also revealed that five per cent of unfit accused identified as Aboriginal, which is slightly above the national average of all Aboriginal persons.[67] Thus Aboriginal people are only slightly over-represented in the fitness process compared to their massive overrepresentation in other parts of the criminal justice system (often as much as three to seven times more). This difference may in part be explained by a lack of representation in the study from Manitoba and Saskatchewan, which have the highest Aboriginal populations.[68] But a more significant explanation is the likelihood that the Crown, defence, and trial judge raise fitness less often in the case of Aboriginal accused or, if raised, a finding of unfitness is less likely to be made in the case of Aboriginal accused.[69]

Diagnosis

Latimer and Lawrence's study confirmed that a large percentage of those found unfit to stand trial suffer from a major disorder. Approximately three-quarters of those under the Review Board's control (both unfit and insane) have been diagnosed with schizophrenia (fifty-six per cent) or an affective disorder (thirteen per cent) such as bi-polar disorder, schizoaffective disorder, or major depression.[70] Some research has also been conducted comparing the extent of an accused's impairment in respect to the legal criteria for unfitness based upon their different disorders. One study found defendants 'with broad types of psychotic disorders demonstrated high levels of impaired legal abilities in comparison to nonpsychotic defendants'.[71] Furthermore, a relationship was found between defendants with psychotic disorders, IQ scores, and their understanding of the nature and object of the criminal proceedings. The authors also found affective disorders without psychotic features, such as depression had a relatively weak relationship to legal impairment, whereas bipolar disorders were more highly correlated.[72] Research into schizophrenia and fitness has also indicated that schizophrenic persons, overall, do not perform as well

[65] Latimer and Lawrence, *The Review Board Systems in Canada* (n 57) 13. [66] ibid.
[67] ibid 20. [68] ibid 14. [69] ibid.
[70] ibid 20. Diagnoses were reported by primary diagnosis only, so if an accused suffered from multiple disorders only one was reported.
[71] Jodi L Viljoen et al, 'An Examination of the Relationship between Competency to Stand Trial, Competency to Waive Interrogation Rights, and Psychopathology' (2002) 26 L and Human Behavior 485, 487. All the defendants were recruited from in-patient forensic facilities in the Greater Vancouver area and were given various tests, including the Wechsler Adult Intelligence Scale—Revised, Test of Charter Comprehension, Fitness Interview Test, and Structured Clinical Interview for *DSM-III-R*.
[72] ibid 498.

on fitness evaluations as healthy control participants.[73] Thus, there is some evidence of a strong link between the type of mental illness an accused suffers from and the likelihood of that accused being found unfit to stand trial.

Prior involvement in the criminal justice system

According to Latimer and Lawrence's study more than one-half of unfit accused have had some prior interaction with the criminal justice system. On the other hand, forty-four per cent of unfit accused had no prior convictions, while thirty-eight per cent had between two and ten prior convictions.[74] Of the fifty-six per cent of accused persons with prior convictions, thirty-eight per cent of those prior convictions were for a violent or sexual offence.[75] The study also indicates adults were much more likely than youth to have a prior record, males were more likely than females, and Aboriginal accused were more likely than non-Aboriginal accused.[76] Furthermore, eighty-nine per cent of unfit accused had no prior NCRMD finding and ninety-eight per cent had no prior UST finding.[77]

Current offence

Latimer and Lawrence found that almost sixty per cent of UST accused have generally committed *very* serious violent offences such as murder, attempted murder, assault, sexual assault, criminal harassment, threats, and robbery, whereas these violent offences only represent approximately fifteen per cent of charges in general.[78] Additionally, unfit accused are much more likely to be facing a serious criminal offence than fit accused.[79]

Fitness Assessments

Decision to make an assessment order

An assessment order may only be made if the court has 'reasonable grounds to believe' that an assessment is necessary to determine a fitness issue.[80] The frequency of fitness assessment orders on a national basis is not known.[81] We do know that in

[73] Eleanor Swain, 'Schizophrenia, Insight and Fitness to Plead in Court and Stand Trial', Ph.D. thesis, University College London (2011).
[74] Latimer and Lawrence, *The Review Board Systems in Canada* (n 57) 15. [75] ibid.
[76] ibid 16. [77] ibid. [78] ibid 17. [79] ibid 18.
[80] *Criminal Code*, s 672.11. Evidence of police officers, social workers, court personnel, counsel, or the judge's own observations without any medical evidence may constitute 'reasonable grounds to believe' an assessment is necessary. See Tollefson and Starkman, *Mental Disorder in Criminal Proceedings* (n 14) 64. For a thorough review of fitness assessments, see Barrett and Shandler, *Mental Disorder in Canadian Criminal Law* (n 32) ch 2.
[81] Anne G Crocker et al, 'The National Trajectory Project of Individuals Found Not Criminally Responsible on Account of Mental Disorder in Canada. Part 1: Context and Methods' (2015) 60 Canadian J of Psychiatry 96, 99.

British Columbia in the 2014–15 fiscal year, 1,226 accused persons were assessed for either fitness or the mental disorder defence, or both.[82] During the same year, 36,763 adult criminal cases were completed in British Columbia.[83] Therefore, fitness and/or insanity assessments were ordered in 3.3 per cent of all adult criminal cases that year. Whether that percentage is higher or lower than in other provinces is unknown.

Pursuant to s 672.14, a fitness assessment has to be done within five days, unless the accused and the prosecutor consent to a longer period initially not exceeding thirty days. If a court or Review Board are satisfied that 'compelling circumstances' warrant a longer assessment, then an assessment of up to sixty days can be made. Under s 672.191, the accused is required to appear before the court or the Review Board as soon as practicable after the assessment is completed, but not later than the last day authorised by the assessment order. One concern about mental disorder assessments has surfaced in recent years. When a court makes an in-patient assessment order, the court assumes that the accused will be transmitted forthwith to the forensic hospital. Unfortunately, due to a significant shortage of secure forensic hospital beds, these accused persons are often detained in jail on a priority waiting list for a psychiatric bed.[84]

While an assessment report will be provided to the court or Review Board, as well as the prosecutor, defence counsel, and the accused, the court or the Review Board has a discretion under s 672.51(3) to withhold the report from the accused where they are satisfied that its disclosure would endanger the life or safety of another person or seriously impair the treatment or recovery of the accused.

Protected statements

Section 672.21 establishes an evidentiary privilege applicable to 'protected statements', ie statements made by the accused during a court ordered assessment or treatment. If such statements are made to a person specified in the assessment order, or to anyone acting under that person's direction, as a general rule those statements will not be admissible as proof of guilt at trial.[85] However, evidence of a protected statement is admissible for the purposes of determining whether the accused is unfit

[82] BC Mental Health Services, *Forensic Psychiatric Services Commission 2014–2015 Annual Report* (2015) 12, available at: http://www.bcmhsus.ca/Documents/forensic-psychiatric-services-commission-annual-report-2014-2015.pdf.

[83] Statistics Canada, *Adult Criminal Court Statistics in Canada 2014/15* (Juristat 2015) Table 2, available at: http://www.statcan.gc.ca/pub/85-002-x/2017001/article/14699/tbl/tbl02-eng.htm.

[84] In *R v Hussein* (2004) 191 CCC (3d) 113 (ONSC) [10], [33], the court held that this is a violation of the accused's rights under the *Criminal Code* and ss 7 and 8 of the Charter. In *R v Conception* 2014 SCC 60, [2014] 3 SCR 82, a case dealing with a mandatory treatment order under s 672.58, the majority of the Supreme Court held that the hospital's consent is required in relation to all aspects of the treatment order, including admission. The Supreme Court only left a very small window in which immediate admission for treatment could be compelled by a court.

[85] Tollefson and Starkman, *Mental Disorder in Criminal Proceedings* (n 14) 72; Hy Bloom and Brian T Butler, *Defending Mentally Disordered Persons* (Carswell 1995) 41.

to stand trial[86] or for making a disposition or placement decision in respect to the accused. It should be noted that the court cannot compel the accused to cooperate with the assessment team if the accused chooses to remain silent.[87] This raises the difficult question of whether defence counsel should advise clients to remain silent during a court-ordered assessment.[88]

In- and out-of-custody assessments and assessment tests

To reduce unnecessary hospital detention in respect to conducting mental assessments, s 672.16 establishes a presumption that an assessment order is to be conducted out of custody unless the court or the Review Board is satisfied on the evidence that custody is necessary to assess the accused, or the accused consents to custody. And for accused persons who have been denied bail, the assessment will be in custody.

Since only a brief assessment is often needed to determine an accused's fitness, some clinicians and other commentators suggest that in-patient hospital assessments are unnecessarily costly and burdensome, and that out-patient or jail-based psychiatric evaluations and assessments have made in-patient assessments largely obsolete.[89] Despite the presumption in favour of out-of-custody assessments, accused persons who are ordered to undergo an assessment are usually charged with serious offences where bail has been denied. One estimate is that over ninety-five per cent of assessments are conducted in custody in jails or hospitals.[90] One main advantage of in-hospital assessments is that they provide an opportunity to stabilise the accused's condition (if the accused is voluntarily or involuntarily medicated).[91] However, one suggested down-side, from a defence counsel perspective, is that if the accused is treated at this stage, the accused may return to court appearing so 'recovered' that the credibility of any psychiatric defence advanced at trial would be diminished.[92]

In Canada, there is no one, formalised clinical methodology that is used country-wide to assess whether the accused is mentally fit to stand trial.[93] Mental health professionals use two main methods: clinical assessment and psychometric instruments. Studies have found a very high level of agreement between psychiatric opinions on fitness and court determinations of fitness, with levels of agreement ranging from

[86] As psychiatrists often base their opinions as to the accused's fitness to stand trial on statements made by the accused during the assessment, it may be necessary for the psychiatrists to refer to the accused's statements as background evidence in support of their opinions. See Tollefson and Starkman, *Mental Disorder in Criminal Proceedings* (n 14) 72.

[87] ibid 65.

[88] Bloom and Butler, *Defending Mentally Disordered Persons* (n 85) 42.

[89] Hy Bloom, 'Fitness to Stand Trial' in Hy Bloom and Richard D Schneider (eds), *Law and Mental Disorder: A Comprehensive and Practical Approach* (Irwin Law 2013) 211, 220.

[90] Barrett and Shandler, *Mental Disorder in Canadian Criminal Law*, Release 3 (n 32) 3-26.3.

[91] Bloom and Butler, *Defending Mentally Disordered Persons* (n 85) 45; Bloom, 'Fitness to Stand Trial' (n 89) 214; *Mental Disorder in Canadian Criminal Law* (n 90) 3-26.3–3-26.4.

[92] Bloom and Butler, *Defending Mentally Disordered Persons* (n 85) 46.

[93] Based on questionnaires administered by the Canadian Centre for Justice Statistics in 2013.

seventy-three to ninety-one per cent.[94] One study in Calgary found 99.8 per cent agreement between clinical fitness assessments and court determinations.[95] This high level of agreement is criticised by some commentators on the assertion that judges simply 'rubber-stamp' psychiatric opinions and fail to exercise independent judicial decision making.[96]

Chantler and Heseltine argue that instead of relying on clinical opinions, psychometric assessment instruments should be used when evaluating the fitness of an accused to stand trial.[97] They argue that research suggests that '[c]linical opinion concerning fitness can be unduly influenced by particular client characteristics and diagnoses'.[98] In other words, clinicians tend to equate lack of fitness with a diagnosis of psychosis or other psychiatric opinion assumed to reflect a lack of rational capacity, thereby ignoring the specific cognitive requirements specified in the legislative and judicial definition of fitness.

Fitness Hearings: Rules and Procedures

Presumption of fitness and right to counsel

Section 672.22 of the 1992 amendments states that an accused is presumed fit to stand trial unless the court is satisfied otherwise on a balance of probabilities. There has been no consideration in Canada as to whether the quantum of proof when the prosecutor raises the issues of fitness should be 'beyond a reasonable doubt' as it is in England for verdicts of unfit or insane.[99]

Section 672.24 provides that where the accused is unrepresented and fitness is an issue, the court shall appoint counsel to represent the accused. The cost of counsel

[94] Alan Jager, 'Fitness to Stand Trial: Court Dispositions' (2000) 7 Psychiatry, Psychology and L 227, 228. An important caveat to note when considering the validity of fitness assessment methods is that fitness is a legal construct and there is no objectively correct answer. Therefore, court decisions are typically used as an outcome criterion when evaluating the validity of fitness assessments.

[95] ibid 230. The court agreed with 817 out of 819 clinic assessment recommendations. That study used fitness assessments from the Forensic Inpatient Unit of the Calgary General Hospital between April 1991 and March 1997 and compared those results to the Forensic Unit Log Book record of Court Dispositions. In Calgary, fitness assessments are presented as a clinic assessment report with a psychiatric opinion formed using psychiatric assessment, psychological testing, a psychosocial report and nurses' observations. Jager interpreted this high level of agreement as evidence of the effectiveness of the forensic fitness recommendations (ibid 231–32).

[96] ibid 231.

[97] Fitness Intervention Test-Revised (FIT-R) and Basic Fitness for Trial Test (BFFTT) are the main two fitness psychometric tests used in Canada. For a description of these tests, see Patricia Zapf et al, 'Assessing Fitness to Stand Trial: The Utility of the Fitness Interview Test (Revised Edition)' (2001) 46:5 Can J Psychiatry 426 and Lisa Chantler and Karen Heseltine, 'Fitness: What is the Role of Psychometric Assessment?' (2007) 14:2 Psychiatry, Psychology and L 349. The usefulness of these tests is critiqued by Jager, 'Fitness to Stand Trial' (n 94).

[98] Chantler and Heseltine, 'Fitness: What is the Role of Psychometric Assessment?' (n 97) 354.

[99] Mackay, chapter 2 at page 25.

is to be borne by either legal aid or the Attorney General of the relevant province, to the extent that the accused is unable to pay for counsel.

Postponing a fitness hearing

A fitness hearing may be postponed until the end of the Crown's case (either at a preliminary inquiry or at trial). The purpose of the postponement is to ensure that the Crown in fact has sufficient evidence to convict the accused. This discretionary power is set out in s 672.25 of the *Criminal Code*. Defence counsel can concede at the outset that the Crown has a *prima facie* case, or make no such concession and compel the prosecution to establish an evidentiary basis for the alleged offence. If a fitness hearing during the trial is postponed to the end of the Crown's case, the accused may then make a motion for a directed verdict of acquittal on the basis that the Crown has failed to establish a *prima facie* case (ie, evidence which if believed by the trier of fact would be sufficient to convict the accused). If the motion for a directed verdict fails, the trial judge still has a discretion under s 725(2)(b) to postpone the fitness hearing beyond the end of the Crown's case to 'any later time that the court may direct' if the accused so requests. Thus, if the accused does request a postponement, the court can postpone the fitness hearing to any stage 'before a verdict is rendered'.[100]

Trial of fitness: judge or jury

The fitness issue will be tried by either a judge or jury, depending on the nature of the proceedings. Under s 672.27 of the *Criminal Code*, the court shall try the issue of fitness and render a verdict at all stages of the proceedings except, according to s 672.26, where the accused is being tried or is to be tried by a court composed of a judge and jury, in which case the jury will decide the issue. Where an accused has been 'given in charge to the jury' and the jury finds the accused is fit, the trial shall continue before the same jury as if the issue of fitness had never arisen. This means the trial jury has heard information in the course of the fitness hearing that would not be admissible at trial and therefore would not have been heard by the jury had there been no fitness hearing. That information the jury heard may be prejudicial to the accused on issues at trial.

There has been little or no discussion in Canada of whether the trial of the issue of fitness should always be done by a judge rather than a jury.[101] The issue

[100] There are no reported cases which discuss the possibility of postponing the fitness hearing until after the accused has presented any defence evidence he or she wishes. The leading cases on the factors that are relevant in respect to a judge's discretion to postpone a fitness hearing until the end of the Crown's case are *Taylor* (n 32) and *R v Le* (2004) 187 CCC (3d) 283, para 15. If an accused has pleaded guilty and evidence arises before or at sentencing that the accused may have been unfit to plead, the sentencing judge may hold a fitness hearing and set aside the guilty plea if the accused was unfit then: *R v Proulx* (2011) 273 CCC (3d) 367 (Sask PC).

[101] But see Richard S Fowler, 'Fitness to Stand Trial', Continuing Legal Education seminar, Criminal Law and Mental Health Issues, Vancouver, 24 May 2008, 5.2.3.

of fitness is now determined by the judge, not the jury, in England[102] and New Zealand,[103] and that change has also been recommended in the Australian state of Victoria.[104]

Disposition Hearings and Options for Accused Found Unfit

Disposition hearings and procedures

Where an accused is found unfit to stand trial, a disposition hearing will be held by a court or Review Board for the purpose of making a disposition order. There are three possible disposition orders; they are described in section 'Disposition Options for the Unfit Accused' below. Section 672.45 of the *Criminal Code* states that *a court may* hold a disposition hearing and shall make a determination with respect to the accused, 'if it is satisfied that it can readily do so and that a disposition should be made without delay'. A court may do this when it is obvious that the unfit accused is not a danger to the community and may be released into the community on simple treatment conditions. However, the court may choose not to hold a disposition hearing and instead refer the matter to the Review Board. The Review Board will have more resources to fully assess the accused's mental health needs. It has been suggested that courts defer the disposition hearing to the Review Board in the 'great majority' of cases, especially where the charges involve serious crimes of violence.[105] If the courts do refer the case to the Review Board, the Board must hold a hearing and make a disposition within forty-five days of the verdict of unfit to stand trial, absent any exceptional circumstances which require an extension of time.[106] Even if the court does make a disposition, the court's disposition must be reviewed by the Review Board under s 672.47(3) within ninety days after that disposition. The disposition provisions are designed to ensure that an unfit accused is given the best medical disposition, while also trying to ensure that once an accused is fit, the accused will be returned to court as expeditiously as possible to complete their trial.[107] The rules of procedure and the accused's rights at disposition hearings (such as the right to counsel, to disclosure, to cross-examine witnesses, and to be present throughout the hearing) are designed to protect the accused person's liberty interests. In addition, an accused has a right of appeal from a finding of unfitness or from a disposition by a court or Review Board.[108]

[102] Criminal Procedure (Insanity) Act 1964, s 4(5), as amended by Domestic Violence, Crime and Victims Act 2004 (c 28), s 22(2).

[103] Criminal Procedure (Mentally Impaired Persons) Act 2003, No 115 (2003), s 14.

[104] Victorian Law Reform Commission, *Review of the Crimes (Mental Impairment and Unfitness to be Tried) Act 1997* (n 46) 232.

[105] Nielsen, 'A Primer for Defence Counsel at Review Board Hearings' (n 53) 1.3.8.

[106] See *Criminal Code*, s 672.47.

[107] Tollefson and Starkman, *Mental Disorder in Criminal Proceedings* (n 14) 101.

[108] For a full explanation of the unfit accused's rights of appeal, see ibid 129–38 and Barrett and Shandler, *Mental Disorder in Canadian Criminal Law* (n 32) ch 11.

Disposition options for the unfit accused

Three possible disposition options exist for an accused who has been found unfit to stand trial: (1) a conditional discharge into the community under s 672.54(b); (2) an order for detention in custody in a hospital under s 672.54(c); and (3) a mandatory treatment order for up to sixty days under s 672.58–672.62. In selecting from these options, s 672.54 stipulates that a court or Review Board must take into account the mental condition of the accused, the reintegration of the accused into society and other needs of the accused, and finally, public safety, which is described as the paramount consideration. It should be noted that there is no onus on any party with regard to the dispositions set out in s 672.54. This omission was intentional,[109] based on the belief that disposition options, like sentences, are better suited for courts and Review Boards to make by balancing all relevant factors, without a burden of proof on either party.[110]

The first significant decision the court or Review Board must make is whether the unfit accused can be released into the community on conditions or whether public safety dictates that a hospital detention order is necessary. There is no available data on exactly how many unfit accused are given a conditional release order *by the court*, but we know the vast majority are not. Latimer and Lawrence do have data on persons found unfit and referred to a Review Board for disposition. In their twelve-year sample, the Board gave (a) a conditional discharge to nine per cent; (b) a detention order to forty-eight per cent; and (3) forty per cent were considered to be sufficiently improved to be returned to court for a judicial determination of whether they were now fit.[111] Latimer and Lawrence also followed the progress of their 1994/1995 cohort for a ten-year period and reported the following results:

- nearly forty per cent stayed in the unfit category for less than six months;
- another forty-three per cent stayed within the unfit category between six months and one year; and
- no unfit accused stayed in the unfit category for more than five years.[112]

This data should allay defence counsel's concerns, at least on a statistical basis, that a finding of fitness will result in very long or even indefinite detention. The authors also found that males, Aboriginal persons, those with affective disorders, and sex offenders were detained for the longest periods of time.[113]

[109] Tollefson and Starkman, *Mental Disorder in Criminal Proceedings* (n 14) 87.
[110] ibid 100.
[111] Latimer and Lawrence, *The Review Board Systems in Canada* (n 57) 24. There were other dispositions in 2% of the cases, such as charges being stayed or withdrawn, cases transferred out of province, or the accused died.
[112] ibid 34. [113] ibid 20–25.

Mandatory treatment order

Section 672.55(1) states that an accused found unfit or NCRMD shall not be required to submit to any treatment, but s 672.58 provides one limited exception in respect to unfit accused. It states that a court (but not a Review Board) can make a treatment order, excluding electro-convulsive therapy (ECT) and psychosurgery, for a period of up to sixty days, provided the treatment is designed to make the accused fit. The treatment order may be carried out on an out-patient or in-patient basis. The rationale for mandatory treatment is that it is in the public interest to require an accused to undergo treatment if doing so would render that person fit and thus able to resume the trial process.[114] Section 672.59 sets strict criteria for making treatment orders. They can only be made when a medical practitioner testifies, after conducting an assessment of the accused, that a *specific treatment* should be administered to render the accused fit to stand trial. The unfit accused has the opportunity to question the doctor on the suggested treatment and possible alternative courses of action. The practitioner's testimony must be based on a set of statutory grounds listed in s 672.59(2) which are directed to the interests of the accused, ensuring the treatment will in fact render the accused fit to stand trial, and that the treatment is the least intrusive possible.[115]

While mandatory judicial treatment orders for unfit accused are carefully limited, there are two other ways that an unfit accused may be treated involuntarily or without free choice. First, in some provinces, an unfit accused will be civilly committed as a danger to himself or others under the provincial Mental Health Act and many of those Acts authorise involuntary treatment of civilly committed patients. Secondly, even without civil commitment, Review Boards may inform an unfit patient that they will release him or her from hospital custody if, and only if, the patient agrees to accept and abide by a recommended treatment plan. While a patient may accept this release agreement it can hardly be said that they have in all such cases 'voluntarily' consented to this treatment.

114 Bloom, 'Fitness to Stand Trial' (n 89) 228.

115 All competent adults including accused or convicted persons have the right to refuse medical treatment except in rare instances where there is an overriding societal interest. No constitutional challenge has been brought against mandatory treatment of the unfit as prescribed in ss 672.58 and 672.59. Such a challenge is likely to fail even though courts have held non-consensual treatment to be unconstitutional in various other situations in the past. See Tollefson and Starkman, *Mental Disorder in Criminal Proceedings* (n 14) 91; Simon N Verdun-Jones and Michelle S Lawrence, 'The *Charter* Right to Refuse Psychiatric Treatment: A Comparative Analysis of the Laws of Ontario and British Columbia concerning the Right of Mental-Health Patients to Refuse Psychiatric Treatment' (2013) 46 UBC L Rev 489.

Reviews of and Maximum Limits on Unfit Status

Mandatory review

Section 672.81(1) requires the Review Board to hold regular hearings to review a disposition (other than an absolute discharge) made in respect of the accused. The first hearing must take place no later than twelve months after making a disposition, and subsequent hearings must be held every twelve months for as long as the disposition remains in force. However, under s 672.81(1.1), if the accused is represented by counsel and both the accused and the Attorney General consent to an extension, the Review Board may extend the time for holding a hearing to a maximum of twenty-four months.[116] However, if the person in charge of the place where the accused is detained requests a review, such a review shall be held as soon as practicable.

In addition, the Review Board must hold a review hearing as soon as practicable after receiving a notice under s 672.56(2) that the place where the accused is detained has significantly increased restrictions on the accused's liberty for more than seven days.[117]

Discretionary review of unfit status

Section 672.82 permits the Review Board to hold review hearings at any time on its own motion or at the request of the accused or any other party. If the Review Board decides to have a review hearing on its own motion, it is required to give notice to the prosecutor, the accused, and any other party. If the hearing is held at the request of a party, the party is deemed to abandon any appeal against the disposition taken under s 672.72.

Maximum length of time an unfit accused can be held as unfit

The 1992 mental disorder amendments introduced a partial safeguard in s 672.33 against unfit accused being held inappropriately under their status as an unfit accused. Section 672.33 requires the prosecutor to establish every two years that the prosecutor still has sufficient evidence to put the accused on trial. Where the prosecutor cannot do so, the court shall acquit the accused.

A second provision in the 1992 amendments was s 672.64, which introduced a maximum length of time (ie, a cap) that an unfit or NCRMD person could be held under their unfit or NCRMD status. For offences punishable by life, the cap was life; for designated serious offences, the cap was the maximum sentence for the offence or ten years, whichever is shorter; and for non-designated offences, the cap was the maximum sentence for the offence or two years, whichever is shorter. If

[116] See also *Criminal Code*, s 672.81(2), which allows for reviews every second year in limited circumstances.

[117] *Criminal Code*, s 672.81(2.1).

NCRMD or unfit accused persons were a danger to themselves or others after these periods, they would be subject to civil commitment under the applicable provincial Mental Health Act. Given the lack of uniformity in provincial Mental Health Acts and the lack of facilities and treatment personnel to deal with such persons in most provinces, the federal government announced that it would not proclaim the capping provisions until the provinces had been given a reasonable time to amend their laws as required.[118] Because of the increased costs that the capping provisions would impose on provinces, there was continued resistance to proclaiming these provisions. Indeed, the capping provisions remained unproclaimed and were repealed in 2005. At that time, the government introduced s 672.851, which provided relief to some, but not all, long-term or permanently unfit persons.[119] Section 672.851(7) allows a court to grant a permanent stay of proceedings if, after an inquiry, the Court is satisfied:

(a) on the basis of clear information, that the accused remains unfit to stand trial and is not likely to ever become fit to stand trial;
(b) that the accused does not pose a significant threat to the safety of the public; and
(c) that a stay is in the interests of the proper administration of justice.

Subsection 672.851(8) states that the court shall consider the following factors in deciding whether a stay is in 'the interests of the proper administration of justice':

(a) the nature and seriousness of the alleged offence;
(b) the salutary and deleterious effects of the order for a stay of proceedings, including any effect on public confidence in the administration of justice;
(c) the time that has elapsed since the commission of the alleged offence and whether an inquiry has been held under s 672.33 to decide whether sufficient evidence can be adduced to put the accused on trial; and
(d) any other factor that the court considers relevant.

Conclusion

It has been twenty-five years since Canada has had a thorough review of the law and procedures for dealing with fitness to stand trial. Such a review is long overdue. First, the most glaring fault in Canadian law is the incomplete and inadequate test for fitness, particularly in comparison to actual changes or proposals for change in several other common jurisdictions including England, Victoria, and New South Wales. Secondly, there is a need for the collection of statistics on all aspects of the fitness process, including how long accused persons are held unfit whether in custody or

118 Standing Committee on Justice and Human Rights, Report No 14 (n 48) 18.
119 This amendment was necessitated by the decision in *R v Demers* 2004 SCC 46, [2004] 2 SCR 489.

out of custody. Likewise, an examination of whether the significantly higher judicial findings of unfit to stand trial in the case of women, older accused, persons charged with violent offences, and persons with psychotic disorders are in fact warranted in light of the legal criteria for fitness. Thirdly, it is time for Canada to consider abolition of fitness-to-stand-trial hearings by juries and instead have all fitness decisions made by judges alone, and to consider raising the quantum of proof to 'beyond a reasonable doubt' when the issue of fitness is raised by the prosecutor. And finally, Canada needs to revisit the issue of capping the maximum period of time that an unfit accused can be held unfit whether in or out of custody.

7

The Development of Unfitness to Stand Trial in New Zealand

Warren Brookbanks

Introduction

The rules governing 'unfitness to stand trial' in New Zealand are a combination of statute and common law, including decisions from courts in New Zealand, Australia, Canada, and the United Kingdom. Although laws governing unfitness have existed in New Zealand for well over 100 years, it is principally since 2003 that unfitness to stand trial[1] has become a major aspect of trial procedure. The year 2003 marked a watershed in the way New Zealand law deals with mentally impaired offenders, with the enactment of the Criminal Procedure (Mentally Impaired Persons) Act 2003 (CP(MIP) Act) and the Intellectual Disability (Compulsory Care and Rehabilitation) Act 2003 (ID(CCR) Act). The CP(MIP) Act redefined the criteria for determining unfitness to stand trial, and other procedures for the management and disposition of mentally impaired offenders. The ID(CCR) Act established a novel statutory regime for the compulsory care and rehabilitation of persons with an intellectual disability, who have been charged with, or convicted of, an offence. In practice, much of the recent case law on unfitness to stand trial has involved intellectually disabled offenders.

Building on this recent history, the purpose of this chapter is to provide an overview of the main developments in the theory and practice of unfitness to plead in New Zealand since 2003. The chapter examines legal developments and is not a critique of current research on socio-demographic or clinical and court-related factors associated with unfitness. These matters are dealt with in a burgeoning literature that may be considered independently of the concerns of this chapter,[2] which begins

[1] The expression preferred in the New Zealand legislation. See Criminal Procedure (Mentally Impaired Persons) Act 2003 (NZ).

[2] See, eg, G Pirelli et al, 'A Meta-analytic Review of Competency to Stand Trial Research' (2011) 17 Psychology, Public Policy and Law 1–53; JA Sakdalan and V Egan, 'Fitness to Stand Trial in New Zealand: Different Factors Associated with Fitness to Stand Trial between Mentally Disordered and Intellectually Disabled Defendants in the New Zealand Criminal Justice System' (2014) 21(5) Psychiatry, Psychology and Law 658–668; J O'Leary et al, 'Exploring Juvenile Fitness for Trial in Queensland' (2013) 20(6) Psychiatry, Psychology and Law 853–66; AJ White et al, 'Fitness to Stand Trial: Views of Criminal Lawyers and Forensic Mental Health Experts regarding the Role of Neuropsychological

Fitness to Plead: International and Comparative Perspectives. First Edition. Edited by Ronnie Mackay and Warren Brookbanks. Chapter 7 © Warren Brookbanks 2018. Published 2018 by Oxford University Press.

with an overview of the current regime. This is followed by a more detailed examination of the statutory process for determining fitness, including a critical examination of issues around the procedure for determining 'evidential sufficiency', the equivalent of the 'trial/examination of the facts' procedures in England and Scotland. Other idiosyncratic issues relating to the determination of unfitness to stand trial in New Zealand are also considered here. Finally, issues around the determination of unfitness post-conviction are examined, a relatively recent consideration in New Zealand. The chapter concludes with some observations concerning the direction of future reforms.

Overview of the Current Law

Unfitness to stand trial in New Zealand has been statutorily defined since the mid 1950s. Up until that time the issue was largely determined by English common law principles, although it seldom arose as a trial issue in New Zealand.[3] Until as late as the early 1990s reported New Zealand case law on unfitness to stand trial was effectively non-existent. During this period intellectually disabled persons, who in the developing law of unfitness to stand trial have been at a higher risk of unfitness to plead findings,[4] in New Zealand were liable to detention in protective custody under generic mental health legislation. They seldom appeared before the courts to face criminal charges. Following the enactment of the Mental Health (Compulsory Assessment & Treatment) Act 1992, offenders with an intellectual disability began to appear on a regular basis in New Zealand criminal courts. This was a 'downstream' effect of legislative changes aimed at excluding persons with an intellectual disability from statutory procedures for the compulsory assessment and treatment of mental disorder, a necessary prerequisite to a finding of unfitness.[5] Not being legally 'mentally disordered' they could not be compulsorily detained in protective custody and were required to be discharged into the community. Some, without adequate supervision, committed serious crimes. This led to an increase in investigations of fitness to stand trial. The legal difficulties encountered by this cohort were a major catalyst for the eventual enactment of the Intellectual Disability (Compulsory Care and Rehabilitation) Act 2003.

Assessment' (2015) 22(6) Psychiatry, Psychology and Law 880–89; AJ White et al, 'Fitness to Stand Trial in One Australian Jurisdiction: The Role of Cognitive Abilities, Neurological Dysfunction and Psychiatric Disorders' (2016) 23:4 Psychiatry, Psychology and Law 499–511.

[3] See Brookbanks, 'A Contemporary Analysis of the Doctrine of Fitness to Plead' (1982) Recent Law 84.

[4] See Sakdalan and Egan, 'Fitness to Stand Trial in New Zealand: Different Factors Associated with Fitness to Stand Trial between Mentally Disordered and Intellectually Disabled Defendants in the New Zealand Criminal Justice System (n 2) 658, 662–68.

[5] See Mental Health (Compulsory Assessment & Treatment) Act 1992, s 4. The section defined matters which alone could not invoke the compulsory assessment and treatment procedures of the Mental Health Act. 'Intellectual disability' was one of the personal attributes which, considered alone, does not constitute mental disorder.

Various amendments to criminal justice legislation since the 1950s have refined the wording of the statutory test for unfitness to stand trial, which was originally based on the common law *Pritchard*[6] test. Unfitness to plead in New Zealand, following English terminology, was described as being 'under disability' and the test remained substantially unchanged from 1954 to 2003. However, the reforms of 2003 incorporated an amended, and extended, definition of 'unfit to stand trial', which had the effect of liberalising the reach of the fitness-to-plead rules and expanding the scope of the fitness procedure. The courts were to be engaged in a more nuanced investigation of relevant trial capacities which tested for the presence of 'mental impairment', the 'adequacy' of trial understanding, and ability to give instructions. The current definition states:[7]

unfit to stand trial, in relation to a defendant,–

(a) means a defendant who is unable, due to mental impairment, to conduct a defence or to instruct counsel to do so; and
(b) includes a defendant who, due to mental impairment, is unable–
  (i) to plead:
  (ii) to adequately understand the nature or purpose or possible consequences of the proceedings:
  (iii) to communicate adequately with counsel for the purposes of conducting a defence.

The implications of this new definition are discussed in more detail later in the chapter. This is a performance-based standard which tests an offender's ability to function meaningfully in the nominated domains. It exclusively defines the criteria for determining trial competence in New Zealand at every stage of criminal proceedings, including the assessment of fitness post-conviction. It has been held to apply equally to the situation where an option for the court is to determine an issue of fitness *after* a guilty plea has been entered, as to determining fitness *before*, or in the course of, a trial.[8] In New Zealand there is now an accepted distinction between fitness to plead guilty and be sentenced and fitness to stand trial and conduct a defence, although the full implications of this distinction have not been explored by the courts. In *Britz v R*,[9] the New Zealand Court of Appeal said:

> … [T]he entering of guilty pleas does not require an ability to give adequate instructions to counsel during a trial, nor is there any need to process information and arrange one's thoughts as would be necessary in the more stressful context of a trial.

This would seem to imply that in the future New Zealand is likely to see more defendants pleading guilty to charges, who would not otherwise be capable of defending the same charges, on the basis that they have been judged fit to enter a guilty plea

[6] *R v Pritchard* (1836) 7 Car & P 303, 173 ER 135. For a fuller discussion of the history of unfitness to stand trial in New Zealand, see W Brookbanks, *Competencies of Trial: Fitness to Plead in New Zealand* (LexisNexis 2011) 13–42.

[7] See Criminal Procedure (Mentally Impaired Persons) Act 2003, s 4.

[8] *R v Komene* [2013] NZHC 1347.

[9] [2012] NZCA 606 [113].

and on the basis that fitness to plead guilty requires a less demanding set of capacities than fitness to stand trial and defend charges.[10] This is, of course, a contestable claim. Many commentators would argue that the capacities to waive the right to counsel or to plead guilty may require a higher level of functioning than is needed to stand trial, because the offender is effectively waiving the right to be tried and to remain silent. This important issue is discussed in more detail in other chapters in this volume, but is not considered further in this context.

The definition changed the previously stated test[11] in three respects:

(i) the precondition for a finding of unfit to stand trial was changed from 'mental *disorder*' to 'mental *impairment*'.
(ii) The traditional three capacities an accused person must have remain as requirements, but it is clear that the unfitness inquiry is not necessarily limited to those three factors.
(iii) The qualifier 'adequately', already part of the ability to *communicate* inquiry, is added to the ability to *understand* inquiry.[12]

The meaning of 'mental impairment' is discussed in detail in the section 'Determining Fitness' In the opinion of the Court of Appeal it is 'not heralded anywhere as a significant change'.[13]

The substitution of 'includes' for 'means' in the statutory test permits consideration of a 'more discriminating' list of incapacities, beyond the text of the statutory test.[14] These are also considered in more detail in the section 'Unfitness to Stand Trial' They serve to illuminate, the definition in s 4(1) of the CP(MIP) Act[15] but do not derogate from the statutory test, which remains the ultimate question.[16] They may help to focus the inquiry.[17]

'Evidential sufficiency' hearing

Central to the revised procedure for determining unfitness in New Zealand is the so-called 'evidential sufficiency' hearing, the procedure for which is defined in s 9 of the CP(MIP) Act. This procedure is an innovation in the 2003 Act, but, as the later discussion will show, has not been without its problems. The meaning of s 9 has given rise to great difficulty.[18]

The s 9 inquiry is the first step in an inflexible codified procedure laid down in Subpart 1 of Part 2 of the Act. There is no jurisdiction for a court to abandon the process once the issue of fitness has been properly raised.[19] This excludes any possibility of judicial discretion to determine that further investigation of the fitness issue

[10] *R v Komene* (n 8) [18] and [19]. [11] See Criminal Justice Act 1985, s 108.
[12] *Solicitor-General v Dougherty* CA 492/2011 [2012] 3 NZLR 586 [42]. [13] ibid [44].
[14] *P v Police* [2007] 2 NZLR 528 [43], per Baragwanath J. [15] ibid.
[16] *Solicitor-General v Dougherty* (n 12) [57]. [17] ibid [57].
[18] *Jones v R* CA 293/2014 [2015] NZCA 601, per Kos J at n 4. See also discussion in *R v Hemopo* [2014] NZHC 1423 [4]–[7].
[19] *R v McKay* [2009] NZCA 378, [2010] 1 NZLR 441.

is not warranted. Where this inquiry occurs *before* trial the Act determines which evidence may be submitted by the prosecutor or the defendant[20] and also defines what evidence can be heard during a Judge-alone trial[21] or in the course of a jury trial.[22]At such hearings there is a discretion to permit cross-examination but there is no absolute right.[23]

An accused person who is the subject of a s 9 finding has a right of appeal under s 16 of the CP(MIP) Act. A judge making a s 9 finding should give sufficient reasons for the decision to allow the accused person to assess the chances of success in an appeal and for the appeal court to fairly consider the appeal.[24]

The fitness-to-plead hearing

Where the evidential sufficiency hearing under s 9 has concluded with an affirmative finding that the accused did the act or omission forming the basis of the offences charged, the matter must proceed to a fitness-to-plead hearing under s 14 of the CP(MIP) Act. If not, the charges against the defendant must be dismissed, which is deemed to be an acquittal of the charge.[25] The s 14 hearing itself envisages six steps, beginning with the obtaining of health assessor reports (if not already available to the Court), and includes giving each side the opportunity to present evidence on mental impairment and/or unfitness to plead, and the opportunity to make submissions. The steps conclude with one of the findings in s 14(3). These are:

(i) that the defendant is not mentally impaired, and is therefore fit to stand trial; or

(ii) that the defendant is mentally impaired but nonetheless fit to stand trial; or

(iii) that the defendant is mentally impaired and unfit to stand trial.

The Court must make one of those findings. There is no authority for the Court to ignore the steps or to craft an alternative non-statutory option. Where the matter does proceed to trial, judges can be expected to take steps to ensure suitable accommodations are made, especially where it is clear that this is necessary for offenders with intellectual or other disabilities at various stages of the trial process.[26] But where a finding is made in terms of (iii) above, the Court must proceed to a disposition ruling in terms of Subpart 3 of the CP(MIP) Act.

20 Criminal Procedure (Mentally Impaired Persons) Act 2003, s 10(3), as inserted by the Schedule to the Criminal Procedure (Mentally Impaired Persons) Amendment Act 2011.

21 ibid. 22 ibid. 23 *R v Jeffries* CA728/2010, [2012] NZCA 608 [36].

24 *R v Te Moni* [2009] NZCA 560 [35].

25 Section 13(3) of the CP(MIP) Act, which stated that 'a discharge under subsection (2) does not amount to an acquittal', was repealed as from 1 July 2013 by s 4 of the Criminal Procedure (Mentally Impaired Persons) Amendment Act 2011. The amendment substituted 'dismiss the charge under s 147 Criminal Procedure act 2011' for 'discharge the defendant'. Under s 147(6), if a charge is dismissed under the section the defendant is 'deemed to be acquitted of that charge'.

26 See *R v Jeffries* (n 23) [52].

Disposition

Where a person has been found unfit to stand trial, the Court must order inquiries to be made to determine the most suitable method of dealing with the person under s 24 or s 25 of the CP(MIP) Act.[27] In many cases the need for a further inquiry will be unnecessary because the Court will already have recent health assessor reports which address that issue. Section 24 authorises detention as a special patient or special care recipient, wherever such detention is necessary in the interests of the public or any class of persons who may be affected by the decision. An order under s 25 is the statutory default where detention as a special patient or special care recipient is not 'necessary'. It authorises detention as either a 'patient' under mental health legislation or as a 'care recipient' under intellectual disability legislation, or immediate release where no other type of order is appropriate.

Generally, special patient/special care recipient status will be ordered where the offender is considered to pose a high risk to the public in the areas of sexual offending, physical aggression, and absconding. Special patient/care recipient status guarantees a higher level of care and removes the potential for dangerous situations. Where an order is made under s 24, the Minister of Health determines how long the order is to remain in force.[28] However, the maximum period an offender found unfit to stand trial can be detained as a special patient or special care recipient is half the maximum term of imprisonment to which the person would have been liable if convicted of the offence charged.[29] The period is a maximum of ten years if the offender is charged with an offence punishable by life imprisonment.[30] Different rules govern offenders acquitted on account of insanity and are not considered here.

Determining Fitness

Mental impairment

Before examining in more detail the way in which fitness to plead is determined in New Zealand, it is necessary to make some observations about the concept of 'mental impairment'. Although the expression is undefined in the statute, judges have not been constrained in extending its ambit as circumstances have dictated. Importantly, an enquiry into whether or not a person is fit to stand trial is an enquiry into whether he or she is 'mentally impaired' as distinct from 'mentally disordered' or 'insane'. In *R v Roberts (No 2)*[31] Fogarty J held that a person who is mentally disordered and/or insane and/or intellectually disabled, will be mentally impaired. The Court said:

> The judgment has to be made in the context. It is not satisfied by the accused demonstrating some fundamentals of rationality. So, the question is whether or not [the defendant] is

[27] CP(MIP) Act, s 23. [28] ibid, s 31(3). [29] ibid, s 30(1)(a).
[30] ibid, s 30(1)(a). [31] HC Auckland CRI-2005-092-14492, 22 November 2006 [56].

'unable, due to mental impairment, to conduct a [rational] defence or to instruct counsel to do so', in this case.[32]

This suggests that unfitness to stand trial is a highly contextualised inquiry. The dictum in *Roberts* was approved by the Court of Appeal in *SR v R*.[33] It was also considered, but disapproved, by a differently constituted Court of Appeal, in *Solicitor-General v Dougherty*.[34] The Court there rejected the test formulated by Fogarty J on the basis that the addition of the word 'rational' could have been interpreted as the court intending to indicate that decisional competence, or a 'best interests' inquiry, was part of the fitness-to-stand-trial test, contrary to the intention of Parliament. This issue is considered in more detail later in the chapter.

However, it might equally be argued that the intention of Parliament in substituting 'mental impairment' for 'mental disorder' was precisely to free relevant mental conditions from the shackles of a purely cognitive understanding of the nature of mental dysfunction and to permit a more nuanced understanding of the effects of such mental dysfunction *in context*. While the Court of Appeal has accepted that the issue of fitness to stand trial is a case-specific contextual assessment 'that must have regard to the nature of the impairment, how it manifests itself and the complexity of the nature of the charges being faced',[35] thus far it has been unwilling to concede that a more inclusive concept of mental impairment is also apt to embrace issues of rationality as well as cognition.

As a practical matter it is difficult to imagine that an accused person who suffers from a major mental disorder (eg, paranoid schizophrenia) leading to persecutory and grandiose delusions, and accompanied by hallucinations and depression, would not also lack the rational capacity to make proper trial decisions and/or instruct counsel.[36] Yet separating out rational capacity to instruct counsel, because it engages notions of decisional competence, from the simple cognitive ability to participate in proceedings, which infuses the notion of trial competence, seems strangely discordant. It is likely to lead to a bifurcated analysis whereby evidence of even profound irrationality in the conduct of the trial will be discounted where a defendant demonstrates some rudimentary cognitive skills thought to be sufficient to engage the trial process at a very basic level.

With respect, it seems doubtful that this is what the New Zealand Parliament would have intended.

Case law has clarified the meaning of mental impairment in the context of assessing fitness for trial. It now seems clear enough that a person suffering from a personality disorder *may* be mentally impaired. However, this would normally only be the case where personality dysfunction was so severe as to prevent the person from functioning in the ways required to participate in a criminal trial.[37] The question will always be whether the mental impairment, whatever its nature and whether or

[32] ibid [57] [emphasis in original text].
[33] CA 783/2010 [2011] 3 NZLR 638 [158].
[34] CA 492/2011 [2012] 3 NZLR 586 [13] and [40].
[35] *Solicitor-General v Dougherty* (n 12) [56].
[36] See *R v Cunningham* HC Gisborne CRI 2011-016-000048, 10 November 2011.
[37] ibid [154].

not it meets the definitional requirements of any other mental construct, *has the effect* of rendering the person incapable of understanding the implications of a plea and the sentencing process,[38] or of conducting a defence, or instructing a lawyer to do so.[39] Courts in other jurisdictions have held that schizoaffective disorder[40] and Alzheimer's disease[41] may be sufficient to establish a relevant mental impairment, but not amnesia per se.[42]

As the Court of Appeal observed in the case of *SR v R,* in some cases where an accused has been found to be insane, or suffering from a recognised mental illness, or having a legal intellectual disability, a finding that he or she was 'mentally impaired' sufficiently to render them unfit to stand trial 'will be practically inevitable'.[43] At the same time there may be other less severe forms of mental impairment which may not have the effect of making the person unfit to stand trial.[44] In the final analysis, whether an offender is relevantly 'mentally impaired' is a matter for judicial determination guided by expert evidence and assessed against the statutory definition of 'unfit to stand trial'.[45]

Quite apart from the issue of what constitutes a mental impairment, the need for a clinical finding of unfitness to be specifically linked to the defined criteria for fitness to plead was underscored in *R v Walls.*[46] On an appeal against conviction on the ground that the Court should admit fresh evidence that the appellant was unfit to plead at the trial, the English Court of Appeal rejected the evidence of one psychiatric assessor because, amongst other things, he had failed to address the criteria for fitness to plead in his report. The Court said (emphasis added):[47]

> ... we consider that, save in clear cases, a court must *rigorously examine* evidence of psychiatrists adduced before them and then subject that evidence to careful analysis against the [fitness to plead] criteria ... the fact that psychiatrists agree is not enough ...; a court would be failing in its duty to both the public and the defendant if it did not rigorously examine the evidence and reach its own conclusion.

This would include failing to identify precisely what mental impairment it was that the offender suffered from.

Within the New Zealand statutory framework 'mental impairment' is not relevant to the s 9 inquiry per se but is essential to the determination of unfitness to stand trial. Its relevance is not only to an accused's ability to understand and make a rational plea decision, but to all aspects of conducting a defence.

38 *R v Komene* (n 8) [18].

39 *R v Roberts* (n 31) [56]–[57] (Fogarty J). See also *R v Cunningham* (n 36) (Andrews J), where paranoid schizophrenia causing the offender to have persecutory and grandiose delusions, hallucinations and depression, was held to mean that he was unable to give satisfactory instructions to his lawyer or participate meaningfully in a Court hearing ([26]).

40 See *R v Bailey* [2011] NSWSC 1228, 11 October 2011.

41 *The State of Western Australia v Stubley [No 2]* [2011] WASC 292, 24 October 2011.

42 *D-G, Department of Environment, Climate Change and Water v Source & Resources Pty Ltd* [2011] NSWLEC 87, 23 May 2011.

43 *SR v R* (n 33) [160].

44 ibid.

45 ibid.

46 [2011] EWCA Crim 443.

47 ibid [38].

New Zealand courts have accepted a two-stage inquiry in assessing mental impairment as applied to the task of assessing fitness:

(1) Determining that there are recognisable impediments to a person's rationality (ie, that he or she is mentally impaired);
(2) Determining whether the impairment is sufficient to render the person unfit to stand trial.[48] It is *not,* however, a question of comparing the defendant's mental faculties with the mentally healthy population and concluding that he/she is mentally impaired. In *SR v R*, the Court of Appeal rightly observed that such an approach would 'broaden the concept of mental impairment beyond that which is warranted in this statutory context'.[49] By implication, mental impairment, despite being undefined, has boundaries, although these are by no means clear.

A useful summary of scope of the concept is provided in *Barton v Police.*[50] There the Court noted that 'mental impairment' has been held to include:

(i) 'Intellectual disability' as defined in s 7 ID (CCR) Act;[51]
(ii) intellectual disability of a degree of seriousness described in s 7, but not fitting the definition in the ID(CCR) Act;[52]
(iii) cognitive functional deficits falling short of either mental disorder or intellectual disability limiting verbal comprehension and expression;[53]
(iv) mild mental retardation arising from brain damage related to fetal alcohol exposure and exposure to domestic violence;[54]
(v) functional disorder arising from profound deafness.[55]

What is clear is that the categories of what may constitute 'mental impairment' are not closed. It is up to the courts to determine the scope of the expression having regard to the facts of particular cases and the tasks expected of the defendant. It ought to remain broadly inclusive to be able to embrace mental states outside of the conventional definitions of mental disorder and intellectual impairment.

Raising the Issue

An important question is knowing when the issue of unfitness to stand trial has been 'raised' as a factual question for determination. In New Zealand, this has become a controversial question in determining unfitness to stand trial. While relative

[48] See *SR v R* (n 33) [158]. [49] ibid [158].
[50] DC Palmerston North CRI 2008-054-003750, 14 November 2011, Judge Garland.
[51] *S v Police* HC Palmerston North CRI 2005-454-47, 8 December 2005, Mackenzie J.
[52] ibid.
[53] *Police v TS* DC Manukau CRI 2009-292-593, 20 September 2010, Judge Hikaka.
[54] *R v BMS (young person)* DC Whangarei, 29 September 2010, Judge Druce.
[55] *R v Paea* DC Christchurch CRN 0508705503, Judge Spear.

certainty now exists around *when* the issue may be raised, some uncertainty still surrounds the question of *how* the process is 'triggered', and by *whom.*

The CP(MIP) Act does not specifically state what is needed to trigger the procedures under Subpart 1 of Part 2 of the Act. This question has been determined by the courts, although a contestable distinction has developed between 'raising the issue' and 'triggering the Subpart 1 procedure'. This distinction has important implications in determining whether there is, in effect, a *locus poentitentiae*, whereby an issue of fitness having been 'raised', can be disavowed or discontinued because there is not a real issue for the court to address.

As regards *how* the issue is raised the courts in New Zealand have opted for a simple test. This was articulated in *R v McKay*[56] after the Court of Appeal had surveyed a range of alternative tests, principally from Australia. The Court concluded:

> … the procedure should be triggered if the accused, his or her counsel, or the Crown raises a question as to the accused's fitness to stand trial.[57]

The Court found that the procedure *may* even be triggered in absence of an application by counsel, where the Court considers the accused's conduct at trial or before trial was so 'bizarre' as to raise concern about his fitness to stand trial.[58] The test was said to set a 'low standard' and was dependent on the 'integrity and good judgment of counsel'.[59] The Court held that it was a standard that was less demanding than requiring a 'clear evidential foundation'.[60]

A question that has arisen post-*McKay* concerns whether the issue of fitness can be 'raised' without triggering the Subpart 1 procedure. This has become a matter of practical importance because of the so-called 'clunkiness' of the procedure and the desirability of 'avoid[ing] jumping on the conveyor belt [of the fitness procedure] on a whim'.[61] However, as matters stand there is a conflict of judicial opinion. In *R v Kimura*[62] the Court of Appeal favoured an approach which suggested that the issue had been conclusively 'raised' when the District Court Judge received a psychiatric report, despite the conclusion of the report writer in that case that the appellant was neither unfit nor insane. Nevertheless, this was enough for the Court of Appeal to conclude that there was 'sufficient merit' to engage (trigger) the statutory process.

This decision contrasts with *R v Latimer*,[63] where the High Court concluded that 'informal assessments', as had occurred, were merely part of an initial screening process and were not directed at the ultimate question of unfitness to stand trial. Rather, they were directed at whether there was a 'real and substantial' question of the accused's fitness to stand trial. Because there was no record of a *request* to determine the issue, it was held that the issue had not been raised and, therefore, the Subpart 1 procedure was not engaged. There was no 'real and substantial question' for determination.

[56] See n 19, 378. [57] ibid [34]. [58] ibid [40]. [59] ibid [39].
[60] See *R v Codd* [2006] 3 NZLR 562 [23].
[61] See R Chambers, 'Trial Rights for the Mentally Impaired' (2011) 24 NZULR 478, 486.
[62] CA 15/2011, [2011] NZCA 238.
[63] HC Auckland CRI 2011-404-000015, 21 June 2011, Venning J.

The latter approach makes good sense in that it allows for an uncommitted discussion of unfitness arising tangentially in a court report, to be treated as an informal or 'screening' assessment.[64] This may assist counsel to decide whether to make a formal application for determination of the issue of fitness, but does not create an obligation for the court to investigate the matter further.

The adoption of the 'real and substantial question' test, although discounted in *R v McKay*, illustrates the fluid nature of legal developments in this area. While it confirms the view that unfitness to plead or stand trial must be based on more than a whimsical notion of mental impairment, and must be rooted in a credible narrative that the offender is more than merely 'unwell', the fact is that the decision in *Kimura* binds all New Zealand High and District Court judges on this point. Importantly, the *Kimura* decision undermines any precedential value that *Latimer* might have had, although the *Latimer* approach is preferable and better accords with common sense. The discussion points to the need for legislative clarification of what it means to 'raise' the fitness issue.

The Evidential Sufficiency Hearing

The elements of the evidential sufficiency hearing procedure are defined in s 9 of the CP(MIP) Act 2003. Section 9 states:

9 Court must be satisfied of defendant's involvement in offence

A court may not make a finding as to whether a defendant is unfit to stand trial unless the court is satisfied, on the balance of probabilities, that the evidence against the defendant is sufficient to establish that the defendant caused the act or omission that forms the basis of the offence with which the defendant is charged.

Section 9 reflected the need for some process or procedure to test an offender's responsibility for the *actus reus* elements, to avoid the risk of factually innocent offenders being found unfit to stand trial. No such procedure previously existed in New Zealand law. To this extent, it broadly corresponds to the 'trial of the facts' procedure in England and Wales and the 'special hearing' model in some Australian states. As a result of recent statutory amendments, if the Court is not satisfied of the matter specified in s 9 it must dismiss the charge. Dismissal of charges is deemed to be an acquittal.[65] The section requires that before a court can make a finding as to whether a defendant is unfit to stand trial, it must satisfy itself that the evidence establishes that the defendant 'caused the act or omission that forms the basis of the offence' (s 9). It is commonly referred to as an 'evidential sufficiency' hearing or an 'involvement hearing', and is aimed at determining the sufficiency or adequacy of evidence concerning the *actus reus* elements of an offence allegedly committed by the accused.[66] Early speculation that the requirements of s 9 could be satisfied on the

[64] *Latimer v Police* HC Auckland CRI 2011-404-000015, 21 June 2011 [23].

[65] See CP(MIP) Act, s 13 as amended by s 4 Criminal Procedure (Mentally Impaired Persons) Amendment Act 2011and s 147(6) Criminal Procedure Act 2011.

[66] See, eg, *Trow v Police* HC, Auckland, CRI 2004-404-208, 10 September 2004.

basis of hand-up briefs have proven to be wide of the mark. The fact that the procedure has tended to become an early testing ground for determining issues of criminal responsibility that might otherwise have been dealt with only at a trial or hearing of the substantive issues has tended to dictate its adversarial character.

Because the s 9 hearing will often be the only opportunity for the defendant to test the prosecution evidence, where there might otherwise be a later finding of unfitness, the hearings tend to be approached with full evidential rigour.[67] Typically, the evidence relied on for the purposes of the hearing might include a transcript of a police interview, forensic evidence relating to DNA evidence (especially where sexual offending is alleged), and identification evidence from a police witness.[68] However, other categories of evidence are regularly presented at such hearings, including propensity evidence,[69] complainant video evidence,[70] and oral complainant evidence.[71]

The wording of s 9 requires the Crown to bear the burden of proving the relevant facts, to a balance-of-probabilities standard. The s 9 hearing must be held at any stage of the trial process at which the issue of the defendant's unfitness to stand trial arises, up until the stage where all the evidence is concluded.[72] However, case law has established that this may include the period post-committal but before a trial has commenced[73] and where a plea of guilty has been entered.[74]

Because the s 9 hearing is not dependent upon a prior finding of unfitness to stand trial, and cannot simply be regarded as an inquiry into a 'preliminary matter', a full adversarial hearing of the substantive issue of responsibility for the *actus reus* has become the norm in many such hearings.[75] The practice has developed that the issues of *physical responsibility* in s 9 and the determination of fitness to stand trial in s 14 are treated as separate enquiries, so that only after the issue of physical responsibility has been determined is the court required to address the issue of trial competence.

As far as the hearing itself is concerned, New Zealand courts have accepted the view that it is 'a more relaxed evidential enquiry in which any evidence (in any form) which assists the Court in making a determination on a core issue ought to be admissible, subject to the requirements of natural justice and the ability to test any evidence which may be inherently unreliable'.[76]

[67] See, eg, *Police v KP* DC Auckland CRN–09004027463, 21 July 2010 (Judge Roderick Joyce QC).

[68] See *R v Rajsic* HC Auckland CRI-2012-004-2810, 11 October 2012 (Priestley J).

[69] *Police v Palu* HC Auckland CRI 2008-404-0083, 8 June 2009 (Priestley J).

[70] *Police v Espanto* DC North Shore CRI 2008-044-009415, 1 May 2009.

[71] See *R v Te Moni* (n 24); *R v Cann* DC Whangarei CRI-2009-024-001269, 14 April 2011; *Police v KP* (n 67).

[72] CP(MIP) Act, s 7(1).

[73] *R v McKay* (n 19); *R v Te Moni* (n 24).

[74] *R v Komene* (n 8).

[75] There is agreement that special hearings cannot be conducted on the basis of hand-up briefs, without the opportunity to examine and cross-examine witnesses.

[76] WJ Brookbanks, 'Special Hearings under CPMIPA' [2009] NZLJ 30, cited with approval in *R v McKay* (n 19), where the Court said the writer's conclusions were 'probably right' ([48]) and in *R v Lyttleton* HC Auckland CRI 2008-044-009466, 4 November 2009 [22].

However, the placement of the 'evidential sufficiency' hearing *before* the determination of unfitness to stand trial has created its own problems. These were discussed in *R v Te Moni*,[77] where the New Zealand Court of Appeal observed that the current provision effectively requires an accused person, whose fitness is in doubt, to undergo a form of trial as part of a process to determine whether he or she is fit to do so. The Court noted that if the s 9 hearing happened *after* the assessment of fitness to stand trial, the process could be tailored to deal with the reality that the accused person could not properly participate. It would also mean that complainants in sex cases would not be required to give evidence twice.[78] These are suggestions that may warrant further investigation as part of any future review of the legislation.

'Act or omission'

Another area of controversy in relation to s 9 hearings concerns the interpretation of the phrase 'caused the act or omission that forms the basis of the offence'. The expression is based on the phrase 'did the act or omission charged against him as the defence' in s 4A Criminal Procedure (Insanity) Act 1964 (UK), added by s 4 Criminal Procedure (Insanity and Fitness to Plead) Act 1991(UK).[79] As was anticipated in early commentary on these provisions,[80] New Zealand courts have been influenced by the interpretative approach of their English counterparts in determining the scope and content of the expression. When the provision was first enacted it was anticipated that the courts would take a narrow approach to the interpretation of the section, so that the new procedure would only assess whether there is sufficient evidence of an accused's '*physical* responsibility' for the offence charged. This implied that only issues of *actus reus* would need to be determined at such hearings.[81] While some New Zealand judges have followed English jurisprudence, in preferring the view that the choice of 'act' rather than 'offence' in s 9 was intended as an indication that the court was not to consider the mental ingredients of the offence,[82] others have taken a broader approach which permits limited consideration of *mens rea* questions.

In *R v Te Moni*[83] the Court of Appeal, drawing on *Ardler*, identified three possibilities.[84] The act or omission might be no more than the physical act essential to the offence, or it could be both the *actus reus* and *mens rea* elements of the offence. The third approach, ultimately favoured by the Court, was recognition that the phrase 'acts which constitute the offence' describes something unlawful in a broad sense, so

[77] See n 24. [78] ibid [96].

[79] For a full account of the operation of the English provisions, see chapter 2, 'The Development of Unfitness to Plead in English Law' by Professor RD Mackay.

[80] See WJ Brookbanks, 'Mentally Impaired Offenders in New Zealand—Recent Developments' in The New Regime of Criminal Procedures and Compulsory Care Governing Mentally Impaired and Intellectually Disabled Persons, New Zealand Law Society Seminar, Auckland, 2004.

[81] This was the approach taken in an early decision on s 9 in *Trow v Police* (n 66) (Nicholson J).

[82] See *R v H* [2003] 1 All ER 497; *R v Antoine* [2000] 2 All ER 208, and see *R v Lyttleton* (n 76) (Wylie J).

[83] See n 24 [75]. [84] See *R v Ardler* [2004] ACTCA (30 March 2004) para 76.

as to be an offence or an element of an offence, but not to require proof of the full mental element necessary in law to establish the commission of the offence.

In *R v Cumming*[85] French J held that while the focus should, as far as possible, be on the physical act constituting the offence, defences of mistake, accident, or self defence, which also have a mental element, must be negatived to the balance of probabilities. In contrast, in *R v Lyttleton*[86] Wylie J held that s 9 only required a focus on the physical acts or omissions, exclusive of *mens rea* considerations.

In *Te Moni* the Court held that where sexual violation by rape is alleged, the court must be satisfied under s 9 that non-consensual penetration took place, on the basis that 'non-consensual penetration is qualitatively different from consensual penetration: they are different acts'.[87] The same approach in cases of sexual violation has been followed in two recent High Court decisions.[88]

In *Te Moni* the Court of Appeal noted that the approach requires difficult distinctions to be made.[89] Such distinctions, the Court found, would be unnecessary if the s 9 inquiry was limited to proof that the defendant committed the *physical* acts that form the basis of the offence, as opposed to the *actus reus*. However, the Court found that the approach of limiting a s 9 inquiry to consideration of whether the accused committed *the physical* acts only, fails to set a sufficiently high threshold to meet the objective of s 9. This was held to be to ensure that a court has made a finding of criminal culpability before the sanctions which can apply to a person who is unfit to stand trial can be imposed on that person. While the Court of Appeal was not required to determine the issue, which had not been argued before it, it nevertheless expressed concern at the lack of clarity in s 9.

This is clearly another area where further reform is required.

Unfitness to stand trial

Unfitness to stand trial in New Zealand can only be determined after there has been a finding that the accused *did* do the act or omission which constitutes the basis of the offence charged, as specified in s 9 CP(MIP) Act. The procedure for determining unfitness per se is prescribed in s 14 of the CP(MIP) Act, informed by the definition of unfit to stand trial in s 4. The definition is similar to the provision it replaced, subject, in particular, to the addition of the word 'includes' and the substitution of 'mental impairment', as discussed earlier in this chapter.[90]

The drafting of the new formula was intended to give the courts freedom to consider other factors which have not been specifically expressed in the legislation. Yet a comment in an early Supplementary Order Paper (SOP) suggested that the legislature's intention was that defendants who, due to mental impairment, are unable to make an informed decision whether or not to give evidence, are to be excluded

[85] HC Christchurch CRI-2001-009-835552, 15 June 2009 [89].
[86] See n 76.
[87] *R v Te Moni* (n 24) [81].
[88] See *R v R* [2015] NZHC 783 [7]; *R v Wira* [2016] NZHC 869 [15].
[89] *R v Te Moni* (n 24) [79].
[90] See s 108 Criminal Justice Act 1985.

from the ambit of the meaning of 'unfit to stand trial'.[91] No reason is given for this proposed exclusion. Nor is there any principled reason why such an important inability should not be privileged in determining trial incapacity. In any event, case law since the enactment of the CP(MIP) Act may have overtaken the restriction foreshadowed in the SOP, for reasons which are discussed below.

While it was initially unclear what other factors, in addition to those expressly stated in the definition, could be considered in determining whether an offender lacks trial capacity, guidance has come from other jurisdictions. Several Australian states have incorporated a broader range of relevant capacities into their statutory tests consistent with developments in the common law. For example, the Mental Health (Treatment & Care) Act 1994 (ACT) follows the list of incapacities laid down by Smith J in *R v Presser*[92] and later approved by the High Court of Australia in *R v Ngatayi.*[93] As defined in the 1994 Act the incapacities are:

... whether the accused was capable of:

(a) understanding what it is that he has been charged with;
(b) pleading to the charge and exercising his right of challenge;
(c) understanding that the proceedings before the Supreme Court would be an inquiry as to whether or not he did what he was charged with;
(d) following, in general terms, the course of the proceedings before the Court;
(e) understanding the substantial effect of the evidence given against him;
(f) making a defence to, or answering the charge;
(g) deciding what defence he would rely on;
(h) giving instructions to his legal representative (if any) and;
(i) making his version of the facts known to the Court and to his legal representative, if any.

Considering the incapacity in (i) above, there would appear to be little difference, at least in a psychological sense, between an offender who is unable to make his version of the facts known to the court and one who lacks the capacity to make an informed decision to give evidence. If the first incapacity is privileged, as the above list suggests, so should the second be privileged. If these criteria represent broadly accepted common law standards for trial competence, it is arguable that each of those criteria enumerated in *Ngatayi*, although *not* part of the statutory list in New Zealand, are, nevertheless, implied criteria which may be 'read into' the statutory test.[94] This approach has, in fact, been accepted and applied by the Courts in New Zealand in determining trial competence.[95] In *Port v R*[96] the Court of Appeal observed that assessment of an offender's disability (unfitness to stand trial) is always nuanced, and seldom turns on one particular indicia of disability.[97] Yet it is generally agreed that a

[91] See Supplementary Order Paper, Criminal Justice Amendment Bill (No 7), PCO 2317c/6, *Explanatory Note,* 43.

[92] [1958] VR 45, 48.

[93] (1980) 147 CLR 1, 8.

[94] See Brookbanks, 'Mentally Impaired Offenders in New Zealand—Recent Developments' (n 80) 11.

[95] See *P v Police* (n 14) [24] and [43]; *Barton v Police* (n 50) [20]; *R v Harvey* HC Auckland CRI-2011-044-6714, 30 May 2012 [10] and [12]; *R v Rajsic* (n 68) [6].

[96] [2012] NZCA 429.

[97] ibid [8].

deficit in just one of the agreed criteria for trial competence will render an offender legally unfit to stand trial. In this area of the law, as we have already seen, context is everything and invariably determines whether a person is unfit to stand trial, regardless of the number of functional incapacities that may be in issue. As was noted earlier, consideration of the impact of 'mental impairment' must be applied '*against the task expected of the accused person*'[98] and cannot be satisfied merely by 'demonstrating some fundamentals of rationality'.[99]

While the New Zealand Court of Appeal has, at least for the meantime, eschewed the idea of expanding the threshold test for unfitness to include a 'best interests' component, it has, nevertheless, conceded that the listed statutory incapacities in s 4 of the CP(MIP) Act are 'not necessarily conclusive of fitness to stand trial. Other considerations are possible.'[100] The Court does not go on to suggest what such other considerations might be. However, it does not consider that the change in s 4(b) of the definition, which establishes that the three traditional capacities are not necessarily the only inquiries, is 'a significant change'.[101]

From the perspective of the statutory language used this is undoubtedly true. It is, nevertheless, clear that judges have interpreted the minimalist statutory formula in a creative manner in order to breathe life into 'old bones' by employing non-statutory considerations that are 'more discriminating'[102] than the traditional simple, single issue of the common law test first enunciated in *R v Pritchard*[103] 180 years ago. While the process of augmenting the statutory criteria by common law 'add-ons' may have begun, it almost certainly has not been concluded. It is clear that in applying the test for unfitness to stand trial in New Zealand, judges have chosen not to be constrained by the statutory language in ways that might inhibit the development of the doctrine. They have moved beyond a prescriptive approach to the interpretation of the provisions and, at least in relation to the application of s 7 of the CPMIP Act and what it means to 'raise' the issue of fitness, have preferred an approach which is dependent on the integrity and good judgment of counsel.[104] It would also seem that this pragmatic approach has informed judicial decision making in other aspects of statutory interpretation around unfitness to stand trial. Although the CPMIP Act is a statutory code, sometimes the provisions have lacked sufficient detail and the courts have had to supply what is missing in order to make the legislation work.[105]

Decisional competence

Decisional competence has been a contested notion in the New Zealand fitness-to-plead jurisprudence. The Court of Appeal has indicated it does not see it as part of the test for unfitness to stand trial. What then is 'decisional competence' that it represents such a threat to settled notions of unfitness to stand trial? Is it subversive? It is an approach to determining trial competence developed by Professor Richard

[98] *R v Roberts (No 2)* (n 31) [57] (Fogarty J). [99] ibid.
[100] *Solicitor-General v Dougherty* (n 12) [54]. [101] ibid [44].
[102] *P v Police* (n 14) [43] (Baragwanath J). [103] See n 6.
[104] See *R v McKay* (n 19) [39]. [105] ibid [92].

Bonnie. Essentially, a distinction is drawn between the *foundational* notion of 'competence to assist counsel' and the *contextualized* notion of 'decisional competence'. The idea is that a defendant who is *provisionally* competent to assist counsel, may lack competence to make specific decisions likely to be encountered as the trial process unfolds. Thus, competence is measured, not simply by an accused's ability to perform cognitive tasks (eg, to understand who the judge or prosecutor is, to know what a lawyer is and be able to communicate with him or her, and know that he is facing a criminal charge in a court), but also the ability to understand and choose amongst alternative courses of action. This may, or may not, involve the ability to make trial decisions which are consistent with an offender's best interests. However, decisional competence is by no means limited to determining whether a course of action is in the defendant's best interests. It may, for example, involve understanding what 'giving instructions' means or what it means to make one's version of the facts known to the Court, where the defendant may have thought there was only (ever) one version of the facts. These inquiries may have nothing to do with the idea of 'best interests', but go to the question of whether *this* defendant has the capacity to make decisions that are fundamental to having a fair trial.

The problem for reform of this area of the law is that the common law has generally eschewed a 'rational capacity' standard for trial competence, requiring simply that the accused have a *rudimentary understanding* of the trial process. On this basis, it has been held in English cases like *R v Robertson* and *R v Berry* that an accused person should be free to make decisions even though they are not in his or her best interests, even where the offender suffers from a high degree of abnormality.[106] This approach has been adopted in New Zealand. In *R v Power*,[107] the Court of Appeal held that the statutory test for 'under disability' in s 108 Criminal Justice Act 1985, did not require that the appellant actually give instructions that are in his or her best interests. The Court further held that a *high* threshold of fitness, including a best interests component, would derogate from the fundamental principle that accused persons are entitled to choose their own defences and to present them as they choose.[108] In *Solicitor-General v Dougherty*[109] the Court of Appeal has affirmed *Power* as 'settled law' in New Zealand and has not been persuaded that the decision needs to be re-visited.[110] Yet the 'low-threshold' model fails to appreciate that the critical issue is whether the defendant has the *capacity* to make such choices at all, not simply whether they are against his or her interests.

At first blush the decision in *Dougherty* would appear to have spelt the end to any prospect of adopting 'decisional competence' in New Zealand. However, linking decisional competence exclusively to the question of whether a defendant is able to assess rationally what defence would be in his or her interests and being able to choose that defence, confines the concept in a manner that would, almost certainly,

[106] See, eg, *R v Robertson* [1968] 3 All ER 557; *R v Berry* (1977) 66 Cr App R 156 (CA).

[107] CA 187/96, 22 October 1996.

[108] See also *R v Ngahooro* CA 201/98, 9 November 1998 (Goddard J): 'The threshold of fitness is low, as was confirmed in *Power's* case, but it must nevertheless be founded on an evidential basis.'

[109] See n 100.

[110] *Solicitor-General v Dougherty* (n 12) [40].

have surprised its founder. As noted above, the concept of decisional competence was first articulated by Professor Richard Bonnie twenty-five years ago.[111] It is a construct which seeks to affirm the *reliability* rationale for barring adjudication on the grounds of a defendant's incompetence. As Bonnie observed, to proceed against a defendant who lacks the capacity to recognise and communicate relevant information to his or her counsel and to the court would be unfair to the defendant and would undermine society's independent interest in the *reliability* of its criminal process.[112] This concern goes somewhat further than simply asking whether a defendant is capable of choosing a defence that is in his or her best interests.

Furthermore, the Court of Appeal's reliance on *Power* as stating the threshold test for determinations of fitness to stand trial requires further consideration. *Power* was not directly concerned with unfitness to stand trial. Counsel for the appellant had conceded that there was no ground for contending that he was 'under a disability' (unfit to stand trial). Given that the Court had heard no argument on the question of unfitness to stand trial, which was not relevant to the issues for determination, it is surprising that the Court of Appeal in *Dougherty* should have professed its preference for the decision as articulating a test for fitness that is still binding on all lower courts. It is unfortunate that the Court of Appeal did not take the opportunity to reconsider the legal efficacy of its earlier decision which, while it is said to represent the law in both England and New Zealand on this question, is hardly an adequate account of the complexities inherent in the 'best interests' debate. In addition, the Court in *Power* gave no explanation or reasoning for its ruling. Nor did it seek to justify it with reference to decided case law or relevant academic commentary. While it has been accepted as 'settled law', it is doubtful whether it represents a strong authority as to where the threshold for unfitness to stand trial should be set.

There are some important practical consequences of the ruling. As Baragwanath J observed in *P v Police,*[113] entitlement to choose implies capacity to do so. Thus, a defendant who lacks the capacity to choose between two courses of action runs the risk of an unfair trial, regardless of whether he actually gives instructions which may be considered to be in his best interests. The issue is not the nature of the instructions given, but whether, whatever they are, they are given by a *capacitated* defendant. This point has been affirmed in recent years by the Judicial Committee of the Privy Council. In *Taitt v The State*[114] their Lordships noted, with reference to *Robertson,* that the *quality* of the offender's instructions to counsel or any evidence that he or she may wish to give is not to the point. 'The emphasis is on his ability, or his inability, to do those things.'[115] The broader principle is that any instructions given by an incapacitated defendant are necessarily unreliable. They should be barred by holding the defendant unfit to stand trial.

In *Dougherty* the Court of Appeal expressed the view that there was no 'discernible statutory intention' to move away from the settled principle that fitness to plead

[111] See RJ Bonnie, 'The Competence of Criminal Defendants: A Theoretical Reformulation' (1992) 10 Behavioral Sciences and Law 291.

[112] ibid 295. [113] See n 14 [20]. [114] [2012] UKPC 38, per Lord Hope.

[115] ibid [16].

does not include an inquiry into whether the accused will act in his or her best interests.[116] It has found that there is no statutory support for a change in relation to decisional competence, a change which it considers should not be implemented by the Courts. Yet it may be that a form of the decisional competence concept has already been applied in New Zealand. In *R v Cumming*[117] the Court of Appeal dismissed an appeal against conviction and found the appellant fit to make the relevant choice to represent himself, albeit the choice he made was 'probably not in his best interests'.[118] Nevertheless, the Court appeared to accept that there was a distinction in principle between capacity, at a *basic level*, to participate directly in a trial through questioning witnesses and communicating the defence to the court, and a separate *decisional capacity*, that is engaged following a finding that an accused person is fit to plead 'but unfit, due to psychological condition or any other reason to exercise the right to represent himself or herself personally at the trial … '. Fogarty J in *R v Roberts* also noted this distinction.[119] Its significance, as applied to circumstances which prevailed in *Cumming*, was that the Court found that the statutory right to self-representation had to be denied 'because the fundamental right to a fair trial will not be upheld if the accused is permitted to proceed to trial without counsel'.[120]

Although the Court's reasoning falls short of a clear articulation of Bonnie's distinction between *basic* and *decisional* competence, it is, arguably, implicit in the language of the Court; and it reflects the commonsense notion that a person who has the present capacity to assist counsel (ie, by meeting the minimum conditions necessary for participating in one's own defence) may lack the more nuanced capacity (decisional competence), for example, to make the decision to dismiss counsel and represent himself, with all that that implies.

Importantly, for the purposes of the developing jurisprudence on unfitness to stand trial in New Zealand, the decision in *Dougherty* has re-ignited debate on the wider purposes of the fitness-to-stand-trial determination. As the New Zealand Court of Appeal recognised in *Port v R*,[121] the assessment of an offender's disability 'is always nuanced, and seldom turns on one particular indicia of disability'. Clearly, the introduction of a notion of 'decisional competence' into New Zealand law would raise the stakes in fitness determinations and would be a challenge to settled law. However, the notion is now well embedded in the thinking of some judges. It permits a proper discrimination to be made between the ability to make low-level decisions about process and the more demanding sorts of decisions which enable the trial process to proceed in a rational and dignified manner.

Indeed, more recent judicial thinking appears to have embraced the idea that the defendant should have a rational understanding of the proceedings as evidence of an ability to participate effectively in the trial. In *N v The Queen*[122] the Court of Appeal observed that the 'effective participation inquiry' is a contextual inquiry, recognising

116 *Solicitor-General v Dougherty* (n 12) [40].
117 [2006] 2 NZLR 597 (CA).
118 ibid [68].
119 *R v Roberts* HC Auckland CRI-2005-092-14492, 22 November 2006 [17].
120 *R v Cumming* (n 117) [50].
121 See n 96 [8], per Asher J.
122 CA610/2015 [2017] NZCA 170.

that a defendant may have the capacity to participate effectively in a simple proceeding like pleading guilty to shoplifting, but may lack ability to participate effectively in more complex proceedings. Such proceedings may require an ability to process information in real time and communicate effectively so as to advance a defence.[123] The Court drew support for the idea of assessing a defendant's fitness to stand trial by focusing on their ability to participate effectively in their trial from the decision in *R v Cumming*,[124] where the Court of Appeal linked a defendant's ability to *effectively* defend charges to his or her ability to *rationally* understand the proceedings and ability functionally to defend the proceedings through *participation* in the trial process.[125]

The Court of Appeal's newly expressed preference for a test based on rational understanding as being 'an important ingredient in the fitness to stand trial requirements of this country', and implying that a defendant's understanding should not be adversely affected by delusional thoughts,[126] is a significant development in the fitness-to-plead jurisprudence in New Zealand. At the very least it re-engages the debate raised in *Solicitor-General* v *Dougherty*[127] as to whether decisional competence is, or ought to be, part of the test for unfitness to stand trial. Although the Court in *R v The Queen* does not refer directly to the concept of decisional competence, it might be argued that its acknowledgement of 'decision making' as one of the four different types of intellectual capacity required for effective participation in a trial,[128] suggests an implicit leaning towards the decisional competence model. In any event it is a debate that needs to be thoroughly aired at the highest level.[129] Perhaps the 'nuanced' approach may also infect official thinking around the 'best interests' issue, so that the idea of decisional competence is ultimately endorsed as a tool for identifying and operationalising capacitated decision making in this area of law and practice.

Ordering inquiries

Where a person has been found unfit to stand trial, the next step as prescribed by s 23 of the CP(MIP) Act, is to bail or remand the person to a hospital or secure facility for inquiries to be undertaken as to the most suitable method of dealing with the person under ss 24 and 25. The direction that the court 'must order that inquiries be made' has been interpreted to mean that *fresh* inquiries must be initiated, regardless of whether earlier health assessors' reports may have clearly recommended a particular disposition, and regardless of whether that disposition may be obvious to the court.[130] In *Moore*, Gendall J interpreted the requirement to mean that he was unable to formally make a special patient order under s 24 of the CP(MIP) Act until

[123] ibid [31]. [124] See n 117. [125] ibid [38] (McGrath J).

[126] *N v The Queen* (n 122) (fn 15). [127] See n 100.

[128] *N v The Queen* (n 122) [30].

[129] It is curious to note that the decision in *Dougherty* is not mentioned in *N v The Queen* (ibid), despite the clear commonality of the substantive issues under discussion in both cases.

[130] See *R v Moore* HC, Palmerston North, CRI- 2003-031-1183, 13 September 2004, per Gendall J.

the fresh report has been received from the health assessor. His Honour suggested that an amendment to the legislation might obviate the 'unnecessary situation' of psychiatrists knowing what is required in terms of disposition and having given such evidence to the court, but still being required to make further inquiries under s 23.[131]

While this concern is well founded, the wording of the section is sufficiently broad to permit evidence from such new inquiries being presented orally, as opposed to requiring a fresh written report.[132]

Raising the Issue Post-conviction

While much of the early jurisprudence around fitness since 2003 has concerned the operation of s 9, in recent years a new focus has emerged, namely, the extent to which the issue of unfitness may be raised post-conviction. Several recent cases have been litigated as late appeals against conviction, challenging convictions based on guilty pleas for offending, often many years earlier. Although local courts and courts in other jurisdictions have emphasised the evidential difficulties in determining unfitness to stand trial many years after the event, this has not prevented determined counsel from advancing these issues for the consideration of the court.

The cases fall into two broad categories: first, cases where a failure to properly assess the true extent of the offender's trial capacities has led to the person being convicted, usually following a guilty plea, where, upon a later assessment, the person is found to be clearly unfit to stand trial. In such cases unfitness is, in effect, unassailable. The second category is cases where current assessments of fitness to stand trial have raised questions about fitness on an earlier occasion, where the issue was either not tested or was dismissed. Here the claims of unfitness are more equivocal. Recent decisions suggest that New Zealand judges do not hesitate to find a miscarriage of justice in the former case. However, in those cases where the issue of fitness has been raised for the first time on an appeal, after a long delay, retrospective assessments are more complex and less likely to succeed.

The practical and policy issues raised by this problem are well illustrated in the case of *Lawler and the Queen*,[133] a case in the second category above. Although the timing of the index offences meant that the issue of unfitness to stand trial would have had to be determined pursuant to Part 7 of the Criminal Justice Act 1985 (NZ), the evidential issues that arose in the case serve to illustrate well the complexities arising when the question of unfitness to stand trial is tested after conviction.

The appellant was serving a sentence of preventive detention imposed in 1994 following convictions for sexual offending against young girls. There were previous convictions for sexual offences in 1987 and 1990. The appeal involved three applications for extension of time to appeal against the convictions in 1987, 1990, and

131 ibid [10].
132 See, eg, *R v Sao Ene Yee* HC, Wellington, CRI- 2004-091-980, 21 February 2005, per Gendall J.
133 CA 777 / 2010 [2013] NZCA 308.

1994. All convictions related to charges of indecent assault or unlawful sexual connection with young children. In each case the basis of the intended appeal was that the appellant was not fit to plead and therefore did not receive a fair trial, resulting in either a nullity or a miscarriage of justice.

At the time of all the previous convictions the law relating to fitness to plead in New Zealand was contained in Part 7 of the Criminal Justice Act 1985. Earlier, in *Ferguson v R*,[134] the Court of Appeal had noted that determination of whether a miscarriage of justice occurred at the time convictions were entered must be determined on the law that was in force at the relevant time. The test for determining fitness to plead was set out in s 108 of the Criminal Justice Act 1985. This provided a test which is substantially the same as the new test set out in s 4 of the CP(MIP) Act. The principal difference between the two provisions was that the threshold for unfitness in the 1985 Act was based on the finding that the offender was 'mentally disordered', an expression defined in mental health legislation, whereas the threshold under the 2003 Act was 'mental impairment'. This expression is undefined. Under the former provision the fact that the appellant was intellectually disabled, rather than suffering from a mental disorder, potentially created a problem in that an intellectual impairment of the kind the appellant suffered from did not fit the concept of 'mental disorder' for the purposes of the 'under disability' definition in the 1985 statute.[135] The procedure for determining fitness to plead was defined in s 111 of the Criminal Justice Act 1985. However, the Court agreed that even if the statutory regime in ss 108 and 111 of the Criminal Justice Act 1985 did not apply in the case of intellectual disability, the High Court could invoke its inherent jurisdiction to grant a stay of proceedings in circumstances where a fair trial was not possible.[136]

The appeal against all the convictions was based on the sole ground that the appellant was not fit to stand trial and that, therefore, the convictions were a nullity or, if not, a miscarriage of justice had occurred. Since the appellant had pleaded guilty on each occasion, his case was that when he entered his pleas he was mentally disordered and that the disorder was such that he was unable to plead or understand the nature or purpose of the proceedings or communicate adequately with counsel for the purpose of conducting a defence. As the court observed, if that case was made out a miscarriage of justice would have occurred and the appeal standard in s 385 (1) of the Crimes Act 1961 would have been met.

The Court found that there was no evidential basis for it to interfere with the processes undertaken in accordance with the law at the time in relation to the three convictions under appeal. The Court reiterated the difficulty it faced in trying to reconstruct events some twenty years later, a problem compounded by the paucity of information about what occurred and the inability of lawyers acting at the time to recall events of the time (at [64]):

[134] [2010] NZCA 2. [135] See Criminal Justice Act 1985, s 108.

[136] See *R v L* [1998] 2 NZLR 141. As to the historical difficulties associated with determining unfitness for an offender with an intellectual disability, see *R v T [a mental patient]* [1993] DCR 600 and *Police v M* [1993] DCR 1119.

All of this emphasizes the importance that concerns about fitness to plead are addressed at the time a person comes before the Court and if they are not, in a promptly brought appeal.

Having undertaken a full analysis of the merits of the appeals, to which there was no Crown objection, the Court granted extensions of time to appeal, but dismissed the appeals. In dismissing the appeal against conviction, the Court held that there was no proper basis for it to intervene in the convictions. Contemporaneous documents suggested that the appellant was assessed as fit to plead at the time of his convictions, and that the new health assessor's reports did not persuade the Court otherwise.

This case raises important questions of public policy and law. It would be objectionable that a person who was presumptively unfit at the time of an earlier conviction, for a crime for which a sentence of imprisonment was imposed, should not be able to challenge the conviction when the matter of unfitness did ultimately come to light. Similarly, after-the-event evaluations of a person's mental state, often many years after the original trial, are extremely difficult to achieve and necessarily involve a fair degree of speculation. As the *Lawler* case demonstrated, difficulties may be compounded when contemporaneous documentation by health assessors is lacking and where the issue of fitness was not raised on the earlier occasions. However, in New Zealand, as in England, there has been a significant increase in the number of cases where the issue of unfitness is raised.[137] These will continue to challenge the courts for the foreseeable future, particularly to the extent that they give rise to a 'separate and distinct' supervisory responsibility of judges to ensure the proper consideration of fitness-to-plead issues when they arise.[138] However, English judges have reiterated that making later reconstructions in order to establish unfitness is extremely difficult, and rarely successful.

A case where a subsequent reconstruction was successful was *R v AA*,[139] where the appellant sought a pardon and commutation of penalty in respect of all her previous convictions for offences of theft, receiving and possession of tainted property. These had occurred over a four-year period. The forty-one-year-old appellant had had a significant intellectual impairment since childhood. Her Full-Scale IQ was in the lowest one per cent of the population. The 'overwhelming inference' from evidence given in two Mental Health Court proceedings was that the appellant was unfit to plead to each of the offences when she pleaded guilty and was sentenced. The Court found that because the appellant was unfit to plead at the time she pleaded guilty and was sentenced to the offences the subject of the appeal, she did not enter the guilty pleas in the exercise of a free choice. Accordingly, it would have been a miscarriage of justice to allow the findings of guilt to stand. The appeals were allowed.

In the New Zealand High Court decision in *Leapai v Police*,[140] the appellant appealed against his entire criminal history comprising fourteen separate convictions. He had pleaded guilty to all the offences he was convicted of and had served sentences, including short periods of imprisonment. At no time was any issue raised

137 See, eg, *R v Walls* (n 46) para 38.
138 *R v Erskine* [2009] EWCA Crim 1425, [2010] 1 WLR 183, para 89.
139 [2010] QCA 305 (5 November 2010).
140 HC Auckland CRI-2011-404-301, 17 April 2012, Potter J.

as to his fitness to plead. The issue of fitness first arose in 2008, when the appellant pleaded guilty to charges of possession of instruments to commit burglary and shoplifting. The issue arose before sentencing and on the basis of three forensic reports the appellant's guilty pleas were vacated. He was found unfit and the criminal proceedings were stayed. However, in 2011 the appellant faced further charges of assault and wilful damage, and the issue of fitness was raised at the outset. He was again found unfit, on the basis of an agreed IQ of fifty-one, and the proceedings were stayed. He was then made subject to a compulsory care order under s 25(1)(b) CP(MIP) Act 2003.

The Court found that in the unique circumstances of the case, and given the unanimity of the expert clinicians, the appellant had never been, and was unlikely ever to be, fit to stand trial, and allowed the appeal.

While the courts are rightly suspicious of claims of historical unfitness, when the matter ought to have been, but was not tested at trial, or where unfitness is claimed in order to bolster a fresh defence that was not advanced at the original trial, exceptional cases like those discussed above justifiably warrant the most careful consideration. The designation of them as cases where the claim of unfitness is 'unassailable' means that in those rare situations where the mental impairment was so profound that the accused could never have been, or ever be, fit to plead and stand trial, the outcome should be a foregone conclusion.

Conclusion

This chapter demonstrates that some of the issues arising from the discourse around s 9 of the CP(MIP) Act are not capable of simple solutions. Two of the matters discussed are good examples and serve to highlight the concerns this chapter has addressed. First, on the question of whether and when a s 9 enquiry is triggered, the critical and overriding issue is whether there is a risk of an incapacitated person being compelled down the road of criminal proceedings when they lack capacity to meaningfully participate in any such proceeding. Such a trial would be properly declared a nullity whenever it occurs. Equally, however, a full fitness-to-plead investigation is a highly intrusive procedure that could, depending on the nature and seriousness of a charge, result in a person's detention, without trial, for a significant period of time. Such an outcome is surely to be avoided unless it is necessary. Permitting a trial judge to have, and to exercise, a limited discretion at the outset of such a procedure to determine that the issue of fitness has not been 'raised' may eliminate the risk, in some of cases, of offenders being made subject to the complicated fitness-to-plead process when it is unnecessary and unjustified.

Secondly, although the concept of *decisional competence* is now well embedded in jurisprudential analysis around unfitness to stand trial if linked to the issue of 'best interests' in decision making, it seems at present to have no role to play. However, decisional competence is a much broader and useful notion that need not be infected by the 'best interests' issue. It serves to permit a more discriminating analysis of the types of incapacities that may impact effective trial participation. Permitting a distinction to be made between *basic* and *decisional* competence may give judges a capacity to make better informed fitness determinations, determinations that are not ultimately decided by whether the defendant makes decisions contrary to his or her best interests. The question is always whether *this* defendant is a capacitated adversary who can *effectively* participate in the legal proceedings as they unfold. That may be an ongoing inquiry that is not necessarily decided on a once-only basis at the beginning of a trial, but may need to be revisited more than once as the trial proceeds.

The chapter has shown that the rules around fitness to stand trial in New Zealand, are fluid, despite their enshrinement in statutory language, and are amenable to robust interpretation by the courts. While judicial interpretation has, for the most part, been an effective means of managing the drafting inadequacies that have from time to time been exposed in the statutory language, some inadequacies are related to statutory procedures and can only be remedied by law reform.

8

Fitness to Stand Trial under Australian Law

Ian Freckelton

Introduction

Australia's law accepts that the threshold of fitness to stand trial is a lynchpin for the fairness of the criminal justice system. Its approach is a recognition of the special vulnerability of persons with mental illness or intellectual disability who come before the courts.[1] Thus, Heydon J in *Eastman v DPP (ACT)*[2] held in 2003 that the rule preventing an accused person from being tried unless fit to plead is 'among the key rules of criminal procedure which seek to ensure that a successful prosecution case rests on reliable evidence. If the accused is not fit to plead and stand trial, there can be no trial.' He observed that if the accused man, who was charged with the murder of an Assistant Commissioner of the Australian Federal Police, had been unfit to stand trial:

> … there could have been no adequate testing of the Crown case in cross-examination; no adequate process of objection to inadmissible Crown evidence; no adequate process of preventing erroneous rulings by the trial judge; no proper attention given to the defence answer to the Crown case or to any proper case which the defence might have been well advised to advance, whether that answer or case be testimonial, documentary or otherwise; and no proper development of defence submissions.[3]

To similar effect in the same case, Gaudron J concluded that:

> If a person stands trial notwithstanding that there is an unresolved issue as to his or her fitness to plead, or, if that issue is not determined in the manner which the law requires, 'no proper trial has taken place [and the] trial is a nullity.' To put the matter another way, there is a fundamental failure in the trial process.[4]

A conviction that is the result of an erroneous determination of fitness to stand trial has been classified as constituting a miscarriage of justice and is sometimes described as a nullity.[5]

[1] See *Lunt v Police* [2013] SASC 25 [25]. [2] (2003) 214 CLR 318 [114].
[3] ibid [115]. [4] ibid [62]. [5] *R v NCT* [2009] VSCA 240 [11].

Fitness to Plead: International and Comparative Perspectives. First Edition. Edited by Ronnie Mackay and Warren Brookbanks. Chapter 8 © Ian Freckelton 2018. Published 2018 by Oxford University Press.

Australia's law on fitness to stand trial is derivative of that existing at reception of English law.[6] However, the common law has evolved in a distinctive albeit variable way, with disuniformity in important respects amongst its eight jurisdictions. There is extensive case law interpreting the concept of fitness/unfitness. Notably, for the most part this does not incorporate the requirement that an accused person be able to exercise rationality or reasonableness. Australia is especially variable in relation to what form of hearing can take place when an accused person is found unfit to stand trial, what dispositions courts can impose after determinations of unfitness, and the processes that exist for persons who have been found unable to stand trial to resume their place in the community. An aspect of this diversity has attracted condemnation by the United Nations Committee on the Rights of Persons with Disabilities.[7]

This chapter reviews Australia's law on fitness to stand trial, as well as recent law reform initiatives in the area. It argues that further reform in the area is needed.

The Concept of Unfitness

Australia's modern law on fitness to stand trial is based upon the reasoning by Smith J, who determined part of the way through a trial to empanel a jury to assess whether the accused man continued to be fit to stand trial. In *R v Presser*[8] he held that:

> [T]he question … is whether the accused, because of mental defect, fails to come up to certain minimum standards which he needs to equal before he can be tried without unfairness or injustice to him. He needs, I think, to be able to understand what it is that he is charged with. He needs to be able to plead to the charge and to exercise his right of challenge. He needs to understand generally the nature of the proceeding, namely, that it is an inquiry as to whether he did what he is charged with. He needs to be able to follow the course of the proceedings so as to understand what is going on in court in a general sense, though he need not, of course, understand the purpose of all the various court formalities. He needs to be able to understand, I think, the substantial effect of any evidence that may be given against him; and he needs to be able to make his defence or answer to the charge. Where he has counsel he needs to be able to do this through his counsel by giving any necessary instructions and by letting his counsel know what his version of the facts is and, if necessary, telling the court what it is. He need not, of course, be conversant with court procedure and he need not have the mental capacity to make an able defence; but he must, I think, have sufficient capacity to be able to decide what defence he will rely upon and to make his defence and his version of the facts known to the court and to his counsel, if any.

The *Presser* test is based on the explanation given by Alderson B to the jury in the English authority of R *v Pritchard*.[9] Smith J applied the presumption of sanity and regarded a fitness trial as one where technically there was no issue joined between the parties, and therefore declined to apply an onus of proof to either the prosecution

[6] In particular, the Criminal Lunatics Act 1800 (39 & 40 Geo III c94) was received into the law of the Australian states: see *R v Draoui* [2015] SASCFC 50 [93].

[7] See I Freckelton and P Keyzer, 'Fitness to Stand Trial and Disability Discrimination: An International Critique of Australia' (2017) 25 Psychiatry, Psychology and Law 770–83.

[8] [1958] VR 45.

[9] (1836) Eng R 540; (1836) 7 Car & P 303; 173 ER 135.

or the defence. The accused man was found fit to stand trial and in due course guilty of manslaughter.

The presumption is that an accused person is fit to stand trial. The question of fitness is a question of fact to be determined on the balance of probabilities by a jury empanelled for the purpose. If the question of a person's fitness to stand trial is raised by the prosecution or the defence, the better view (*Presser* notwithstanding) is that the party raising it bears the onus of rebutting the presumption of fitness.[10] If the question is raised by the trial judge, the prosecution has carriage of the matter, but no party bears any onus of proof in relation to it.[11] Once the issue of unfitness is raised, a judge can only accept a plea of guilty if satisfied that no reasonable jury, reasonably instructed, could find the accused unfit to stand trial.[12]

The *Presser* criteria contain few adjectives or adverbs—for instance, which mandate the level or quality of understanding required. This has the outcome that the *Presser* requirements are relatively low level for an accused person to be brought to trial, although it has been accepted that the relevant impairment may arise from either a physical or a mental condition,[13] including where the person has suffered substantial head injuries.[14] The test should be employed in a 'reasonable and common sense manner',[15] not in an extreme or over-literal sense:[16] 'If an accused realises, in general terms, what it is to be put on trial and *can make sense of the evidence* against him he can take a sufficient part in proceedings for the trial to proceed' (emphasis added).[17] However, what making sense of the evidence means and how it is to be gauged are not so clear.

The requirements have consistently been applied to persons with developmental and intellectual disabilities, as well as to those with psychiatric symptomatology.[18] Considerations of rationality, lucidity, and reasonableness, by contrast with the *Dusky/Drope* approach in the United States,[19] are not explicitly incorporated into what is essentially a capacity for comprehension[20] and communication test.[21] The

[10] Crimes (Mental Impairment and Unfitness to be Tried) Act 1996 (Vic), s 7(2)–(3). See *R v McKellar* [2012] NSWSC 1567 [3].

[11] Crimes (Mental Impairment and Unfitness to be Tried) Act 1996 (Vic), s 7(4)–(5).

[12] *Kesavarajah v The Queen* [1994] HCA 41; (1994) 181 CLR 230, 245 and *R v Enright* [1990] 1 Qd R 563; *Heapes v The Queen* [2000] TASSC 77 [17].

[13] See *R v Abdulla* [2005] SASC 399 [15], [48].

[14] See, eg, *R v Bradley (No 2)* (1986) 85 FLR 111.

[15] *R v Presser* (n 8) 48; *Ngatayi v The Queen* (1980) 147 CLR 1, 9; *R v Taylor* [2014] SASCFC 112 [46].

[16] *Egan, Hawkins and Burr v JG* [2010] ACTSC 53 [69].

[17] *R v T* (2000) 109 A Crim R 559 [22]; *Egan, Hawkins and Burr v JG*, ibid [90].

[18] See, eg, *R v Mailes* (2001) 53 NSWLR 251 [213]–[214]; *R v Abdulla* (n 13) [24].

[19] See *Dusky v United States*, 362 US 402 (1960); *Drope v Missouri*, 420 US 162 (1975). See further I Freckelton, 'Rationality and Flexibility in Assessment of Fitness to Stand Trial' (1996) 19 International Journal of Law and Psychiatry 39.

[20] In *R v Larizza* [2004] SASC 360 [24] Gray J observed that 'lack of comprehension, regardless of cause is the relevant criterion to determine unfitness for trial'.

[21] A partial exception exists in South Australia, where s 269H of the Criminal Law Consolidation Act 1935 (SA) provides that 'A person is mentally unfit to stand trial on a charge of an offence if the person's mental processes are so disordered or impaired that the person is (a) unable to understand, or to respond rationally to, the charge or the allegations on which the charge is based; or (b) unable to exercise

Australian approach has been pragmatic, although an important Western Australian judgment spoke in terms of 'the ability to consider in an informed way and make rational choices about defences that are reasonably open on the evidence and the submissions that should be made by the defence in respect of the evidence presented by the prosecution'.[22] This means that in principle other factors may result in unfitness to be tried, including language difficulties that may prevent an accused from being able to make a good defence and no interpreter can be made available.[23]

The *Presser* criteria have been absorbed into legislative provisions in most jurisdictions,[24] and have been applied consistently in New South Wales[25], Queensland[26] and South Australia.[27] The '*Presser* test' is part of the statutory law of the Commonwealth[28] and of all state[29] and territory[30] jurisdictions, although diversely expressed. An example is Queensland, where 'fit for trial' is defined in the schedule to the Mental Health Act 2000 (Qld) as meaning 'fit to plead at the person's trial and to instruct counsel and endure the person's trial, with serious adverse consequences to the person's mental condition unlikely'. The *Presser* test has been described as incorporating the 'minimum requirements for a fair trial'.[31]

The fitness of an accused person to stand trial is determined at the date of the trial but having regard to the likely length of the trial and to 'what the accused's condition will or is likely to be during the course of the trial'.[32] The role of the trial judge in the fitness-to-stand-trial procedure has been described as 'significantly different and intended to be more investigative than would be the case during a conventional criminal trial', at least under Victoria's statutory provisions.[33]

(or to give rational instructions about the exercise of) procedural rights (such as, for example, the right to challenge jurors); or (c) unable to understand the nature of the proceedings, or to follow the evidence or the course of the proceedings.'

[22] *State of Western Australia v Tekle* [2017] WASC 170 [93].

[23] See, eg, *R v Grant* [1975] WAR 163; *Ngatayi v The Queen* (n 15) 9; *R v Abdulla* (n 13) [70]; *R v Willie* (1885) 7 QLJ (NC) 108.

[24] Crimes Act 1900 (ACT), s 311; Criminal Code (NT) s 43J; Criminal Law Consolidation Act 1935 (SA) s 269H; Criminal Justice (Mental Impairment) Act 1999 (Tas) s 8; Crimes (Mental Impairment and Unfitness to Be Tried) Act 1997 (Vic) s 6; Criminal Law (Mentally Impaired Accused) Act 1996 (WA) s 9.

[25] See, eg, *R v Haines* [2013] NSWSC 1609 [7]; *R v Krbavac* [2013] NSWSC 313 [4]; *R v Peterson* [2013] NSWSC 1002 [9]; *R v Feili* [2013] NSWSC 492 [11]; *R v Thomas* [2014] NSWSC 1181 [40]; *Prothonotary of the Supreme Court of New South Wales v Yau Hang Cha*n [2015] 1177 [38]; *R v Wilson* [2015] NSWSC 1538 [4]; *R v Azar* [2016] NSWSC 480 [11]; *R v Crnobrnja* [2016] NSWSC 1034 [8]; *R v Whittall* [2016] NSWSC 691 [3]; *R v Blackman* [2016] NSWSC 1579 [4].

[26] See, eg, *R v Mathews* [2013] QCA 203 [29]; *R v Lee* [2014] QCA 36 [38]; *Berg v DPP* [2014] QCA 281; *Berg v DPP* [2015] QCA 196 [54].

[27] See, eg, *R v Hayles* [2017] SASC 182 [15].

[28] Crimes Act 1914 (Cth) Pt IB, Div 6.

[29] Mental Health (Forensic Provisions) Act 1990 (NSW), Part 2; Mental Health Act 2000 (Qld), Ch 7, Parts 4 & 6; Criminal Law Consolidation Act 1935 (SA), Part 8A, Div 3; Criminal Justice (Mental Impairment) Act 1999 (Tas), Part 2; Crimes (Mental Impairment and Unfitness to Be Tried) Act 1997 (Vic), Part 2; Criminal Law (Mentally Impaired Accused) Act 1996 (WA), Part 3.

[30] Crimes Act 1900 (ACT), Part 13; Criminal Code Act 1983 (NT), Sch I, Part IIA, Div 3.

[31] *R v Rivkin* (2004) 59 NSWLR 284 [296], [301]; *Wills v The Queen* (2007) 173 A Crim R 209 [61], [64]; *Berg v DPP* (n 27) [44].

[32] *Kesavarajah v The Queen* (n 12) 246; *R v Miller [No 2]* [2000] SASC 463 [8].

[33] *R v Langley* [2008] VSCA 81 [24] per Lasry AJA.

The mere fact that an accused person has a psychiatric disorder, an intellectual disability or a brain injury is not determinative of the issue of fitness.[34] Nor is the fact that the person's mental disorder is such as to prevent him or her having an amicable, trusting relationship with their legal representatives.[35] In *Eastman v The Queen*,[36] for instance, Gleeson CJ noted that the following propositions, enunciated in the Canadian decision of *R v Taylor*[37] were 'sound, and ... consistent with the statutory test':

(a) The fact that an accused person suffers from a delusion does not, of itself, render him or her unfit to stand trial, even if that delusion relates to the subject matter of the trial.
(b) The fact that a person suffers from a mental disorder which may cause him or her to conduct a defence in a manner which the court considers to be contrary to his or her best interests does not, of itself, lead to the conclusion that the person is unfit to stand trial.
(c) The fact that an accused person's mental disorder may produce behaviour which will disrupt the orderly flow of a trial does not render that person unfit to stand trial.
(d) The fact that a person's mental disorder prevents him or her from having an amicable, trusting relationship with counsel does not mean that the person is unfit to stand trial.

However, where an accused person's lack of insight into their medical condition means that they are unable to give instructions to their lawyers at the trial, they may be adjudged unfit to stand trial.[38]

The ability of an accused person to follow the course of the trial, and to understand the substantial effect of the evidence, is contextual—it will depend on the complexity of the trial.[39] For example, a greater degree of understanding and capacity may be required for a complex fraud trial than for a trial in which the issues are narrow and well defined.[40] The jury should take the resource of legal assistance into account in determining whether he or she is, or will be, able to understand and follow the trial processes.[41] Mere loss of memory will not be sufficient to deprive a person of capacity to stand trial.[42]

It has been held not to be necessary for an accused person to give an account to his or her lawyers; rather, it is enough if he or she personally understands the substantial effect of evidence so as to answer the charge.[43] It is not necessary for the accused to understand the law or the legal effect on admissions, simply that he or she can instruct counsel in relation to the admissions they may have made and whether they were truthful or untruthful.[44] In *R v House*,[45] Connolly J held that capacity to instruct counsel:

[34] *State of Western Australia v Tekle* [2017] WASC 170; *State of Western Australia v Tekle (No 2)* [2017] WASC351 [46].

[35] *State of Western Australia v Tekle (No 2)* [2017] WASC351 [46].

[36] [2000] HCA 29; (2000) 203 CLR 1 [26]–[27].

[37] (1992) 77 CCC (3d) 551, 564–65.

[38] See *Wills v The Queen* (n 32) [80].

[39] See *R v Stevens* (2010) 107 SASR 456, 468; *R v Taylor* (n 15) [13]; *R v Polanski* [1999] NSWSC 433 [54].

[40] *R v Wahlstedt* (2003) 231 LSJS 140; *R v Gillard* [2006] SASC 46.

[41] *Ngatayi v The Queen* (n 9); *R v Miller [No 2]* (n 34) 152; *R v P* (1991) 105 FLR 12.

[42] *R v Dennison*, unreported, New South Wales Court of Criminal Appeal, 3 March 1998; Criminal Justice (Mental Impairment) Act 1999 (Tas) s 8(2).

[43] *Re T* (2000) 109 A Crim R 559 [31].

[44] See *R v Dunne* [2001] WASC 263 [43].

[45] [1986] 2 Qd R 415, 422.

involves understanding the evidence which is led so as to be able to inform counsel whether it is true or not and whether there are other facts which qualify or explain the evidence adduced. It does not involve understanding the law especially if, as in this case, he had the benefit of counsel.

To similar effect de Jersey CJ in *R v M*[46] concluded that:

Fitness for trial, in relation to the capacity to instruct counsel, posits a reasonable grasp of the evidence given, capacity to indicate a response, ability to apprise counsel of the accused's own position in relation to the facts, and capacity to understand counsel's advice and make decisions in relation to the course of the proceedings.

However, he emphasised that:

It does not extend to close comprehension of the forensic dynamics of the courtroom, whether as to the factual or legal contest. For a person represented by counsel, fitness for trial of course assumes that counsel will represent the client on the basis of the client's instructions. That the giving of such instructions may take longer because of intellectual deficit is a feature with which courts should and do bear.[47]

One of Australia's most significant analyses of the impact of intellectual disability upon an accused person's fitness for trial occurred in the decision by Bampton J in *R v Hayles*,[48] where the accused man who was charged with murder had an IQ of 63. Bampton J held that the capacity to follow the evidence at trial 'must require a capacity to retrieve stored memory of the evidence when required'.[49] He concluded on the basis of neuropsychological assessments that while the accused could respond to individual questions, he lacked the capacity to store what he understood in the moment to his memory, recall and comprehend it. In addition, he found that the accused had the capacity to tell his version of events but it was unclear what questions he misinterpreted, what confused him, and at what point his responses to questions were compromised by impaired memory function and concrete thinking. This led Bampton J to make a finding of unfitness to stand trial.[50]

The potential for medication to assist the accused's capacity to function in the trial environment can be taken into account, but there are occasions where this may come at too high a cost. Thus Nyland J concluded in *R v Gillard*:[51]

I am satisfied that the large doses of medication required to control Gillard's schizophrenia add to his difficulty in concentration and ability to give instructions. It would also affect his ability to give rational evidence at his trial. Although a reduction in that medication would probably assist Gillard in being more alert at the trial, I accept [psychiatric] evidence that such a reduction would be likely to cause a relapse of the psychosis.

If the accused person's attention span is seriously impaired to the point where they cannot in substance follow the evidence, such as by reason of thought disorder or pre-occupation, this may go to whether they are unfit to stand trial.[52]

[46] [2002] QCA 464 [13]. [47] ibid. [48] [2017] SASC 182. [49] ibid [122].

[50] See I Freckelton, 'Subtle Effects of Intellectual Disability for Fitness to Stand Trial' (2018) 25 *Psychiatry, Psychology and Law* (in press).

[51] See n 44 [48].

[52] See *R v McKitterick* (2004) 36 SR (WA) 115 [24]; *R v Polanski* (n 43) [53].

The fact that the accused could perform better against some of the *Presser* considerations if he or she had greater intelligence, or received additional treatment, is not determinative. The critical question has been held to be whether the accused meets the minimum requirements for fitness.[53] In addition, the fact that an accused person has made surprising or counter-productive forensic decisions does not in itself render the person unfit to stand trial.[54] In addition, the fact that an accused person has declined to rely on the defence of mental impairment, which may be open on the evidence, does not mean that he or she is unfit to stand trial. A person may rationally reject such an option out of concern for the consequences of a finding of not guilty by reason of mental impairment.[55]

As in England[56] and Canada,[57] Australian courts have drawn a distinction between an accused person being highly abnormal, eccentric, delusional, psychotic, or having a mental disorder, on the one hand, and being unfit to stand trial on the other.[58] The courts have been alert to the potential for an accused person to manipulate the circumstances and to exaggerate or even fabricate psychotic symptomatology in order to avoid going to trial.[59] Similarly, it has been observed that a distinction should be drawn between the state of an accused person at the time of alleged commission of an offence and their state at the time of trial, the latter being the relevant issue for fitness to stand trial.[60] It has been noted too that ordinarily, given the consequences that flow from a finding of unfitness, it is in the interests of an accused person to be brought to trial.[61]

High Court Guidance

The Australian High Court has engaged with the issue of fitness to stand trial on a small number of occasions.

In *Sinclair v The Queen*[62] the High Court heard an appeal from a conviction of a man for murder committed when Sinclair was seventeen years of age. A jury found him fit to be tried eleven years after the murder, at a time when he had spent a period in a criminal lunatic asylum after being certified insane following his committal for trial. The appeal focused upon the admissibility of confessional evidence. However, Dixon J noted in the context of fitness for trial that the matters to be considered 'are whether the form of insanity of the prisoner arraigned allows him to comprehend the course of the proceedings so as to make a proper defence, to challenge any juror to whom he may wish to object and to comprehend the details of the evidence'.[63]

[53] *R v Rivkin* (n 33); *Clarkson v The Queen* [2007] NSWCCA 70.

[54] See, eg, *Heffernan v The Queen* (2005) 194 FLR 370; *Eastman v The Queen* (n 40); *Kesavarajah v The Queen* (n 12).

[55] *R v Bridge* [2005] NSWCCA 122.

[56] See *Berry* (1977) 66 Cr App R 156, 158.

[57] *R v Taylor* (n 41).

[58] See, eg, *Eastman v The Queen* (n 40) [27] per Gleeson CJ; *Kesavarajah v The Queen* (n 12) 249; *R v Khallouf* [1981] VR 360.

[59] See, eg, *Eastman v The Queen* (n 40).

[60] ibid [24] per Gaudron J; *R v Steurer* [2009] ACTSC 150 [28].

[61] *Eastman v The Queen* (n 40) [24] per Gleeson CJ.

[62] (1946) 73 CLR 316.

[63] ibid 334.

He commented that it did not seem to have been noticed by text writers how high a degree of intelligence the test might require if literally applied, but observed that:

> in none of the cases or treatises apparently is the matter discussed on the footing that a plea of guilty may be tendered by the prisoner whose sanity is in doubt. That he will undergo a trial is assumed. Probably this is because of the traditional practice of questioning such a plea when there is any doubt about it and taking measures to secure the substitution of the entry of a plea of not guilty.[64]

In *Ngatayi v The Queen*[65] the High Court heard an appeal from the Western Australian Supreme Court in relation to an Aboriginal man who had been found guilty of murder. At trial, his counsel had sought a jury empanelled to determine Ngatayi's fitness for trial on the basis that:

> ... he does not understand white men's law. In his law a man who kills is always guilty and there is no amelioration. He just cannot understand that in our law if a man is drunk and kills we have gradations of wilful murder, murder, manslaughter. This concept he cannot understand.

The trial judge declined to empanel a jury for such a purpose and the accused pleaded guilty. However, the trial judge declined to accept the plea and entered a plea of not guilty on his behalf. Ultimately, Ngatayi gave incoherent evidence and was found guilty. The High Court concluded that there was no reason to doubt that Ngatayi understood the nature of the proceedings of the evidence. It concluded that the fact that he could not understand the law under which he was tried did not mean that he was unable to make a proper defence with the assistance of counsel.

The Court reviewed prior English and Australian authority and commented on the observations of Dixon J in *Sinclair v The Queen* that:

> ... it cannot be thought that he was suggesting that the test should be literally applied. The test looks to the capacity of the accused to understand the proceedings, but complete understanding may require intelligence of quite a high order, particularly in cases where intricate legal questions arise. It is notorious that many crimes are committed by persons of low intelligence, but it has never been thought that a person can escape trial simply by showing that he is of low intelligence. We respectfully agree with the view expressed by Smith J in *R v Presser* (at 48) that the test needs to be applied 'in a reasonable and common sense fashion'.

In *Kesavarajah v The Queen*[66] the accused in a drug importation trial presented in a grandiose and irritable manner, maintaining that he was the reincarnation of Vishnu and that he could control the sun and the planets. He was described by a psychiatrist who examined him as having an elevated mood and being disorientated in time, place, and person, with impaired attention and concentration span and an inability to understand why he was in prison. However, another psychiatrist expressed the view that notwithstanding the accused man's grandiosity and cosmological and religiose delusions he was logical and rational thinking. He made the point that the accused's psychosis had the potential to flare up in such a way as to

[64] ibid. [65] See n 15. [66] See n 12.

render him unfit to be tried. The trial judge concluded that there was no serious issue to be tried in relation to the accused man's fitness to be tried, a proposition with which the accused at the time concurred. However, issues arose in the course of the trial in relation to the accused's mental state and Mason CJ, Toohey, and Gaudron JJ concluded that the trial judge had erred in failing to place the accused man's fitness to be tried before the jury:

> In the context of a trial, fitness to be tried is to be determined by reference to the factors mentioned by Smith J in *Presser* and by reference to the length of the trial. It makes no sense to determine the question of fitness to be tried by reference to the accused's condition immediately prior to the commencement of the trial without having regard to what the accused's condition will or is likely to be during the course of the trial. There is simply no point in embarking on a lengthy trial with all the expense and inconvenience to jurors that it may entail if it is to be interrupted by reason of some manifestation or exacerbation of a debilitating condition which can affect the accused's fitness to be tried.[67]

They also observed that when the accused's mental state deteriorated, it was still necessary that he be able to understand the nature of the charges and the proceedings, understand the substantial effect of the evidence, and follow the course of the rest of the proceedings:

> For example, it could not be said that the appellant was fit to be tried if he were unable to understand the nature of the jury's finding and the effect of a conviction. That could hardly be the case if the appellant believed, as the trial judge had been informed, that he could influence other people including the court proceedings.
>
> Notwithstanding that the trial was drawing to its close, the possibility remained that the appellant might be called upon to participate in the proceedings to protect his own interests. There was the taking of exceptions to the charge, the possibility that the jury might ask questions or make requests, e.g., for transcripts of tape-recordings, and the further possibility that the jury might not be able to reach a verdict with the consequence that the judge might be required to take some action after giving consideration to submissions from the parties.[68]

In *Eastman v The Queen*[69] the High Court dealt with an appeal from a public servant who had been found guilty by a jury of murdering an Assistant Commissioner of Australia's Federal Police. During the trial, his behaviour was very difficult. It was violent, abusive, and disruptive and incorporated phases where the accused appeared on his own behalf after terminating the services of his legal representatives. However, as Gleeson CJ observed, 'At the time when he was conducting his own defence he appeared to have a clear understanding of the issues in the case, the nature of the charge against him, and the nature of his answers to the charge.'[70] The view of the trial judge was that Eastman's behaviour was manipulative:

> As the trial progressed, the cogency of the Crown case became clear. Regrettably, however, from the outset of the trial the prisoner attempted to avoid the consequences of the damning nature of the Crown evidence by adopting a process of manipulating the trial process and attempting to frustrate its progression in any conventional manner. Despite the persistence

[67] ibid [35]. [68] ibid [37]–[38]. [69] See n 32. [70] ibid [30].

of this approach, the trial process nevertheless managed to overcome the obstacles presented and reached finality.[71]

Before the High Court the principal question was whether fresh expert evidence could be adduced about what was asserted on appeal (but had not been at trial, nor before the Court of Appeal) to be Eastman's unfitness. The court reaffirmed that before it is appropriate for a question as to unfitness to be referred to jury there must be a 'real and substantial question' as to the accused person's unfitness.[72]

Special Hearings

In all state and territory jurisdictions in Australia, save for Queensland and Western Australia,[73] there is legislative provision for 'special hearings' to be conducted[74] to determine whether the physical elements of criminal offences have been proved beyond reasonable doubt.[75] Thus, under s 15 of the Crimes (Mental Impairment and Unfitness to Stand Trial) Act 1997 (Vic) the purpose of a special hearing is stated to be to determine whether the accused (a) is not guilty of the offence; (b) is not guilty of the offence because of mental impairment; or (c) committed the offence charged or an offence available as an alternative.[76] It is orthodox for the accused to be taken to have pleaded not guilty. The rules of evidence apply and the trial is conducted as closely as possible to that of a criminal trial,[77] including with a formal arraignment of the accused.[78] In Victoria, it was held by majority that a judge-alone procedure is available for a special hearing.[79]

In *Subramaniam v The Queen*[80] the High Court held that the purpose of special hearings is:

> ... to see that justice is done, as best as it can be in the circumstances, to the accused person and the prosecution. She is put on trial so that a determination can be made of the case against her. The prosecution representing the community has an interest also in seeing that justice be done. A special hearing gives an accused person an opportunity of being found not guilty in

[71] ibid [32]. [72] ibid [46] per Gleeson CJ. See too *R v Khallouf* (n 65).

[73] However, see the recommendations for such a procedure in Law Reform Commission of Western Australia, *The Criminal Process and Persons Suffering from Mental Illness*, WALRC 69 (WALRC 1991) para 4.10.

[74] See Crimes Act 1900 (ACT) ss 315C–319A; Mental Health (Forensic Provisions) Act 1990 (NSW), s 19; Criminal Code (NT) pt IIA div 4; Criminal Law Consolidation Act 1935 (SA), ss 269M–269N; Criminal Justice (Mental Impairment) Act 1999 (Tas), s 15; Crimes (Mental Impairment and Unfitness to Be Tried) Act 1997 (Vic), Part 3.

[75] See *DPP v Khoury* [2014] NSWCA 15. Compare Criminal Procedure (Insanity) Act 1964 (UK), s 4A. See, however, s 20B of the Crimes Act 1914 (Cth), which provides that where a person's fitness to be tried is raised by the prosecution, the magistrate must refer to the proceedings to the court to which the proceedings would have been referred had the person been committed for trial, and where the person is found unfit to be tried, the court 'must determine whether there has been established a prima facie case that the person committed the offence'. See *Agoston v The Queen* [2008] NSWCCA 116.

[76] In relation to the defence of mental impairment in the ACT, compare *R v Steurer* (n 67) [28].

[77] See *EK v The Queen* [2010] NSWCCA 199 [38].

[78] *R v Zvonaric* [2001] NSWCCA 505 [38].

[79] *SM v The Queen* [2013] VSCA 342 [28]. [80] (2004) 79 ALJR 116 [40].

which event the charge will cease to hang over her head, and if she requires further treatment that it may be given to her outside the criminal justice system.

Similarly, in *McDonald v The Queen*[81] Redlich and Beale JJA held that:

There is always a public interest in having a formal determination of the guilt or innocence of a person in a special hearing. It serves to maintain public confidence in the administration of justice and ... provides an opportunity for the complainants to be vindicated regardless of the fact that an accused's mental state may be such that they could play no meaningful role in the proceeding.[82]

In R v Ardler[83] the Court of Appeal of the Australian Capital Territory reviewed English authority,[84] determined that when a special hearing is embarked upon the prosecution is required to prove beyond reasonable doubt the physical acts of the offence charged which would constitute an offence if done intentionally and voluntarily, and with any particular intent or knowledge specified as an element of the offence. However, it held that the prosecution is not required to negative lack of mental capacity to act intentionally or voluntarily or to have the specific knowledge or intention specified as an element of the offence unless there is objective evidence which raises such an issue, including mistake, accident, lack of any specific intent, or knowledge of the particularity necessary to constitute the offence that is an element of the offence or self-defence, in which case the prosecution must negative that issue beyond reasonable doubt.

It applied previous authority that there is no legal presumption that acts are done voluntarily and intentionally,[85] but concluded that in the absence of evidence to the contrary a jury (or a judge alone) is entitled to infer that the act engaged in by the accused was voluntary and intentional.[86] Its determination was that 'lack of intent, specific or general, arising from mental impairment, or, where relevant, diminished responsibility, falls outside the scope of acts "constituting the offence", the issue before the court in the Australian Capital Territory on a special hearing'.[87] It is likely that this approach will generally be followed by Australian courts.

Fitness to Stand Trial in Different Levels of Courts

In the Australian Capital Territory,[88] South Australia,[89] Tasmania,[90] and Western Australia[91] the legislative scheme that applies in relation to fitness to stand trial in the Supreme Court also applies in the lower courts. By contrast, in the

81 [2016] VSCA 304 [44]. 82 See too *Dupas v The Queen* (2010) 2141 CLR 237 [37].

83 [2004] ACTCA 4; (2004) 144 A Crim R 552; see too R *v Aleer* [2016] ACTSC 75.

84 In particular, *R v Antoine* [2001] AC 340; *Attorney-General's Reference (No 3 of 1998)* [2000] QB 401.

85 *Parker v The Queen* (1963) 111 CLR 610. 86 [2004] ACTCA 4 [83].

87 ibid [86]. 88 Crimes Act 1900 (ACT), Part 13 divs 13.1–13.2, 13.6.

89 Criminal Law Consolidation Act 1935 (SA), Part 8A.

90 Criminal Justice (Mental Impairment) Act 1999 (Tas), s 4(1), Part 2.

91 Criminal Law (Mentally Impaired Accused) Act 1996 (WA), Part 3.

fitness-to-stand-trial regimes in the Northern Territory[92] and Queensland[93] and in New South Wales and Victoria there is no provision for a finding of unfitness to stand trial in the Magistrates' Court.

Consequences of Findings of Unfitness

Major changes were implemented in many parts of Australia out of recognition of the unfairness of detention at the Governor's pleasure of persons found unfit to stand trial.[94] The modern era of Australian reform in the area commenced with a report in 1995 by the Parliamentary Community Development Committee in Victoria.[95]

Currently, in New South Wales,[96] the Northern Territory,[97] Tasmania,[98] and Victoria[99] a sentencing court must decide between whether a person should be made subject to a custodial or non-custodial supervision order in the community after a finding in a special hearing. However, detention after a finding of unfitness is until released by an order of the Governor in Western Australia,[100] while in Queensland[101] the discretionary power to release is that of the Mental Health Tribunal, and in Tasmania[102] the decision is that of the Supreme Court, although the Mental Health Tribunal reviews custodial orders annually.

In New South Wales and South Australia, when a court makes a custodial order after a finding of unfitness and a special hearing, a court must set a limiting term. That is 'the best estimate of the sentence the Court would have considered appropriate if the special hearing had been a normal trial of criminal proceedings against a person who was to be tried for that offence and the person had been found guilty of that offence'.[103] When the limiting term expires, the person who has been detained ceases to be a 'forensic patient' and is able to leave the facility where they have been detained unless an application is made for an extension of the term.[104]

[92] Criminal Code (NT), s 43L. [93] Mental Health Act 2000 (Qld), s 256.

[94] See A Freiberg, ' "Out of Mind, Out of Sight": The Disposition of Mentally Disordered Persons Involved in Criminal Proceedings' (1976) 3(2) Monash University Law Review 134.

[95] See Parliament of Victoria, Community Development Committee, *Review of Legislation under which Persons are Detained at the Governor's Pleasure in Victoria* (VGPS 1995); see also S Delaney, 'Controlling the Governor's Pleasure—Some Gain, Some Pain' (1998) Law Institute Journal 46; J Lightfoot, 'Striking the Balance— Abolition of the Governor's Pleasure System' (1998) 5(2) Psychiatry, Psychology and Law 265; B McSherry, 'Criminal Detention of Those with Mental Impairment' (1999) 6 Journal of Law and Medicine 216; *Re LN* [2000] VSC 159.

[96] Mental Health (Forensic Provisions) Act 1990 (NSW), s 23(2).

[97] Criminal Code (NT), s 43ZA(1).

[98] Criminal Justice (Mental Impairment) Act 1999 (Tas), s 18(2).

[99] Crimes (Mental Impairment and Unfitness to be Tried) Act 1997 (Vic), s 26(2).

[100] Criminal Law (Mentally Impaired Accused) Act 1996 (WA), s 24(1).

[101] Mental Health Act 2000 (Qld), s 203(1).

[102] Criminal Justice (Mental Impairment) Act 1999 (Tas), ss 24, 26.

[103] Mental Health (Forensic Provisions) Act 1990 (NSW) s 23(1)(b); Criminal Law Consolidation Act 1935 (SA) s 269O(2).

[104] See, eg, Mental Health (Forensic Provisions) Act 1990 (NSW), Sch 1.

In the Northern Territory[105] and Victoria,[106] at the time that a custodial supervision order is set, a court must order a person to be reviewed (in a 'major review') at the expiration of the 'nominal term'. In Victoria, the nominal term is prescribed by statute (twenty-five years for murder and the maximum term of imprisonment for other offences[107]), while in the Northern Territory a court must fix a term that is 'equivalent to the period of imprisonment or supervision (or aggregate period of imprisonment and supervision) that would, in the court's opinion, have been the appropriate sentence to impose on the supervised person if he or she had been found guilty of the offence charged'.[108]

Another approach is taken by the Commonwealth and the Australian Capital Territory. Under s 20BC of the Crimes Act 1914 (Cth), if a court determines that a person is unfit to be tried and will not become fit to be tried within twelve months, it can order that the person be detained in a hospital (if treatment is available, and the person agrees to be transferred to a hospital) or other place (including a prison). However, the person can only be detained for a specified period 'not exceeding the maximum period of imprisonment that could have been imposed if the person had been convicted of the offence charged'.[109] In the Australian Capital Territory, if the court makes a custodial order and would have imposed imprisonment if the hearing were a normal criminal hearing, it must indicate a sentence that would have been appropriate, and the person cannot be detained for longer than this term.[110]

An extensive and somewhat inaccessible jurisprudence[111] has evolved in relation to release of persons by courts after they have been found unfit to stand trial or not guilty by reason of mental impairment.[112] The essential question is whether they pose a serious risk to themselves or others, if downgraded in supervisory status from custodial to non-custodial or if their supervisory status is relinquished or revoked by the courts. It has been held that such an evaluation is a discretionary one,[113] which makes an appeal against such a judgment as to risk difficult.[114] It requires an assessment of the potential for endangerment—both its seriousness and the likelihood of a risk materialising.[115]

The better view is that no onus of proof applies and that a common-sense approach to evidence applies.[116] A step-by-step process has often been employed by courts in order to test out the extent to which a person has responded to pharmacotherapy,

[105] Criminal Code (NT), s 43ZG(6).

[106] Crimes (Mental Impairment and Unfitness to be Tried) Act 1997 (Vic), s 35.

[107] Crimes (Mental Impairment and Unfitness to be Tried) Act 1997 (Vic), s 28(1).

[108] Criminal Code (NT), s 43ZG(2).

[109] Crimes Act 1914 (Cth), s 20BC(2).

[110] Mental Health Act 2015 (ACT), s 183.

[111] Many of the decisions are marked 'not to be reported'.

[112] See I Freckelton, 'Involuntary Detention of Persons Found Not Guilty of Murder by Reason of Mental Impairment or Found Unfit to Stand Trial: A New Jurisprudence from Victoria' in K Diesfeld and I Freckelton (eds), *Involuntary Detention and Therapeutic Jurisprudence: International Perspectives on Civil Commitment* (Ashgate 2003).

[113] *RDM v DPP* [1999] 2 VR 270.

[114] See *NOM v DPP* [2012] VSCA 198 [44]–[45], [48].

[115] See *In the Matters of Major Reviews of Percy, Farrell and RJO* (1998) VSC 70.

[116] See *NOM v DPP* (n 114) [84].

acquired insight into their mental illness, and the need to take medication for it, shown a capacity to abstain from abuse of alcohol or drugs, and been able to reintegrate into the community without conflict or preoccupations of the kind that contributed to their previous offending. Often a relatively longitudinal evaluation is possible as persons found either unfit to stand trial or not guilty by reason of mental impairment are retained in either custodial or non-custodial supervision for extended periods of time. Such evaluations are highly influenced by the expert evidence of the clinicians with responsibility for their in-patient or out-patient forensic care. It is a question of evaluating the degree of risk because such risk can never be eliminated.[117] As Winneke P observed in *RDM v DPP*:

> a decision made by a judge . . . not to release a mentally impaired person unconditionally from supervision seems to me to be a decision made in the exercise of a discretion of a discretely different character. The function which the court is to perform is essentially an inquisitorial or administrative one in which it is not bound by defined rules or practices but may inform itself in any manner it thinks fit. . . . The court is required by the statute, amongst other things, to balance the competing interests of the detainee and the public and, in doing so, to assess risk factors which, in turn, depend upon value judgments in respect of which reasonable minds might differ. In that sense, it seems to me to be a discretionary exercise which does not lend itself as readily to review as the exercise of a sentencing discretion.[118]

However, the exercise of such discretion is not readily amenable to appellate review.

Controversies

A number of Australian cases have become notorious in recent years in terms of showing injustice in the system for responding to indigenous persons' unfitness to stand trial. The Rosie Anne Fulton and Marlon Noble cases are particularly illustrative.

The Rosie Anne Fulton case

Rosie Anne Fulton was an indigenous woman held in a Kalgoorlie prison for twenty-one months after being charged in 2012 with property crimes related to a motor vehicle. She was found unfit to stand trial due to her level of cognitive impairment, which arose from fetal alcohol spectrum disorder, and was held in a prison because of the absence of any other suitable environment:[119] there were no relevant female-specific facilities or services and the secure facility for people with an intellectual disability and challenging behaviours was unsuitable because the other detainees were male and there were safety risks.[120] Lateline 'broke' her

[117] See *Re SKD* [2009] VSC 363; *NOM v DPP* (n 121). [118] [1999] VSCA 86 [64].

[119] See L Steele, 'Disabling Forensic Mental Health Detention: The Carcerality of the Disabled Body' (2016) 19(3) Punishment and Society 327; [2016] UTSLRS 31.

[120] See 'Disabled Aboriginal Woman Rosie Fulton Arrested again Days after being Freed from WA Jail' (8 July 2014) *ABC News*, available at: http://www.abc.net.au/news/2014-07-08/nt-woman-at-centre-of-petition-rosie-fulton-assaults-three-poli/5580400.

story[121] after a decision by her public guardian to make her circumstances public (in consultation with her) after an extended period of endeavouring to negotiate her release from indefinite detention and to secure her access to disability support services. The Aboriginal Disability Justice Campaign, at the time, maintained that there were at least thirty Aboriginal people in Fulton's situation Australia-wide.

The Marlon Noble case

Marlon Noble was a nineteen-year-old indigenous man charged in 2001 with sexual assault offences against a child. These were never proven because he was found unfit to stand trial and made subject to a custody order with responsibility for oversight over his circumstances shifting to the Mentally Impaired Accused Review Board, which determined that he should be detained in custody at the correctional centre of Greenough Regional Prison. He remained there until 2012, although he was permitted overnight stays outside the prison subject to supervision. In 2010 a report from a forensic psychologist determined that Noble was competent to stand trial, subject to his receiving assistance during it. However, the Western Australian Director of Public Prosecutions determined not to proceed with any further prosecution on the basis of the passage of time and the limited prospects of securing a conviction because of the low quality of the evidence available. He spent over ten years in prison before being released.

Noble made a communication to the United Nations Committee on the Rights of Persons with Disabilities ('the Committee'),[122] arguing that the Criminal Law (Mentally Impaired Defendants) Act 1996 (WA) ('the MID Act') was a discriminatory status-based law in violation of Art 5 of the Convention on the Rights of Persons with Disabilities ('the Convention'); that he had been deprived of his entitlement to exercise his legal capacity and enter a plea of not guilty and test the evidence against him in violation of Arts 12(3) and 13(1) of the Convention; that he had been deprived of his liberty on the basis of his disability in violation of Art 14 of the Convention; and that whilst he was detained in prison he was at significant risk of harm from other prisoners and that by virtue of the conditions imposed upon him which imposed unjustifiable restrictions on his liberty in violation of Arts 14 and 15.

The Committee found that throughout Noble's detention he was not given any possibility to plead not guilty and test the evidence submitted against him, and that the government had not provided Noble with the support or accommodation he required to exercise his legal capacity: 'As a result of the application of the MID Act, the author's rights to a fair trial were instead fully suspended, depriving him of

[121] See F McGaughey et al, 'UN Decision on Marlon Noble Case: Imprisonment of an Aboriginal Man with Intellectual Disability Found Unfit to Stand Trial in Western Australia' (2017) 42(1) *Alternative Law Journal* 67: 67–70; J Stewart, 'Jailed without Conviction' (12 March 2004) *Lateline*, available at: http://www.abc.net.au/lateline/content/2014/s3962171.htm.

[122] See Freckelton and Keyzer, 'Fitness to Stand Trial and Disability Discrimination' (n 7).

the protection and equal benefit of the law.'[123] This meant that the MID Act had resulted in discriminatory treatment of Noble in violation of Art 5(1) and (2) of the Convention.

In addition, the Committee concluded that Noble was unfit to plead because of his intellectual and mental disability, which resulted in a denial of his right to exercise his legal capacity to plead not guilty and test the evidence presented against him. It found that:

> No adequate form of support was provided by State party's authorities to enable him to stand trial and plead non-guilty, despite of his clear intention to do so. He therefore never had the opportunity to have his criminal charges against him determined, and his status as an alleged sexual offender potentially cleared. The Committee considers that while States parties have a certain margin of appreciation to determine the procedural arrangements to enable persons with disabilities to exercise their legal capacity. This did not happen in the author's case, as he had no possibility and was not provided with adequate support or accommodation to exercise his rights to access to justice and fair trial.[124]

This meant that Noble's rights under Arts 12(2)–(3) and 13(1) of the Convention had been violated.

The Committee found that Noble's detention was decided on the basis of the assessment by the government of potential consequences of his intellectual disability in the absence of any criminal conviction, thereby converting his disability into the 'core cause of his detention'. This led the Committee to conclude that Noble's detention amounted to a violation of Art 14(1)(b) of the Convention, according to which 'the existence of a disability shall in no case justify a deprivation of liberty'.[125] It also found that as the conditions subject to which Noble was released were determined upon as a direct consequence of his detention, they too were in violation of Art 14(1)(b) of the Convention.[126]

In respect of Noble's contention that his Art 15 rights had been violated by reason of the conditions of his detention, the Committee emphasised the vulnerability of persons with a disability in the penal system and stated that:

> State party authorities must pay special attention to the particular needs and possible vulnerability of the person concerned.... In the present case, the Committee notes the author's allegations that he was subject to frequent incidents of violence and abuse, that his disability prevented him from protecting himself against such acts, and that State party authorities did not take any measure to sanction and prevent them, or to protect the author therefrom.'[127] Taking into account the fact that Noble's detention was indefinite, and in fact extended for a period in excess of 10 years, and the 'irreparable psychological effects that such indefinite detention can have on the detained person', the Committee concluded that the detention to which Noble was subject amounted to inhuman and degrading treatment in breach of article 15 of the Convention.

[123] *Noble v Australia*, Decision by the United Nations Committee on the Rights of Persons with Disabilities, 2 September 2016, 8.4.
[124] ibid 8.6. [125] ibid 8.7. [126] ibid 8.8. [127] ibid 8.9.

The Committee made a series of recommendations to the state party, Australia:

(a) Concerning Mr Noble: the state party is under an obligation:
   (i) To provide him with an effective remedy, including reimbursement of any legal costs incurred by him, together with compensation.
   (ii) To revoke immediately the 10 conditions of Mr Noble's release Order replacing them with all necessary support measures for his inclusion in the community.
   (iii) To publish the Committee's Views and circulate them widely in accessible formats so that they are available to all sectors of the population.

(b) General measures: the State party is under an obligation to take measures to prevent similar violations in the future. In this regard, the Committee refers to its recommendations as contained in paragraph 32 of its concluding observations and requires the State party:
   (i) To adopt the necessary amendments of the MID Act (WA), and all equivalent or related Federal and state legislations, in close consultation with persons with disabilities and their representative organizations, ensuring its compliance with the principles of the Convention and the Committee's Guidelines on article 14 of the Convention on the Rights of Persons with Disabilities;
   (ii) To ensure that adequate support and accommodation measures are provided to persons with mental and intellectual disability to enable them to exercise their legal capacity before the courts whenever necessary;
   (iii) To ensure that appropriate and regular training on the scope of the Convention and its Optional Protocol, including on the exercise of legal capacity by persons with intellectual and mental disabilities, is provided to staff of the Review Board, members of the Law Reform Commission and the Parliament, judicial officers and staff involved in facilitating the work of the judiciary.

The Committee also required the State party to submit a written response to the Committee within six months including information as to any action taken in the light of the Views and Recommendations of the Committee. The Commonwealth complied with this obligation,[128] but did not accept in any respect that the Committee's decision had merit. The Western Australian government reviewed the legislation that applied to Noble and made no recommendations for reform in respect of the introduction of a fixed-term custody order or the implementation of a special hearing system.[129]

Law Reform

A number of high-profile recent law reform reports have dealt with the way in which the Australian criminal justice system deals with persons who are unfit to stand trial.

[128] https://www.ag.gov.au/RightsAndProtections/HumanRights/Documents/Noble-v-Australia-Australian-Government-Response.PDF. For a summary of the response, see Freckelton and Keyzer, 'Fitness to Stand Trial and Disability Discrimination' (n 7).

[129] http://www.parliament.wa.gov.au/publications/tabledpapers.nsf/displaypaper/3914071ad16451df7e0990bf48257f8e000e532a/$file/4071.pdf.

The NSWLRC Report

In 2013 the New South Wales Law Reform Commission (NSWLRC) published its report on *People with Cognitive and Mental Health Impairments in the Criminal Justice System: Criminal Responsibility and Consequences*.[130] It recommended that the standards for determining fitness to be updated and incorporated into statute[131] and that the legal system go as far as possible to provide a fair trial or to establish whether the person committed the acts constituting the criminal offence with which they had been charged.

The NSWLRC proposed that those found unfit but likely to resume fitness within twelve months be referred to the Mental Health Review Tribunal (MHRT) for up to twelve months so that the MHRT could review their fitness periodically. If the MHRT found the person to have become fit, the presumption of fitness should be restored and the trial process could continue but if they remained unfit, the Commission proposed the person be referred to the relevant court for a special hearing. It recommended that in respect of persons found unfit and not acquitted at a special hearing (and those found not guilty by reason of mental imprisonment), a court should first determine if they would have been sentenced to imprisonment if found guilty at a normal trial.[132] If they would have been imprisoned, it proposed a court be obliged to nominate a 'limiting term', this being the best estimate of the sentence that would have been imposed at a normal trial, taking into account the person's cognitive or mental situation, which may mean that they cannot demonstrate the mitigating or discounting factor available to other defendants. At the end of the limiting term, it proposed that persons cease to be forensic patients. It recommended that the initial determination about the detention and treatment of forensic patients be made by the MHRT, with the court only making an interim order pending MHRT review, which should occur within two months of referral.

The NSWLRC recommended reform to the law so that the MHRT could only make an order for leave or release if satisfied that the person's release would not pose a significant risk of serious physical or psychological harm to others.[133] It proposed that the MHRT be permitted to order leave or release in the rare circumstances where the forensic patient posed a risk of harm solely to themselves, not to others, with them being managed in the civil mental health system or the guardianship system. It recommended that the principle of least restriction be regarded as relevant to decisions about persons found unfit to stand trial, with the MHRT being obliged to provide the least restrictive environment possible to protect against serious harm to the forensic patient or to others.[134]

[130] Report No 138, available at: http://www.lawreform.justice.nsw.gov.au/Documents/Publications/Reports/Report-138.pdf.

[131] Recommendation 2.1.

[132] Recommendation 7.2.

[133] Recommendation 8.1.

[134] Recommendation 8.3.

The VLRC Report

In a 2014 report into Victoria's mental impairment and unfitness-to-be-tried legislation the Victorian Law Reform Commission (VLRC) observed:

> An accused person with a mental illness, for example, may have no trouble having a factual or an intellectual understanding of their right to challenge a juror, but their delusional beliefs may hinder them from making decisions to exercise that right (or having a 'decision-making capacity'). On the other hand, an accused person with a cognitive impairment or intellectual disability may have more trouble than an accused person with a mental illness to understand this right. This raises the question of whether the current criteria are suitable for people with a mental illness and whether the threshold for unfitness to stand trial is currently set at the right level for these people.[135]

In its consultative process, the VLRC asked, among other things, whether the test for unfitness to stand trial should include a consideration of a defendant's decision-making capacity, effective participation in the trial, or capacity to be rational. It recommended that:

- the legal tests for unfitness to stand trial and the defence of mental impairment be revised, including adding a definition of mental impairment to the law;
- the application of the law be extended to the Magistrates' Court and Children's Court;[136]
- the role of juries in determining the defence of mental impairment be extended and the complexity in the content of jury directions under the law be reduced;
- how community interests are represented in court hearings be improved;
- the decision-making framework for review, leave, and release of people subject to indefinite supervision orders be strengthened;
- a new youth forensic facility for treating and supervising young people and a new medium-secure forensic mental health hospital be established; and
- equal treatment of people with an intellectual disability or other cognitive impairment under the supervision regime be assured.

In terms of the test for unfitness, the VLRC's proposal was that a person be accounted unfit to be tried if

> because the person's mental processes are disordered or impaired, the person is or, at some time during the hearing, will be:
>
> (a) unable to understand the nature of the charge
> (b) unable to understand the actual significance of entering a plea to the charge
> (c) unable to enter a plea to the charge

[135] http://www.lawreform.vic.gov.au/sites/default/files/Review_of_the_Crimes_Mental_Impairment_and_Unfitness_to_be_Tried_Act_0.pdf.
[136] See *CL (a minor) v Lee* [2010] VSC 517.

(d) unable to understand the nature of the hearing (that it is an inquiry as to whether the person committed the offence)
(e) unable to follow the course of the hearing
(f) unable to understand the substantial effect of any evidence that may be given in support of the prosecution
(g) unable to decide whether to give evidence in support of his or her case
(h) unable to give evidence in support of his or her case, if he or she wishes to do so, or
(i) unable to communicate meaningful instructions to his or her legal practitioner.[137]

It also proposed that the government establish an expert advisory group to determine:

(a) who should conduct assessments of unfitness to stand trial
(b) whether the group of people identified under paragraph (a) should be registered or accredited by a professional body, and if so, the requirements for registration or accreditation
(c) whether guidelines should be developed or experts should undergo training on applying the test for unfitness to stand trial, and if so, the content of the guidelines or training
(d) whether assessments should be standardised to a greater extent and the extent to which these should be standardised
(e) whether legislative or other requirements should be introduced to require the application of the process in relation to assessments of unfitness, and
(f) how to promote better communication techniques in the conduct of assessments.[138]

The VLRC proposed the introduction of a new system of five-year 'progress reviews' to replace the nominal term system to ensure that the review of orders and duration of supervision are more explicitly linked to the actual decrease or increase in the risk posed by the person and any improvements or decline in the person's progress or recovery. It regarded such an approach to be consistent with the principle of least restriction, the point at which a person's supervision should be reduced can be monitored and identified more accurately, and protects against arbitrary detention.

The VLRC proposals were translated to the Crimes (Mental Impairment and Unfitness to be Tried) Amendment Bill 2016 (Vic). Amongst other things, it slightly reformulated the unfitness test (cl 8) and replaced the 'serious endangerment' test with respect to decisions made under the Crimes (Mental Impairment (Vic) and Unfitness to be Tried) Act 1997 with an 'unacceptable risk' test (cl 3B). For a court or decision maker to find there is an unacceptable risk of a person causing harm, there must be 'sufficient likelihood' of the person doing so when all relevant factors, including the nature and seriousness of the harm, are considered. The Bill enables it to be possible to find an unacceptable risk of a person causing harm 'even if the likelihood of the person doing so is less than the likelihood of more likely than not'.

It also requires decision-makers to consider, where relevant:

- the restrictions on a person's freedom and personal autonomy;
- the impact on all stakeholders, including the victim, the accused, and their respective families;
- the safety of the community;

[137] ibid, Recommendation 15. [138] ibid, Recommendation 23.

- the rights of the accused; and
- the potential for unreasonable delays.

The Bill removes from juries the decision as to whether a person is fit to stand trial and transfers the functions of the Forensic Leave Panel (whose task it is to determine whether persons on custodial supervision orders are given leave) to the Mental Health Tribunal (cl 105) and institutes a system of five yearly 'progress reviews' for persons found unfit to stand trial. It also creates procedures for children to be found unfit to stand trial (cl 52).

The ALRC Equality, Capacity, and Disability Report

In 2014 the Australian Law Reform Commission (ALRC) published its report on *Equality, Capacity and Disability in Commonwealth Laws*.[139] It argued that the current (*Presser*) legal test for unfitness to stand trial needed to be reformed to avoid unfairness and maintain the integrity of criminal trials 'while ensuring that people with disability are entitled to equal recognition before the law, and to participate fully in legal processes'.[140]

The ALRC Incarceration Rates Discussion Paper

In July 2017, the Australian Law Reform Commission published its Discussion Paper on Incarceration Rates of Aboriginal and Torres Strait Islander Peoples.[141] It focused upon the use of 'limiting terms' and noted that it had been informed that in jurisdictions without limiting terms:

> … fitness to stand trial may not be raised because an accused person may end up held in indefinite detention without trial. In these circumstances, the ALRC has been advised that the accused person may instead enter a plea of guilty or stand trial in order to receive a fixed term of imprisonment with a release date.

This means that some people—particularly Aboriginal and Torres Strait Islander peoples—with cognitive impairments or mental health issues, who may not have the capacity to understand the consequences of a guilty plea or court processes, are entering the criminal justice system, instead of the forensic mental health system, and are not receiving the required treatment or care. This may affect the likelihood of recidivism and runs counter to legal principles that underpin fair trials and access to justice.[142]

[139] Report 124, available at: https://www.alrc.gov.au/sites/default/files/pdfs/publications/alrc_124_whole_pdf_file.pdf.

[140] ibid 7.13.

[141] DP 84, available at: https://www.alrc.gov.au/sites/default/files/pdfs/publications/discussion_paper_84_compressed_cover2.pdf.

[142] ibid 11.52–11.54.

Conclusion

There is significant lack of uniformity amongst Australian jurisdictions in relation to the statutory provisions relating to fitness to stand trial. Most importantly, there is a deficit in terms of the facility for a special trial for persons found unfit to stand trial in Western Australia and in Queensland. This deficit in Western Australia was the subject of controversial castigation by the United Nations Committee on the Rights of Persons with Disabilities in relation to Marlon Noble, as discussed above. The federal and Western Australian jurisdictions have not been responsive to this criticism. There is also variation in the provisions for care of persons found unfit to stand trial and for review of their suitability for release. This impacts upon the uptake of the option for use of the plea of unfitness to stand trial and has been the subject of criticism on human rights grounds.[143] It is likely that the 2016 Victorian Bill (which as of February 2018 had yet to pass Parliament) will constitute a model for a further, nuanced generation of law reform in relation to Australian fitness-to-stand-trial legislation.

[143] See Law Society of Western Australian Briefing Paper: Mentally Impaired Accused (December 2016), available at: https://www.lawsocietywa.asn.au/wp-content/uploads/2015/10/Law-Society-Briefing-Papers-Mentally-Impaired-Accused.pdf; P Gooding et al, 'Unfitness to Stand Trial and the Indefinite Detention of Persons with Cognitive Disabilities in Australia: Human Rights Challenges and Proposals for Change' (2017) 40 Melbourne University Law Review 816.

9

Fitness for Criminal Adjudication

The Emerging Significance of Decisional Competence in the United States

*Richard J Bonnie**

The practice of assessing and adjudicating fitness to plead (or competence to stand trial as it is often called in the United States) developed largely without assistance from the US Supreme Court or other appellate courts for most of the nineteenth and twentieth centuries. However, the need for appellate guidance became evident in the 1980s, especially regarding the significance of mental or emotional conditions that can impair capacity for rational decision making. In the early 1990s, the author called attention to these emerging issues and pointed the way towards possible solutions. During the past twenty-five years, several governing principles have come into view, but important issues remain unresolved. After a brief review of the historical and conceptual foundations of the competence requirement, the chapter summarizes the current state of the law in the United States, focusing on two recent decisions by the United States Supreme Court, and offers suggestions for future development.

Brief History of the Competence Requirement in the United States

At least since the fourteenth century, common-law courts have declined to proceed against criminal defendants who are "unfit" or "incompetent" to be brought before the court for adjudication.[1] The evolution of common-law doctrine is apparent in the court's description of the elements of "fitness to stand trial" in *R v Pritchard*[2] in 1836, a famous case involving a defendant who was deaf and dumb:

> First, whether the prisoner is mute of malice or not; secondly, whether he can plead to the indictment or not; thirdly, whether he is of sufficient intellect to comprehend the

[1] Don Grubin, *Fitness to Plead in England and Wales* (Psychology Press 1996) 9.
[2] (1836) 7 C & P 303.

Fitness to Plead: International and Comparative Perspectives. First Edition. Edited by Ronnie Mackay and Warren Brookbanks. Chapter 9 © Richard J Bonnie 2018. Published 2018 by Oxford University Press.

course of proceedings on the trial, so as to make a proper defense—to know that he might challenge [jurors] to whom he may object—and to comprehend the details of the evidence.... It is not enough that he may have a general capacity of communicating in ordinary matters.[3]

Although the medieval interest in whether a defendant remained "mute by malice" no longer has any legal importance, the two other key components of the *Pritchard* formulation (ability to understand the proceedings and to interact with the court in a meaningful way) have continuing significance in applying the "incompetency plea." These two ideas are reflected in the "test" for competence to stand trial enunciated by the US Supreme Court for use by the federal courts in *Dusky v United States*[4] in 1960: "*whether the defendant has sufficient present ability to consult with his lawyer with a reasonable degree of rational understanding—and whether he has a rational as well as factual understanding of the proceedings against him.*"[5] It is worth noting that by the time *Dusky* was decided, it was generally recognized that indigent criminal defendants charged with felonies were entitled to representation by counsel, a right later extended to misdemeanors under most circumstances.[6] This fundamental change in the adversary system explains the shift of emphasis from communication with the court to communication with counsel.

Fifteen years after *Dusky*, in *Drope v Missouri*[7] the Supreme Court[8] held that the incompetence doctrine was "so fundamental to an adversary system of justice," that conviction of an incompetent defendant, or failure to adhere to procedures designed to assess a defendant's competence when doubt has been raised, violates the due process clause of the federal Constitution.[9] According to *Drope*: "It has long been accepted that a person whose mental condition is such that he lacks the capacity to understand the nature and object of the proceedings against him, to consult with counsel, and to assist in preparing his defense may not be subjected to a trial." And, it should be added, such a defendant is not competent to enter a plea of guilty in lieu of a trial.[10] The essential point is that incompetence bars adjudication, whether by plea or trial, and this includes any pre-trial proceedings that may be adverse to the defendant's interests. For the sake of brevity, the term "adjudicative competence" will be used to refer to this requirement.[11]

[3] ibid. [4] 362 US 402 (1960). [5] ibid.

[6] *Powell v Alabama* 287 US 45 (1932); *Gideon v Wainwright* 372 US 335 (1963); *Argersinger v Hamlin*; 407 US 25 (1972).

[7] 420 US 162 (1975).

[8] Elsewhere in the chapter, "the Court" or "the Supreme Court," when capitalized, refers to the United States Supreme Court.

[9] Unless otherwise specified, "the Constitution" refers to the United States Constitution. References to state constitutions are specifically noted and not capitalized.

[10] *Godinez v Moran* 509 US 389, 398 (1993).

[11] Vocabulary bearing on fitness for adjudication varies not only among English-speaking nations, but also within the United States. (In)competence and (in)capacity tend to be used interchangeably in both legal and scientific discourse. In this chapter, "capacity" is generally used to refer to specific legally relevant abilities (eg, capacity to understand the proceedings), while "competence" is used to refer to the legal and/or moral judgment that the defendant is or is not "fit" to proceed.

The concept of adjudicative competence thus far described conveys a fairly passive view of the defendant's role in contemporary criminal proceedings. A prosecution cannot proceed unless the defendant understands his jeopardy and is able to consult with and advise the lawyer who is representing him. In the picture that emerges, the defendant responds, consults, and assists, but the active adversaries in the litigation are the prosecutor and the defense attorney. This may be an accurate picture of many—if not most—criminal proceedings, but it is an incomplete picture of the *rights* accorded to the defendant under the constitution, and of the values embedded in the requirement of adjudicative competence. Under the US system of criminal justice, a criminal defendant may decline representation by counsel and represent himself, even in a full-fledged criminal trial presenting the most extreme legal jeopardy. In *Faretta v California*,[12] the Supreme Court ruled that the Sixth Amendment to the Constitution, which assures the right to assistance of counsel, also confers a right to decline assistance of counsel and to represent oneself.

Very few defendants choose to represent themselves under *Faretta*, but important questions sometimes arise regarding the allocation of authority between the client and the attorney representing him or her. Clearly, the law accords the defendant personal control over some aspects of the case, even when represented by counsel. The most important of these is whether to plead guilty instead of proceeding to trial. In the US criminal justice system, when more than ninety per cent of cases are resolved by negotiated pleas, the decision whether to plead guilty to one or more charges is highly consequential. Other decisions that must be made personally by the defendant are whether to be tried before a jury, or to testify if the case goes to trial. The basis for these rules is self-evident—each entails a waiver of a basic constitutional right: the right to a trial by jury;[13] the right not incriminate oneself;[14] and the right not to be convicted unless the state proves one's guilt beyond a reasonable doubt.[15] The scope of a represented defendant's authority to direct or control the defense of the case is unclear and will be discussed later in this chapter.[16] For present purposes, however, it is enough to point out that disputes sometimes arise between clients and counsel about key decisions in the case (I refer to these disagreements as "autonomy fights") and that many of them also raise questions about whether the defendant has the mental capacity to make the requisite decision (assuming that the responsibility for making the decision lies with the defendant in the first place). Over the past thirty years, a large proportion of the appellate litigation in the United States bearing on adjudicative competence relates to the resolution of disputes between criminal defendants and their attorneys over control of the defense.

[12] 422 US 806 (1975). It is noteworthy that three Justices dissented.

[13] *Duncan v Louisiana* 391 US 145 (1988).

[14] *Palko v Connecticut* 302 US 319 (1937).

[15] *In re Winship* 397 US 358 (1970).

[16] See generally Erica Hashimoto, "Resurrecting Autonomy: The Criminal Defendant's Right to Control the Case" (2010) 90 Boston College L Rev 1147; Richard Uviller, "Calling the Shots: The Allocation of Choice between the Accused and Counsel in the Defense of a Criminal Case" (2000) 52 Rutgers L Rev 719.

Values Served by the Competence Requirement

When viewed from a contemporary perspective, the requirement of adjudicative competence in criminal proceedings serves three conceptually independent social purposes: preserving the dignity or integrity of the criminal process; reducing the risk of erroneous convictions; and respecting the defendant's decision-making autonomy. The *dignity* of the criminal process is undermined if the defendant lacks a basic moral understanding of the nature and purpose of the proceedings against him or her. The *accuracy* or reliability of the adjudication is threatened if the defendant is unable to assist in the development and presentation of a defense. Finally, to the extent that decisions about the course of adjudication must be made personally, by the defendant, he or she must have the abilities needed to exercise decision-making *autonomy*.

Dignity

A person who lacks a rudimentary understanding of the nature and purpose of the proceedings against her is a not a "fit" subject for criminal prosecution and punishment. To proceed against such a person offends the moral dignity of the process because it treats the defendant not as an accountable person, but as an object of the state's effort to carry out its promises. Only cases involving defendants who lack a meaningful moral understanding of wrongdoing and punishment, or the nature of the jeopardy to which they are exposed in a criminal prosecution, implicate the dignity rationale. These cases implicate not only the legal interest of the defendant in avoiding unfair or unjust punishment but also—and perhaps even more importantly—the independent interest of the society in the moral integrity of the criminal process. To make the point plainly, suppose a defendant, while competent, signs a witnessed document authorizing the state to try him and, if warranted by the evidence, to convict him, even if he were to become unaware of the nature of the proceeding due to unconsciousness or delusion. This advance directive would not be honored. Pronouncing an unconscious or insane defendant "guilty" offends human dignity and the integrity of the judicial process, even if the evidence leaves no doubt about his guilt.[17] Similarly, a court should not allow a deluded defendant, proceeding *pro se*, to question a witness about the defendant's own behavior at the crime scene while referring to himself in the third person.[18]

[17] Lists of purposes served by the incompetence doctrine typically include the need to preserve the decorum of the courtroom and the dignity of the trial process. See, eg, "Incompetency to Stand Trial" (1967) 81 Harvard L Rev 454. However, courtroom decorum is not, standing alone, a viable rationale for a bar against adjudication. If necessary, a disruptive defendant can be removed from the courtroom and an otherwise competent defendant can waive her right to be present. Moreover, judges should be very tolerant of "disturbing" behavior in the courtroom during plea proceedings and bench trials.

[18] In a 1995 trial for killing six people on a Long Island Railroad train, a demonstrably delusional Colin Ferguson was allowed to represent himself. See Bruce Arrigo and Mark Bardwell, "Law, Psychology and Competency to Stand Trial: Problems with and Implications of High-Profile Cases"

Accuracy

Beyond the minimal demands of the dignity rationale, the bar against adverse adjudication in cases involving incompetent defendants serves as a critically important prophylactic protection against erroneous convictions. Just as the assistance of competent counsel is regarded as a prerequisite to reliable adjudication, so too is the participation of a competent defendant. As stated by Henry Weihofen in 1954,[19] a mentally impaired defendant might be unfairly convicted if he "alone has knowledge" of certain facts but does "not appreciate the value of such facts, or the propriety of communicating them to his counsel."[20] To proceed against a defendant who lacks the capacity to recognize and communicate relevant information to his attorney and to the court would be fundamentally unfair to the defendant and would undermine society's independent interest in the reliability of its criminal process. This basic intuition provides the basis for the Supreme Court's statement in *Drope v Missouri* that the bar against trying the incompetent defendant "is fundamental to an adversary system of justice."[21]

Autonomy

A third feature of the competence construct, conceptually independent of the two aspects thus far mentioned, derives from legal rules that establish that the defendant must make or have the prerogative to make certain decisions regarding the defense or disposition of the case. As mentioned above, a construct of "decisional competence" is an inherent, though derivative, feature of any legal doctrine that prescribes a norm of client autonomy. In theory, one could imagine a system of criminal adjudication that leaves no room for client self-determination—one that bars self-representation,

(2002) 11 Criminal Justice and Policy Review 15; Richard J Bonnie, "Ferguson Spectacle Demeaned System" (March 13, 1995) National L J A23–A24.

[19] Henry Weihofen, *Mental Disorder as a Criminal Defence* (Dennis & Co 1954) 429–30.

[20] William Blackstone, *Commentaries* 4 Bl Comm 24. In his *Commentaries*, William Blackstone described the rationale for the incompetence plea as follows:

> [I]f a man in his sound memory commits a capital offence, and, before arraignment for it, he becomes mad, he ought not to be arraigned for it, because he is not able to plead to it with that advice and caution that he ought. And if, after he had pleaded, the prisoner becomes mad, he shall not be tried; for how can he make his defense? If, after he be tried and found guilty, he loses his senses before judgment, judgment shall not be pronounced; and if, after judgment, he becomes of non-sane memory, execution shall be stayed. . . .

[21] *Drope v Missouri* (n 7) 171–72: "It has long been accepted that a person whose mental condition is such that he lacks the capacity to understand the nature and object of the proceedings against him, to consult with counsel, and to assist in preparing his defence may not be subjected to a trial." Social scientists should note that courts use reliability in constitutional adjudication as a synonym for "validity" or accuracy of outcome. The system's commitment to a fair "balance" in the adversary system underlies the right to counsel, the protections of the fifth Amendment, and the principle of proof beyond a reasonable doubt. As a practical matter, the functional meaning of competence must be operationalized in the context of the attorney–client relationship. Thus, to the extent that the meaning of incompetence derives from its instrumental function, it refers to the capacity to provide whatever assistance counsel requires in order to explore and present an adequate defense, as the idea has evolved in progressive understanding of fairness.

does not permit guilty pleas, and commits all decisions regarding defense of the case to counsel rather than to the defendant.[22] Under these legal arrangements, a defendant's decisional competence would not be relevant. But this does not describe our system.

Our law commits some decisions regarding the defense or disposition of the case to the defendant and not to the attorney. According to all authorities, these decisions include whether to plead guilty or not guilty; if the case is to be tried, whether it should be tried before a jury; whether the defendant attends the proceedings in person or remotely; and whether the defendant testifies.[23] For some of these decisions (ie, those involving waivers of constitutional rights), the obligation imposed on courts to conduct a formal colloquy with the defendant to ensure that the defendant's decision has been made knowingly, intelligently, and voluntarily made reinforces the principle of self-determination.[24] Not surprisingly, judicial scrutiny is likely to be most intensive when the defendant decides to represent himself.[25]

There is a considerable realm of uncertainty regarding allocation of authority between attorney and client in criminal defense. Ethical canons often declare that the lawyer shall abide by a client's decisions concerning the "objectives" of representation, while the lawyer controls decisions about the "means by which they are to be pursued, including technical or tactical issues such as whether to call or cross-examine a particular witness.[26] But some issues are not easy to classify: what about the basic theory of defense (eg, whether to contest the state's prima facie case or raise a claim of justification or excuse)? Or what about issues with a highly personal valence, such as whether or not to ask the defendant's mother to testify? The greater the sphere of client autonomy, the greater the likelihood that autonomy fights will arise and that the defendant's decisional competence will be called into question.

[22] *Faretta v California* (n 12), holding that a defendant is constitutionally entitled to waive assistance of counsel and to represent himself, makes such a system constitutionally implausible, but it is noteworthy that three Justices dissented.

[23] See, eg, *Rock v Arkansas*, 483 US 44, 52–53 (1987) (regarding whether to testify); *Brookhart v Janis*, 384 US 1, 7–8 (1966) (regarding whether to plead guilty); *Adams v United States ex rel McCann*, 317 US 269, 275 (1942) (regarding waiver of jury trial). See generally American Bar Association, *ABA Standards for Criminal Justice: Prosecution and Defense Function*, s 4-5.2(a) (4th edn, American Bar Association 2015); American Bar Association, *Model Rules of Professional Conduct*, Rule 1.2 (a) (American Bar Association 2017).

[24] See *Boykin v Alabama*, 395 US 238, 242 (1969); *Johnson v Zerbst*, 304 US 458, 464–65 (1938).

[25] See, eg, *United States v Mooney*, 123 F Supp 2d 442 (ND Ill 2000) and *People v Welch*, 976 P 2d 754 (Cal 1999).

[26] Regarding " 'objectives' versus 'means' of representation," see American Bar Association, *Model Rules of Professional Conduct* (n 23), Rule 1.2(a). American Bar Association, ABA *Standards of Criminal Justice* (n 23), s 4-5.2(c) state that "strategic or tactical decisions should be made by defense counsel after consultation with the client where feasible and appropriate." These decisions "include how to pursue plea negotiations, how to craft and respond to motions and, at hearing or trial, what witnesses to call, whether and how to conduct cross-examination, what jurors to accept or strike, what motions and objections should be made, what stipulations if any to agree to, and what and how evidence should be introduced."

Components of Adjudicative Competence

"Keeping in mind these three rationales for barring criminal adjudication in cases involving 'incompetent' defendants, and drawing on the language of *Dusky v United States* and other appellate decisions that interpret and apply *Dusky*, it is possible to specify the competence-related abilities required for adjudicative competence. In my view, it is helpful to conceptualize adjudicative competence as encompassing two related but separable components: 'competence to assist counsel' and decisional competence."[27]

Competence to assist counsel

The first component is a foundational requirement, relating generally to understanding one's legal jeopardy, and becomes legally relevant from the moment a person is criminally accused. I use the phrase because the traditional label for the competence requirement (competence to stand trial) diverts attention from the *pre-trial* interactions with counsel and the court that implicate most directly the fairness of the process and the reliability of its outcome. This observation also highlights another key feature of the competence requirement—it is a highly contextualized inquiry under which the clinical–legal judgment about whether the defendant is competent depends on the demands of the particular case.[28] In general, the "foundational" requirement of competence to assist counsel entails capacities (a) to understand the charges and the basic elements of the adversary system (understanding); (b) to appreciate one's situation as a defendant in a criminal prosecution (appreciation); and (c) to relate pertinent information to counsel concerning the facts of the case (reasoning). These three psycho-legal abilities, taken together, operationalize *Dusky*'s stated requirements that the defendant must have a "rational as well as factual understanding of the proceedings" and that he or she be able "to consult with counsel with a reasonable degree of rational understanding."[29] The competence-to-assist-counsel component of adjudicative competence, summarized in this way, serves the dignity and accuracy rationales mentioned above, and the law clearly precludes any adjudication adverse to a defendant who lacks the abilities required to assist in his or her own defense.

[27] See Richard J Bonnie, "The Competence of Criminal Defendants: Beyond *Dusky* and *Drope*" (1993) 47 U of Miami L Rev 540; and Richard J Bonnie, "The Competence of Criminal Defendants: A Theoretical Reformulation" (1992) 10 Behavioral Science and the L 291.

[28] I have referred to this foundational construct as "competence to assist counsel" in order to emphasize that the ability to interact rationally with counsel in presenting a defense is the determinative functional consideration in pre-trial competence determinations and to distinguish it conceptually from the defendant's role in decision making. However, no consensus has emerged among commentators or courts regarding a phrase to denote the aspects of "competence" or fitness that do not relate to decision making. The ABA Task Force that recently revised the *ABA Standards on Mental Health and Criminal Justice*, on which I served, concluded that the phrase "competence to proceed" (at any stage of the proceedings) is a more useful phrase for denoting this foundational requirement.

[29] *Dusky v United States* (n 4).

Decisional competence

In most cases, questions about "competence to assist counsel" arise at the outset of the process, before significant interactions with counsel have occurred and before strategic decisions regarding defense of the case have been encountered or considered. However, in other cases, questions about the defendant's competence are not formally raised until late in the process when doubts are raised, typically by the defense attorney, regarding whether the defendant is competent to make specific decisions regarding defense of the case that are encountered as the process of criminal adjudication has unfolded. These cases implicate the second component of adjudicative competence, which I have labeled "decisional competence."

Decision making involves cognitive tasks in addition to those required for assisting counsel, but the abilities required to establish decisional competence have not yet been definitively established. The Supreme Court's formulation of the competence requirement in *Dusky* does not mention decision making, and courts often seem uncertain about how to apply the *Dusky* formula to cases in which the defendant's capacity to make particular decisions is being questioned, often by defense counsel (eg, refusing to plead insanity, pleading guilty, choosing to testify). In a series of articles in the 1990s, I suggested that decisional competence had not received adequate theoretical attention and sought to initiate a scholarly conversation about the concept and the possible criteria for decisional competence in the context of criminal adjudication, drawing on the then-developing literature of competence to make medical decisions. I do not intend to rehearse my full argument here, but three claims are pertinent to the narrative line of this chapter. First, the core value served by the requirement of decisional competence is assuring that the defendant has the capacities necessary to make rational, self-interested decisions on those matters that the law places within the prerogative of the defendant, rather than counsel. Secondly, questions about decisional competence are not likely to be brought to judicial attention unless an "autonomy fight" has developed between the defendant and counsel, or unless the attorney has profound doubts about the defendant's capacity to understand the nature and consequences of decisions that the defendant is expected to make, especially waivers of constitutional rights.[30] This implies that specific evaluation of the defendant's competence to make a particular decision is likely to be required late in the case.

[30] Attorneys are not likely to seek clinical or judicial assistance in resolving the "autonomy fight" unless the stakes are high and the attorney disagrees with the defendant's decision and has doubts about his or her decisional competence. This empirical observation underlies my view, spelled out in RJ Bonnie "The Competence of Criminal Defendants beyond *Dusky* and *Drope*" (1993) 47 Miami L R 577–82, that if the de facto standard of decisional competence is elevated in such cases a "closer look" is needed than if it were a routine decision or if the attorney is vouching for the defendant's competence rather than contesting it. Some have questioned this claim, but I stand by it both on ethical grounds and as a prediction of judicial outcomes.

One test of competence or multiple tests?

In light of these theoretical and practical differences between competence to assist counsel under the *Dusky* formulation (factual and rational understanding of the proceedings) and decisional competence, it might be sensible to regard them as legally separate constructs rather than as two component parts of a single highly contextualized legal test of adjudicative competence. That is the view I propounded in 1993, thinking it would facilitate greater conceptual clarity and clinical precision. The issue, as I saw it then, is that the capacities needed for decision making might differ in important respects, at least in some cases, from those needed to assist counsel and a higher level of capacity might be needed, normatively speaking, for one type of decision than for others. Indeed, state and federal appellate courts were divided in the 1980s over whether certain decisions—such as pleas of guilty or waiver of counsel—required a "higher" level of decisional capacity than the level implicitly embedded in the *Dusky* standard, assuming that *Dusky* required decisional capacity at all.[31] Although they used different phrases, most state and federal decisions embraced the view that, unlike guilty pleas, waivers of counsel *do* require a higher level of competence.[32]

However, in a 1993 decision, *Godinez v Moran*,[33] the Supreme Court explicitly held that decisional competence (capacity to make rational decisions) is encompassed *within* the *Dusky* test (specifically, capacities to understand and make rational decisions regarding waivers of constitutional rights) and that *Dusky* states the applicable test of competence in all cases, even if the defendant wants to waive counsel and plead guilty.

Although the Court did not articulate which abilities are required for decisional competence under *Dusky*, the most plausible extrapolation of the *Dusky* standard to cover decision making entails the following abilities: (a) capacity to understand information relevant to the specific decision at issue (understanding); (b) capacity to appreciate the significance of the decision as applied to one's own situation (appreciation); (c) capacity to think rationally (logically) about the alternative courses of action (reasoning); and (d) capacity to express a choice among alternatives (choice). Taken together, these four criteria operationalize the "capacity for rational decision-making" implied by the *Dusky* formula (see Table 9.1 below).

Notwithstanding the Supreme Court's decision in *Godinez v Moran*, many questions remain about decisional competence and the legal sufficiency of the *Dusky* test. First, the *Godinez* decision stated clearly that the *Dusky* test sets a constitutional *floor*, and that states are free to adopt more a demanding standard of competence for making

[31] Compare *Sieling v Eyman*, 478 F.2d 211 (9th Cir 1973) with *Allard v Hellgemoe*, 572 F.2d 1 (1st Cir 1978). The cases are summarized in *Godinez v Moran* (n 10).

[32] In 1993, I endorsed the view that, while guilty pleas should not ordinarily require a higher level of decisional capacity, waiver of counsel should not be permitted if the defendant's decision is substantially affected by psychopathological factors. Under this approach, the higher standard would also have to be met if the defendant sought to make a decision over counsel's objection (such as refusing to plead insanity or refusing to introduce mitigating evidence in a capital case).

[33] *Godinez v Moran* (n 10).

Table 9.1 Translation of *Dusky* Language after *Godinez v Moran*

Competence-related ability	**Original *Dusky* language**[1] **(Competence to proceed and assist counsel)**	**Implications of *Godinez v Moran*[2] (Decision making)**
Understanding	"Factual understanding of proceedings"	Capacity to understand nature and consequences of a specific decision [within defendant's prerogative]
Appreciation	"Rational understanding of proceedings"	Rational understanding (appreciation) of the nature and consequences of a specific decision
Reasoning	Capacity to "consult with lawyer with reasonable degree of rational understanding" [logically]	Capacity to reason logically about required decisions [and ability to make a choice]

1. Refers explicitly to competence to proceed or assist counsel (the foundational component of adjudicative competence) in the Bonnie/MacArthur Network vocabulary.
2. Refers to decisional competence in the Bonnie/McArthur Network vocabulary.

certain decisions, especially waiver of counsel. Secondly, *Godinez* did not, by its terms, apply to a case where a defendant seeks to exercise his right under *Faretta* to represent himself at trial. Indeed, the Court subsequently ruled, in *Edwards v Indiana* (2008), that a defendant who is competent under *Dusky* and *Godinez* to waive his right to counsel may nonetheless be found incompetent to represent himself at trial. In those cases, at least, the competence standard *is* more demanding than the test set forth in *Dusky*. Finally, *Godinez* by its own terms does not address other decisions that lie within the defendant's sphere of control, such as deciding whether to plead insanity[34] or introduce mitigating evidence in a capital case.[35] As the law continues to develop, I expect an increasing number of state courts to rule that the *Dusky* test is not sufficient for a finding of decisional competence when the defendant chooses to waive counsel, represent himself at trial, or otherwise to nullify counsel's fundamental strategic decisions about defense of the case. The recently promulgated *Criminal Justice Mental Health Standards* of the American Bar Association reflect this general point of view.[36]

Unresolved issues regarding decisional competence

The fundamental question at issue in both *Godinez* and *Edwards* was whether the Constitution embodies a unitary standard (the *Dusky* formula) for being "competent" for all aspects of criminal adjudication. This represents the nub of the disagreement between the majority and dissenting opinions in both cases. The Court said "yes" in *Godinez* and "no" in *Edwards*. In my opinion, the Court was wrong in

[34] See *Treece v Maryland*, 547 A 2d 1054 (Md 1988).
[35] Richard J Bonnie, "Dignity of the Condemned" (1988) 74 Virginia L Rev 1363.
[36] American Bar Association, *Criminal Justice Standards on Mental Health* (American Bar Association 2016) Standard 7-5.2. See below in section "The 2016 American Bar Association Standards."

Godinez and right in *Edwards*. In *Godinez*, the Court should have ruled that competence to decide to waive counsel is subject to a "higher" or more demanding standard than the standard set forth in *Dusky*. Admittedly, the two decisions can be reconciled because the higher standard set forth in *Edwards* applies when a defendant decides to represent himself at a contested trial, while *Godinez* applies when a defendant waives counsel in order to plead guilty. However, the current law is unstable and I think it is likely that *Edwards* will have a spillover effect by empowering counsel in cases involving autonomy fights with decisionally impaired clients by taking away the client's option of self-representation.

Godinez v Moran

The Supreme Court's decision in *Godinez* merits detailed analysis. This section describes the context in which the case arose, analyzes the Court's ruling and the dissenting opinion, and highlights the issues that remain unresolved. As noted above, before the Court decided *Godinez,* federal circuit courts were divided on what I regard as an easy issue—the standard for competence to plead guilty. Some circuits, including the federal courts of appeal for the Ninth and DC Circuits, had ruled that the standard for competence to plead guilty was "higher than" the *Dusky* standard, and that the defendant had to have the capacity not only to understand the nature and consequences of the plea, but also to make a "reasoned choice" about whether or not to enter it. As I had written in several articles beginning in 1990,[37] requiring capacity to make a reasoned choice, taking into account the advantages and disadvantages of each option in light of the probabilities of conviction at trial would be too demanding a standard—it would be out of alignment with the fairly thin constitutional requirements for a valid plea, and it would tend to deny the advantages of plea bargaining to defendants with intellectual deficits. In my opinion, the test for pleading guilty should be essentially the same as the *Dusky* standard, as adapted for application to a decision-making context—rational understanding of the nature and consequences of the plea—but the Ninth Circuit ruled otherwise in *Godinez.* And that's why the Supreme Court agreed to hear the state's appeal in *Godinez*—it took the case for the purpose of reversing the Ninth Circuit's ruling that the standard for competence to plead guilty was "higher than" or different from the standard for competence to stand trial.

The problem, however, is that *Godinez* was not a simple guilty plea case: It involved a *defendant* (Richard Moran) *who had waived his right to counsel in order to plead guilty 4.5 months after his arrest for capital homicide and had announced that he had no intention of introducing mitigating evidence at his sentencing proceeding.* He had attempted suicide, was highly remorseful and depressed, and wanted to die. In my view, the right answer in this case was for the Court to extend the *Dusky*

[37] Richard J Bonnie, "The Competence of Criminal Defendants with Mental Retardation to Participate in their Own Defense" (1990) 81 J Crim L and Criminology 419; Bonnie, "The Competence of Criminal Defendants: A Theoretical Reformulation" (n 27); Bonnie, "The Competence of Criminal Defendants: Beyond *Dusky* and *Drope*" (n 27).

standard (rational understanding of the nature and consequences of the plea) to ordinary guilty pleas while applying a distinct and specific requirement of decisional competence when the defendant has waived counsel (and, I would suggest, in other contexts where a defendant seeks to make highly consequential decisions, especially against the advice of counsel).

Facts and context

Richard Moran had been charged with three counts of capital murder in Nevada for killing two people in a bar on August 2, 1984 and for shooting his former wife in a separate incident seven days later. Immediately after shooting his wife, Moran attempted suicide by shooting himself in the abdomen and slashing his wrists. While in the hospital recovering from his wounds, he summoned the police and confessed to all three homicides. Soon after discharge from the hospital, he was referred for forensic assessment of his competence to stand trial, and two examining psychiatrists interviewed him separately on September 12 and September 17. Each psychiatrist concluded that Moran understood the charges and was able to assist his attorney. Taking note of his depression and remorse, however, one of the psychiatrists observed that "Moran may not make the effort necessary to assist counsel in his own defense." The other psychiatrist also found Moran to be "in full control of his faculties insofar as his ability to aid counsel, assist in his own defense, recall evidence and to give testimony if called upon to do so." However, he, too, expressed reservations, observing: "Psychologically, and perhaps legally speaking, [Moran], because he is expressing and feeling considerable remorse and guilt, may be inclined to exert less effort towards his own defense."

In November 1984, just three months after his suicide attempt, Moran appeared in court seeking to discharge his public defender, waive his right to counsel, and plead guilty to all three charges of capital murder. The trial judge accepted Moran's waiver of counsel and his guilty pleas after posing a series of routine questions regarding his understanding of his legal rights and the offenses, to which Moran gave largely monosyllabic answers. In a string of affirmative responses, Moran acknowledged that he knew the import of waiving his constitutional rights, that he understood the charges against him, and that he was, in fact, guilty of those charges. The trial judge concluded that he was competent to stand trial and that he voluntarily and intelligently had waived his right to counsel. Accordingly, Moran was allowed to plead guilty and appear without counsel at his sentencing hearing. Moran presented no defense, called no witness, and offered no mitigating evidence on his own behalf. Not surprisingly, he was sentenced to death.

Wholesale capitulation by remorseful capital defendants is not unusual.[38] Such defendants typically insist on pleading guilty against counsel's advice and instruct counsel to refrain from introducing any evidence in mitigation, or like Richard Moran, they discharge their attorneys and plead guilty while unrepresented. These

[38] Bonnie, "Dignity of the Condemned" (n 35).

defendants also frequently request sentences of death. This behavior presents puzzling and controversial questions regarding the ethical and legal obligations of defense attorneys and trial judges.[39]

Capital defendants who have failed to defend themselves or seek leniency at trial and who have received death sentences often regret their behavior thereafter. They then file appeals or *habeas* petitions seeking to nullify the convictions and death sentences they had so ardently sought. The possibility of strategic behavior in such cases cannot be altogether ruled out, but the most likely explanation is that medication, counseling, and the passage of time have alleviated the prisoners' acute distress and that they eventually come to prefer life, even with suffering and guilt, to death. Moran filed his state *habeas* petition in July of 1987. Among other claims, he alleged that he had not been competent to waive counsel, or to enter valid guilty pleas in November of 1984 and that, in any event, the trial court had not undertaken a constitutionally adequate inquiry regarding his competence to do so.

Lower court ruling and critique

After an evidentiary hearing, the state *habeas* court concluded that Moran had been competent to waive counsel and to enter his guilty pleas, relying exclusively on the reports of the two psychiatrists who had found Moran competent to stand trial in September of 1984. The Nevada Supreme Court affirmed, and Moran then filed his federal *habeas* petition. After relief was denied in the federal district court, the Ninth Circuit reversed, ruling that the state *habeas* court's finding that Moran had been competent at the time of his plea was not binding because both the examiners and the judge had applied an incorrect legal standard of competence. The legal standard used to determine a defendant's competency to stand trial is different from the standard used to determine competency to waive constitutional rights. A defendant is competent to waive counsel or plead guilty only if he has the capacity for "reasoned choice" among the alternatives available to him. By contrast, a defendant is competent to stand trial if he merely has a rational and factual understanding of the proceedings and is capable of assisting his counsel. Competency to waive constitutional rights requires a higher level of mental functioning than that required to stand trial. The court went on to examine the record and concluded that it could not "support a finding that Moran was mentally capable of the reasoned choice required for a valid waiver of constitutional rights" at the time of his guilty pleas. The state of Nevada asked the Supreme Court to review the case and the Supreme Court agreed to do so in late 1992.

I was not pleased when the Supreme Court chose to review the Ninth Circuit's decision in *Godinez*. It seemed clear to me, as noted above, that the Court had agreed to review the case for the purpose of reversing the Ninth Circuit's decision. As a scholar who had become interested in adjudicative competence only recently (in 1989), I was convinced that the topic was ripe for theoretical exploration as well as

[39] ibid.

empirical investigation, but I also realized that the few decisions in the lower courts on decisional competence had not positioned the case well for Supreme Court review. The MacArthur Foundation Research Network on Mental Health and the Law—on which I was serving—had just begun an ambitious empirical research program aiming to ascertain how competence inquiries were conducted in practice and to develop a structured instrument for assessing and measuring competence-related abilities, including decisional capacity. For the Supreme Court to wade into this area was unfortunately premature.

When the Court decided to hear the case, my exploratory manuscript highlighting the importance of decisional competence was still in press. In that article, however, I critiqued the Ninth Circuit's decision in *Moran v Godinez* and pointed the way toward what I still regard as the proper resolution of that case:

> On the facts of this case, the Ninth Circuit's analysis is sound. First, even if Moran was competent to assist counsel (in both September and November), this finding does not suffice to establish that he was competent to waive counsel and plead guilty in November. The latter finding pertains to Moran's decisional competence, a distinct issue. Second, in this context—when a capital defendant waives counsel and enters a guilty plea without (or against) counsel's advice—the criteria for decisional competence must be especially demanding. "Capacity for reasoned choice among alternatives" provides a sensible formulation of the competence standard in this context.
>
> On the first point, the Supreme Court should explicitly endorse the proposition that "competence" in criminal defense is not a unitary construct. The *Dusky/Drope* test does not encompass the abilities required for competent decision making, and it would be unwise to reformulate the *Dusky/Drope* test so that decision-making abilities are encompassed within a single competence formula. Any criterion of decisional competence used in the unitary test would be too demanding in some contexts and not demanding enough in others....
>
> Efficiency and finality provide the only possible advantages of a unitary test. Yet even these advantages will not likely result because sequential assessment and repeated judicial inquiries would be required under even a unitary test. An analysis of the facts of *Moran* illustrates the need for sequential assessment. At the time that the doctors evaluated Moran, he and his lawyer had not yet had extensive interactions, and it would have been premature and speculative for these examiners to address Moran's possible competence to waive counsel, to plead guilty, or to make any other decision that might be anticipated. The initial evaluation, which was properly focused on competence to assist counsel, could not have definitively resolved any doubts that might—and in fact did—subsequently arise regarding Moran's competence to make particular decisions regarding his defense or the disposition of the case. This is why decisional competence must be sequentially evaluated, regardless of how the standard is defined. In sum, little would be gained, and much would be lost, by a ruling that "competence" is a single construct, encompassing abilities required to make decisions and waive constitutional rights, as well as the foundational abilities required to assist counsel.
>
> Assuming that decisional competence and competence to assist counsel are understood as separate constructs, the further question is whether the criteria for competence to waive counsel and plead guilty (without or against counsel's advice) should be as demanding as the Ninth Circuit has required. If the Supreme Court addresses this question at all, it need only decide that the "reasoned choice" formula applies to the following situations: (a) waiver of counsel and a decision to represent oneself at trial under *Faretta*; (b) waiver of counsel and a decision to enter a guilty plea without advice of counsel; and (c) entry of a guilty plea against

advice of counsel. In these situations, the obligations of the trial court and counsel can be clearly stated. Moreover, incompetence does not bar adjudication because default rules are available—if the defendant is not competent to waive counsel, counsel can be provided; if defendant's competence to make a "reasoned choice" to plead guilty without or against counsel's advice is doubted, the case can be tried.[40]

The manuscript of this article was quoted in Moran's brief and formally submitted to the Court in support of affirmance.[41] The approach taken in the article was also embraced in *amicus* briefs filed by the American Psychiatric Association and the American Civil Liberties Union.[42]

Supreme Court ruling

Only two Justices (Justices Blackmun and Stevens) agreed with this analysis. Instead, the majority, in an opinion by Justice Thomas, declared that:

Requiring that a criminal defendant be competent has a modest aim: It seeks to ensure that he has the capacity to understand the proceedings and to assist counsel. While psychiatrists and scholars may find it useful to classify the various kinds and degrees of competence, and while states are free to adopt competency standards that are more elaborate than the *Dusky* formulation, the due process clause does not impose these additional requirements.[43]

Godinez held that *Dusky* establishes the standard for assessing competence to plead guilty, waive counsel, or waive other constitutional rights. So, if a defendant (like Moran) has been found to meet the *Dusky* standard, he has already been found to have the requisite competence to waive constitutional rights. To the extent that the argument in this case was that the standard for competence to waive constitutional rights should be "higher" than the *Dusky* standard, the Court said it could see no difference between the requirement of "rational understanding" in *Dusky* and the "reasoned choice" standard articulated by the Ninth Circuit. And even if there is a difference, the Court said, it could see no persuasive reasons why the standard for these decisions should be higher than for other decisions involving exercising or waiving constitutional rights that criminal defendants are expected to make in the course of a criminal trial (emphasis added):

[E]ven assuming that there is some meaningful distinction between the capacity for "reasoned choice" and a "rational understanding" of the proceedings, we reject the notion that competence to plead guilty or to waive the right to counsel must be measured by a standard that is higher than (or even different from) the *Dusky* standard.

We begin with the guilty plea. A defendant who stands trial is likely to be presented with choices that entail relinquishment of the same rights that are relinquished by a defendant

[40] A 1992 article sketching my conceptual approach to adjudicative competence, but not discussing Moran, was also before the Court and was referenced by Justice Blackmun's opinion. Bonnie, "The Competence of Criminal Defendants: A Theoretical Reformulation" (n 27).

[41] Moran brief, on file with author. [42] Briefs on file with author.

[43] Justices Kennedy and Scalia were even more emphatic in a separate concurring opinion: "The due process clause does not mandate different standards of competence at various stages of or for different decisions made during criminal proceedings" (*Godinez v. Moran* (n 10)).

who pleads guilty: He will ordinarily have to decide whether to waive his "privilege against compulsory self-incrimination," by taking the witness stand; if the option is available, he may have to decide whether to waive his "right to trial by jury," and, in consultation with counsel, he may have to decide whether to waive his "right to confront [his] accusers," by declining to cross-examine witnesses for the prosecution. A defendant who pleads not guilty, moreover, faces still other strategic choices: In consultation with his attorney, he may be called upon to decide, among other things, whether (and how) to put on a defense and whether to raise one or more affirmative defenses. *In sum, all criminal defendants—not merely those who plead guilty—may be required to make important decisions once criminal proceedings have been initiated.* And while the decision to plead guilty is undeniably a profound one, it is no more complicated than the sum total of decisions that a defendant may be called upon to make during the course of a trial. (The decision to plead guilty is also made over a shorter period of time, without the distraction and burden of a trial.) This being so, we can conceive of no basis for demanding a higher level of competence for those defendants who choose to plead guilty. If the *Dusky* standard is adequate for defendants who plead not guilty, it is necessarily adequate for those who plead guilty.

This strikes me as the crucial part of the *Godinez* opinion: It seems to say that "rational understanding" of the decisions that a defendant may be called on to make is a *Dusky* requirement. In this respect, the Court declared in *Godinez* that *decisional competence is already part of the Dusky formula.*

The Court's reasoning is sound and, in retrospect, I have accordingly retreated from the position that decisional competence should be regarded as an altogether independent construct rather than being folded into the *Dusky* formula. I say this primarily because encompassing decisional competence within the *Dusky* formula improves routine forensic practice and thereby furthers the values protected by the competence requirement: It has invited forensic researchers to operationalize the relevant capacities and develop instruments for measuring it, and has become an accepted component of clinical guidelines for forensic assessment.[44] It has also highlighted the longitudinal dimension of competence assessment, thereby increasing the likelihood that decisional competence is specifically addressed when it has been become clinically pertinent in a particular case.

That said, folding decisional competence into the *Dusky* formula will not satisfy the demands of due process in all situations. In some cases, a heightened standard of decisional competence is required. As explained above, one of these situations is when a mentally disturbed defendant waives assistance of counsel and seeks to represent himself and plead guilty. On this aspect of Richard Moran's case, the Supreme Court reached the wrong decision, in my view: Immediately following the excerpt quoted above regarding common decision-making tasks in criminal cases, including guilty pleas by defendants represented by counsel, Justice Thomas stated:

Nor do we think that a defendant who waives his right to the assistance of counsel must be more competent than a defendant who does not, since there is no reason to believe that the decision to waive counsel requires an appreciably higher level of mental functioning than the

[44] "The MacArthur Adjudicative Competence Study", MacArthur Research Network on Mental Health and the L, available at: http://www.macarthur.virginia.edu/adjudicate.html.

decision to waive other constitutional rights. Respondent suggests that a higher competency standard is necessary because a defendant who represents himself "must have greater powers of comprehension, judgment, and reason than would be necessary to stand trial with the aid of an attorney." But this argument has a flawed premise; the competence that is required of a defendant seeking to waive his right to counsel is the competence to *waive the right*, not the competence to represent himself.... Thus, while "[i]t is undeniable that in most criminal prosecutions defendants could better defend with counsel's guidance than by their own unskilled efforts," a criminal defendant's ability to represent himself has no bearing upon his competence to *choose* self-representation.[45]

Conceptually, this is a very important passage. Justice Thomas is correct in saying that the key question in Moran's case was whether he was *competent to choose self-representation*, a decision that was inextricably bound up with his decisions to plead guilty and seek a death sentence. In answering that question, was it sufficient to find that he had the capacity to understand the legal significance and consequences of his decisions, and that he in fact understood them—ie, that his waiver of his rights was "knowing and intelligent?"[46] If so, folding "competence to understand and waive his rights" into the *Dusky* formula would be an efficient and sensible approach—as long as the defendant's understanding is specifically evaluated at the time within reasonable proximity to the entry of the plea and waiver. However, the Court's reasoning rests on a mistaken premise: Mere understanding is *not* sufficient to establish decisional competence in this context or, indeed, under *Dusky* itself. Altogether missing from the Court's analysis is any mention of Moran's *reasons or motivations for the decisions* he is making and whether they are affected by mental illness. In relation to the *Dusky* language, are his decisions grounded in "rational thinking"? Where, if at all, does the Court's analysis of competence and waiver take into account claims that the defendant's reasons or motivations for the decision to waive the right were grounded in mental illness? Of what legal significance is proof that a defendant lacked a *rational* understanding of the consequence of his plea (hypothetically due, for example, to a delusional belief that he would be reunited with his

[45] *Godinez v Moran* (n 10).

[46] The court properly emphasizes that the validity of the waiver of constitutional rights is an independent inquiry—ie, separate from the competence inquiry:

> 'A finding that a defendant is competent to stand trial, however, is not all that is necessary before he may be permitted to plead guilty or waive his right to counsel. In addition to determining that a defendant who seeks to plead guilty or waive counsel is competent, a trial court must satisfy itself that the waiver of his constitutional rights is knowing and voluntary. In this sense there *is* a 'heightened' standard for pleading guilty and for waiving the right to counsel, but it is not a heightened standard of *competence*. ... [W]hen a defendant seeks to waive his right to counsel, a determination that he is competent to stand trial is not enough; the waiver must also be intelligent and voluntary before it can be accepted.

As discussed in the text, the waiver inquiry is important because it focuses on the defendant's actual understanding of the nature and consequences of his decisions, but it does not address the reasons for his decisions except insofar as those reasons suggest such coercion or other external influence that should render the waiver involuntary. However, reasons or motivations grounded in mental illness do not negate the voluntariness of the waiver. See generally, *Colorado v. Connelly*, 479 US 157 (1986). They must be considered, if at all, in connection with the 'competence' inquiry—which, under *Godinez* is governed by the *Dusky* test.

deceased mother after serving his time) or that his spiraling depression precluded rational consideration of alternative courses of action?

The evidence in Richard Moran's case suggests that his decisions were driven by profound despair and were not rooted in reasoned choice. The waiver colloquy is designed to assure that the defendant understands the consequences of his choices waiving constitutional rights. But the waiver colloquy does not, by its terms, cover the defendant's reasons for making the choice(s) he made. In Moran's case, however, he specifically explained to the judge his remorseful motivation and his desire to receive a death sentence, factors not relevant to the legal test for a valid waiver. However, these factors are possibly relevant to his "competence" to make the decisions he made, especially if they were rooted in severe mental illness (delusional thinking) or a profound suicidal depression. In this respect, a court might rule that he lacked capacity to make a reasoned choice (or even a "rational" one)—especially if the defendant's mental illness was treatable. The problem in Moran's case was that he was permitted to waive all of his constitutional protections, including representation by counsel, during the throes of acute emotional distress four months after his arrest.[47]

Summary

Godinez declared that adjudicative competence, as defined in the *Dusky* formula, is a unitary construct that encompasses abilities required for assisting counsel and for making decisions. Once it is clear that decision making is included in the formula, it is necessary to translate *Dusky*'s requirement of a "rational understanding" of the proceedings into a "rational understanding" of the nature and consequences of the decisions the defendant is expected to make during the course of the proceedings. When the Court decided *Godinez,* the MacArthur Research Network on Mental Health Law was in the process of conceptualizing the abilities required for adjudicative competence and developing measures for them. In the wake of the decision in *Godinez,* the Network decided to use a hypothetical guilty plea as the

[47] It is not possible to say, based on the existing record, whether Moran was able to make a "reasoned choice among alternatives" in November of 1984. Even if the right questions had been asked at that time, the trial court might have concluded that he had rational, coherent reasons for deciding not to contest his guilt or seek leniency (he felt guilty and remorseful); that he was able, notwithstanding his acute depressive symptoms, to understand the possible consequences of these decisions and the arguments against them (including the possibility of later regret); and that he was able to weigh these considerations in a reasoned manner. Obviously, the mere fact that Moran regretted his decision three years later does not demonstrate that he lacked competence to make a reasoned choice in November of 1984. On the other hand, a contemporaneous clinical investigation of his mental and emotional state conceivably could have raised a reasonable suspicion that his decision to capitulate was anchored in transient emotional distress and unresolved conflict. Under these circumstances, therapeutic intervention might have helped to resolve the problem relatively quickly. Years later, there is simply no way of knowing. This further indicates why the decisional competence of a defendant who insists on waiving counsel and pleading guilty—and in a death penalty case, foregoing presentation of a case in mitigation—should be fully explored as early as possible in the trial court. If the issue is ignored in the trial court, it is likely to receive—and should receive—critical attention in federal *habeas* proceedings.

context for assessing the cognitive abilities needed to understand the legal effects of a guilty plea and to rationally decide ("reason about") whether or not to plead guilty.[48] Presumably, if these cognitive abilities are unimpaired in a forensic interview focused on a hypothetical guilty plea, the defendant is likely to have the requisite capacity to make most decisions that he will be called on to make in the criminal proceedings.

However, a general assessment of cognitive decision-making abilities in a routine pretrial competence examination will *not* be sufficient in cases where defendant's generally intact cognitive understanding and logical reasoning ability are distorted by delusional beliefs or affective factors that impair his or her ability to "appreciate" the meaning or consequences of the decision, or its risks and benefits, *in his own situation*. Some impairments of "appreciation" may infect the defendant's global understanding of the nature and seriousness of the jeopardy to which he is exposed, or the defendant's relationship with counsel. In those cases, the problems will be apparent early in the process and the defendant will likely be found incompetent to stand trial, lacking a "rational" understanding of the process or of his legal jeopardy. In other contexts, however, the deficit may not manifest itself until it affects a particular decision as the case unfolds, precipitating an "autonomy fight" between the client and counsel and leading the defense attorney to seek a competence assessment much later in the proceedings. In many such situations, the defendant's decisional competence may be the *only* ground for the competence assessment and adjudication. In these cases, the defendant's "appreciation" of the nature and consequences of a particular decision, or his "rational understanding" of it, to use the *Dusky* language, has to be assessed in the context of a specific decision when it actually arises, as it did in Richard Moran's case.

By broadening the *Dusky* formula to encompass decisional capacity, *Godinez* made a valuable contribution to the development of legal principles governing competence assessment and adjudication, both conceptually and in the practice of forensic assessment. While the Court assumed, without evidence, that decision-making abilities were encompassed within routine forensic assessment, that assumption was probably not an accurate description of routine practice at the time. Practice has probably changed, largely in response to the work of the MacArthur Foundation Research Network on Mental Health and the Law, which was grounded in the *Godinez* Court's reinterpretation of meaning of *Dusky*. Unfortunately, the Supreme Court never specifically addressed the motivational and affective dimensions of Moran's decision making and ruled, mistakenly, that the *Dusky* formula is legally sufficient in all contexts. Correcting this mistake remains unfinished business in the law of adjudicative competence.

Edwards v Indiana

In July 1999, Ahmad Edwards tried to steal a pair of shoes from an Indiana department store. After he was discovered, he drew a gun, fired at a store security officer,

[48] N Poythress et al, *Adjudicative Competence: The MacArthur Studies* (Kluwer Academic/Plenum Publishers 2002) 103.

and wounded a bystander. He was charged with attempted murder, battery with a deadly weapon, criminal recklessness, and theft. Due to ongoing concerns about his competence, he did not come to trial until June 2005, six years after his arrest.

Just before trial, Edwards requested the court to allow him to proceed *pro se.* The trial judge appears to have found that Edwards knowingly and intelligently waived his right to counsel. However, Edwards withdrew his request after he was denied a continuance. Edwards was then tried while represented by counsel. The jury convicted him of criminal recklessness and theft but failed to reach a verdict on the charges of attempted murder and battery. The state decided to retry him on the attempted murder and battery charges. On August 3, Edwards again asked the court to permit him to represent himself and his attorney moved to withdraw. The trial court granted counsel's motion to withdraw and appointed new counsel. However, on August 31, Edwards moved again to proceed *pro se*. Referring to the lengthy record of psychiatric reports, the trial court noted that Edwards still suffered from schizophrenia and concluded that "[w]ith these findings, he's competent to stand trial but I'm not going to find he's competent to defend himself," and accordingly denied Edwards request for self-representation.[49] At the retrial, the jury convicted him on both of the remaining counts.

Edwards appealed to Indiana's intermediate appellate court, arguing that the trial court's refusal to permit him to represent himself at his retrial deprived him of his constitutional right of self-representation under *Faretta v California*. The court of appeals agreed and ordered a new trial. The Indiana Supreme Court reluctantly affirmed this ruling, holding that *Faretta* and *Godinez v Moran,* taken together, left them no choice. Under the ruling in *Godinez*, the court reasoned, if Edwards was competent to stand trial under *Dusky*, he was also competent to waive his right to counsel and to invoke his right under *Faretta* to represent himself. In a 7–2 decision in *Edwards v Indiana*, the US Supreme Court reversed, holding that Edwards did not have a constitutional right to represent himself at trial.

Justice Breyer's majority opinion and Justice Scalia's dissenting opinion provide a rich opportunity to explore the logic of autonomy in criminal adjudication and its implications for the competence requirement. Two questions warrant attention.

1. Does either of these precedents (*Godinez* and *Faretta*) control the outcome in *Edwards*, vindicating his right to represent himself, as the Indiana courts thought? The answer, in short is that the Supreme Court's contrary ruling in *Edwards* is consistent with the holdings and reasoning of both *Godinez* and *Faretta.*
2. What is the proper test for competence for self-representation at trial? The answer is that the Court did not attempt to define one and left the matter open for further judicial development in case-by-case adjudication.

[49] *Indiana v Edwards* 554 US 164, 169 (2008). The court implicitly found that Edwards knowingly and voluntarily waived his right to counsel before denying his *Faretta* motion.

What does *Godinez* require or permit?

The hornbook summary of the law after *Godinez* seemed to be that "competence" for criminal adjudication is governed solely by the *Dusky* test. One could read *Godinez* to declare that the *Dusky* test applies to all stages of a criminal proceeding and to all decisions. However, as Justice Breyer correctly observed, competence to represent oneself *at trial* was not before the Court in *Godinez*. Richard Moran waived representation by counsel in order to plead guilty. Indeed, his sole objective in waiving his right to counsel was to waive his right to a trial—on guilt as well as on the facts necessary to justify a death sentence.

It is also important to remember that Justice Thomas's opinion for the Court in *Godinez* acknowledged the states' prerogative to adopt a more demanding standard than *Dusky* for particular purposes (eg, guilty pleas or waivers of counsel), thereby allowing the states to provide greater protection than the due process clause requires to defendants with deficits related to mental disorder.[50] If this is so, why doesn't Indiana have the authority to make the standard of competence for self-representation as high as it wants? The answer is raising the bar too high would nullify the Faretta right itself. This principle is not contested by anyone who accepts *Faretta*.[51] The question raised in *Edwards* is simply what "competence" means in this particular context. The argument put forth on behalf of Ahmad Edwards is that *Dusky* (as explicated in *Godinez*) sets the correct threshold for establishing competence for self-representation under *Faretta*. Justice Breyer's majority opinion rejected this argument, while Justice Scalia's dissent embraced it.

Does self-representation at trial require a different standard of competence?

Self-representation at trial poses different, and more substantial, challenges for criminal defendants than proceeding to trial while represented by counsel or pleading guilty without counsel. But the question is whether it is sufficiently different to warrant a different (and possibly "higher") standard of competence in the face of the

[50] *Godinez v Moran* (n 10).

[51] In its effort to defend the trial judge's ruling denying Edwards' request to proceed to trial *pro se*, Indiana asked the Court to overrule *Faretta*. In *Indiana v Edwards* (n 49) 178, the Court declined to do so:

> We recognize that judges have sometimes expressed concern that *Faretta,* contrary to its intent, has led to trials that are unfair. But recent empirical research suggests that such instances are not common.... At the same time, instances in which the trial's fairness is in doubt may well be concentrated in the 20 percent or so of self-representation cases where the mental competence of the defendant is also at issue. If so, today's opinion, assuring trial judges the authority to deal appropriately with cases in the latter category, may well alleviate those fair trial concerns.

Like every autonomy-affirming right, the right to represent oneself is subject to a competence limitation. The ruling in *Indiana v Edwards* is nothing more than a tentative refinement of what it means for a severely mentally ill defendant to be competent in this specific context.

Court's preference, stated so clearly in *Godinez*, for a single competence standard. Why is a standard different from *Dusky* warranted in this context?

The efficiency argument against proliferation of competence tests—which a majority of the Court had found so persuasive in *Godinez*—does not seem persuasive in the context of self-representation. The rate of requests for self-representation is low, especially in felony cases.[52] So the question is whether any of the values at stake in either *Dusky* or *Faretta* would be served by allowing Edwards to represent himself. Writing for a substantial majority of the Court, Justice Breyer concluded that allowing self-representation by marginally competent defendants who satisfy the *Dusky* standard would undermine both the accuracy and integrity of the judicial process.

The *Dusky* formula, in its modern context, focuses on the capacities needed to enable *counsel* to provide effective representation. Self-representation at trial is an entirely different legal context. With that point established, Justice Breyer goes on, quite properly, to point out that standards of competence for legal purposes are meant to be functional and are highly dependent on the nature of the tasks that are required in particular legal contexts:

> [T]he nature of the problem before us cautions against the use of a single mental competency standard for deciding both (1) whether a defendant who is represented by counsel can proceed to trial and (2) whether a defendant who goes to trial must be permitted to represent himself. Mental illness itself is not a unitary concept. It varies in degree. It can vary over time. It interferes with an individual's functioning at different times in different ways. The history of this case illustrates the complexity of the problem. In certain instances an individual may well be able to satisfy *Dusky*'s mental competence standard, for he will be able to work with counsel at trial, yet at the same time he may be unable to carry out the basic tasks needed to present his own defense without the help of counsel.[53]

Here Justice Breyer refers specifically to the MacArthur Research Network's studies and its effort to operationalize and measure the relevant abilities, and specifically the distinction drawn between competence to assist counsel drawn by the author and the MacArthur Research Network between competence to assist counsel and decisional competence.[54] Based on this reasoning, Justice Breyer continued:

> [We] conclude that the Constitution permits judges to take realistic account of the particular defendant's mental capacities by asking whether a defendant who seeks to conduct his own defense at trial is mentally competent to do so. That is to say, the constitution permits states to insist upon representation by counsel for those competent enough to stand trial under *Dusky* but who still suffer from severe mental illness to the point where they are not competent to conduct trial proceedings by themselves. . . .

[52] See Erica J Hashimoto, "Defending the Right of Self Representation: An Empirical Look at the Pro Se Defendant' (2007) 85 NC L Rev 424.

[53] *Indiana v Edwards* (n 49) 175.

[54] See, eg, Poythress et al, *Adjudicative Competence* (n 48): "[w]ithin each domain of adjudicative competence (competence to assist counsel; decisional competence) the data indicate that understanding, reasoning, and appreciation [of the charges against a defendant] are separable and somewhat independent aspects of functional legal ability."

The fundamental intuition underlying the majority opinion in *Edwards* is that the fairness and integrity of the proceedings are threatened by allowing defendants with serious mental illness to represent themselves based simply on a finding that they are competent to assist counsel under the *Dusky* standard:

> [I]nsofar as a defendant's lack of capacity threatens an improper conviction or sentence, self-representation in that exceptional context undercuts the most basic of the Constitution's criminal law objectives, providing a fair trial....
>
> Further, proceedings must not only be fair, they must "appear fair to all who observe them." ... The application of *Dusky*'s basic mental competence standard can help in part to avoid this result. But given the different capacities needed to proceed to trial without counsel, there is little reason to believe that *Dusky* alone is sufficient.[55]

In short, Justice Breyer says, allowing *pro se* representation by a defendant who is marginally competent to stand trial would present a substantial risk of undermining the accuracy and integrity of the criminal process.[56] Surely the defendant who is unable to carry out these tasks is running a higher risk of a legally erroneous outcome than one who is able to carry them out. The proceedings are less likely to be fair and, as Justice Breyer observed, they are less likely to be perceived as fair because they would lack even the minimum requirements of procedural regularity and orderly deliberation that *Dusky* itself seeks to assure though effective representation by counsel for a client capable of providing assistance. Accordingly, the finding that Edwards was competent to stand trial while represented by counsel was not sufficient to demonstrate that he was competent to represent himself at trial.

How could anyone think otherwise? Importantly, Justice Scalia doesn't seem to contest or dispute Justice Breyer's concerns about fairness and integrity of the process. Instead, his answer is, quite baldly, that respect for the defendant's autonomy overrides these otherwise compelling concerns about fairness that the competence requirement aims to protect. It is up to the admittedly mentally ill defendant to decide what is "fair" (to him) when he decides to invoke *Faretta.*

What does *Faretta* require?

Is this a proper understanding *of Faretta*? Justice Stewart's opinion for a closely divided Court in *Faretta*,[57] explicitly privileges autonomy—"the lifeblood of the law"—over the "objective" fairness of the proceedings or the reliability of the outcome. The Court acknowledges that a defendant who chooses to go it alone runs a

[55] *Indiana v Edwards* (n 49) 176–77.

[56] To illustrate these concerns about the accuracy and integrity of the judicial process, Justice Breyer referred to incoherent and confused motions and documents that Edwards had prepared in the case and appended one of them to the Court's opinion. Justice Scalia observed, in response, that Edwards' condition fluctuated over the course of the proceedings and that he also filed several intelligible pleadings and motions.

[57] *Faretta v California* (n 12). *Faretta* was a 5–4 decision.

greater risk of an unfair conviction simply because he lacks the technical skill and knowledge of a lawyer:

> It is undeniable that in most criminal prosecutions defendants could better defend with counsel's guidance than by their own unskilled efforts. . . . When an accused manages his own defense, he relinquishes, as a purely factual matter, many of the traditional benefits associated with the right to counsel. For this reason, in order to represent himself, the accused must "knowingly and intelligently" forgo those relinquished benefits. Although a defendant need not himself have the skill and experience of a lawyer in order competently and intelligently to choose self-representation, he should be made aware of the dangers and disadvantages of self-representation, so that the record will establish that "he knows what he is doing and his choice is made with eyes open."[58]

Faretta stands clearly and unambiguously for the ennobling proposition that the well-informed and mentally competent defendant is entitled to stand up against the power of the state whatever the risk to his life or liberty, if she chooses to do so:

> To force a lawyer on a defendant can only lead him to believe that the law contrives against him. Moreover, it is not inconceivable that in some rare instances, the defendant might in fact present his case more effectively by conducting his own defense. Personal liberties are not rooted in the law of averages. The right to defend is personal. The defendant, and not his lawyer or the state, will bear the personal consequences of a conviction. It is the defendant, therefore, who must be free personally to decide whether in his particular case counsel is to his advantage. And although he may conduct his own defense ultimately to his own detriment, his choice must be honored out of "that respect for the individual which is the lifeblood of the law."[59]

Let us assume that Ahmad Edwards, though properly diagnosed with a serious mental illness (and a "gray area" or borderline case under *Dusky* in Justice Breyer's words), had the ability to understand the risks of self-representation, chose, after rational deliberation, to proceed *pro se,* and was therefore competent to waive his right to counsel, as the trial court appears to have found. Justice Scalia insists that trial judges who deny *Faretta* motions in such cases would be substituting their own perceptions about what is "fair" for the defendant's own judgment. He says that the defendant has the right not only to make a fool of himself but also to make an "incoherent defense." What is at stake, Scalia insists, is the supreme dignity of being master of one's fate rather than a ward of the state—the dignity of individual choice.[60]

[58] ibid 834–35.

[59] ibid 834. I assume here that Edwards was properly found to be competent to waive counsel. However, I argue below that the heightened stakes of self-representation should require a more exacting inquiry regarding the defendant's decisional capacity to waive representation by counsel than the Court required in *Godinez.* But even if *Godinez*'s waiver holding is thought to govern, a state may require a more demanding test for waiver than the Court required in *Godinez* and, in any case, a specific finding of a valid waiver was never made.

[60] In *Indiana v Edwards* (n 49) 176, Justice Breyer correctly observed:

> In our view, a right of self-representation at trial will not "affirm the dignity" of a defendant who lacks the mental capacity to conduct his defence without the assistance of counsel. To the contrary, given that defendant's uncertain mental state, the spectacle that could well result from his self-representation at trial is at least as likely to prove humiliating as ennobling.

Justice Scalia's stirring endorsement of autonomy begs the underlying question. What are the capacities that are prerequisite to genuine "autonomy?" I presume that even Justice Scalia would admit that there is *some* floor on performance capacity to exercise one's *Faretta* right. The only question is where that floor should be set, and the answer to that question should take into account *all* the interests at stake, not only the right to be master of one's fate. Why assume that *Dusky* draws the right line *in this context?*

Does a legally valid waiver of counsel by a *Dusky*-competent defendant erase all valid concerns about the defendant's appreciation of the consequences of his choice? What if a defendant fully understands the risks of self-representation in the abstract but does not appreciate the incoherence of his own advocacy, as may have been true of Ahmad Edwards? What if his reality testing is intact at the time of the waiver colloquy, but frays and deteriorates under the stress of the trial? The waiver colloquy provides only a snapshot of the defendant's capacities and does not take into account the longitudinal demands of self-representation. In short, the defendant may not be the best judge of what is "fair" to him.

Another factor is the society's independent interest in the integrity of the judicial process. Perhaps the most disturbing scenario is self-representation by a defendant whose defense is grounded in delusional thinking. One vivid example is Colin Ferguson, whose cross-examination of witnesses and direct examination of himself in his trial for killings of passengers on the Long Island Railroad in 1994 was a bizarre spectacle that surely brought tears to the blindfolded eyes of the Maiden of Justice. Is the society's independent interest in the integrity and reliability of the adjudication process no longer relevant at all once a defendant "intelligently" waives his right to counsel? Even a fully competent defendant is not permitted to plead guilty without a factual foundation for the plea. Nor may a fully competent defendant convicted of a capital crime stipulate to the existence of the statutory predicates for a death sentence or waive the right to appellate review of the validity of a death sentence. All of these rules show that even though "autonomy is the lifeblood of the law," it is not absolute and does not trump the basic integrity of the criminal process.

The decision in *Edwards* does not invite trial judges to eviscerate *Faretta*. Nor does it liberate them to override the prerogative of headstrong and misguided defendants who are in a tug of war with counsel or the court and foolishly exercise their *Faretta* rights to show who is in charge. There is no slippery slope here. Edwards does not represent a retreat from *Faretta* any more than treatment of a grossly psychotic person over his or her objection represents disrespect for the competent person's right to refuse unwanted medical treatment.

Justice Scalia chastises the Court for "singling out mentally ill defendants" for the special treatment of being denied their right to stand up for themselves, noting somewhat snidely that doing so lacks "the questionable virtue of being politically correct." He claims that the majority's holding in *Edwards* discriminates against

I agree. *Faretta* affirms the dignity of choice and control, but respecting the choice of a seriously mentally incapacitated person is an affront to human dignity, not an affirmation of it.

people with mental illness. Admittedly, mental health law may occasionally lean too heavily toward paternalism. I would argue most emphatically, however, that *Edwards* is not such a case. The narrow issue raised in *Edwards* is what competence for self-representation in a judicial proceeding means in the context of a severely mentally ill person who is marginally competent to stand trial at all, even with assistance of counsel. The nub of the matter is that Ahmad Edwards is, in Breyer's phrase a "gray-area" defendant. He is severely mentally ill, and the authority of trial judges recognized in Edwards is narrowly focused on defendants who are marginally competent for adjudication to begin with.

Faretta itself embraces the overriding importance of respecting human dignity—the prerogative of a free person to stand up to the state, with all of its power, insisting that justice be done. But allowing a severely mentally ill person, who is confused, disorganized, possibly delusional, to represent himself in a criminal trial where his liberty, and maybe even his life, may be in jeopardy is an affront to the dignity of the defendant himself and to the integrity of the criminal process.

What does competence for self-representation mean?

What, then does the Court mean by "competence to represent oneself at trial?" The tasks that a *pro se* defendant is expected to perform at a trial are more demanding than the tasks required of a defendant who is observing, and perhaps assisting, an attorney performing these tasks. What capacities are required to carry out these tasks in a manner that respects the defendant's autonomy without compromising the integrity of the judicial process? The Court declines to address this question in any depth, leaving further elaboration to forensic witnesses and the lower courts:

> Indiana has also asked us to adopt, as a measure of a defendant's ability to conduct a trial, a more specific standard that would "deny a criminal defendant the right to represent himself at trial where the defendant cannot communicate coherently with the court or a jury." We are sufficiently uncertain, however, as to how that particular standard would work in practice to refrain from endorsing it as a federal constitutional standard here. We need not now, and we do not, adopt it.

Although the Court declined to try to develop competence criteria for self-representation at trial, some essential factors seem self-evident. Competence for self-representation is rooted in attentional and decisional capacities needed to formulate and exercise control over the defense, tasks that otherwise would be carried out by counsel. At a minimum, the defendant needs cognitive capacities to sustain attention and to maintain mental coherence (including the capacity for logical thinking) over the course of a trial, not only at a given moment.[61] The capacity to sustain attention and mental coherence bears on all the moment-to-moment decisions that

[61] The American Psychiatric Association (APA) filed an *amicus* brief in *Indiana v Edwards* (support of neither party), observing that "[d]isorganized thinking, deficits in sustaining attention and concentration, impaired expressive abilities, anxiety, and other common symptoms of severe mental illnesses can impair the defendant's ability to play the significantly expanded role required for self-representation even if he can play the lesser role of represented defendant."

the defendant needs to make, as well on the capacity to present arguments in support of his or her positions. This would be especially difficult for many marginally competent defendants (in the "gray zone") like Edwards, under the stresses of a trial, when the accompanying anxiety can be expected to make it more difficult for such a defendant to sustain attention and to maintain mental and emotional equilibrium (ie, "hold it together").

I want to emphasize that I am not referring to cognitive and emotional capacities, not knowledge or technical sophistication. *Faretta* made it clear that the defendant is entitled to represent himself despite the lack of technical knowledge and skill as long as he understands that he lacks technical knowledge and skill. However, at a minimum, the defendant needs the capacity to pay attention and *maintain orderly mental operations*. This longitudinal feature distinguishes the task of self-representation at trial from the tasks needed to assist counsel before trial (counsel can postpone important conversations if the defendant is confused, distracted, or distraught). A defendant proceeding *pro se* at trial must be "on alert" continuously in order "to control the content and organization of the defense, to make motions, to argue points of law, to participate in voir dire, to question witnesses, and to address the court and the jury . . . ,"[62] all of which he is entitled to do under *Faretta*. None of this is necessary for the represented defendant, whose active consultation or participation in decision making may not be needed most of the time.

It is also important to emphasize that the core abilities needed for self-representation relate to exercising control over the defense, not necessarily to conducting the defense. As Professor Lea Johnston has shown, Indiana's proposed focus on the ability to communicate coherently is a bit off the mark because many defendants with communication disabilities can make the decisions needed to instruct stand-by counsel or hybrid counsel. The *pro se* defendant requires sufficient communication abilities to communicate with the court or with standby or hybrid counsel to enable that person to communicate the defendant's wishes or positions to the court.[63]

The missing piece: decisional competence

One of the problems underlying counsel's repeated requests for competence assessment in *Edwards* appears to have been a disagreement about the basic theory of defense to the attempted murder charge. The attorney's line of defense was that Edwards lacked the intent to kill required for attempted murder, while Edwards apparently preferred to raise a defense that would avoid criminal conviction and imprisonment altogether. When Edwards sought unsuccessfully to proceed *pro se* in his first trial, he apparently wanted to raise an insanity defense. In his second trial,

62 *McKaskle v Wiggins*, 465 US 168, 174 (1984).

63 E Lea Johnston, "Communication and Competence for Self-Representation" [2016] 84 Fordham L Rev. 2121; E Lea Johnston, "Representational Competence: Defining the Limits of the Right to Self-representation at Trial" (2011) 86 Notre Dame L Rev 523.

he wanted to claim self-defense. Who controls the defense in these situations—the client or the attorney?

Some professional canons aiming to provide ethical guidance in allocating authority between client and counsel in criminal defense proclaim that decisions about the "basic theory of defense" are reserved for the client.[64] If that had been the governing rule in Indiana, the trial court's ruling that Edwards was competent to stand trial would have bound the defense attorney to follow Edwards' instructions at trial, whether or not it was a plausible defense.[65] However, because the decision is apparently counsel's to make under Indiana ethics rules, Edwards decided to take the only course then remaining to him to assert his autonomy—waiving counsel and seeking to represent himself. When the case is seen in that light, the underlying controversy in *Edwards* relates to the limits of client autonomy in criminal defense.

It has become clear in recent years that an attorney may not raise an insanity defense over a competent defendant's objection.[66] However, attorneys are probably *not* obligated to pursue an insanity defense simply because the defendant wants to do so. If, as in *Edwards*, the attorney is not willing to raise what she regards as an unsupported or imprudent defense, the dissatisfied defendant's only option is to invoke *Faretta*. In sum, if the defendant wants to go to trial, the attorney is in charge except for a few decisions that must be made personally by the defendant—whether or not to plead guilty, waive a jury trial, or testify. Setting those decisions to one side, a defendant who wants to be in charge of trial strategy and tactics must yield to the attorney unless he represents himself. *Faretta* is the defendant's trump card in resolving autonomy fights in criminal defense.

Against this backdrop, the practical significance of *Edwards* comes into clearer view. One way of understanding the legal effect of the ruling is that it shifts the default rule in client–counsel autonomy fights from the defendant to the attorney in the class of cases involving defendants with substantial mental or emotional impairments who are nonetheless *Dusky*-competent. If the trial court finds that the defendant is not "competent to proceed pro se to trial," the defense attorney will have the firm legal prerogative to make all decisions that are not by law reserved to the defendant. From this perspective, an implicit consideration in "competence" for self-representation is whether the defendant has the capacity to make rational, self-interested decisions in defending the case. In other words, concerns about decisional competence are likely to be a key consideration in the assessment of competence for self-representation. *Edwards* is a case in point.[67]

64 *Model Rule of Professional Conduct* (n 23), Rule 1.2 (a).

65 One can rightly wonder whether the trial court would have found Edwards to be competent if this had been the legal effect of doing so.

66 If the defendant is not *Dusky*-competent, the case cannot proceed. If the defendant is competent (however defined), then the defense may not be raised over his objection. Possibly important issues are what "competent" means in this context, and whether a *Dusky*-competent defendant is necessarily competent to preclude what the attorney believes to be a valid insanity plea. Most courts would probably rule, citing *Godinez*, that a *Dusky*-competent defendant may preclude an insanity defense.

67 An alternative rationale in *Indiana v Edwards* is that he lacked capacity to make a reasoned choice or was unable to appreciate the consequences of the decision to waive counsel and proceed on the basis of

Beyond *Godinez* and *Edwards*: The 2016 American Bar Association Standards

The law governing adjudicative competence in the United States remains somewhat unsettled—and in transition—in the wake of the Supreme Court's decisions in *Godinez v Moran* and *Indiana v Edwards*. It is important to recognize that each of these decisions left the state courts wide latitude in developing principles and procedures governing assessment and adjudication of fitness to proceed, and particularly relating to decisional competence. While holding in *Godinez* that the federal constitution did not require states to apply an elevated standard for pleas of guilty or waiver of counsel, the Court left states free to do so. Similarly, *Edwards* allowed states to raise the bar beyond *Dusky* for establishing competence for self-representation at trial, but did not require them to do so. In areas where such flexibility is allowed, "expert" professional bodies play an important role in formulating authoritative guidelines and standards for courts, prosecutors, law enforcement agencies, and the defense bar. One such non-judicial standard-setting body is the American Bar Association (ABA), acting through its highly influential *Standards for Criminal Justice*.

The first edition of *Criminal Justice Mental Health Standards*, approved by the ABA in 1984, was drafted by seven multi-disciplinary task forces with funding from the MacArthur Foundation. These *Standards*, now called the *Criminal Justice Standards on Mental Health*, were recently (2012–15) revised and updated by a twelve-member interdisciplinary task force and were officially approved by the ABA in August 2016.[68] One important contribution of the revised *Standards* is to specify criteria and procedures relating to assessment and adjudication of decisional competence. The *Standards* codify the *Dusky* criteria for "competence to proceed" when the defendant is represented by counsel[69] and specify a contextualized version of *Dusky* for guilty pleas.[70] However, the *Standards* recognize explicitly that "special competence issues arise" when "the defense counsel has good faith doubts about the

self-defense. As the case was framed by the trial court ruling, Edwards was found to be *Dusky*-competent and to have understood the consequences of waiving his right to counsel. However, the trial court did not inquire into his reasons for waiving counsel, and particularly the basis for the disagreement about the main line of defense, presumably because *Godinez* does not require such an inquiry. As argued above, *Godinez* was wrongly decided on this point. Waiver of counsel to plead guilty or to go it alone at trial should not be allowed unless the defendant is capable of making a reasoned, self-interested decision unimpaired by serious psychopathology. Although the record is not clear about Edwards' decisional capacity, it does seem possible that motivation for pursuing a self-defense claim was rooted in delusional or magical thinking and that he may have lacked the requisite decisional competence under the proper standard. See Christopher Slobogin, "Mental Illness, and Self-representation: *Faretta, Godinez* and *Edwards*" (2009) 7 Ohio State J Crim Law 391. It is noteworthy that Professor Slobogin sided with Justice Scalia rather than Justice Breyer and the majority on the issue that was actually decided in *Edwards*.

[68] American Bar Association, *Criminal Justice Standards on Mental Health* (n 36). The chapter author served on the Task Force.

[69] ibid, Standard 7-4.1(b).

[70] ibid, Standard 7-4.2(a)(ii).

defendant's ability to make significant decisions" in the case and when "the defendant wants to proceed *pro se*."[71]

Standard 7-5.2 (c) provides:

(c) If the defense attorney has a good faith doubt concerning the defendant's competence to make decisions within the defendant's sphere of control, ... the defense attorney may make a motion to determine the defendant's competence to proceed ... even if the defendant has previously been found competent to proceed in the case.... Upon such motion, the court should order a mental health evaluation, if necessary, ... and indicate the specific decisional issue in question. If, after a hearing, the court finds the defendant competent to proceed, defense counsel should follow the defendant's direction on matters within the defendant's sphere of control. If the defendant is found incompetent, the court should order treatment....

Decisions within the defendant's sphere of control include decisions to plead guilty, assert an insanity defense, and waive the rights to jury trial, testify, and appeal, but may include others that governing legal rules or ethical principles allocate to the defendant. The test for determining whether the defendant is competent to make a decision regarding control and direction of the case is "whether the defendant has sufficient present ability to consult with counsel with a reasonable degree of rational understanding and whether the defendant has a rational as well as factual understanding of the nature and consequences of the decision or decisions under consideration." As discussed above, "rational understanding" of the consequences of a decision should be understood to encompass deficits in weighing the benefits and risks or pros and cons of a decision attributable to either cognitive or affective impairments.

Standard 7-5.3 addresses the two facets of the problem that were intertwined in *Edwards*—competence to decide whether to waive counsel and proceed *pro se*; and, assuming the defendant is decisionally competent, competence to carry out the tasks of self-representation. First, under subsection 7-5.3(b), the test for determining *competence to elect to proceed without representation by counsel* includes three elements—(i) being competent to proceed under the general *Dusky* standard; (ii) understanding the consequences of doing so ("has a rational and factual understanding of the possible consequences of proceeding without legal representation, including difficulties the defendant may experience due to his or her mental or emotional condition or lack of knowledge about the legal process"); and (iii) being able to make a rational choice ('has the ability to make a voluntary, knowing, and rational decision to waive representation by counsel'). Taken together, components (ii) and (iii) establish an elevated standard of decisional competence. As noted above, Ahmad Edwards may not have been competent to elect to proceed *pro se* under this standard.

Secondly, subsection 7-5.3(d) addresses the issue actually decided in *Edwards*—competence to represent oneself. Even if the defendant is "competent to elect to proceed *pro se*," the court may deny his or her request for self-representation upon finding that, as a result of mental disorder, "the defendant lacks the capacity to carry out the minimum tasks required for self-representation at trial to such a substantial

[71] ibid, Standard 7-5.1.

extent as to compromise the dignity or fairness of the proceeding. . . ." Following the lead of the Supreme Court, the drafters of the ABA *Standards* decided not to attempt to formulate criteria for competence for self-representation.

The ABA *Criminal Justice Standards on Mental Health* have made an important contribution by clarifying the independent significance of decisional competence and providing a conceptual roadmap of the intersecting issues of competence to proceed, waiver, and decisional competence. The Standards take the law on a sound path beyond the decisions in *Godinez* and *Edwards*, while being fully compatible with them.

10
Involuntary Competence in United States Criminal Law

*Stephen J Morse**

Introduction

This chapter addresses whether in the United States the state has the right to forcibly medicate an incompetent defendant or prisoner to restore competence, including competence to stand trial, competence to plead guilty and to waive trial rights, competence to represent oneself, and competence to be sentenced.[1] Other legal systems may treat this as primarily a mental health law question addressed best by mental health laws, but in the United States, it is a criminal law question, although some courts are very deferential to the judgment of mental health professionals.

The chapter first presents the legal and mental health background concerning incompetence and the right of prisoners generally to refuse psychotropic medication. Although the relevant cases are important and deserve sustained analysis in their own right, for the purposes of this chapter they are presented only as the basis for addressing the chapter's central question. The chapter then turns specifically to the claim that the state does have the right forcibly to treat, primarily to medicate with psychotropic substances, solely to restore various competencies. The general thesis is that in appropriate cases finality in the criminal process is such an important value that the state should have the power to forcibly medicate an incompetent defendant or prisoner who refuses medication. Thus, there is inevitable and deep tension between an individual's common law and constitutional rights to be free

* Stephen J Morse, JD, PhD, is Ferdinand Wakeman Hubbell Professor of Law, Professor of Psychology and Law in Psychiatry, and Associate Director of the Center for Neuroscience and Society at the University of Pennsylvania, Philadelphia, PA, USA. Thanks are due to Ed Greenlee and Ben Meltzer for their assistance.

[1] Forcible medication to restore competence to be executed is an issue in the United States, but since this volume will be read by many people who live in countries that do not impose capital punishment, the editors have asked me to omit discussion of this issue to conform to the volume's word limits. I have discussed the issue in Stephen J Morse, "Mental Disorder and Criminal Law" (2011) 101 Journal of Criminal Law and Criminology 895.

Fitness to Plead: International and Comparative Perspectives. First Edition. Edited by Ronnie Mackay and Warren Brookbanks. Chapter 10 © Stephen J Morse 2018. Published 2018 by Oxford University Press.

of unwanted medical interventions and the legitimate needs of the criminal justice system.

Legal and Mental Health Background

This section of the chapter addresses various competencies, the permissibility of involuntary medication generally, some general procedural issues, and concludes with information about the mental health and treatment issues.

Criminal competencies

Other chapters explore the competence doctrines themselves, so I shall only provide sufficient information to motivate the main question of involuntary treatment. I will not explore in any depth the theoretical bases for these doctrines, which have been ably addressed by Bonnie, Saks, and Schopp.[2] For the purposes of the chapter, I shall assume that a defendant has properly been found incompetent according to the applicable standard in the jurisdiction and will not address the wisdom of various different competence tests.

In three important cases, *Dusky v United States, Pate v Robinson*, and *Drope v Missouri*,[3] the United States Supreme Court created the federal constitutional doctrine governing incompetence to stand criminal trial. The first, a brief *per curiam* opinion, involved a statutory interpretation of the then applicable incompetence-to-stand-trial provision of the federal code. The Court held that it was not sufficient to find competence simply because "the defendant [is] oriented to time and place and [has] some recollection of events." Rather, the test was:

> Whether he has sufficient present ability to consult with his lawyer with a reasonable degree of rational understanding—and whether he has a rational as well as factual understanding of the proceedings against him.[4]

Although the case did not impose this standard on the states as an invariant constitutional requirement, the standard it adopted for federal criminal cases has been very influential with legislatures and courts that have addressed the issue. The current federal standard is similar. A defendant will be found mentally incompetent to stand trial if the defendant:

[2] Richard J Bonnie, "The Competence of Criminal Defendants: A Theoretical Reformulation" (1992) 10 Behavioral Sciences and the Law 291; Richard J Bonnie, "The Competence of Criminal Defendants: Beyond *Dusky* and *Drope*" (1993) 47 University of Miami Law Review 539; Elyn R Saks, *Refusing Care: Treatment and the Rights of the Mentally Ill* (University of Chicago 2002); Robert F Schopp, "Involuntary Treatment and Competence to Proceed in the Criminal Process: Capital and Noncapital Cases" (2006) 24 Behavioral Sciences and the Law 495.

[3] *Dusky v United States* 36 US 402 (1960); *Pate v Robinson* 383 US 375 (1966); *Drope v Missouri* 420 US 162 (1974).

[4] *Dusky v United States* (n 2) 402.

is presently [sic] suffering from a mental disease or defect rendering him mentally incompetent to the extent that he is unable to understand the nature and consequences of the proceedings against him or to assist properly in his defense.

Pate held that the failure to observe procedures adequate to protect a defendant's right not to be tried or convicted while incompetent violated the due process right to a fair trial, thus cementing the constitutional status of the prohibition against trying an incompetent defendant. The Court also observed that it was contradictory to claim that an incompetent defendant could waive the right to have his competence determined. *Drope* noted that the prohibition against trying incompetent defendants is fundamental to an adversary process. The Court held that due process requires that, at any time during criminal proceedings that a defendant's competence is in question, further inquiry is required. The Court wrote that, "There are … no fixed or immutable signs which invariably indicate the need for further inquiry …",[5] and that deciding to do so was often a difficult inquiry, calling for the exercise of judgment.

The rationale for the constitutional doctrine, which is rooted in the Fifth, Sixth, and Fourteenth Amendments, appears straightforward: A defendant cannot receive a fair trial if he or she is incompetent. If a defendant does not understand what is happening or cannot assist counsel, the defendant's ability to help guide his or her own defense will be substantially impaired because the defendant will not be able rationally to make crucial decisions, such as whether to testify in his own defense or to raise various claims, and he will not be able to assist counsel to defeat the prosecution's case. Accuracy and autonomy interests are therefore compromised. Moreover, it undermines the dignity of the criminal trial process to try an incompetent defendant. Although these are undoubtedly weighty concerns, there is reason to believe that the defendant's competence may not be as practically important to achieving a fair trial as the Court implicitly assumed.[6] Nevertheless, the constitutional prohibition against trying incompetent defendants is now clear and settled. As Justice Blackmun wrote, "It is axiomatic by now that criminal prosecution of an incompetent defendant offends the Due Process Clause of the Fourteenth Amendment."[7]

In *Godinez*, the Court considered whether the standard for competence to plead guilty or to waive the right to counsel should differ from the standard for competence to stand trial. Pleading guilty waives all of a defendant's criminal justice rights, including the right to be tried and the right to remain silent. Although the Supreme Court has held that criminal defendants have a constitutional right to waive counsel and to represent themselves,[8] waiver of the right to counsel is weighty because counsel usually plays a crucial role in mounting an effective criminal defense. Therefore, the waiver must be knowing and intelligent. The Ninth Circuit Court of Appeals had held that waiving these rights required a higher level of mental functioning than

[5] *Drope v Missouri* (n 3) 180.

[6] See, eg, Robert A Burt and Norval Morris, "A Proposal for the Abolition of the Incompetency Plea" (1972) 40 Chicago Law Review 66; see also Bruce J Winick, "Incompetence to Stand Trial: An Assessment of Costs and Benefits, and a Proposal for Reform" (1987) 39 Rutgers Law Review 243.

[7] *Godinez v Moran* 509 US 389 (1993).

[8] *Faretta v California* 422 US 806 (1975).

that needed to stand trial, and it imposed a standard of "reasoned choice" among the available alternatives, rather than the *Dusky* rational understanding standard.[9]

In a controversial decision, the Supreme Court reversed, holding that the same standard—rational understanding—should apply, and questioning whether the reasoned choice test was really a higher standard. There were substantial arguments suggesting that a different, higher standard should be required for competence to plead guilty and to waive counsel,[10] many of which the dissent addressed. Although different "skills" may in theory be necessary successfully to accomplish different tasks, such as assisting counsel and deciding whether to plead guilty, it is not clear that the allegedly higher standard that the Court rejected, "reasoned choice," would make much difference in practice. Rational understanding and reasoned choice are both vague formulations that provide little guidance. Whichever words are used to express the standard, the test should be a functional and context-dependent rationality standard, focusing on what skills are demanded in a particular context. Waiver of distinct constitutional rights implicates distinct rational understandings of each right waived. Thus, a defendant who appears to have general rational understanding may appear on close examination to lack that understanding for a particular trial right. If the trial court makes a careful inquiry concerning whether a particular waiver is knowing and voluntary, the more general and specific inquiries should merge, as the *Godinez* dissent recognized. Once again, however, what is necessary is not a distinct formulation for competence to plead guilty or to waive the right to counsel, but a context-dependent evaluation by the trial court of the defendant's rational capacities necessary in each context.

Finally, if a different or higher standard had been imposed, it is by no means clear that trial courts would have behaved much differently, and appellate courts would seldom overturn a trial court's substantive determination that a defendant was or was not competent. In any case, then, for constitutional purposes, once again the issue is settled. Rational understanding and the ability to assist counsel are constitutionally sufficient standards for competence to stand trial, to plead guilty, and to waive one's rights. Congress or the states are, of course, entitled to impose higher standards for any aspect of competence in criminal pre-trial and trial proceedings, but the Constitution requires no more.

Should a criminal defendant who meets the *Godinez* standard for waiving the right to counsel, which is essentially the competence to stand trial standard, be permitted to proceed *pro se* if he suffers from serious mental disorder? The constitutional right to proceed *pro se* announced by the Supreme Court in *Faretta v California*[11] does not depend on the defendant's ability to function as an able defense counsel. As long as the defendant understands the consequences of representing himself, he is entitled to do so. Consequently, one would have thought that as long as a defendant with severe mental disorder understood what he was doing, he would be entitled to represent himself.

[9] *Moran v Godinez* 972 F2d 263, 266 (9th Cir 1992).
[10] Bonnie, "The Competence of Criminal Defendants: A Theoretical Reformulation" (n 2).
[11] *Faretta v California* (n 8).

Nevertheless, in *Indiana v Edwards*,[12] the Supreme Court held otherwise, in my view unpersuasively distinguishing *Godinez* on the grounds that the issue of self-representation was not raised in the previous case and that *Godinez* involved permitting a defendant to represent himself, whereas the instant case involved a state trying to prevent the defendant from doing so. Writing for the majority, Justice Breyer cautioned against trying to apply a unitary competence standard to address two very different questions: Whether a represented defendant is capable of going to trial and "whether a defendant who goes to trial must be permitted to represent himself."[13] Instead, Justice Breyer tried to apply a more nuanced understanding of competency that properly considered context. He recognized that a defendant with mental disorder might be able to assist counsel but might nonetheless be too disabled to perform basic trial tasks at even a minimal level. He therefore worried that an apparently unfair trial could result. Discretion was left in the hands of trial judges to decide if a defendant is competent to represent himself, even if he is competent to stand trial.

The United States Supreme Court has never addressed the constitutional standard, if any, for competence to be sentenced. This issue does not arise with great frequency because any offender about to be sentenced was competent to plead guilty or to stand trial. Nonetheless, an offender's mental condition may have deteriorated between plea or trial and sentencing, or there may be a specific problem about understanding sentencing although the convict retains plea or trial competence. Criteria vary, but the essential question is whether the defendant is capable of understanding what is happening to him and why, and is able to speak for himself and to assist counsel. Lower courts have essentially employed the test for competence to be executed adopted by the Supreme Court in *Ford v Wainwright*,[14] which requires that the prisoner is able to understand what sentence is being imposed and why. Some lower courts and commentators have also imposed or suggested further requirements.[15] I believe it is fair to say that the necessity of sentencing competence is assumed for some of the same reasons that support the bar on trying an incompetent defendant. It is inconsistent with both the offender's dignity and autonomy and the dignity of the law to impose a punishment on an offender who does not understand what is happening. Perhaps more important, an incompetent offender cannot adequately participate in the sentencing process, which may make it more difficult for the defense to argue for mitigation, thus reducing the fairness of the sentencing process.

Involuntary psychotropic medication

In *Washington v Harper*,[16] the Supreme Court considered whether the state may involuntarily treat a prison inmate with psychotropic medication. The Court held

[12] *Indiana v Edwards* 554 US 164 (2008). [13] ibid 175.

[14] *Ford v Wainwright* 477 US 399 (1986).

[15] John Parry and Eric Y Drogin, *Criminal Mental Health and Disability Law, Evidence and Testimony* (American Bar Association 2009) 103–04.

[16] *Washington v Harper* 494 US 211 (1990).

that although Harper had a substantive liberty right under the Due Process Clause to be free of unwanted medication, the state also had a legitimate interest in reducing the danger a mentally disordered, violent inmate poses. The Due Process Clause therefore permits involuntary treatment with antipsychotic medication if the inmate is a danger to himself or others and the treatment is medically justified in the inmate's interest. In brief, the state's interest sometimes outweighed the prisoner's liberty interest, and antipsychotic medication was found to be a rational means to effectuate the state interest. Moreover, the Court did not require a prior finding of incompetence and judicial approval of the treatment using a substituted judgment standard. Finally, the Court found that potential alternatives to antipsychotic medication, such as seclusion or restraints, had not been shown to protect the inmate's liberty interest in freedom from medication at minimal cost to penological interests.

The most important Supreme Court decision prior to *Sell v United States*[17] bearing on the state's right involuntarily to medicate a criminal defendant who is incompetent to stand trial is *Riggins v Nevada*.[18] In *Riggins*, the Supreme Court considered whether the forced administration of antipsychotic medication to a defendant during trial violated rights guaranteed by the Sixth and Fourteenth Amendments. The Court re-affirmed the *Harper* reasoning and holding and wrote that the Fourteenth Amendment provides "at least as much protection" to criminal defendants as to inmates.

Writing for the majority, Justice O'Connor found that there was a substantial probability that Riggins' trial for murder may have been prejudiced by the heavy doses of medication he was forced to take during trial. Although the treatment was medically indicated, Nevada had provided no evidence that involuntary medication was "necessary to accomplish an essential state policy" that would justify the potential prejudice to Riggins. As examples of such prejudice, the Court noted the possibility of untoward effects on Riggins' own testimony, on his interaction with counsel, and on his ability to comprehend the trial proceedings. The majority thus explicitly recognized the possibility that antipsychotic medication might prejudice a criminal defendant's rights at trial. It also noted that, "... the State *might* have been able to justify medically appropriate, involuntary treatment with the drug by establishing that it could not obtain an adjudication of ... guilt or innocence by using less intrusive means"[19] (emphasis added) and that "trial prejudice can sometimes be justified by an essential state interest."[20] Thus, the majority strongly implied that adjudication of guilt or innocence might be an essential state interest that would justify involuntary medication in some cases, even if prejudice might result. The Court specifically declined to decide "whether a competent criminal defendant may refuse antipsychotic medication if cessation of medication would render him incompetent at trial"[21] because the issue did not arise in this case. Finally, the Court did not adopt any standard of review for deciding such questions. In sum, the majority left open the standard of review to be applied and whether adjudication of guilt or innocence

[17] *Sell v United States* 539 US 166 (2003). [18] *Riggins v Nevada* 504 US 127 (1992).
[19] ibid 135 (emphasis added). [20] ibid 138. [21] ibid 136.

was such an essential state interest that it would outweigh a competent defendant's liberty interest in refusing medication and his interest in avoiding prejudice at trial.

In his concurrence in the judgment, Justice Kennedy wrote that "... the medical and pharmacological data ... indicate that involuntary medication with antipsychotic drugs poses a serious threat to a defendant's right to a fair trial."[22] He expressed the opinion that the state would therefore have to make an "extraordinary showing"[23] before it could involuntarily medicate a defendant for the purpose of restoring competence, and he expressly doubted that this showing could be made in most cases, considering the properties of the drugs then available. Justice Kennedy likened forcible medication that changed a defendant's behavior to the prosecution's manipulation of material evidence. He wrote that the state would need to show that there is "no significant risk that the medication would impair or alter in any material way the defendant's capacity or willingness to react to the testimony at trial or to assist his counsel."[24]

Justice Kennedy also worried that altering the defendant's demeanor might have an outcome-influencing, prejudicial effect on the defendant's constitutional rights at all stages of the proceedings, especially the right to testify in his own defense, and that side effects might hamper the attorney–client relation, " ... preventing effective communication and rendering the defendant less able or willing to take part in his defense."[25] Justice Kennedy closed his concurrence, however, by noting that psychopharmacological treatment was evolving and by recognizing that future treatments might not cause the behavioral alterations that concerned him.

Procedural issues

The state must adopt valid procedures to determine when involuntary medication is appropriate and necessary to restore the defendant's competence and, in appropriate cases, whether medication will unduly prejudice the defendant. It also seems clear that appellate courts have jurisdiction to review non-final, trial court authorizations of involuntary medication. The most important questions are whether there must be a judicial hearing before forcibly medicating the incompetent defendant, and, if so, what burden of persuasion the state should meet. As a matter of constitutional law, deciding what procedure is due usually involves consideration of four factors: the individual interests; the state interests; the value of the proposed procedures; and the risk of erroneous deprivation of rights the current procedures may pose.[26] Given the importance of the individual right to liberty that will be abridged, it seems clear that some form of hearing is required and that the exercise of reasonable professional judgment, although important on the issues of the medical appropriateness and necessity of medication, will not be sufficient (compare *Vitek v Jones*, with *Youngberg v Romeo*).[27]

[22] ibid 138. [23] ibid 139. [24] ibid 141. [25] ibid 144.
[26] See *Matthews v Eldridge* 424 US 319 (1976).
[27] cf *Vitek v Jones* 445 US 480 (1980) with *Youngberg v Romeo* 457 US 307 (1982).

In the contexts of transfer from prison to a mental hospital (*Vitek*),[28] the commitment of minors (*Parham v J.R.*),[29] the involuntary treatment of mentally disordered and dangerous prisoners (*Harper*),[30] and the right of civilly committed patients to refuse treatment,[31] administrative hearings have been held sufficient. Although an advisor is often required, there is generally no right to be represented by counsel or by a truly independent advisor.[32] The usual rationale for these holdings is that the decision being made is essentially medical and that requiring a full judicial hearing would be unnecessary for accurate determination and inefficient.

The context of involuntary medication to restore competence is arguably distinguishable, however. Although the precedents in the other contexts suggest that the determination has substantial medical aspects, deciding whether the governmental interest is sufficient to override the defendant's autonomy and bodily integrity and thus to medicate to restore competence is a core legal question. What is at issue is not simply a question of medical appropriateness and institutional management (and even these are ultimately legal questions). For examples, as *Riggins*[33] first made clear, legal rights are in question, and, deciding whether medication will unduly prejudice trial rights is a purely legal question. Thus, there will be substantial value in permitting a genuine adversary process before a neutral judge, with defendant represented by counsel.

There is little authority on the government's burden of persuasion concerning involuntary medication. Although the defendant's interest in avoiding an unfair trial is strong, it is constitutional for the state to place the burden of persuasion to prove incompetence to stand trial on the defendant (*Medina v California*;[34] but compare *Cooper v Oklahoma*,[35] holding unconstitutional the requirement that the defendant must prove incompetence by the intermediate, clear and convincing evidence standard). This might suggest that the preponderance standard would be sufficient to determine whether the defendant might be involuntarily medicated. On the other hand, involuntary medication involves both the risk of an unfair trial and a basic intrusion on autonomy and liberty. The individual's interest in being free of unwanted medication is substantial, as is the risk of error and harm. Although not as serious as a criminal conviction, involuntary medication is a serious abridgement

[28] *Vitek v Jones* (n 27).
[29] *Parham v JR* 442 US 584 (1979).
[30] *Washington v Harper* (n 16).
[31] See, eg, *Rennie v Klein* 462 F Supp 1131 (D NJ 1973).
[32] In *McWilliams v Dunn* 137 S Ct 1790 (2017), the United States Supreme Court granted review to decide if an indigent criminal defendant with a colorable mental state issue involving mental disorder related to culpability or punishment was entitled to the provision of a genuine defense expert or only to an evaluation and possible assistance by a neutral expert available to both the defense and the prosecution, a question left open by *Ake v Oklahoma*, 470 US 1985 (1985). In the event, the Court decided the case on very case-specific grounds that enabled the Court to avoid the more general question, but left lower courts uncertain about the reach of *Ake*. I assume that the Court would find the issues of guilt and punishment distinguishable from the question of competence, but, as a normative matter, the issue of competence is sufficiently important to warrant the provision of a mental health professional dedicated to the defendant or prisoner to assist him to contest the involuntary administration of psychotropic medication.
[33] *Riggins v Nevada* (n 18).
[34] *Medina v California* 505 US 437 (1992).
[35] *Cooper v Oklahoma* 517 US 348 (1996).

of liberty and the individual and the state should seemingly not have to share the risk of error equally. Thus, the state bearing the intermediate, much justification in this context.

A final procedural issue is whether trial courts should appoint a guardian *ad litem* to represent a defendant's medical interests. If the guardian consented, the state could medicate. If the guardian objected, the necessity for medication would still have to be assessed by the trial court. Thus, it is unclear what role the guardian would play. Counsel is presumably capable of developing the medical evidence that might show that medication is not medically appropriate or not likely to restore the defendant's competence.

Mental health and treatment issues

Whether a defendant is incompetent and whether a defendant suffers from mental disorder, which includes intellectual disability (formerly termed developmental disability and mental retardation) are distinct issues. Although criminal defendants might be incompetent to plead or to stand trial for reasons other than mental disorder,[36] such as insufficient education or experience, many incompetence standards require the presence of a mental disorder as a necessary (but not sufficient) condition. Moreover, in practice, problems with competence are usually associated with mental disorder and those found incompetent are typically treated with mental health interventions[37] or in the case of intellectual disability, with psychoeducational methods. Initially, research indicated that incompetence was especially associated with the diagnosis of schizophrenia and psychotic symptoms.[38] More recent research, although confirming the strong association between incompetence and schizophrenia and psychotic symptoms, indicates that other disorders, too, are associated with incompetence.[39] Nonetheless, people with schizophrenia and those suffering from psychotic symptoms generally are the largest group found incompetent to stand trial. This chapter therefore addresses only the involuntary antipsychotic medication of incompetent defendants with psychotic symptoms, who are being medicated solely for the purpose of restoring competence.

Even after antipsychotic medication became available, the Supreme Court's opinion in *Jackson v Indiana*,[40] which prohibited indefinite involuntary civil confinement solely for the purpose of restoring competence to stand trial unless there was a reasonable chance of restoration, suggested that large numbers of incompetent defendants could not be restored to competence. Nonetheless, for the past four

[36] Jodi Viljoen et al, "An Examination of the Relationship between Competency to Stand Trial, Competency to Waive Interrogation Rights, and Psychopathology" (2002) 26 Law and Human Behavior 481.

[37] Norman Poythress et al, *Adjudicative Competence: The MacArthur Studies* (Kluwer-Plenum 2002).

[38] Robert Nicholson and Karen Kugler, "Competent and Incompetent Defendants: A Quantitative Review of Comparative Research" (1991) 109 Psychological Bulletin 355.

[39] Poythress et al, *Adjudicative Competence* (n 37).

[40] *Jackson v Indiana* 406 US 715 (1972).

decades, antipsychotic medication has provided the most efficient means to restore a psychotic defendant's competence, although not the only means.

Psychotropic medication is not a panacea, however. A substantial number of patients do not respond, even to the most effective agents. All the drugs have side effects that can be extremely serious and unpleasant, and the drugs do not provide life skills that the person did not formerly possess. Antipsychotic treatment has changed considerably since *Riggins* was decided. The newer, so-called atypical antipsychotic medications are now widely in use, and can be effective even for those patients refractory to the traditional drugs. Most informed professionals believe that they are the first-line treatment of choice for people with schizophrenia. It now appears, however, that they are generally not more effective than the first generation of antipsychotic medications and the side-effect profile is less benign than originally thought.[41] About forty per cent of voluntary patients taking either generation of antipsychotic drugs discontinue use, primarily because of side effects. Antipsychotic medication for the purpose of restoring competence will be administered for a relatively brief period of time, however, thus reducing the risk of the deleterious consequences of long-term treatment that some antipsychotic medications present.

If a defendant who is a candidate for antipsychotic medication refuses to take it, administration requires either particularly intrusive, forcible oral administration or a forcible injection of agents that can be administered this way. The risks of side effects will never disappear. In appropriate pre-trial cases, such as if the defendant is not dangerous and poses no flight risk, there is no need for inpatient commitment. Medication can be provided on an outpatient basis. If the defendant does not comply with appointments, hospitalization can then be ordered. Even if the person responds well to psychotropic medication and regains reasonable cognitive control, some educational interventions may also be necessary to prepare the defendant for a criminal trial. These, too, can be provided on an outpatient basis in appropriate cases.

Despite the difficulties, medication will be the first treatment of choice for most defendants who are incompetent because they are out of touch with reality. Prescription of psychotropic medication is usually empirically based because there are few established links between a specific diagnostic assessment and a specific drug. The therapist typically starts with one from among a class of drugs that has the highest benefit–cost profile. After a trial of a few months, if the patient does not respond, a different drug is tried, and so on. If the patient who is incompetent as a result of psychosis has not responded to any drug over the course of six months, then the therapist can order clozapine. Clozapine is effective with a high percentage of nonresponders but has extremely dangerous, potentially fatal side effects, which require careful monitoring. If the patient still fails to respond, then it is reasonably safe to conclude that none of the available drug therapies is likely to restore the person's

[41] Jeffrey A Lieberman et al, "Effectiveness of Antipsychotic Drugs in Patients with Chronic Schizophrenia" (2005) 353 New England Journal of Medicine 1209; Peter B Jones et al, "Randomized Controlled Trial of the Effect on Quality of Life of Second- vs First-generation Antipsychotic Drugs in Schizophrenia" (2006) 63 Archives of General Psychiatry 1079.

contact with reality.[42] In virtually all cases, a determination can be made within six to nine months that the defendant is or is not treatable. Most defendants are restored to competence within six months.[43] Nonetheless, the potential for lengthy commitment remains and can be abused, but there is no need for longer commitment to restore any competence. A conclusion of irreversibility can be reached and further commitment for restoration is unjustified.

Whether antipsychotic medication is medically appropriate and *necessary* to restore competence are essentially medical and psychological questions that mental health professionals can best judge. Indeed, the Supreme Court has recognized that such questions are primarily medical or psychological. As long as professional judgment is adequately exercised, courts will and should be unwilling to override professional judgment on this issue. The state's interest, balanced against the defendant's substantial liberty interest, would not require certainty that forcible antipsychotic medication would restore competence. It would be sufficient if competent professional judgment was reasonably exercised. Of course, the ultimate question of whether the defendant must be forcibly medicated is nonetheless legal.

On the other hand, professionals and courts will need to be sensitive to the possibility of using less intrusive means than medication to restore competence. As noted, the risk/benefit ratio of antipsychotic agents is acceptable for transient treatment, but they must be administered highly intrusively to defendants who refuse to consent to treatment. In contrast, psychosocial or educational methods may enable the restoration of competence without medication or with less medication than would otherwise be required,[44] and such methods are almost always less intrusive than forcible medication.[45] If such methods are potentially useful, they should be tried first because medication must be necessary to justify forcible administration. Courts will evaluate whether medication is necessary, but it is doubtful that they will override professional judgment that is adequately exercised. *Sell* has once again adopted this position in the context of trial competence, but it should be applied broadly.

Before turning to the doctrines and arguments concerning involuntary competence, let us consider whether a defendant who is incompetent in some part of the criminal process may nonetheless be competent to make a treatment decision, including the refusal of psychotropic medication. As we have seen, these agents can have serious side effects and there can be good reasons to refuse, unrelated to a tactical decision concerning the criminal process. Objections based on religious belief

[42] Beng-Choon Ho et al, "Schizophrenia and other Psychotic Disorders" in Robert E Hales and Stuart C Yudofksy (eds), *Textbook of Clinical Psychiatry* (4th edn, American Psychiatric Publishing Inc 2003); Lauren B Marangell, "Psychopharmacology and Electroconvulsive Therapy" in Robert E Hales and Stuart C Yudofksy (eds), *Textbook of Clinical Psychiatry* (4th edn, American Psychiatric Publishing Inc 2003).

[43] Poythress et al, *Adjudicative Competence* (n 37) 51.

[44] Kirk Heilbrun et al, "The Debate on Treating Individuals Incompetent for Execution" (1992) 149 American Journal of Psychiatry 596; Alex Siegel and Amiram Elwork, "Treating Incompetence to Stand Trial" (1990) 14 Law and Human Behavior 57.

[45] Winick, "Incompetence to Stand Trial: An Assessment of Costs and Benefits, and a Proposal for Reform" (n 6).

are a classic example. In theory, it is possible that a defendant with mental disorder might be incompetent to stand trial but competent to refuse medication. The modern view of competence generally is that it can be relatively domain-specific, with diminished competence in some areas of functioning and not in others. On the other hand, Robert Schopp has argued convincingly that an incompetent defendant will also be incompetent to refuse treatment in virtually all cases.[46] I shall argue that in almost all contexts, the government should have the right to treat incompetent defendants whether or not they are competent to refuse treatment.

Involuntary Competence

This section begins with consideration of the general issues underlying whether it is permissible to medicate a defendant solely for the purpose of restoring competence. Then it turns to the discrete doctrinal contexts in which the issue arises.

Individual interests

Harper and *Riggins* confirm what was already clear: Involuntary antipsychotic medication administered for the purpose of restoring competence implicates important individual and state interests, both of which must be considered to determine whether this practice is constitutionally acceptable. In *Harper,* the Court referred to the citizen's interest in avoiding unwanted administration of antipsychotic medication as a "significant liberty interest." Whether the Court was signaling that this interest is fundamental, thus necessitating strict scrutiny of its abridgment in some contexts, is unclear, but it certainly means that this is an important interest. *Harper* nonetheless applied only rational basis review in upholding involuntary medication. As many courts have pointed out, however, *Harper* is distinguishable from cases involving involuntary medication to restore competence because *Harper* concerned prison administration, a context in which deference is granted to the needs of prison administration, rather than crucial, trial-related rights.

Even if antipsychotic treatment is medically appropriate and the benefit–risk ratio is quite favorable, the individual's interest in refusing unwanted treatment is weighty because it includes the rights to dignity, bodily integrity, and autonomy. In our political and legal system, no one has the right to invade another's body or to make medical decisions for another without the agent's consent if the agent is competent. People can refuse even the most sensible medical treatments for any reason they wish, including for no reason at all. In this instance, there may be many good reasons for refusing indicated antipsychotic medication, including the fear of unpleasant and sometimes disabling and even fatal side effects. In our political, moral, and legal culture, it is widely believed that respect for the agent's autonomy is a deontological

[46] Schopp, "Involuntary Treatment and Competence to Proceed in the Criminal Process: Capital and Noncapital Cases" (n 2).

good. Thus, even apparently irrational decisions will be respected. It is also believed that in general agents are the best judges of their own interests. Medicating solely to restore competence is distinguishable from cases in which treatment is sought for the patient's own good or for the safety of others. The state is medicating so that it may proceed with the criminal justice process. There is thus an undoubted invasion of the defendant's dignity, bodily integrity, and autonomy. The issue is whether the state's interests justify such an invasion.

Some believe, and many courts have held, that involuntary psychotropic medication also infringes upon First Amendment rights to freedom of thought and expression.[47] Antipsychotic medication does affect cognition and thus thought and expression. Further, if one denies the disease concept of mental disorder and the status of psychotic mentation and perception as symptoms, a once popular but now minority view at best, then the First Amendment argument gains strength. Moreover, at the margins, distinguishing psychotic thought from idiosyncratic or unusual thought may sometimes be difficult. In addition, some people with psychosis may rationally prefer to remain psychotic because the psychotic state seems more desirable than more realistic recognition of their life situation.[48]

The First Amendment rationale for objecting to involuntary psychotropic medication has been intensely criticized, despite its initial plausibility.[49] Reducing usually ego-alien psychotic symptoms of undoubted thought disorder that cause significant distress or dysfunction would appear to increase freedom of thought rather than to decrease it. Rather than producing "synthetic sanity," in most cases the medication returns the sufferer to a baseline condition of more normal functioning, much as other medicines do for physical diseases. Most mental health professionals understand the difference between disorder and mere difference, and manifestly psychotic thinking is seldom hard to recognize. In most cases, the "freedom" to be psychotic does not seem to be a freedom worth having, or freedom at all. In the present context, defendants are refusing medication to remain incompetent, not to achieve the subjective benefits of remaining psychotic (or to avoid aversive side effects). Finally, in some cases, such as incompetence to stand trial, the defendant can refuse medication after competence is restored and the process—for example, plea, trial, sentencing—has concluded (unless the state has another sufficient interest to medicate forcibly). In sum, the First Amendment claim seems weak in this context.

Criminal defendants (and society) have an undeniable interest in receiving fair processes, including the avoidance of prejudice at trial. The primary rationale supporting the prohibition against trying incompetent defendants is that incompetence prevents them from receiving a fair trial. It would seem be inconsistent, however, to employ methods to permit a trial to proceed that would themselves unduly

47 Winick, "Incompetence to Stand Trial: An Assessment of Costs and Benefits, and a Proposal for Reform" (n 6).

48 Theodore van Putten et al, "Drug Refusal—Schizophrenia and the Wish to be Crazy" (1976) 33 Archives of General Psychiatry 1443.

49 See, eg, Thomas Gutheil and Paul Appelbaum, "'Mind Control,' 'Synthetic Sanity,' 'Artificial Competence,' and Genuine Confusion: Legally Relevant Effects of Antipsychotic Medication" (1983) 12 Hoffstra Law Review 77.

compromise fairness. The question, then, is whether involuntary antipsychotic medication would so prejudice the defendant's right to a fair trial that Due Process would be violated, even if the state has an essential interest.

In the United States the vast majority of criminal defendants, especially in federal cases, do not go to trial, but plead guilty instead. Thus, although most discussion of prejudice has focused on trial prejudice, the issue will arise in relatively few cases. Moreover, we may assume that antipsychotic medication that restores competence to plead guilty or to waive rights will virtually never prejudice the hearings that consider these issues. At plea and waiver hearings, judges are being asked whether or not to accept a plea or waiver and not to adjudicate guilt. This decision is unlikely to be prejudiced by the types of problem that will occur at trial itself.

As *Riggins* indicated, antipsychotic medication could affect many trial rights by interfering with the defendant's memory, ability to consult with counsel, and the ability to testify. Altering demeanor might also interfere with other trial rights. First, it might undermine the persuasiveness of an insanity defense by making the defendant appear "normal." Some empirical research demonstrates that juries that believe the defendant is manifesting psychotic symptoms at trial are more likely to acquit by reason of insanity than jurors who believe the defendant is free of symptoms at trial.[50] Second, altering demeanor might also generally prejudice the factfinder by making the defendant appear lacking in remorse or concern, an issue that also plays a role at sentencing.

These are serious concerns, as Justice Kennedy indicated in *Riggins*. Antipsychotic medication at proper dosage levels typically does not sedate the defendant or otherwise impair a person's abilities. Rather, if effective, it restores cognitive functioning and should enhance the defendant's performance. Courts must clearly assess the potential for prejudice and should apply any reasonable remedies, including instructions, that might reduce such prejudice. And many of these concerns can be alleviated by effective advocacy. Lower courts have assumed that undue prejudice can be avoided in most cases.

It seems clear that a defendant should *not* have a constitutionally protected right to refuse psychotropic medication solely for the purpose of avoiding criminal trial or otherwise to delay or impede the criminal process. Some defendants would understandably prefer to delay or to avoid trial for tactical purposes or for other reasons concerning personal comfort, and such motives surely cause some defendants to raise the issue of incompetence. Nonetheless, a defendant has no legitimate right to "game" the system by refusing a treatment that might restore him or her to competence, no matter who raises the issue of competence. Moreover, a defendant who could be restored to competence may in some cases, such as incompetence to stand trial, remain committed under *Jackson*, thus forcing the state to bear the expense of costly confinement. The state should not have to absorb such a cost unless there is strong justification for it. Now, there are many justifiable reasons a defendant might

[50] Karen E Whittemore and James RP Ogloff, "Factors that Influence Jury Decision Making: Disposition Instructions and Mental State at the Time of the Trial" (1995) 19 Law and Human Behavior 283.

want to refuse antipsychotic medication, such as fear of side effects, but refusing medically appropriate treatment solely for the purpose of delaying or avoiding a criminal trial does not seem justifiable.

Standing alone, the psychotic individual's interest in bodily integrity and autonomy are strong, but the interest in freedom of thought seems less powerful. The defendant also has a substantial interest in avoiding trial prejudice, but little legally cognizable interest in refusing medically appropriate treatment solely for the purpose of preventing trial or the continuation of the criminal process.

State interests

The state interest in adjudicating guilt and innocence and achieving finality in the criminal process is concededly "essential" or important. In *Riggins,* for example, Justice O'Connor quotes Justice Brennan's concurrence in *Allen v Illinois*:[51] "Constitutional power to bring an accused to trial is fundamental to scheme of 'ordered liberty' and prerequisite to social justice and peace."[52] *US v Weston*,[53] which presents a thorough and representative discussion of the state interests, concluded that it is "essential." The opinion pointed to the many statements by the Supreme Court that the government has a compelling interest in apprehending, convicting, and punishing criminals. The state interest is not only incapacitation, but also "demonstrating that transgressions of society's prohibitions will be met with an appropriate response by punishing offenders."[54] The opinion rejects civil commitment as a viable alternative because civil commitment assumes that the government's essential penological interests lie only in incapacitating dangerous offenders. It ignores the other functions of the criminal justice system such as retribution, deterrence, communication, and investigation, which serve to insure offenders receive their just deserts, to make clear that offenses entail consequences, and to discover what happened through the public mechanism of trial.[55] Acquittal of the innocent is also achieved only in the criminal justice system. *Weston* concluded that trying a defendant is the only constitutionally acceptable means for the state to further the essential interest in adjudicating guilt and innocence.

To assess the importance of this interest, consider an analogous problem.[56] Suppose that obtaining the testimony of the sole material witness to a crime was the only effective means by which a state could effectively try a defendant. Not only does the state have the right to compel such testimony (by providing immunity, if necessary, and by the threat of contempt), but the state also has the right to incarcerate a material witness who will flee the jurisdiction. The state interest in trying a criminal defendant must be weighty if it justifies such substantial intrusions on the liberty of a person other than the defendant and who may be entirely innocent. Indeed, the

[51] *Allen v Illinois* 397 US 337 (1970).
[52] *Riggins v Nevada* (n 18) 136, quoting *Allen v Illinois*, ibid 347.
[53] *US v Weston* 255 F 3d 873 (DC Cir 2001). [54] ibid 880. [55] ibid 882.
[56] This analogy was suggested to me by Professor Adam Candeub.

state interest might even be sufficient to medicate the material witness involuntarily if this were the only means to restore competence to testify.

Assuming that the state interest in adjudicating guilt or innocence may be essential, must it always be essential? For example, *US v Brandon*[57] held that the state interest would not be essential in less serious crimes. *Weston* took no position on that issue because defendant Weston was charged with multiple murders and the government's interest in prevention of danger is unparalleled in such cases of obvious threat. *Weston* implied, however, that the seriousness of the crime might be a criterion for deciding whether the state interest was substantial. *US v Gomes*[58] rejected a bright-line rule in favor of case-specific weighing, and pointed to the breadth of the harm a type of crime created and to the dangerousness of the defendant as the most important factors. As we shall see below, *Sell* at least theoretically settled this question for the purpose of restoring competence to stand trial.

Incapacitation is less weighty for less serious crimes, but some of the other interests, such as retribution, adjudication, and communication, would be equally well served by trying less serious cases. Moreover, it is not clear what should count as a serious crime. In *United States v Jones*,[59] for example, the Supreme Court considered whether the Constitution permitted indefinite confinement of a person who was committed following a verdict of not guilty by reason of insanity on a charge of shoplifting a jacket. The Court was unwilling to limit indefinite commitment for dangerousness to those who had committed crimes of "violence" and was willing to characterize non-violent theft as sufficiently dangerous constitutionally to justify potentially life-long confinement to protect the public. It is reasonable to conclude that the state's interest in trying all defendants is as strong as the state's interest in protecting the public from mentally disordered, non-violent people who shoplift. Moreover, potentially indefinite confinement is a much greater infringement of liberty than transient antipsychotic treatment for the purpose of restoring competence. Nonetheless, if one is balancing the interests, state interests are diminished as the seriousness of the crime or the dangerousness of the criminal decreases.

The most general, implicit objection to the state's strong interest in finality is that involuntary medication to restore competence violates the basic integrity of the American system of accusatorial, adversarial criminal justice because one party, the state, is permitted to intervene involuntarily in the mental processes of its adversary, the defendant. Although plausible, this objection seems unpersuasive. The essential state interest in adjudicating guilt or innocence and pursuing the consequences of guilt to their conclusion, and the interest of all parties in fair process are undeniable. The defendant has no right to avoid adjudication if there is probable cause to believe a crime has been committed, or to avoid the consequences of guilt if the defendant pleads guilty or is convicted. Thus, the only question is whether involuntary medication of the defendant undermines the fairness of trial or the defendant's ability to help produce the strongest possible defense. If it does not, then the state will meet a

[57] *US v Brandon* 158 F 3d 947 (6th Cir 1998).

[58] *US v Gomes* 289 F 3d 71 (2d Cir 2002).

[59] *US v Jones* 463 US 354 (1983).

fully adversarial defense. Indeed, to the extent that the defendant's mental capacities are improved by the medication, it is likely to improve the quality of the defense. Involuntary medication does not compromise the independence of the defense. As long as the medication is medically appropriate and is being used solely for the legitimate purpose of restoring competence, involuntary medication by the state seems neither unseemly on its face nor a violation of the values of the adversarial system.

Competence to stand trial

In *Sell v United States*,[60] the Supreme Court addressed whether and under what conditions the state could forcibly medicate an incompetent defendant for the purpose of restoring the defendant's competence to stand trial. The Court agreed, as it had previously in *Harper*, that citizens have a strong liberty interest in being free of unwanted medical interventions. The Court nonetheless held that an incompetent defendant could be involuntarily medicated if four conditions were met: the treatment was medically appropriate; the governmental interest was strong because the charges were serious; the treatment would not cause trial prejudice; and less restrictive means of restoring competence were not effective. The Court did express a preference for treating the defendant under an independent and less fraught rationale, however, such as the *Harper* rationale based on the defendant's dangerousness. Not all incompetent defendants satisfy such an independent rationale for involuntary treatment, and trial courts have to apply the *Sell* criteria. Although *Sell* appears to put serious restrictions on the state's ability to forcibly medicate, in practice the limitations are not substantial, especially in federal cases.[61]

Three of *Sell*'s conditions are appropriate, although the issue of trial prejudice is best addressed at trial, as I suggest below. I would go further, however, and argue that the government's interest in trying an accused is sufficiently strong in the case of any felony or violent misdemeanor to justify forcible medication of an incompetent defendant for the purpose of restoring competence. All felonies and violent misdemeanors are serious crimes because both have the potential to result in stigma and serious prison time, the interests *In re Winship*[62] adduced when holding that the constitution required the state to bear the burden of persuasion beyond a reasonable doubt on all the elements of the crime. A criminal prosecution is an extremely serious matter. Neither the case nor the prosecution and defense should remain in limbo while an incompetent defendant languishes in a hospital untreated. The incompetence standards and consequences are not meant to be used strategically by either side. What is the point of keeping an incompetent defendant in a hospital to restore competence if restoration is made impossible by treatment refusal or by refusal to treat without informed consent? The intrusion of forcible medication is not trivial, to be sure, but neither is it so extensive that it should block the progress of the case.

[60] *Sell v United States* (n 17).

[61] Christopher Slobogin, "Sell's Conundrums: The Right of Incompetent Defendants to Refuse Anti-psychotic Medication" (2012) 89 Washington University Law Review 1523.

[62] *In re Winship* 397 US 358 (1970).

It is not a form of thought control or any other type of unjustifiable intervention. Forcible medication simply tries to restore the person's cognitive control and ability to test reality. Moreover, hospitalization is expensive and should be terminated as soon as possible. Finally, no good alternative usually presents itself.

Professor Christopher Slobogin[63] proposed that the criteria should be simplified to permit forcible medication if the defendant is charged with a felony and if it is medically appropriate. I have already argued that violent misdemeanants should also be included and I think he gives too little weight to the possibility of trial prejudice. So few defendants go to trial that that this is not a serious practical problem, but in the relatively few cases in which it is a problem, it should be addressed, albeit at trial and not in the initial medication decision. Thus, we may not disagree on this issue. Professor Slobogin also worries reasonably that the *Harper* rule, whereby prisoners who are mentally disordered and dangerous may be medicated, can be used to undermine the integrity of *Sell*'s limiting criteria, primarily because the meaning of dangerousness is not clear. Consider again the Supreme Court's *Jones* decision in which shoplifting was considered sufficient danger to justify indefinite post-insanity acquittal commitment. In other words, the state may use *Harper* as a pretext for avoiding *Sell* to restore competence. I agree that this is a problem that needs clarification. If *Harper* is being used for that pretextual purpose, it is an abuse that must be ceased. If there is no pretense, then the state has two independent justifications for forcible medication that may be used in appropriate cases. Non-pretextual use of *Harper* forcibly to medicate that restores competence as a side benefit is not an abusive practice.

Many defendants have been and will be medicated, so we must address in detail how possible prejudice can be avoided. Appropriately dosed medication is more likely to restore the defendant's ability to appear and respond appropriately, rather than to flatten his or her affect to a degree that conveys a potentially deleterious impression of unconcern. If altered demeanor does seem to risk undue prejudice, either to an insanity defense or more generally, there are reasonable remedies. Expert witnesses can explain the effects of the drugs to the jury and the judge can issue cautionary instructions. If there is a bench trial, the dangers would be further reduced. On the other hand, cautionary instructions are often ineffective, and expert testimony may be less salient than the appearance of the defendant.

It would be optimum if the trial judge held a brief hearing just prior to trial to evaluate whether undue prejudice was likely to result from the competent defendant's medicated condition, but for resolving most potential prejudice issues other than the ability to communicate with counsel effectively, this determination will be difficult to make in a context other than the trial itself. Consequently, these potential problems can be best monitored at trial, when the judge will have the opportunity carefully to observe the defendant's particular response to medication. Thus, in most cases, defendants who are competent on medication should be tried and the effects of potential prejudice should be assessed by the trial judge at trial.

[63] Slobogin, "Sell's Conundrums: The Right of Incompetent Defendants to Refuse Anti-psychotic Medication" (n 61).

If prejudice seems too great at trial, the judge may have to halt the proceedings. If too much prejudice has already been created or if the defendant cannot be restored to competence by means that do not create undue prejudice within a short period of time, the judge will have to declare a mistrial. The question then is whether this mistrial is occasioned by "manifest necessity" (that is, conditions under which it is not unjust to re-try the defendant) and double jeopardy does not obtain. Trial judges have great discretion in these matters. On the one hand, the defendant has been medicated at the prosecution's request and the defendant may not have moved for a mistrial. On the other hand, the state interest in adjudicating guilt or innocence is substantial, and the request for forcible medication is not done to gain a tactical advantage but to advance a constitutionally important value. Thus, manifest necessity should apply and the defendant should be tried again if he can be restored to competence without creating too much prejudice. Even if it is constitutionally permissible for a state to re-try a defendant under these circumstances, a state may impose more restrictive rules if it wishes. If the defendant cannot be restored to competence without creating prejudice, the defendant should be declared permanently incompetent.

If the defendant can prevent restoration or simply cannot be restored without prejudice, rendering him permanently incompetent, then the government must dismiss the charges, presumably with prejudice, and seek involuntary civil commitment. This is an imperfect remedy because civil commitment terms are relatively brief and not geared to people for whom there is probably cause to believe a serious crime has been committed. Perhaps a special form of commitment is needed. For example, some jurisdictions already have special forms of lengthy commitment for certain classes of especially dangerous people who have been charged with a crime but have not been convicted, and who are non-responsible and dangerous to others.[64] Such commitments are a clear instance of preventive detention, but without necessary treatment, they are simply warehousing.

If this type of scheme were adopted, we should insist that the state prove that the defendant did commit the crime to differentiate the subject from the subject of traditional involuntary commitment. In addition, the state should prove that the defendant is mentally disordered and dangerous, and the defendant should have full due process protections and the right to periodic review.[65] For example, the types of protections applied to sexual predator commitments, including the right to full adversary counsel and proof beyond a reasonable doubt, should be provided because so much loss of liberty is at stake. Automatic review should be frequent, the review should be thorough and include a hearing, and some provision for permitting the

[64] California Welfare and Institutions Code, ss 5008(h)(1)(B) and 5350 (West 2010), providing for "conservatorships" for people who are permanently incompetent to stand trial: conservatorships are for a year and may be renewed annually—the placement may be in a secure facility if necessary.

[65] Some dangerous people might still be uncommittable. Imagine a defendant who invalidly waives his right to silence as a result of mental disorder and the state needs the evidence unlawfully obtained by the waiver to secure a conviction. Between the waiver and the commitment, however, the defendant regains his mental health and is no longer committable. I assume that, as a technical matter, such a person would have to be released. I also assume that it would almost never happen.

person committed to challenge the commitment between automatic reviews should be available. If the person could be forcibly treated in involuntary civil commitment or in some form of special commitment under a different rationale, then perhaps trial competence would be restored.

Finally, consider a question that *Riggins* explicitly reserved and *Sell* did not address: Whether a defendant restored to competence may waive his right to be competent by ceasing medication, assuming that cessation is for the limited purpose of demonstrating his unmedicated mental state to the factfinder. *Weston* argued that the defendant claiming a mental state defense has no absolute right to replicate on the witness stand his mental state at the time of the crime. *Weston* used the following analogies: A defendant claiming a reduction to voluntary manslaughter from murder based on a theory of provocation and passion does not have the right to be enraged on the stand, and a defendant claiming an intoxication-based doctrine does not have the right to appear in court drunk. On the other hand, most finders of fact probably have experience with rage and intoxication, but much less experience with manifest psychotic behavior. There may be particular evidentiary value in observing the defendant unmedicated. Therefore, unless the defendant's behavior would be unduly disruptive, perhaps the defendant should be permitted to waive the right to be competent on a temporary basis.[66] This may appear inconsistent with the rationale for prohibiting trying incompetent defendants, but neither accuracy nor autonomy seems substantially compromised in these limited circumstances. If this were to be allowed, the trial judge would have to make a careful inquiry into the validity of the waiver, which could be temporary, with medication continuing after the finder of fact has observed the unmedicated state. This would be time consuming and cumbersome, however, and I suspect it would seldom arise.

Unless the Supreme Court reverses decades of incompetence jurisprudence, it is not possible to try incompetent defendants, even in those cases in which they could receive a fair trial. To permit this, however, would solve many of the problems raised by *Sell* or by cases of seeming permanent incompetence, allowing final resolution of the criminal justice process. One may fairly ask how we could be sure that the trial would be fair, but I suggest that this could be resolved at pre-trial hearings. Everything depends on how complicated the issues are and whether difficult strategic choices will be necessary in which the defendant would be likely to disagree with the attorney's advice. We could also adopt various prophylactic rules, such as requiring the prosecution to disclose evidence that may not pass the *Brady v Maryland*[67] threshold of actual innocence evidence, but which arguably favors the defense. In any case, the issue will not arise frequently because most state and federal cases are resolved by plea bargains. Nonetheless, the incompetence process would be rationalized in those cases in which going to trial seems optimal, and a fair trial would be possible despite incompetence. I recognize that this is a controversial suggestion and the procedural requirements to guarantee fairness would be complex, but, in principle, this is a reform that could work.

[66] See *State v Hayes* 389 A 2d 1379 (NH 1978).
[67] *Brady v Maryland* 373 US 83 (1963).

Competence to plead guilty and to waive rights

In *Godinez,* recall that the Supreme Court was asked to impose a standard of a so-called reasoned choice for cases involving competence to plead guilty and to waive the right to counsel, a test that was allegedly different and higher than the standard for incompetence to stand trial. The argument for doing so was that pleading is more complicated than going to trial and therefore a different and presumably higher standard was required to satisfy due process. The Court refused to adopt a different test, holding that the competence-to-stand-trial standard was sufficient to protect the defendant's rights as long as the waiver of the right to trial and other constitutional protections was actually knowing and voluntary. In his concurrence in *Godinez,* Justice Kennedy characterized the requirement as "knowing, intelligent, and voluntary." After all, a defendant might be competent but might not actually understand what he is doing as a result of confusion, marginal competence, or the like.

Requiring deeper or more detailed rational understanding risks paternalism, but requiring less risks an unjust outcome. I have a preference for limiting paternalism as much as possible and perhaps the Court's recognition that the defendant must actually waive his rights knowingly partially remedies the vagueness of the general test. On the other hand, defining knowing or intelligent is as vulnerable to manipulation as defining competence itself. In short, evaluating any competence case is a normatively fraught and difficult enterprise. I have no easy answer, but simply a policy preference for keeping the bar relatively low to let most defendants over it. This will maximize liberty, but the danger is that it will also unduly risk the defendant's ultimate liberty by potentiating the possibility of an irrational outcome.

If the defendant is not competent to plead and to waive rights because he has failed the competence-to-stand-trial standard or a state-imposed higher standard, the state should have a right to forcibly medicate so the defendant can competently make a choice—to plead guilty—that is open to and overwhelmingly chosen by most competent defendants. All the same reasons to achieve finality that apply to competence to stand trial apply *a fortiori* in this context. Once again, there is no need for lengthy treatment to decide if the defendant is restorable.

Competence to proceed pro se

This issue seems straightforward. If the defendant is competent to stand trial, he is probably going to be competent to make a treatment decision. If he fails an *Edwards* standard and is not permitted to represent himself because he has psychological abnormalities, then he will have every incentive to try to alleviate those abnormalities so that he can represent himself. Thus, the defendant should be told that either he can permit medication and perhaps be able to represent himself, or a lawyer will be appointed to represent him. I see no need for involuntary medication in this situation. The choice he is offered respects his autonomy and dignity.

In the unlikely event that the defendant's abnormalities do render him incompetent to make a treatment decision even though he is competent to stand trial, then a dilemma arises. Presumably his decision to represent himself is competently made. The *Edwards* problem is not incompetence to make a decision; it is that the defendant's psychological abnormalities will prevent him from meeting even the very low threshold for self-representation. If he wants to go forward *pro se* despite having such disabilities, that may indicate that his decision is not rational and perhaps he is not competent to stand trial either. It is simply not clear. In this case, I would permit forcible medication both to insure trial competence and to provide the strongest possibility of the defendant becoming sufficiently capable to overcome *Edwards* concerns.

Competence to be sentenced

It is inconsistent with both the offender's dignity and autonomy and the dignity of the law to impose a punishment on an offender who does not understand what is happening. Moreover, an incompetent offender cannot adequately participate in the sentencing process, which may make it more difficult for the defense to argue for mitigation, thus reducing the fairness of the sentencing process.

Unlike the defendant incompetent to stand trial who is presumed innocent, the defendant incompetent to be sentenced has been convicted and is lawfully in custody (or is perhaps out on bail, but still under criminal justice restraint). The offender has a clear interest in being free of unwanted mind-altering medication, but both the individual's interest and the government's interest in sentencing a convicted defendant are also strong. If the offender is a danger to himself or others in custody, whether in a jail or a hospital, *Harper* permits his involuntary medication, and he may thereby also be restored to competence to be sentenced.

Suppose, however, that there is no *Harper* justification? I would permit the state to medicate the offender as long as it was medically appropriate and less restrictive alternatives, such as psychosocial therapies, were unavailing. Defendants incompetent to be sentenced are probably not competent to refuse treatment for the same reasons that defendants incompetent to stand trial are probably not competent to refuse. Retaining a psychotic, unsentenced convict in a jail is cruel, and hospitalization, which is more expensive than a prison, is an unjustified use of resources. If the defendant is on bail and is not dangerous, treatment could be accomplished in the community on an outpatient basis. There is systemic value in reaching final resolution of questions a case presents and a rational convicted defendant also should want finality.

If the offender simply cannot be restored or there is otherwise reason to avoid involuntary medication, the court could impose a conditional sentence and retain the person in a hospital, or perhaps in prison if the latter can manage the person. I assume that, as a practical matter, the sentence would be the maximum for the crime of conviction. If there had been a plea bargain and sentence was part of the agreement, then the sentence would be for the agreed term. If at any point the convict is restored to competence, either by agreeing to take medicine or by spontaneous recovery, the court can then impose a final sentence. If the defendant is never restored to sentencing competence, then he would be released at the end of the conditional sentence.

Conclusion

All individuals, including defendants and prisoners in the criminal justice system, have a strong substantive liberty interest in avoiding unwanted medical interventions, such as psychotropic medication. On the other hand, the state in most cases has a strong interest in adjudicating guilt or innocence and in completing the consequences of guilt, such as sentencing and punishment. I have termed this the state interest in finality. If forcible medication is used appropriately after proper procedures to restore competence, I believe the state interest should prevail.

11

The Right to Fair Preliminary Investigation and Trial for Vulnerable Defendants

The Case of the Netherlands

*PHPHMC van Kempen**

Introduction

The position of the participants in the criminal process and the nature of that process in terms of its inquisitorial and adversarial characteristics are determinative for each other. Thus, a predominantly inquisitorial system expects less activity from the defendant and his counsel and is therefore less dependent on their capabilities than chiefly adversarial proceedings. Intensification of adversariality in the criminal process might therefore mean that the powers and responsibilities of the defence are or need to be strengthened also. Whereas criminal procedure in the Netherlands traditionally was as a modern moderate inquisitorial system, with the responsibility for fairness and truthfulness primarily resting on the courts and a defendant who mainly figures as a subject of criminal investigation, it is increasingly less so as a result of a whole set of developments. In fact, a small revolution is taking place in criminal procedure law relative to the adversarial responsibilities of the defence.

Over the past ten years, those responsibilities have been growing and they will be developed drastically in the near future. This is partly to do with the aim of achieving a more efficient criminal procedure, and partly with quality and fairness through the reinforcement of contestation in criminal proceedings, ie the increasing emphasis on the need for parties to claim and make use of their procedural rights and to respond to, comment on, argue against, and oppose arguments and evidence brought forward during the criminal proceedings. The observation that these objectives are in themselves worth pursuing does not alter the fact that achieving them

* Prof. Dr (Piet Hein) PHPHMC van Kempen (LLM, PhD) is Full Professor of Criminal Law and Criminal Procedure Law, and Dean of the Law School of Radboud University, Nijmegen, the Netherlands. He is also a Justice *ad litem* at the Court of Appeal, 's-Hertogenbosch, the Netherlands and Secretary General of the International Penal and Penitentiary Foundation (IPPF). He can be contacted at: p.h.vankempen@jur.ru.nl.

As for references: *NJ* = *Nederlandse Jurisprudentie* = Netherlands' Case Law; *Staatsblad* = Bulletin of Acts and Decrees.

Fitness to Plead: International and Comparative Perspectives. First Edition. Edited by Ronnie Mackay and Warren Brookbanks. Chapter 11 © Piet Hein van Kempen 2018. Published 2018 by Oxford University Press.

fundamentally changes the nature of criminal procedure. One consequence of these developments is that it leads to a fundamentally different position of the defendant[1] and his counsel in the criminal proceedings compared with the one we have seen until recently in the Code of Criminal Procedure and the practice of criminal justice based on it. The impact of the developments is considerable, because they have been advanced by both the legislator and the Supreme Court's case law.

The question is what this means for adult[2] defendants with only limited and/or inadequate abilities, also known as vulnerable defendants. Can the safeguards for those suspects remain the same? This chapter sets out why this is not the case. It provides fourteen recommendations for what is considered a necessary reinforcement of the legal position of defendants who possess insufficient abilities to adequately participate in criminal proceedings or who are even unfit to stand trial. To that end this chapter pays attention to the development in the Netherlands towards more adversariality and contestation in the criminal justice system. This includes the right to a fair trial in Art 6 of the European Convention on Human Rights (ECHR) and in the case law of the European Court of Human Rights (ECtHR), Directives from the European Union (EU) on the right of access to a lawyer and the right to information in criminal proceedings, and current criminal procedural legislation, as well as the fundamental modernisation of the Code of Criminal Procedure of The Netherlands (CCP). Although the recommendations are made with a view to the criminal justice system of the Netherlands, almost all of them have general value and may be worth considering in other jurisdictions.

Increasing Responsibilities for the Defence

Unlike jurisdictions with an adversarial criminal procedure law system, most non-English-speaking European countries recognise a system which is inquisitorial. Within this dichotomy, criminal law procedure in the Netherlands must be characterised as inquisitorial.[3] However, this qualification is only helpful as a first characterisation, as neither of these systems exists in a pure form, because there are many differences amongst inquisitorial systems, and some phases of a country's criminal procedure system may be more inquisitorial than others.

The pre-trial investigation phase of the Dutch criminal justice system is essentially inquisitorial in nature, with some adversarial elements. The collection of evidence and fact finding is mainly done by the authorities: the police force investigates under the prosecutor's supervision and there is oversight by an investigative judge. In this

[1] This article employs a broad definition of defendants; the term refers to suspects and accused persons in criminal proceedings, whether it be the preliminary inquiry phase or the trial phase, who have been made aware by the competent authorities that they are suspected or accused of having committed a criminal offence.

[2] Defendants who are minors will be excluded from this analysis.

[3] See PHPHMC van Kempen, 'The Protection of Human Rights in Criminal Law Procedure in the Netherlands' (2009) 13(2) Electronic Journal of Comparative Law, available at: http://www.ejcl.org/132/art132-1.pdf, para IV(4). For an explanation of the system, see also MFH Hirsch Ballin, *Anticipative Criminal Investigation. Theory and Counterterrorism Practice in the Netherlands and the United States* (Asser Press/Springer 2012) 37–111.

phase of criminal law procedure, the suspect figures mainly as a subject of investigation and is exposed to all kinds of coercive powers. Although the suspect increasingly possesses all kinds of defence rights during this phase and can even instigate investigations as well, the system is not constructed in such a way that the defence is equally responsible for truth discovery as the authorities. The balance is different in the trial phase, which increasingly puts emphasis on contestation by the parties. Here the position of the prosecution and defence is much more one of equality of arms. Nevertheless, the structure of the trial is still rather inquisitorial: it is the trial court that leads the proceedings and presents the evidence and investigation results in the case file on trial and actively questions the defendant, witnesses, and experts. Furthermore, it reflects modern inquisitorial values as the court also has responsibilities to actively secure the defendant's fundamental rights, including the right to a fair trial. The trial phase is strongly guided by the case file as it was constructed in the rather inquisitorial pre-trial investigation.[4] As a result, for the proceedings as a whole, when qualifying the nature of criminal law procedure in the Netherlands, the pre-trial proceedings have to weigh rather more than the trial phase. Therefore, I would qualify criminal law procedure as a whole as a modern moderate form of inquisitorial proceedings with adversarial elements.

In reality, the criminal procedure system has become rather hybrid. And it is increasingly so due to an expansion in the responsibilities of the defence and a decrease in judicial *ex officio* activity. This has by and large taken place since around 2005, and has accelerated somewhat in the past five years. In honouring defence rights, the Supreme Court of the Netherlands (*de Hoge Raad*, HR) ever more explicitly attaches responsibilities for the defence to enter a defence and submit requests in time, to do so with providing reasons and to be 'to the point', where in most cases the interest that the defence has in it must also be explained adequately. This is apparent, for example, in the case law concerning breaches of procedural requirements,[5] the right to be present at the trial,[6] requests to hear witnesses,[7] requests for a second expert opinion,[8] the use of the right to make a plea,[9] and access to the Supreme Court in cassation.[10]

[4] cf ML Komter and M Malsch, 'The Language of Criminal Trials in an Inquisitorial System: The Case of the Netherlands' in LM Solan and PM Tiersma (eds), *The Oxford Handbook of Language and Law* (Oxford University Press 2012) 408–20.

[5] See Supreme Court 19 February 2013, ECLI:NL:HR:2013:BY5321, *NJ* 2013/308 with case note by BF Keulen. See also Art 359a(1) CCP, according to which the court '*may, if it appears that procedural requirements were not complied with during the preliminary investigation which can no longer be remedied and the law does not provide for the legal consequences thereof, determine*' that the sentence shall be reduced, that evidence shall be excluded, or that there is a bar to the prosecution.

[6] See, eg, Supreme Court 8 September 2015, ECLI:NL:HR:2015:2476.

[7] See Supreme Court 1 July 2014, ECLI:NL:HR:2014:1496, *NJ* 2014/441 with case note by MJ Borgers.

[8] See, eg, Supreme Court 12 March 2013, ECLI:NL:HR:2013:BZ3886, *NJ* 2013/179.

[9] See, eg, Supreme Court 26 May 2015, ECLI:NL:HR:2015:1340, *NJ* 2015/299 with case note by N Rozemond.

[10] See Supreme Court 7 June 2016, ECLI:NL:HR:2016:1005, *NJ* 2016/430 with case note by PHPHMC van Kempen.

Increased responsibilities of the defence and further emphasis on adversariality also came about through criminal procedure legislation. Important in this regard is the introduction of the requirement of the explicitly substantiated point of view in Art 359(2) CCP: this provision holds that courts only have to give reasons when derogating from the positions by the defendant (or the public prosecutor) if these positions are expressly substantiated, as a result of which the defence needs to take clear positions that are supported by arguments and unambiguous conclusions.[11] Furthermore, of importance here is the fact that the essence of the appeal procedure has been fundamentally amended:[12] appeal no longer implies an automatic new, full, and complete consideration of the case by the Court as it used to do, but now concentrates on matters in dispute between the defence and the prosecution. This means that in principle only issues addressed by the defence in the grounds of appeal are discussed in the appeal hearing, and furthermore that the appeal courts offer defendants less *ex officio* legal protection now than under the former appeal regime.[13]

With the intended fundamental modernisation of the Code of Criminal Procedure—which the legislator desires to accomplish through a variety of extensive Bills—the responsibilities for the defence will be significantly further increased. One of the main objectives of that modernisation is that the responsibilities of the defence and the prosecution for a smooth and swift procedure will be laid down in law.[14] The emphasis will be on enabling the defendant to determine his position and strategy regarding his defence. This starts as early as the preliminary inquiry. The defendant's freedom to chart his own course in the procedure, however, also means that the defendant may be bound by the choices made by him and that these choices may have further legal consequences.[15]

Nearly every reinforcement of defence rights and possibilities is accompanied by an increase in defence responsibilities. To illustrate that there is indeed a reinforcement of rights, it is notable that, in addition to the fact that defendants have quite recently acquired the right to legal aid during police questioning,[16] they have also acquired the right to information about their rights (among other things the

[11] Act of 10 November 2004, *Staatsblad* 2004/580 (entry into force 1 January 2005), and Supreme Court 11 April 2006, ECLI:NL:HR:2006:AU9130, *NJ* 2006/393 with case note by Y Buruma.

[12] Act of 5 October 2005, *Staatsblad* 2006/470 (entry into force 1 March 2007 and 1 July 2007), and regarding this with respect to submitting objections by defence Supreme Court 6 March 2012, ECLI:NL:HR:2012:BU3614, *NJ* 2012/610.

[13] van Kempen, 'The Protection of Human Rights in Criminal Law Procedure in the Netherlands' (n 3). See also JW Fokkens and N Kirkels-Vrijman, 'The Dutch System of Legal Remedies' in MS Groenhuijsen and T Kooijmans (eds), *The Reform of the Dutch Code of Criminal Procedure in Comparative Perspective* (Brill 2012) 19–24.

[14] *Parliamentary Documents II* 2015–16, 29 279, no 278, 4 (Letter of the Minister of Justice on the modernisation of the Code of Criminal Procedure and Outline Policy).

[15] ibid 6; with regard to these legal effects see also ibid, 12, 14, 17, 79–80, and 93.

[16] The right to assistance from counsel during police questioning has first been recognised by the Supreme Court (Supreme Court 22 December 2015, ECLI:NL:HR:2015:3608, *NJ* 2016/52 with case note by AH Klip) and was later implemented through Art 28d CCP by Act of 17 November 2016 (implementation of the European Parliament and Council Directive 2013/48/EU of 22 October 2013 on the right of access to a lawyer in criminal proceedings [2013] OJ L294/1), *Staatsblad* 2016/475 and 2017/66 (entry into force 1 March 2017).

so-called 'letter of rights').[17] The modernisation provides for further expanding the possibilities of the defence to specify their wishes regarding the inquiry at an early stage of the proceedings, to receive file documents pertaining to the case, to exert influence on the presentation of the statement by the defendant in the police report, and the possibility for the defendant to be present more often during witness examinations.[18]

The fact that the defendant and his counsel are consequently given a position to assess earlier and better whether the inquiry is complete and adequate, so they can submit requests and pleas, entails that in all sorts of situations they are actually expected to use these opportunities adequately—on pain of forfeiture of rights. As a result, the adversarial quality of the defence is much more decisive for the course of the proceedings than it has ever been before.

Increased Importance of Capabilities of Defendant and Counsel

The above-mentioned developments show that the defence is increasingly responsible for the fairness and veracity of the criminal proceedings. That does not necessarily mean that the responsibilities of the trial court for the completeness of the investigation and the correctness of its decision have also legally diminished.[19] However, because it is easier to remain passive in the case of shared responsibility, the degree to which the trial court actually takes responsibility could decrease.[20] The quality of the criminal procedure then comes to depend on the capabilities of the defence even more. This seems a genuine risk, particularly when the judiciary is under pressure to meet production targets and/or when it is being faced with an influx of new judges who are less inclined to adhere to the traditional process culture with inquisitorial legal protection.

However, even if such a scenario does not unfold, the increasing responsibilities for the defence still require considerable capabilities on the part of the defendant and his counsel. From a dogmatic as well as a practical point of view, the emphasis on those responsibilities results in a fundamental repositioning of the defence in criminal justice. Where the defendant is concerned, the system increasingly assumes the defendant to be a genuinely (and not merely ideally) autonomous, legally capable, assertive, and fully fledged participant in the proceedings.[21]

[17] See Art 27c CCP, which was implemented by the Act of 5 November 2014 (implementation of European Parliament and Council Directive 2012/13/EU of 22 May 2012 on the right to information in criminal proceedings [2002] OJ L142/1), *Staatsblad* 2014/433 and 434.

[18] *Parliamentary Documents II* 2015–16, 29 279, no 278 (n 14), 7, 31, 37, 43, 104–05.

[19] ibid 14, 17, 80, and 107, where the government argues that the trial court must fully retain its responsibility for the completion of the investigation and the correctness of its decision.

[20] cf AA Franken, 'Instemming en afstand (Consent and Waiver)' [2015] Delikt en Delinkwent 1, who is of the opinion that the image of the active criminal judge is no longer adequate and correct for the practice of criminal justice these days and that this image therefore needs adjusting.

[21] For such a positioning, see also MS Groenhuijsen and G Knigge, 'Afronding en Verantwoording. Algemeen deel (Completion and Accountability). General Part' in MS Groenhuijsen and G Knigge (eds), *Afronding en verantwoording. Onderzoeksproject strafvordering 2001: Eindrapport* (*Completion and Accountability. Research Project Criminal Procedure 2001: Final Report*) (Kluwer 2004) 3–185, 78–86.

Additionally, that system implies the need for an alert, active, legally and practically knowledgeable counsel who has sufficient time to devote to the case.[22] The increase in responsibilities in the defence therefore requires qualities in the defendant and counsel that formerly—in the system that did not rely on contestation and forfeiture of rights as much—were less important. Meanwhile, the capabilities of defendant and counsel cannot be seen in isolation. What matters is the combination: the quality of the defence will increasingly often depend on the capabilities of both counsel and his client and the cooperation between the two.

With an increasing responsibility for the defence, this means that shortcomings in the capabilities of one of them or in the defence as such are more likely to be detrimental to the defendant than previously.[23] Attaching consequences to what the defence submits, or conversely fails to submit, also means that the defendant can miss out on legal protection that he previously would have obtained, be it directly or indirectly.[24] In a modern inquisitorial system, flaws in the defence tend to be less detrimental to the defendant than in a system that leans more heavily on adversarial principles.

It is also important that the creation of more rights and responsibilities for the defence does not only result in a reinforcement of contestation in criminal proceedings, but also introduces an important adversarial element because of the inherent threat of forfeiture of rights. This is the development that is currently well underway in criminal procedural law and the practice of criminal proceedings in the Netherlands. It is, therefore, remarkable that there is hardly any increase in attention given to the qualities of the defendant and counsel in a general sense within the case law of the Dutch Supreme Court,[25] while the preparatory documents for the fundamental modernisation of the Code of Criminal Procedure do not even discuss it.[26]

The question, therefore, is whether defendants and counsel are capable of adequately discharging the responsibilities assigned to them and are actually endowed with the capabilities they supposedly have. If that is the case, the reinforcement of the rights and responsibilities of the defence may constitute a boost to the quality, fairness, and efficiency of criminal justice. To that extent, the developments vis-a-vis the responsibilities of the defence merit approval. However, it is a different matter when the defence in general or in specific cases is not sufficiently capable of

[22] For the position of the counsel, see ibid 86–93.

[23] For an example where passivity on the part of the defence seems to have resulted in the defendant missing out on legal protection, see Supreme Court 3 February 2015, ECLI:NL:HR:2015:194, *NJ* 2015/134 with case note by PHPHMC van Kempen (see para 6 of the case note).

[24] See, eg, the following case law and the accompanying case notes: ibid (direct); Supreme Court 17 September 2013, ECLI:NL:HR:2013:708, *NJ* 2014/288 with case note by PHPHMC van Kempen (direct); Supreme Court 10 February 2015, ECLI:NL:HR:2015:268, *NJ* 2015/137 with case note by PHPHMC van Kempen (indirect).

[25] However, see Supreme Court 12 June 2001, ECLI:NL:HR:2001:AB2064, *NJ* 2001/696 with case note by J de Hullu (excusable failure to meet the appeal deadline by a suspect with psychosis); Supreme Court 17 November 2009, ECLI:NL:HR:2009:BI2315, *NJ* 2010/143 with case note by TMCJ Schalken (waiver of right to legal aid during trial for a serious offence involving defendant with probably limited development of mental faculties), but also: Supreme Court 18 November 2014, ECLI:NL:HR:2014:3288, *NJ* 2015/49 with case note by JM Reijntjes.

[26] *Parliamentary Documents II* 2015–16, 29 279, no 278 (n 14) 4.

exercising its rights effectively. In those cases, the trend towards more adversarial proceedings will actually result in a loss of quality, fairness, and eventually efficiency as well.

Defendants with Limited Abilities and Article 6 ECHR

Article 6 ECHR does not say anything about the abilities of the defendant as a prerequisite for a fair procedure. The first paragraph of this Article, however, recognises the right to a fair hearing of the case and the third paragraph under 'c' creates the right to defend oneself or to be assisted by counsel. It is particularly here that the ECtHR derives various rights for defendants and obligations for the authorities that are relevant if a defendant is not, or is insufficiently capable of, adequately contributing to looking after his interests in criminal proceedings.

Guarantees for effective participation by defendants during trial

The right to a fair process implies the right for the defendant to effective participation in the criminal proceedings.[27] This includes in general the right to be present during the examination of the case, and to hear and follow proceedings.[28] According to the ECtHR, these rights are enshrined in the concept of 'adversarial procedure'. More precisely, it concerns the following with respect to the required capabilities:

> 'Effective participation' in this context presupposes that the accused has a broad understanding of the nature of the trial process and of what is at stake for him or her, including the significance of any penalty which may be imposed. The defendant should be able, *inter alia*, to explain to his own lawyer his version of events, point out any statements with which he disagrees and make them aware of any facts which should be put forward in his defence.[29]
>
> It also requires that he or she, if necessary with the assistance of, for example, an interpreter, lawyer, social worker or friend, should be able to understand the general thrust of what is said in court.[30]
>
> The defendant should be able to follow what is said by the prosecution witnesses.[31]

The standard applied by the Court with regard to the degree of understanding the defendant needs to achieve is not particularly rigorous. It only concerns a broad awareness or a general insight[32] into the nature of the trial, what it will deal with,

[27] See, among other sources, with further references *Liebreich v Germany* App no 30443/03 ECtHR, 8 January 2008, para 2(a); *Pylnev v Russia* App no 3038/03 ECtHR, 9 February 2010, para 3(b).

[28] If necessary, this can be done by video link, provided it is of sufficient quality and works without interruptions and its use does not hinder the confidential communication between the defendant and counsel; see *Gennadiy Medvedev v Russia* App no. 34184/03, ECtHR, 24 April 2012, paras 30, 37–38 (no violation); and in more detail *Marcello Viola v Italy* App no 45106/04 ECtHR, 5 October 2006, paras 63–77 (no violation).

[29] See, eg, *Liebreich v Germany* (n 27) para 2(a); *Pylnev v Russia* (n 27) para 3(b).

[30] In this sense, see *Güveç v Turkey* App no 70337/01 ECtHR, 20 January 2009, para 124; *SC v UK* App no 60958/00 ECtHR, 15 June 2004, para 29.

[31] *SC v UK* (n 30) para 29.

[32] Sometimes the following wording is used: 'that the accused understands in general the character of the proceedings'; in that sense *Tarasov v Ukraine* App no 17416/03 ECtHR, 31 October 2013, para 98.

and what is at stake. Still, this minimum requirement for the level of understanding is strict in the sense that there can be no effective participation if the defendant does not meet this requirement. Such a lack of understanding on the part of the defendant cannot be compensated for by adequate legal aid from competent and experienced counsel, for example.[33] A fair criminal procedure simply is not feasible in that situation. The defendant will then be found unfit to stand trial[34] and the criminal proceedings discontinued under those circumstances.

Nevertheless, the ECtHR opts for a fairly general and flexible approach with the above-mentioned standard. The International Criminal Court shows that other approaches are possible. With a view to the right to a fair trial, this Court requires among other things that the defendant understands the nature, cause, and content of the accusation against him in detail, is able to follow the proceedings, able to instruct counsel, understands the consequences of the proceedings, and is capable of making a statement.[35] Ultimately, the level of guarantee required by the ECtHR is actually more in line with this approach than appears at first sight. After all, it appears from the ECtHR case law quoted above that the defendant will have to be able to understand the case to such a degree that he can instruct his counsel in a meaningful way about essential parts of the case. If the defendant is not capable of doing that, he does not meet the required minimum level of understanding. This does not alter the fact that it will not be necessary for the defendant to understand fully all legal and evidential complexities and all exchanges during the proceedings.[36]

The capacities required by the ECtHR for effective participation by the defendant include his physical condition,[37] mental state,[38] hearing,[39] language competence,[40]

[33] See *T v UK* App no 24724/94 ECtHR, 16 December 1999, paras 88–89; *SC v UK* (n 30) paras 25, 29–30, 34, and 37. Also when a defendant has an insufficient command of the language in which the trial is conducted and in the absence of an interpreter, this obstacle to effective participation cannot be compensated for by the presence of counsel; see *Cuscani v UK* App no 32771/96 ECtHR, 24 September 2002, paras 34–40.

[34] Also see P Bal and F Koenraadt, *Het psychisch onvermogen terecht te staan. Waarborg of belemmering van het recht op een eerlijk proces* (*The Psychological Inability to Stand Trial. Safeguard or Obstacle to the Right to a Fair Trial*) (Boom Juridische uitgevers 2004) 53–54.

[35] In relation to other international courts, see also I Freckelton and M Karagiannakis, 'Fitness to Stand Trial under International Criminal Law. Challenges for Law and Policy' (2014) 12 Journal of International Criminal Justice 705, 722.

[36] *SC v UK* (n 30) para 29.

[37] *Tarasov v Ukraine* (n 32) paras 98–101 (violation regarding a defendant who was unable to walk and sit and had to be brought in on a stretcher and lie there during the entire trial, and who was not able to deliver a closing statement); *Bortnik v Ukraine* App no 39582/04 ECtHR, 27 January 2011, para 43 (violation in the case of an alcoholic defendant with a physical handicap, from a disadvantaged group); *Pylnev v Russia* (n 27) para 3(b) (no violation).

[38] *Güveç v Turkey* (n 30) paras 123–33 (violation involving a minor with psychological problems without counsel); *Liebreich v Germany* (n 27) para 2(a) (no violation involving a depressed defendant under the influence of medication).

[39] See with further references—*Grigoryevskikh v Russia* App no 22/03 ECtHR, 9 April 2009, paras 78–94 (violation); *Timergaliyev v Russia* App no 40631/02 ECtHR, 14 October 2008 (violation).

[40] See, eg, *Baytar v Turkey* App no 45440/04 ECtHR, 14 October 2014, paras 46–59 (violation because of the absence of an interpreter during police questioning); *Cuscani v UK* (n 33) paras 34–40 (violation because of the absence of an interpreter, as a consequence of which the defendant could not be fully involved in the criminal proceedings).

and intellectual abilities,[41] so that the defendant's immaturity,[42] age, and social background can also play a part.[43] Also relevant are the possibilities of using resources such as notes they may have prepared, regardless of whether the defendant has legal aid or not.[44] With regard to shortcomings in these abilities, the defence must have the opportunity to demonstrate effectively—and with sufficient substantiation[45]—that the defendant is unable to stand trial.[46]

However, this is not to say that each limitation of the above-mentioned abilities must immediately be considered an obstacle to effective participation.[47] The authorities will have to assess to what extent effective participation is compromised and whether compensatory measures are therefore required. In general, it falls to the state to decide how—within its national legal system—the possibility of effective participation is ensured.[48] This will have to be done in a genuinely effective manner, though.[49] The authorities and the judge in particular can therefore be required to take positive measures in a specific case, which will truly enable the defendant to participate effectively in the proceedings.[50]

This may involve both remedial and compensatory measures. Measures that can counteract shortcomings in abilities include the provision of medicines to suppress pain or psychoses for example, an interpreter, extra explanation for the defendant, and closing the doors, so that effective participation is not rendered impossible as a consequence of intimidation by the public. Compensation can consist of providing aid by counsel, provided that—as discussed above—the defendant at least meets the required minimum level of understanding. In the final analysis, the benchmark is whether the defendant can sufficiently participate effectively. For defendants who are sufficiently capable of doing so, but nevertheless have limited mental or

[41] *SC v UK* (n 30) paras 26–37 (violation involving an eleven-year-old with limited intellectual abilities); *Vaudelle v France* App no 35683/97 ECtHR, 30 January 2001, paras 50–66 (violation involving a defendant who had been deemed to be unfit to defend himself in earlier civil proceedings).

[42] See, eg, *Blokhin v Russia* App no 47152/06 ECtHR, 14 November 2013, para 157.

[43] See *Botnik v Ukraine* App no 39582/04 ECtHR, 27 January 2011, para 43.

[44] *Mościcki v Poland* App no 52443/07 ECtHR, 14 June 2011, para 42 (violation); *Pullicino v Malta* App no 45441/99 ECtHR, 15 June 2000, para A(3) (no violation, because the procedure as a whole was fair, thanks to the assistance from counsel, among other things).

[45] See, eg, *Andrey Yakovenko v Ukraine* App no 63727/11 ECtHR, 13 March 2014, para 117 (insufficient substantiation); *Liebreich v Germany* (n 27) para 2 (idem); and the more general *Vasiliy Ivashchenko v Ukraine* App no 760/03 ECtHR, 26 July 2012, para 88.

[46] It also follows from the fact that—as we have seen above—a fair trial is not possible against a defendant who is not sufficiently capable of effective participation; see, among other sources, *SC v UK* (n 30) paras 26–37. Also compare *Aswat v UK* App no 62176/14 ECtHR, 6 January 2015, para 30, where the Court in its conclusion that extradition does not contravene Art 3 ECHR also takes into consideration that 'Although there is currently no suggestion that the applicant is unfit to plead, concerns regarding his fitness to plead have been answered in that it would be open to him to immediately challenge his fitness to stand trial'; *Kerr v UK* App no 63356/00 ECtHR, 23 September 2003 (requirements regarding fairness for persons who cannot participate effectively carry more weight in criminal cases than in civil cases).

[47] *Pylnev v Russia* (n 27) para 3(b) (poor health and distraction caused by pain did not impede effective participation).

[48] *Gennadiy Medvedev v Russia* (n 28) para 30. [49] ibid.

[50] See, eg, *Liebreich v Germany* (n 27)) para 2(a); *Pylnev v Russia* (n 27) para 3(b).

intellectual abilities, the authorities may be obliged to provide such assistance. This applies even if the defendant declines such assistance.[51]

In addition, the authorities' duty to take positive measures to ensure the right to effective participation is supported by Art 13 of the UN Convention on the Rights of Persons with Disabilities.[52] This provision states, among other things, that states parties must ensure that persons with disabilities can play an effective part as direct and indirect participant in all legal proceedings, including at investigative and other preliminary stages.

Safeguards for fairness during police questioning of defendants with limited abilities

Where the position of the defendant in the preliminary enquiry is already vulnerable in general, this is all the more so relative to police questioning. This is one of the reasons for the recognition of the right to legal assistance prior to questioning.[53] Such vulnerability exists *a fortiori* in the case of a defendant with insufficient abilities. For such defendants, states are therefore required to provide additional safeguards with respect to the right of access to counsel. In principle, the obligation on this point can apply to limitations of all the above-mentioned abilities: physical condition, mental state, hearing, language competence, intellectual abilities, and maturity. Vulnerabilities in these areas may also present because the defendant is blind,[54] or under the influence of alcohol for example, or because he is addicted.[55]

First, it is important that the limitations of abilities of the defendant may be such that he is not allowed to be questioned by the police without the assistance of legal counsel. This also means that if the defendant, having been informed of his right to legal aid, decides not to exercise this right, it cannot be assumed as easily as usual that the right to legal counsel was waived in a legally valid way.[56] In the case of serious incapacitation of the defendant, it must even be assumed that a conscious and intelligent choice of 'waiver' is not possible.[57] Consequently,

[51] *Prezec v Croatia* App no 48185/07 ECtHR, 15 October 2009, paras 25–32 (defendant with serious and permanent personality disorder with paranoid personality disorder, schizophrenic disorder, and a distinctly narcissistic pathology, as well as a strong tendency towards destructive and self-destructive behaviour); compare *Bortnik v Ukraine* (n 37) paras 43–44. See also Supreme Court 20 November 2011, ECLI:NL:HR:2011:BT6406, *NJ* 2012/29.

[52] *Convention on the Rights of Persons with Disabilities*, New York, 13 December 2006, *UN doc* A/RES/61/106 Annex I.

[53] See *Salduz v Turkey* App no 36391/02 ECtHR, (GC) 27 November 2008, paras 54–55.

[54] *Todorov v Ukraine* App no 16717/05 ECtHR, 12 January 2012, paras 74–81.

[55] *Plonka v Poland* App no 20310/02 ECtHR, 31 March 2009, para 38; *Bortnik v Ukraine* (n 37) para 43.

[56] *Omelchenko v Ukraine* App no 34592/06 ECtHR, 17 July 2014, para 49 (written and signed declaration of waiver by a vulnerable arrested suspect not legally valid); *Płonka v Poland* (n 55) paras 37–42 (no legally valid waiver by an arrested alcoholic suspect who had been drinking heavily the day before being questioned and who had been informed of her right to legal aid and had subsequently not requested such aid).

[57] See *Kravchenko v Ukraine* App no 23275/06 ECtHR, 24 June 2014, paras 60–62 (waiver by a schizophrenic suspect who had been declared legally incapacitated was voluntary but not conscious nor intelligent).

the authorities will in principle have to ensure actively that the right to counsel during questioning is effected in the case of less capable and/or vulnerable defendants.[58] That obligation is indeed not necessarily limited to defendants who have been deprived of their liberty. It may also apply to persons who have not formally been arrested, and even those who have not formally been designated as suspects.[59]

According to the Court, the requirement that persons who are not able to defend themselves on account of physical or mental limitations be legally represented as soon as the authorities are aware of the limitation is consistent with Art 6 ECHR.[60] This also means that the above-mentioned obligations only actually arise if the suspect or defendant informs the questioning authorities of his limitation or if there are indications, because of which the authorities have to assume that they are dealing with someone with limited abilities.[61]

No right to terminate the trial and no impediment to fair proceedings by suspension

As observed above, it follows from Art 6 ECHR that a criminal procedure cannot continue if the defendant does not meet the required minimum level of understanding and consequently cannot participate effectively. As a result, and only to this extent, a right to suspension of the criminal proceedings ensues from the ECHR, which can be exercised, for example, by suspending the prosecution or the trial inquiry. However, there is no right to a definitive termination of the criminal proceedings on the grounds that the defendant is insufficiently able to stand trial.[62]

Justifiable or necessary suspension of the criminal proceedings because of genuine incapacity of the defendant does not lead to a violation of the requirement regarding a reasonable time either.[63] That is clear. After all, a state would otherwise find it hard to escape a violation of the Convention with an incapable defendant: suspending the proceedings would soon cause a violation of the principle of a reasonable time, whereas continuing the proceedings would be incompatible with the right to effective participation. Moreover, in principle Art 6 ECHR—on account of the 'criminal

[58] See also *Kaçiu and Kotorri v Albania* App no 33192/07 ECtHR, 25 June 2013, para 120.

[59] *Sobko v Ukraine* App no 15102/10 ECtHR, 17 December 2015, paras 12–13 and 54–62 (violation of Art 6(3)(c) ECHR versus a suspect of low intelligence who was originally interviewed as a witness, and was interviewed further at the police station without having been arrested and without him having been told that he was a suspect).

[60] In *Kravchenko v Ukraine* (n 57), para 68 (in connection with 39).

[61] ibid paras 63–70 (therefore in this case no violation of Art 6(3)(c) ECHR).

[62] *Krakolinig v Austria* App no 33992/07 ECtHR, 10 May 2012, para 27; *Antoine v UK* App no 62960/00 ECtHR, 13 May 2003, para 1(B). Nevertheless, for a critical take on the fact that proceedings cannot be terminated definitively if the defendant is permanently insufficiently capable of standing trial, see: *Nichitaylov v Ukraine* App no 36024/03 ECtHR, 15 October 2009, para 36.

[63] *Krakolinig v Austria* (n 62) paras 18–28. However, in those cases where a defendant becomes increasingly less capable, there may be an obligation for the authorities to speed up the proceedings: failure to do so could cause a violation of the principle of reasonable time; according to *Nichitaylov v Ukraine* (n 62) para 39.

charge' requirement—does not apply to procedures taking place after the defendant has been declared unfit to stand trial.[64]

This does not alter the fact that if it is clear that there is not a realistic prospect that the defendant will become sufficiently fit to stand trial, fairness requires—perhaps even the principles of due process[65]—that the prosecuting authorities formally make a decision to abstain from further prosecution.[66]

Preliminary conclusion: task for legislator and legal practice

The gist of the case law of the ECtHR is that each defendant must be able to participate sufficiently effectively in the criminal proceedings against him. Moreover, each defendant must be able to safeguard his own interests sufficiently during questioning in the preliminary enquiry.

First, this means that the system of criminal procedure must be set up and applied in such a way that each defendant actually—not merely defendants in general—has that opportunity. The ECtHR is primarily concerned about participation during the trial in this respect. In the criminal justice system of the Netherlands, however, the immediacy principle (the principle that holds that all evidence has to be produced and discussed at trial in the presence of the defendant and of the judges who decide the case[67]) does not have a strong position, and the emphasis is on the preliminary inquiry. The emphasis on that phase of criminal justice will only increase further as a result of the modernisation of the Code of Criminal Procedure.[68] If the presentation and discussion of the evidence cannot or will not take place during the trial, it must in principle be guaranteed that the defendant's participation in the investigation will be possible prior to the trial. The considerations of the ECtHR quoted above show, for example, that effective participation also applies to witness examinations. When witnesses are examined in the preliminary enquiry rather than at the trial, this means

[64] See *Antoine v UK* (n 62) para 1(B); *Kerr v UK* (n 46) para B. In my opinion, the same applies almost certainly to procedures to assess the defendant's fitness to stand trial, in view of this case law, the Engel criteria (*Engel v Netherlands* App no 5100/71 ECtHR, 8 June 1976, para 82), the decision of the *Mosbeux v Belgique* (1991) 71 DR 269 and the type of procedures which, according to the ECtHR, do not concern a criminal charge; see the list in DJ Harris et al (eds), *Harris, O'Boyle & Warbrick, Law of the European Convention on Human Rights* (3rd edn, OUP 2014) 373.

[65] Within the criminal justice system of the Netherlands, the relevant criterion is that no member of the Public Prosecution Office acting reasonably can claim that any interest protected by enforcement of criminal law would be served by continuing the prosecution; see Supreme Court 16 November 2012, ECLI:NL:HR:2012:BX4280, *NJ* 2013/109 with case note by TMCJ Schalken; Supreme Court 2 July 2013, ECLI:NL:HR:2013:7, *NJ* 2013/563 with case note by PHPHMC van Kempen.

[66] See also Bal and Koenraadt, *Het psychisch onvermogen terecht te staan. Waarborg of belemmering van het recht op een eerlijk proces* (n 34) 46, 71, 82.

[67] See, eg, Marc S Groenhuijsen and Hatice Selçuk, 'The Principle of Immediacy in Dutch Criminal Procedure in the Perspective of European Human Rights Law' (2014) 126(1) Zeitschrift für die gesamte Strafrechtswissenschaft 248. See also *Cutean v Romania* App no 53150/12 ECtHR, 2 December 2014, paras 60–61; *PK v Finland* App no 37442/97 ECtHR, 9 July 2002, para 1(a).

[68] *Parliamentary Documents II* 2015–16, 29 279, no 278 (n 14), 4, 9–11. These proposals are characterised by a 'move forward': the importance of the preliminary investigation gains weight relative to the examination at trial. The same applies for the examination at the trial hearing in first instance relative to the hearing on appeal.

that in principle the defendant will have to be able to follow the witness examination during the preliminary enquiry. Therefore, it is appropriate for the modernisation to result in defendants being able to attend the examination of witnesses more often than is currently the case.[69]

Secondly, the principles in the European Court's case law imply that when the abilities of defendants are less than optimal for effective participation, the system of criminal procedure needs to offer the possibility of taking measures to remedy or compensate for the lack of abilities. It will be the responsibility of the examining magistrate and the trial court in particular to see to this. Compensation for limitations regarding effective participation is not possible however, if the defendant does not at least meet the required minimum level of understanding. This appears to be different in the case of limited abilities on the part of the defendant when questioned during the preliminary enquiry. At that point, compensation must be provided through the assistance of counsel.

Finally, the following deserves attention. With many fundamental rights in the ECHR, a somewhat higher level of safeguards appears to be required when one focuses on the general principles given prominence by the ECtHR in its case law as opposed to when one considers exclusively the details of concrete cases in which the Court establishes a violation of the Convention. Those general principles result not only from a commitment to fairness and veracity, but also from the recognition by the ECtHR that criminal justice must be effective and efficient, and that states must therefore have room to make choices in that respect. It is possible to see the minimum standards arising from the Convention and the relevant case law of the ECtHR primarily as obligations—which they are, to be sure—and to interpret and apply them as parsimoniously as possible by concentrating on the above-mentioned case details in order to ascertain what is required. However, in view of the focus of the general principles on fairness, veracity, efficacy, and discretion for states, it would be valuable for legislators and other authorities to see these principles in a positive light as opportunities for inspiration and quality. This certainly also applies relative to the issue of defendants with limited abilities.

The Need for Reinforcement of the Legal Position of Insufficiently Capable Defendants

The foregoing gives rise to two categories of interconnected arguments to safeguard the position of defendants with limited abilities more effectively in the system of legal procedure: a criminal procedure that is increasingly focused on adversariality and the right to a fair trial as guaranteed by Art 6 ECHR. Now the question is in which concrete areas the legislator must provide better safeguards for the position of defendants with limited abilities. Although the focus will be on the Netherlands,

[69] ibid 31, 37.

many of the following recommendations can be of value to other jurisdictions as well.

Defendants who are unfit to stand trial

Pursuant to Art 6 ECHR, the defendant must display a minimum level of understanding which enables him to comprehend in a general sense the nature of the trial, its subject matter, and what is at stake, to such an extent that he is able to instruct his counsel in a meaningful way about the essential aspects of the case. Although this requirement appears to be minimal from an international point of view, it involves stricter demands on the abilities—the level of understanding—of the defendant than Art 16 of the Code of Criminal Procedure does. This provision states that the court suspends the prosecution of the defendant for the reason that he is unfit to stand trial. A defendant is unfit for trial, according to the provision, if he 'suffers from such mental disease or defect to the extent that he lacks the capacity to understand the purpose of the prosecution instituted against him'. The legislator herewith codified the case law of the Dutch Supreme Court in 1986.[70]

It follows from that case law that unfitness to stand trial in the sense of Art 16 CCP only applies if the defendant suffers from a mental illness to such an extent that he 'is no longer capable of understanding the gist of the prosecution instituted against him'.[71] The Supreme Court thus rejected the requirement used by the district court in this case according to which the defendant is already unfit to stand trial if he is judged to be unable to conduct his defence (or have his defence conducted for him) properly.[72] Taking into account that this criterion therefore does not apply to Art 16 CCP, whereas it does reasonably fit the level of understanding as required by Art 6 ECHR, the conclusion must be drawn that the requirements for the defendant's abilities in Art 16 CCP are too low.

Consequently, currently cases may present themselves in which the defendant is insufficiently capable of participating in proceedings, without there being any room for applying Art 16 CCP. In that case, prosecution would contravene Art 6 ECHR.[73] Although Art 16 CCP already needs to be modified for that reason alone, there are several other objections which give rise to this need, as will shortly become apparent. This leads to the following.

Implication 1. It is desirable to introduce a criterion for suspension of prosecution which would encompass more causes of unfitness to stand trial than is currently the

[70] WECA Valkenburg, 'Commentary to Art 16, annotation 1' in CPM Cleiren et al (eds), *Tekst & Commentaar Strafvordering* (*Commentaries on the Code of Criminal Procedure*) (11th edn, Kluwer 2015).

[71] See paras 5(2)(1) and 5(3) of Supreme Court 5 February 1980, ECLI:NL:HR:1980:AB7357, *NJ* 1980/104 with case note by AL Melai (*Menten Case*).

[72] See also para 2 of the case note to this judgment, by AL Melai. For extensive information on this, see MS Groenhuijsen et al (eds), *Wetboek van Strafvordering* (*Code of Criminal Procedure*) (Kluwer) (unbound/online) commentary to Art 16 CCP, annotation 2 (1 October 1989); see also M van der Wolf et al, 'Understanding and Evaluating Contrasting Unfitness to Stand Trial Practices: A Comparison between Canada and the Netherlands' (2010) 9(3) International Journal of Forensic Mental Health 245, 246–47.

[73] See above, section headed 'Guarantees for effective participation by defendants during trial' at page 237.

case. The foundation for the possibility of suspension is the fairness of the trial. If a fair trial is not compatible with the prosecution of incapacitated persons, the question why they are incapacitated is irrelevant.

Although deficient development or a pathological disorder of mental faculties are the most important categories, there can be more physical causes for an inability to defend oneself, for example if the defendant is a terminal patient and exhausted or has gone both deaf and blind. After all, as we have seen before, the defendant's capacities for effective participation as required by the ECtHR include not only his mental state, intellectual abilities, and maturity, but also his physical condition and hearing.

Meanwhile, the possibility of suspension should not be applicable if the defendant cannot participate effectively for reasons that are nothing to do with mental or physical limitations, for example if the defendant is detained abroad. In view of the above, it may be desirable to limit the legal criterion regarding possible causes of unfitness to stand trial to 'deficient development or pathological disorder of mental faculties' (already excepted by law) but with the addition of 'serious physical illness and limitations'.

Implication 2. Subsequently, the emphasis in that criterion must be on the heart of the matter: the effects of the inability to defend oneself. The decisive question there is whether the defendant is so incapable that he does not have at least a general understanding of the nature, subject, and importance of the criminal proceedings and cannot instruct his counsel about essential aspects of the case. The current criterion for suspension of the prosecution for reason that the defendant is unfit to stand trial in Art 16 CCP is, as has been noted above, that he is not capable of understanding the gist of the criminal proceedings levelled against him. In view of the foregoing, that criterion does not immediately satisfy the requirements of Art 6 ECHR. Moreover, it is also rather inquisitorial in nature, in the sense that the defendant takes centre stage as the subject of prosecution, without expressing the importance of the ability to defend oneself. Given both the trend towards an increasingly adversarial position for the defendant and the requirement of effective participation for a fair trial, it is desirable to include in the criterion for suspension the defendant's ability to make a sufficient contribution to his defence.

Implication 3. From the point of view of the right to effective participation, it is not relevant when the unfitness to stand trial came about. Nevertheless, it is argued by some that the possibility of suspension only needs to exist in those cases where the unfitness to stand trial came about after the commission of the offence, because the offence in cases where that unfitness existed at that time will not be attributed to the defendant, by virtue of Arts 37 and 39 of the Criminal Code (CC) of The Netherlands.[74] Article 37 CC states that 'The court may order the admission of a person, who cannot be held responsible for committing a criminal offence by reason

[74] In that sense Groenhuijsen et al, *Wetboek van Strafvordering* (n 72). On these provisions, see PJP Tak, *The Dutch Criminal Justice System* (Wolf Legal Publishers 2008) 74, 120–22; see also Susanna Radovic et al, 'Introducing a Standard of Legal Insanity: The Case of Sweden compared to the Netherlands' (2015) 40 International Journal of Law and Psychiatry 43, 46.

of deficient development or a pathological disorder of mental faculties, to a psychiatric hospital for a term of one year, but only if he poses a danger to himself, to others, or to the general safety of persons or property.' Article 39 CC provides the so-called insanity defence (an excuse): 'Any person who commits an offence for which he cannot be held responsible by reason of deficient development or pathological disorder of his mental faculties shall not be criminally liable.' The view that the possibility of suspension can be limited to cases where the unfitness to stand trial came about after the commission of the offence is problematic in my opinion, for the following reasons.

First of all, there may be other causes for unfitness to stand trial not covered by Arts 37 and 39 CC, as we saw earlier. Furthermore, before one arrives at the point where these provisions can be applied, there will first have to be a fair trial concerning the criminal charge (although this can be circumvented, see *Implication 4* below). Although the text of Art 16 CCP, since the amendment of the law in 1986, no longer requires that the inability must have arisen after the commission of the offence, it is still a controversial issue in Dutch literature and case law.[75] With the modernisation of the Code of Criminal Procedure, it must be clear without any room for misunderstanding, that the suspension of a trial is possible, regardless of the moment when the defendant became unfit to stand trial.

Implication 4. Does this mean that the application of Art 37 ff. CC (ie, psychiatric hospital order, entrustment order[76]) is ruled out for defendants who are unfit to stand trial? That is not necessarily so. It needs to be arranged in legislation roughly as follows. It should be possible first to declare the defendant to be unfit for trial. Subsequently, the trial should be able to continue, but in the first instance primarily for the purpose of answering the question whether the defendant is accountable for his actions. The judge must then declare the defendant to be wholly criminally unaccountable (in the sense of Art 39 CC) in an interim ruling. If this happens—in which case it is no longer possible to impose a punitive penalty—then, as we have seen before, there is no longer a criminal charge.[77] That means that Art 6 ECHR no longer applies on that ground, nor does the right to effective participation. Regarding the question whether an Art 37 ff. CC measure deserves to be applied, the following can be addressed (possibly by another panel of judges): whether the defendant actually committed the act he is accused of; if so, whether the act constitutes a criminal offence; and if so, which measure is justified.[78] The procedure cannot be allowed to end in a conviction.[79] It merely aims to establish to which non-punitive

[75] See also M van der Wolf et al, 'Understanding and Evaluating Contrasting Unfitness to Stand Trial Practices: A Comparison between Canada and the Netherlands' (n 72) 245, 254.

[76] Art 37a(1) CC sets the conditions under which the court '*may order the detention under an entrustment order of a defendant who at the time of the commission of the offence suffered from deficient development or a pathological disorder of mental faculties*'.

[77] ECHR (n 73).

[78] The Dutch system of sanctions distinguishes between penalties (which are punitive in nature, such as prison sentences, fines, and community service) and measures (which are not meant to be punitive but are aimed at maintaining security and safety or at restoring a state of affairs, such as the psychiatric hospital order in Art 37 CC or the confiscation of illegally obtained profits); see further Tak, *The Dutch Criminal Justice System* (n 74) 111–23.

[79] See *Antoine v UK* (n 62) para 1(B); *Kerr v UK* App (n 46) para B.

measure the person involved must be subjected, given the deficient development or pathological disorder of his mental faculties which grounded his unaccountability. Thus, the foregoing is only meaningful for defendants who are both unfit to stand trial and cannot be held accountable for the act (the fact that the defendant is wholly unaccountable for the offence does not necessarily mean that that defendant will also be unfit to stand trial; ie a person can be criminally non-responsible but not unfit to stand trial). In my opinion, it would be advisable to include this possibility in legislation.

Implication 5. Finally, I believe it is desirable that the defendant who is unfit to stand trial after a certain period should be able to request a definitive end to prosecution if it is no longer possible, taking into account the incapability of the defendant, to initiate further proceedings that may serve any interest protected by enforcement of criminal law. This may happen, for example, in the case of the defendant who is actually definitively unfit to stand trial (or in whose case the procedure described above has been applied). While Art 6 ECHR (strictly speaking) does not require this, as became apparent before, this does not alter the fact that it is a suitable element of decent criminal procedure, also that it creates clarity for any victims and for the defendant's relatives.

Defendants with limited capacity for effective participation during trial

The fact that a defendant can meet the required minimum level of understanding and therefore qualifies as sufficiently fit to stand trial does not necessarily mean that he is also able to exercise his right to effective participation sufficiently—let alone doing that well. Defendants who are fit to stand trial but who nevertheless do have limited—mental or physical—abilities, may require remedial or compensatory measures to be taken. Article 509a–509d CCP provides for possibilities to that effect 'if it is believed that the defendant suffers from deficient development or a pathological disorder of his mental faculties and due to said defect is unable to properly look after his own interests' (Art 509a(1) CCP). If the trial court in its ruling declares that this is the case, an order will be issued to assign legal counsel to the defendant (Art 509c CCP). From the moment of that declaration, all rights and powers that the defendant has are shared by this counsel (Art 509d(3) CCP). There is no place for waiver of the right to legal aid then.[80] This arrangement is both too wide and too narrow in scope.

Implication 6. The legislation of Art 509a ff. CCP is too wide because it can also be applied to defendants that are unfit to stand trial but cannot be recognised as such under the current Art 16 CCP. This applies if one assumes that Art 16 CCP is unusable for incapacities that already existed at the time when the offence was committed, and it certainly applies to the defendant's incapacities of a physical nature. If the defendant cannot meet the required level of understanding because of his

[80] Supreme Court 17 November 2009, ECLI:NL:HR:2009:BI2315, *NJ* 2010/143 (n 25) para 3(3)(3).

incapability, there can be no more effective participation, and trying the defendant would conflict with Art 6 ECHR. As we said, this cannot be compensated for through providing adequate legal aid by a knowledgeable and experienced counsel.[81] The compensation provision—as it is currently defined in Art 509a ff. CCP—should therefore only be applied to defendants with limited capacities who can yet qualify as fit to stand trial. The provisions for suspension of prosecution (currently Art 16 CCP) and those for compulsory legal aid (as currently defined in Art 509a ff. CCP) should therefore be harmonised.

Implication 7. At the same time, the criterion in Art 509a CCP can be said to be too narrow, at least in part. The applicability of the legislation if the defendant is not capable of defending his own interests properly because of his limitations is in principle very compatible with both the right to effective participation in Art 6 ECHR and the increasingly adversarial criminal proceedings. However, the scope is too narrow in that the provisions of Art 509a–509d CCP only apply if the cause of the poor skills to defend himself are rooted in the stunted development or pathological disorder of the mental faculties.

As we discussed in detail above, it may be necessary for realisation of the right to effective participation that other limitations of the defendant—of a physical or gerontological nature, for example—are compensated for. After all, it is not relevant in the context of Art 6 ECHR what the exact cause of the limitation is. That is why the law should also recognise 'physical and gerontological diseases and limitations' as possible causes of limited abilities to defend oneself.

Moreover, the concepts of 'deficient development' and 'pathological disorder' of the mental faculties (sometimes also referred to as mental disease or defect) must be interpreted broadly here. For example, compensatory measures will also need to be taken for defendants who are to such extent less intelligent, alert, or sharp than the average person that they cannot independently conduct an essential active defence for themselves. With this last category, usually action will have to be taken to ensure that at least legal aid is provided.

Implication 8. Apart from the above, the legislation should not be restricted to compensation through (mandatory) legal aid. If there is reason to believe that the defendant can exercise his right to effective participation independently only to a limited extent, legislation must make sure that the court assesses which remedial and compensatory measures are called for, in the light of the specific limitations of the defendant and given the nature of the case.[82] The case law of the ECtHR referred to earlier contains measures such as the provision of medicines to suppress pain or psychoses, an interpreter, extra explanation for the defendant, and closing the doors (in camera), so that effective participation is not rendered impossible as a consequence of intimidation by the public. One could also think of providing assistance to the

[81] See *T v UK* (n 33), paras 88–89; *SC v UK* (n 30) paras 25, 29–30, 34, and 37. Also when a defendant has an insufficient command of the language in which the trial is conducted and in the absence of an interpreter, this obstacle to effective participation cannot be compensated for by the presence of counsel; see *Cuscani v UK* (n 33) paras 34–40.

[82] cf Supreme Court 17 November 2009, ECLI:NL:HR:2009:BI2315, *NJ* 2010/143 (n 25) para 3(4).

defendant from a social worker or psychologist. In my opinion, it is therefore desirable that the law offers an explicit, non-limitative list of measures, so the judge can implement them or have them implemented.

Implication 9. In view of the previous two recommendations, there will have to be room in the procedure for the court to have an investigation carried out into the nature and seriousness of the defendant's limitations, lest it may be established to what extent measures need to be taken and which measures they need to be.

Defendants with limited capacity during police questioning and preliminary enquiry

Both defendants who have been arrested and those who have not are entitled to access to a lawyer *before* they are questioned by the police.[83] Although defendants who have not been arrested may also be eligible for subsidised legal aid under certain circumstances, they are not in any case assigned legal counsel automatically,[84] not even where the defendant has limited capabilities. However, if an arrested so-called vulnerable suspect or vulnerable accused is involved (see below for the meaning of the term), counsel needs to be assigned automatically.[85] According to Art 28c(2) CCP, vulnerable defendants can only waive the right to access to a lawyer after they have been informed of the consequences thereof by counsel.

Furthermore, the right to assistance from counsel *during* police questioning is recognised under Dutch law for arrested defendants; it has first been recognised in case law[86] and subsequently in the legislation that implements the EU Directive on the right to access to a lawyer.[87] The statutory right to assistance during police questioning applies both for defendants who have been arrested and for defendants who have been invited to appear in a specific location in order to be questioned; see Art 28d CCP. The right to assistance when being questioned is not available for defendants who have neither been arrested nor been summoned, not even in the case of a defendant with limited abilities.

Also of importance here is that Art 27c CCP provides defendants the right to information about their rights. Pursuant to this provision, defendants who have not been arrested are also informed about their right to legal assistance at n 53 prior to the first police interview at the latest and if applicable, about the right to interpretation and translation. Additionally, arrested defendants will be provided with information about their other rights during the preliminary enquiry (the so-called 'letter of rights'). The law does not pay specific attention to defendants of limited abilities here.

There is no question that the above-mentioned legislation has led to an improved position of the vulnerable defendant in the preliminary enquiry. Nevertheless,

[83] See Art 28(1) CCP and *Parliamentary Documents II* 2014–15, 34 157, no 2 (Bill), and no 3, 20 (Explanatory memorandum).

[84] *Parliamentary Documents II* 2014–15, 34 157, no 3, 20 (Explanatory memorandum).

[85] See Art 28b(1) CCP.

[86] See Supreme Court 22 December 2015 (n 16).

[87] See Art 28d CCP.

the legislation would benefit from further improvement in a number of respects, among other things with a view to addressing the requirements from the relevant EU Directives and Art 6 ECHR.

Implication 10. Although the wording of the law ('vulnerable defendant'—'kwetsbare verdachte') as such offers enough room to encompass all defendants (suspects and accused) with limited abilities, as they are all vulnerable, the memorandum of explanation indicates that it must be taken to mean 'juvenile suspects and defendants with a mental disorder or mental disability'.[88] This definition, however, is not in accordance with the Directive on the right of access to a lawyer. That does not contain a formal definition, but establishes more materially, and in a significantly broader scope, that 'a fair administration of justice' depends on a 'duty of care' towards defendants 'who are in a potentially weak position' and that the authorities must therefore take into account 'any potential vulnerability' that affects their ability to exercise their right of access to a lawyer, among other things.[89] Moreover, all limitations affecting the defendant's capacity—including alcoholism—could necessitate access to a lawyer pursuant to Art 6 ECHR.[90]

That is why at the very least a wider interpretation of 'vulnerable defendant' should be recognised in the Parliamentary Documents than is currently the case, but it would be better to do so in the actual legislation or, alternatively, in a corresponding implementing rule. At least the following persons should qualify as vulnerable: persons with an (apparent) mental handicap or a disorder of cognitive functions, such as Parkinson's or Alzheimer's disease or a disorder affecting perception, memory, thinking, language/speech, attention, concentration, and executive functions and motor skills. In view of Art 6 ECHR, this will also have to include people with a temporary functional disorder, for example as a result of the influence of medicines, alcohol, or drugs.

Of course, none of this means that each imperfection in a defendant should lead to the measures that are discussed below, or any other ones.[91] The main point is whether the limitation entails that the defendant must be qualified as insufficiently capable. As far as the interview is concerned, the criterion ought to be whether the limitation is of such a nature that the defendant is not capable of adequately and independently looking after his own interests, participating in the interview, and deciding whether or not to use his right to remain silent. For other investigative acts during the preliminary enquiry the criterion is whether the limitation impedes effective participation.

Implication 11. Defendants with limited abilities who have not been arrested do not have the right to be assigned counsel automatically, and do not have the right to assistance during questioning if they are interviewed unexpectedly or, for example,

[88] *Parliamentary Documents II* 2014–15, 34 157, no 3, 40 (Explanatory memorandum).

[89] See consideration 51 of the European Parliament and Council Directive 2013/48/EU of 22 October 2013 (n 16).

[90] See for information on ECHR (n 73) section headed "Safeguards for fairness during police questioning of defendants with limited abilities at page 240".

[91] cf Supreme Court 15 December 2015, ECLI:NL:HR:2015:3580, *NJ* 2016/454 with case note by TMCJ Schalken (pain because of recent burns and the analgesics taken to alleviate the pain did not lead to a reduced awareness, nor to a confession that was not freely made).

at home or in the street. Furthermore, they do not get special protection against waiving their rights and they do not have to receive a 'letter of rights'. The current legislation and modernisation plans make little or no mention of defendants with limited abilities who have not been arrested. Yet, the interview of a defendant with limited abilities who has not been arrested, and for whom access to counsel has not explicitly been realised, may contravene Art 6 ECHR.[92] Apparently, the Dutch Supreme Court also reckons with that possibility.[93]

That is hardly surprising, since the first police interview may be crucial for the subsequent course and outcome of the case. That is exactly why it is appropriate to recognise in legislation the right to assistance during questioning and to have counsel assigned for vulnerable defendants, if they are insufficiently aware of it and/or insufficiently capable of functioning adequately during the interview in cases where they have not been arrested. In that case, the same threshold for waivers should apply as that of Art 28c(2) CCP. This should, however, perhaps only apply to more serious offences. For example, offences that are punishable by a prison sentence for a maximum of twelve years, acts where the victim died or suffered grievous bodily harm, and the more serious sexual offences. Moreover, the interviewing authorities will need to have reasonable cause to believe that they are dealing with someone with limited abilities.

Implication 12. Within the condition mentioned above regarding more serious offences, it is desirable that the defendant with limited abilities who has not been arrested can also have an assigned counsel at other times during the preliminary enquiry. This is the case, for example, when important investigative acts such as examining witnesses are carried out, where the defendant has a right to attend, and legal counsel is needed to safeguard the defendant's right to effective participation.[94] The law should therefore also provide for this.

Implication 13. According to Art 3(2) of the EU Directive on the right to information,[95] 'any particular needs' must be taken into account in the case of vulnerable defendants when they are furnished with information—orally or in writing—about their rights (the right to legal advice and aid, information about the charges, interpretation, and translation, and the right to remain silent). Neither Art 27c CCP nor its parliamentary explanation details how this obligation is fulfilled in the case of adult vulnerable defendants. It is desirable to integrate this obligation in the law, so it is clear that it should be normal practice to consider insufficiently capable defendants. To that end, policies must also be developed, so that information can be furnished to various categories of vulnerable defendants in a meaningful way.

[92] See for information on this ECHR (n 73) section headed "Safeguards for fairness during police questioning of defendants with limited abilities at page 240".

[93] Supreme Court 18 November 2014, ECLI:NL:HR:2014:3288, *NJ* 2015/49 (n 25) para 3(5): 'the question whether and under which circumstances certain general categories of [adult] [...] suspects who have not been arrested have a right to legal aid from a lawyer relative to police questioning should be addressed first and foremost by the legislator'.

[94] For information on the defendant's presence during the witness examination in the preliminary enquiry see also ECHR (n 73) section headed "Preliminary conclusion: task for legislator and legal practice" at page 242.

[95] European Parliament and Council Directive 2012/13/EU (n 17).

Provisions in the law

According to the modernisation project, the objective is to bring the provisions of Art 16 CCP and those of Art 509a ff. CCP together under the special procedures.[96] That seems commendable. In this way, the trial court can determine in the procedure whether the defendant (in view of his limited abilities) will be able to realise the minimum level of understanding required for the right to effective participation. If that is not the case, the defendant—irrespective of when and why the incapacity first manifested itself—must be declared unfit to stand trial. If that is the case, the judge can determine to what extent and which remedial and/or compensatory measures must be taken. Additionally, and finally, the following must be pointed out.

Implication 14. The government's modernisation plans aim to bring about a clear framework for the powers and position in the proceedings of the various participants in criminal justice, where a balanced system of safeguards for rights is provided as well as a proper evaluation of the various interests of these participants.[97] In the light of the foregoing, it is desirable to include a general provision for the legal position of vulnerable defendants in the Code as well. In addition to a sufficiently broad definition of this category of persons, all the defence rights and obligations for the authorities that apply specifically to this category can also be included. Not only would this lead to a more systematically embedded place for them in the Code, it would also emphasise that it is genuinely important to treat each of them carefully.

Conclusion

The principles of fairness, truthfulness, effectiveness, and humanity all require that criminal procedures take into consideration every defendant with no or limited abilities to participate sufficiently independently in police interviews, the preliminary inquiry, and the inquiry at the trial. The need to take these matters into account has increased in the past few years and will increase even further substantially, in the Netherlands as well as in other countries.

This is because first, Dutch case law and the Dutch legislator demonstrate an increasingly strong trend towards developing more adversarial elements in criminal procedures. The increase in defence responsibilities, with the associated threat of forfeiture of rights, constitutes an important—albeit not the only—component. It is therefore important to realise that flaws in the defence in a system that comes to rely more heavily on adversarial principles, among other things, will have a more acutely detrimental effect than in a stricter modern inquisitorial system. More than ever before, there is a reason to reinforce the legal position of the insufficiently capable defendant. Other arguments in favour of this are the right to a fair trial as expressed in Art 6 ECHR and various Directives from the European Union.

[96] *Parliamentary Documents II* 2015–16, 29 279, no 278 (n 14), 76 and 97.
[97] ibid 4 and 7.

In connection with this reinforcement, fourteen substantiated recommendations have been made above. They are primarily aimed at the legislator. That does not change the fact that when all is said and done, it is legal practice that will need to give effective attention to the legal position of defendants with no or only limited capabilities. That means police officers, members of the Public Prosecutions Department, judges, and lawyers will need to be vigilant to ensure that the fairness, truthfulness, effectiveness, and integrity of the criminal justice process are not jeopardised, notably when defendants who are unfit to stand trial still end up being tried, or because insufficient measures were taken for defendants with limited abilities in order for them to participate sufficiently effectively. In other words, there is an important task here for all professional key participants in criminal justice.

12

Competency to Stand Trial in Italy

*Alberto Cadoppi and Mattia Celva**

1. Introduction

Because this chapter is intended for an audience which is unlikely to have much knowledge of the Italian legal system some premises are essential to analyse the way in which 'fitness to plead' is regulated in Italy. It is therefore necessary to clarify some concepts in order to allow a better understanding of the following pages.

First, it should be noted that this issue is regulated by the Code of Criminal Procedure (CPP hereafter). Within the rules governing criminal proceedings, unfitness to stand trial means 'capacity to participate consciously in the trial'. Therefore, such capacity is at the heart of this analysis.[1] Furthermore, in this introduction, it is appropriate to mention that capacity to participate consciously in the trial is of a complex nature. Indeed, recently, some have suggested that such capacity overlaps with the concept of 'procedural capacity'.[2]

However, a similar point of view has been articulated differently by other academics. For example, some believe that the absence of the capacity to participate consciously in the trial does not affect the capacity to be part of the trial as the accused, but instead has an effect on the ability to participate in the trial itself. Usually, these two capacities go hand in hand, but they correspond to two different profiles that

* The authors would like to thank Martina E Salerno (PhD student in Legal Sciences—Criminal Law at the University of Parma) for the valuable collaboration in drafting the English version of this chapter, and Professor Fabio S Cassibba (Associate Professor of Criminal Procedure at the University of Parma) for having proofread the chapter. It should be noted that, after the drafting of this work, the reform mentioned in was approved by the Italian Parliament (Art 1 l, 23 June 2017, 103).

[1] It must be noted that the provisions governing the request for application of the sentence (so-called 'plea bargain') could also be examined, under CPP Art 446, para 5, according to which if the judge believes it is necessary to verify whether the request has been submitted or the consent has been given voluntarily, he shall order the accused to appear before him. However, this aspect will not be dealt with here. For further discussion, see Daniela Vigoni, *L'applicazione della pena su richiesta delle parti* (Giuffrè 2000); Renzo Orlandi, 'Procedimenti speciali' in Giovanni Conso et al (eds), *Compendio di procedura penale* (8th edn, Wolters Kluwer-CEDAM 2016) 593–687. See also Luca Marafioti, *La giustizia penale negoziata* (Giuffrè 1992); Alfredo Gaito, 'Revocabile o invalida la richiesta di «patteggiamento» viziata da errore?' [1996] Diritto penale e processo 1145.

[2] See Mariangela Montagna, 'L'imputato' in Giovanni Dean (ed), *I Soggetti* in Giorgio Spangher (director), *Trattato di procedura penale*, Volume 1 I (UTET Giuridica 2009) 503.

Fitness to Plead: International and Comparative Perspectives. First Edition. Edited by Ronnie Mackay and Warren Brookbanks. Chapter 12 Published 2018 by Oxford University Press.

can be divided: one concerns the legal capacity, the other one refers to the capacity to act. Therefore, the exclusion of the ability to participate consciously in the trial would be able to exclude only the capacity to act, to be intended as a procedural capacity in a technical sense.[3] As will be seen below, a judgment of acquittal, for example, may occur for those who are deemed incapable, in this sense. This is inconsistent with an incapacity to be part of the trial.

Furthermore, it must be pointed out that, except when specific rules are laid down for one situation or another, the CPP considers as equivalent the accused person and the suspect.[4] In other words, the qualification of the accused person refers to those who have been charged, while the qualification of the suspect indicates those that, although subject to preliminary investigations, have not yet had the accusation against them formalised, but are under only a temporary charge.[5] Similarly, a distinction can be made between trial and proceedings: in particular, the latter also includes preliminary investigations. The rules that will be examined take as a point of reference the accused and the trial. In fact, these rules also apply to the suspect and, therefore, to the preliminary investigations. This means that when the terms 'accused' and 'trial' are used, they have to be interpreted as referring, in principle, also to the suspect and the preliminary investigations. An explicit distinction will be made only when necessary.

Finally, it is appropriate briefly to give an outline of the following analysis. First, the provisions which form the legal basis of the regulation of the capacity to participate consciously in the trial in the Italian experience are examined. Then, two fundamental aspects are analysed: the first focuses on the so-called '*eterni giudicabili*' (those who are 'permanently non-justiciable'). In this regard, it must be observed that the Constitutional Court has repeatedly been asked to rule on this issue. For this reason, it is interesting briefly to recall the constitutional jurisprudence on this point.[6] The second aspect worthy of special attention concerns the concept of 'capacity to participate consciously in the trial'.[7] In this respect, an effort is made to define the term 'insanity', which is able to lead to the recognition of the incapacity of the accused to act in the trial against him.

[3] Giovanni Conso, 'Capacità processuale penale' in *Enciclopedia del Diritto VI* (1960) 139–40, 147–48. See also Oreste Dominioni, 'Imputato' in *Enciclopedia del Diritto XX* (1970) 812.

[4] CPP Art 61 establishes that: '1. The rights and safeguards of the accused person extend to the suspected person. 2. Any other provision concerning the accused extends to the suspect, unless otherwise provided.' All the translations of the provisions of the Italian Code of Criminal Procedure are taken by Mitja Gialuz et al (eds), *The Italian Code of Criminal Procedure: Critical Essays and English Translation* (Wolters Kluwer-CEDAM 2014).

[5] See CPP Art 60, according to which:

> 1. A suspect becomes an accused person when he is charged with an offence in a request for committal to trial, immediate trial, criminal decree of conviction, application of punishment under Article 447, paragraph 1, in the decree of direct summons for trial and direct trial. 2. The person maintains the status of accused person at any stage and instance of the proceedings, until the judgment of no grounds to proceed is no longer subject to appellate remedies, the judgment of dismissal or conviction becomes final or the criminal decree of conviction becomes enforceable. 3. The person resumes the status of accused person in case of revocation of the judgement of no grounds to proceed and if a revision of the trial is ordered.

[6] See, in this chapter, section 3.

[7] See, in this chapter, section 4.

2. The Rules on Capacity to Participate Consciously in the Trial

Before analysing the most controversial aspects related to capacity to participate consciously in the trial under the Italian legal system it is necessary briefly to examine the rules on this matter laid down in CPP Arts 70–73.

As many have already highlighted, the Italian legislature has adopted an approach by which those involved in criminal proceedings, as suspected or accused persons, should be able to implement a defensive strategy to oppose the allegations made against them by the Public Prosecutor.[8] As a result, the sensitive position of those who cannot exercise their essential defence rights must be taken into consideration by the rules governing the proceedings. In this context, the CPP is particularly concerned with the protection of those who, by reason of insanity, are not able to assess the procedural events of which they become the main actors.[9] In fact, the ability to make such an assessment constitutes the prerequisite to exercising the right to defend oneself. The latter requires that the person is not only physically present, but also conscious and capable of understanding what is happening in the proceedings against him.

CPP Arts 70–73—which represent the outcome of a difficult legislative process[10]—are based on the 'insanity' of the accused. The concept of 'insanity' is characterised by its vagueness.[11] One of the problems that the Constitutional Court had to resolve concerned the question of whether it was relevant only to mental disorder subsequent to the fact or also to disorder that was already present at the time of the fact. Indeed, on many occasions it has been pointed out that there is a possible conflict between the first solution and Arts 3 and 24 of the Constitution: the former regulates the principle of formal and substantial equality, while the latter concerns the right to defence.[12]

[8] See Guido Colaiacovo, 'L'imputato' in Giorgio Spangher (ed), *Soggetti. Atti. Prove* in Giorgio Spangher et al (directors), *Procedura penale. Teoria e pratica del processo*, Volume I (Wolters Kluwer-UTET Giuridica 2015) 287. See also, in tempi più risalenti e con riferimento al vecchio codice di rito, Giovanni Leone, *Lineamenti di diritto processuale penale* (4th edn, Jovene 1956) 173; Conso, 'Capacità processuale penale' (n 3) 147; Dominioni, 'Imputato' (n 3) 812. More recently, with reference to the new Code of Criminal Procedure, Roberto E Kostoris, 'Commento *sub* art. 70 c.p.p.' in Mario Chiavario (coordinator), *Commento al nuovo codice di procedura penale*, Volume I (UTET 1989) 347–52; Giovanni Paolo Voena, 'Infermità mentale e partecipazione cosciente' in Conso et al (eds), *Compendio di procedura penale* (8th edn, Wolters Kluwer-CEDAM 2016) 101–05.

[9] Colaiacovo, 'L'imputato' (n 8) 287.

[10] For a historical reconstruction, see Maria Gabriella Aimonetto, *L'incapacità dell'imputato per infermità di mente* (Giuffrè 1992) 9–103.

[11] This aspect is analysed in depth below, at section 4.

[12] Article 3 Constitution:

> All citizens have equal social dignity and are equal before the law, without distinction of sex, race, language, religion, political opinion, personal and social conditions. 2. It is the duty of the Republic to remove those obstacles of an economic or social nature which constrain the freedom and equality of citizens, thereby impeding the full development of the human person and the effective participation of all workers in the political, economic and social organisation of the country.

This issue had already arisen with reference to the rules contained in the Code of 1930,[13] since the heading of Art 88, in force at that time, referred to mental disorder subsequent to the fact, although the provisions contained in the text did not specify anything in this regard. However, the Constitutional Court ruled on the constitutional compatibility of this regulation on the basis of two main considerations. First, in terms of equality, the Court held that the different legal treatment between the insanity existing at the *tempus commissi delicti* and subsequently was justified, because the former would have resulted in an acquittal for non-imputability in any case: in fact, CPP Art 88 implicitly assimilated the notion of significant insanity during the trial and the notion taken into account by the substantive criminal law with reference to the total *vizio di mente* (ie, a total lack of capacity in the field of imputability).[14] As for the supposed violation of the right to defence, the Court found that the possibility that the accused person was not able to properly assess the consequences of his procedural behaviour could be balanced, on the one hand, through the assistance of a lawyer and, on the other hand, by the involvement of the judge on the assessment of the evidence offered by the accused himself and the statements made by him.[15]

This problematic aspect has not been removed by the reform of the CPP, which dates back to 1988; indeed, it has been intensified. The new provisions, on the one hand, specified under CPP Art 70, para 1 that mental disorder was only relevant 'subsequent to the fact' and, on the other hand, that the new provisions removed the correspondence between the substantive and the procedural meaning of 'insanity'. It is clear that these differences have increased the doubts concerning compliance with Arts 3 and 24, para 2, of the Constitution. In fact, the loss of symmetry between the total *vizio di mente* and the incapacity to participate consciously in the trial not only limited the relevant insanity to that arising at a time subsequent to the fact, but also prevented the accused person from being acquitted. As a consequence, the constitutional judges have again been called upon to rule on the legality of this regulation. In this context, the Court recognised the incompatibility of CPP Art 70, para 1 with Art 24, para 2 of the Constitution, and held that this provision was unconstitutional, being limited to the words 'subsequent to the fact'.[16] According to the Court,

All the translations of the provisions of the Italian Constitution are those found on the official website of the Italian Senate.

In relation to Art 24 Cost, in this context, of particular relevance is para 2: 'Defense is an inviolable right at every stage and instance of legal proceedings. The poor are entitled by law to proper means for action or defense in all courts.'

[13] See Conso, 'Capacità processuale penale' (n 3) 146–47, n 58; Dominioni, 'Imputato' (n 3) 813. Mario Chiavario, *La sospensione del processo penale* (Giuffrè 1967) 179, believed that CPP Art 88 could be interpreted in the sense to include only the supervening insanity; for the opposite minority opinion, see Vincenzo Cavallari, *La capacità dell'imputato* (Giuffrè 1968) 215–17.

[14] It is worth noting that the total *vizio di mente*, set out in CPP Art 88 excludes the criminal liability. This means that the accused must be acquitted, and therefore the penalty cannot be imposed. Only if he is deemed a danger to the society may a security measure be applied.

[15] C Cost 25 May 1979, 23.

[16] C Cost 20 July 1992, 340. See Maria Gabriella Aimonetto, 'Sospensione del processo penale per infermità di mente dell'imputato' [1992] Giurisprudenza costituzionale 2744; Angelo Giarda, 'Infermità mentale dell'imputato al tempo del fatto e sospensione del processo' [1992] Corriere giuridico 1217.

since the inability to participate consciously in the trial could not be attributed necessarily to a corresponding total *vizio di mente* ('mental defect'), this could affect the interest of the accused to exercise the right of the self-defence: indeed, the non-necessary existence of *vizio di mente* would have not led anyway to an acquittal.[17]

On the assumption that in order to assess the capacity to participate consciously in the trial both the insanity subsequent to the fact and that already existing at the time of the fact are relevant, it is necessary to scrutinise other general aspects of this regulation, laid down in CPP Arts 70–73.

In the first place, it must be noted that what is relevant is a 'mental' disorder. If it is now accepted that various 'physical' diseases are regarded also as 'mental', the specification should be interpreted in the sense that Arts 70–73 require that the accused suffers from a disorder that, although 'physical' in nature, affects his or her ability to participate consciously in defending the charges.[18]

Secondly, if there is reason to believe that, because of his insanity, the accused is not able to understand what happens during the trial and to exercise his rights,[19] the judge—if necessary—can request expert evidence to verify this. It is therefore necessary to take into consideration certain factors. First of all, during preliminary investigations such assessments can only be carried out upon the request of the parties.[20] Moreover, the discipline in question does not concern the judgment before the Court of Cassation, and all the other trials related to the enforcement of the penalty.[21] Finally, the assessment of capacity is carried out only if the judge believes that the court cannot immediately acquit the accused. This is a particularly important aspect, expressing the principle of *favor rei*.[22]

[17] It must be noted that the Constitutional Court in the 1979 judgment (n 15) stated that CPP Art 88 was not incompatible with Art 24 of the Constitution, by virtue of the acquittal resulting from the parallelism between the substantial meaning of insanity (related to the mental disorder) and the procedural one (concerning the ability to participate consciously in the trial).

[18] In C Cost 26 January 2004, 39, the Constitutional Court clarified that, in relation to the provisions object of this examination, not only the diseases defined as psychic in the clinical sense, but also every disease affecting the mental faculties of the accused to the point of making them inadequate for the exercise of his rights of self-defence are of relevance, while only the purely 'physical' pathological conditions may be considered relevant, even if only partially, in other respects; for instance, they may give rise to a legal impediment (CPP Art 420-*ter*), which essentially allows the judge to adjourn the hearing when the accused is absent, due to unforeseeable circumstances, *force majeure*, or legal impediment: see Voena, 'Infermità mentale e partecipazione cosciente' (n 8) 102. On this issue, C Cost (ord) 21 October 2013, 243.

[19] On the capacity to participate consciously in the trial, see Montagna, 'L'imputato' (n 2) 503. See also Luca Bresciani, 'Infermità di mente (profili processuali)' in *Digesto delle discipline penalistiche VI* (4th edn, UTET 1992) 434.

[20] On this issue, see Bresciani, 'Infermità di mente (profili processuali)' (n 19) 435; Kostoris, 'Commento *sub* art. 70 c.p.p.' (n 8) 350.

[21] See, eg, Cass (4) 17 May 2005, 28559; Cass (1) 29 April 1993; Cass (1) 9 March 2007, 22749. It must be observed that in the Italian legal system the Supreme Court of Cassation presides over the judgment of legitimacy of the proceedings, while the Supervisory Penitentiary Tribunal and that of enforcement preside over the implementation of the penalty. In these two latter cases, the accused is no longer present, and specific provisions apply (CPP Art 666, para 8, and Art 148): see Voena, 'Infermità mentale e partecipazione cosciente' (n 8) 103.

[22] See, in particular, CPP Art 129, which establishes that:

1. At any stage and instance of the proceedings, the judge who acknowledges that either the criminal act did not occur or the accused did not commit it or the act does not constitute an offence or it is not

That said, once expert evidence has been ordered and while the technical assessment is performed—assessment in which the consultants of the parties may eventually participate—both the procedural and the investigative activities remain suspended. This consequence seems consistent with the rationale for the rule, since it would be a paradox to perform such activities while having doubts on the ability of the accused to use his or her defence rights.[23] Nevertheless, it must be pointed out that this paralysis of the procedural and investigative activities is not absolute.[24] In fact, according to CPP Art 70, para 2, the lawyer may request the gathering of evidence, which may lead to the dismissal of the accused person and any other evidence requested by the parties, when such gathering may be compromised due to the expiration of the time limit for assessment of the capacity of the accused person. In addition, CPP Art 70, para 3 allows that evidence may be gathered even in circumstances in which it is not required by the conscious participation of the suspect, or in cases provided for in CPP Art 392, which establishes the special evidentiary hearing, when the delay poses a danger.[25]

Once the ascertainment of the capacity of the accused person has been carried out, the judge, according to CPP Art 71, has to rule on the question. The judge remains free to evaluate expert opinions—although he or she must justify departure from the expert opinions[26]—and the decisions may be essentially of two types. The judge may decide to proceed, if it appears that the mental state of the accused does not prevent his or her conscious participation in the proceedings; otherwise, the judge may decide that the proceedings are suspended, provided that a judgment of dismissal cannot be issued or there are no grounds to proceed.

The order of suspension can be appealed to the Court of Cassation[27] and such appeal may produce different effects.[28] At an evidentiary level, the same rules that find application in relation to the gathering of evidence during the ascertainment of

deemed an offence by law or the offence is extinguished or a requirement for prosecution is not met, he shall declare it *ex officio* by issuing a judgment. 2. The judge shall deliver a judgment of either acquittal or no grounds to proceed with the prescribed formula if there is a cause of extinguishment of the offence but it is clearly proven that the criminal act did not occur or the accused did not commit it or the act does not constitute an offence or it is not deemed an offence by law. Furthermore, it must be specified that, during the preliminary hearing, the decision does not take the shape of a judgment of acquittal, but rather of one of no grounds to proceed.

[23] Aimonetto, *L'incapacità dell'imputato per infermità di mente* (n 10) 143–44, which refers to *Relazione al progetto preliminare del codice di procedura penale*.

[24] On the contrary, Montagna, 'L'imputato' (n 2) 507 believes that it is possible to refer to a purely procedural slowdown, which does not necessarily result in a paralysis of the proceedings, while others refer to a procedural stasis, although in different ways. See Aimonetto, *L'incapacità dell'imputato per infermità di mente* (n 10) 152; Kostoris, 'Commento *sub* art. 70 c.p.p.' (n 8) 351; Franco Cordero, *Procedura penale* (9th edn, Giuffrè 2012) 243–44; Voena, 'Infermità mentale e partecipazione cosciente' (n 8) 102.

[25] The special evidentiary hearing, set out in CPP Arts 392 ff., within certain limits, allows the gathering of evidence during the preliminary investigations.

[26] Cordero, *Procedura penale* (n 24) 244.

[27] According to the Supreme Court of Cassation, the decision to proceed further cannot be appealed: Cass (1) 19 February 2004, 9676.

[28] The summary is based on the opinions of Colaiacovo, 'L'imputato' (n 8) 289–91; Voena, 'Infermità mentale e partecipazione cosciente' (n 8) 103–05.

the capacity of the accused apply. Then, a special administrator must be appointed—preferably, the legal representative—who enjoys powers to initiate and intervene in the trial. To this end, the administrator has to receive all the formal notifications addressed to the accused. The administrator may ask to gather evidence that can lead to the acquittal of the accused; he or she may appeal the order of suspension and has also competing legitimacy to challenge other measures; he or she must be present when, for example, the accused person is subject to inspections.[29] Finally, the suspension of the process also involves the suspension of the time limits of the statute of limitations[30] and of procedural terms. Moreover, together with the suspension order, the judge must ensure the separation of the proceedings for any co-accused.[31] Finally, according to CPP Art 71, last para, the 'victim' can abandon the trial—the suspension of which may last for a long time—and continue the civil action in its own context.

CPP Art 72 provides that, once the suspension of the proceedings has been issued and in order to allow—if necessary—the resumption of the trial, the mental state of the accused is further ascertained periodically by an expert. This assessment must be completed at the end of the sixth month after the issuing of the suspension order, or even before that, when the judge considers it necessary. If it is not yet possible for the proceedings to resume their course, the judge shall decide likewise at the end of each successive six-month period. On the other hand, if it appears that the mental state of the accused allows his or her conscious participation in the proceedings, it is mandatory for the suspension order to be revoked; the judge must come to a similar decision, when a judgment of dismissal or no grounds to proceed is to be delivered for the accused. Finally, CPP Art 73 regulates the position where the accused is unable to participate consciously in the trial, since his or her mental state is such that the accused requires psychiatric treatment. In these instances, the judge is obliged to promptly inform the authority competent for the adoption of the measures set by the laws on the medical treatment of mental illnesses. It is, in fact, a fundamental principle according to which, as a general rule, the court may not issue measures affecting the treatment of mental illnesses.[32] Only if the accused poses a danger

[29] See Colaiacovo, 'L'imputato' (n 8) 290.

[30] For a better understanding, it must be observed that the statute of limitations entails the extinguishing of the offence and, therefore, the exemption from punishment of the criminal (from a procedural point of view, it results in a judgment of non-prosecution), when a specific period of time since the offence was committed has elapsed, and the criminal liability of the agent has not been judicially ascertained in a definitive manner. This rule, which in the Italian legal system has a strong connotation in substantial terms, finds its own regulations in CPP Arts 157 ff. In addition, there are mechanisms of suspension or interruption for statutes of limitations. The first applies to the impediments of the accused or the lawyer, and entails a stasis of the proceeding; the limitation period restarts when the cause ceases. The second, linked to a number of other hypotheses, implies that the limitation period resumes from the beginning, without being able to extend beyond a certain limit. It must also be noted that there are offences in which the statute of limitations does not apply. See Paolo Veneziani, *La punibilità. Le conseguenze giuridiche del reato* in Carlo Federico Grosso et al (directors), *Trattato di diritto penale. Parte generale*, Volume III.II (Giuffrè 2014) 323–40.

[31] Roberto E Kostoris, 'Commento *sub* artt. 71–72 c.p.p.' in Mario Chiavario (coordinator), *Commento al nuovo codice di procedura penale*, Volume I (UTET 1989) 355.

[32] Colaiacovo, 'L'imputato' (n 8) 291, n 126. See also Roberto E Kostoris, 'Commento *sub* art. 73 c.p.p.' in Mario Chiavario (coordinator), *Commento al nuovo codice di procedura penale*, Volume I (UTET 1989) 358.

can the judge also order their temporary hospitalisation in a suitable facility of the hospital psychiatric service: this order, which cannot be challenged, ceases to have effect when the decision of such authority is enforced.[33] A similar situation occurs when this need arises during the preliminary investigations: however, the Public Prosecutor can only decide to inform the competent authority, while for a temporary hospitalisation to be ordered he or she must request the judge to make such an order. Finally, where the precautionary detention of the accused person, in a state of mental illness, has been or is to be ordered, the judge may order the temporary hospitalisation in a suitable department of the psychiatric hospital, adopting the necessary requirements to prevent the risk of flight.[34]

3. The Issue of the '*eterni giudicabili*'

The issue of so-called '*eterni giudicabili*' is problematic. By using this expression, the literature has always[35] intended to refer to those whose incapacity to participate consciously in the trial is considered irreversible. With regard to such individuals, the procedural status may last indefinitely. This means that they may be subject to the jurisdiction—at least potentially—until their death. This condition of '*eterno giudicabile*' is regulated by various provisions of both a procedural and a substantive nature.

By virtue of CPP Arts 70 ff., where the proceedings are suspended, as a result of the recognition of the incapacity to participate consciously in the trial of the accused, the assessment of the accused's health status should be repeated at least every six months, until he regains his faculties (at least in a manner that is sufficient to exercise his right of defence). Moreover, a crucial aspect concerns the fact that, until recently, the statute of limitations would not have been available because, as already mentioned, the suspension of the trial—by virtue of CPP Art 159, paragraph 1—involved also the suspension of the statute of limitations.[36] On this basis, only the emergence of the (limited) elements that would enable a ruling of acquittal could put an end to the proceedings against those who were affected by a form of insanity that makes it impossible to regain the capacity to participate consciously in the trial. Potentially, therefore, the accused could remain under the jurisdiction for his entire life.[37] Today, this situation still exists, in the case of indefeasible crime.

[33] See Alessandra Gualazzi, 'Gli accertamenti volti a verificare identità fisica, età e capacità processuale dell'imputato' in Mariangela Montagna (ed), *La giustizia penale differenziata*, Volume III (Gli accertamenti complementari, Giappichelli 2011) 432.

[34] Voena, 'Infermità mentale e partecipazione cosciente' (n 8) 105. According to Alessandra Gualazzi (ibid), this hypothesis is absolutely optional.

[35] This expression has to be attributed to Bruno Franchi, 'Riforma carceraria scientifica, manicomii e misure di sicurezza' [1908] La Scuola positiva 679–80.

[36] See n 30.

[37] Oliviero Mazza, 'L'irragionevole limbo processuale degli imputati "eterni giudicabili"' [2013] Giurisprudenza costituzionale 384.

This mechanism, which caused difficulties[38] between doctrine and judicial practice, often raised issues of constitutional legitimacy and is still relevant. Indeed, as recently as 2015 the Constitutional Court issued an important ruling that has partially reduced the numbers of the '*eterno giudicabile*'. Before analysing this decision, however, a summary will be given of the jurisprudence of the Constitutional Court on this point.

The *'eterni giudicabili'* in the prism of constitutional jurisprudence

a) The traditional self-restraint of the Constitutional Court

Subsequent to the reform of the CPP, the Constitutional Court has been repeatedly called upon to assess the legality of the above-mentioned provisions, of both a procedural and substantive nature, relating to the condition of '*eterno giudicabile*'.[39]

The issues brought to the attention of the Constitutional judges have been varied, and have often taken several provisions of the Constitution as a point of reference. However, the analysis of the constitutionality has often resulted in the re-litigation of similar issues, different only in part. For this reason, rather than undertaking an analysis of each decision, it seems more appropriate to examine, overall, the aspects of possible conflict with the constitutional provisions that have been submitted before the Court on each occasion.

The applicants have referred, essentially, to the constitutional parameters which establish the following principles: equality (Art 3 of the Constitution[40]); the right of defence (Art 24, para 2[41]); the rehabilitative function of punishment (Art 27, para 3[42]); the good performance of public administration (Art 97, para 1[43]); the reasonable duration of the trial (Art 111, para 2[44]); and the mandatory prosecution (Art 112[45]). The provisions that are at risk of being declared unconstitutional have been indicated, depending on the case, in the regulation under CPP Arts 70 ff. or in that of the statute of limitations (especially CPP Art 159, in terms already mentioned).

[38] Mario Chiavario, 'Incapacità processuale e autodifesa: il "*novum*" del codice vigente e gli avalli della Corte costituzionale' in Sergio Vinciguerra and Francesco Dassano (eds), *Scritti in memoria di Giuliano Marini* (Edizioni Scientifiche Italiane 2010) 200.

[39] For a summary, see, eg, Hervé Belluta, 'Il tema degli "eternamente giudicabili" torna davanti alla Corte Costituzionale' (2014) Diritto penale contemporaneo, available at: http://www.penalecontemporaneo.it/d/3056-il-tema-degli-eternamente-giudicabili-torna-davanti-alla-corte-costituzionale; Eleonora AA Dei-Cas, 'Illegittima la disciplina riservata agli "eterni giudicabili"' [2015] Cassazione penale 2557.

[40] See n 12. [41] See n 12.

[42] Article 27, paragraph 3, of the Constitution lays down: 'Punishments may not be inhuman and shall aim at re-educating the convicted.'

[43] According to Article 97, paragraph 1, of the Constitution: 'Public offices are organised according to the provisions of law, so as to ensure the efficiency and impartiality of administration.'

[44] Article 111 of the Constitution, which concerns the principle of the 'fair trial', sets out, at para 2, that: 'All court trials are conducted with adversary proceedings and the parties are entitled to equal conditions before an impartial judge in third party position. The law provides for the reasonable duration of trials.'

[45] Article 112 of the Constitution lays down 'The public prosecutor has the obligation to institute criminal proceedings.'

To summarise the main unconstitutionality issues submitted to the Constitutional Court, first of all there is a possible violation of the equality principle because of the fact that the suspension of the trial would result in a disparity between who is irreversibly unable to participate consciously in the trial and all other indicted people. Indeed, only the former is prevented from obtaining a ruling on the merits and from being tried within a reasonable time: such an impediment is able to extend for an indefinite period of time in the event of irreversible insanity. It is the fact that the accused person may be under the jurisdiction for a period that can extend up to his or her death, in contrast to other constitutional principles. With regard to Art 24, para 2 of the Constitution, it has been argued that, in the absence of pre-defined time limits, the right of defence remains unreasonably blocked and that, accordingly, the passage of time can affect the effectiveness of such right. Also, the rehabilitative function of punishment would be frustrated by the excessive amount of time that could elapse between the commission of the offence and the imposition of the punishment.[46] Similarly, tension can also be found between a situation of this kind and the principle of reasonable duration of the process. In terms of Art 112 of the Constitution, it has been considered that the obligation to prosecute would be, de facto, neutralised by a procedural suspension that, from a structural point of view, contains a potentially unlimited time extension. Finally, as regards the conflict with Art 97 of the Constitution, it has been suggested that CPP Art 72, which provides for the obligation to carry out periodic assessments on the health condition of the accused even when his insanity is irreversible, places an unnecessary financial burden on the Treasury.

The Constitutional Court, however, initially dismissed all questions submitted.[47] Indeed, with reference to Art 97, para 1, of the Constitution, the complaint was deemed unfounded, both because the investigations are aimed at the resumption of the trial and because it is believed that the principle in question does not relate to the exercise of the judicial function.[48] In particular, with reference to the other issues, it must be highlighted—beyond the specificities of each ruling—that the Court is bound, in carrying out its activity, by the need not to invade the sphere of discretion of the legislature.[49] Consequently, given that for solving the problems concerning the condition of the '*eterni giudicabili*' there are several solutions (but none of them

[46] It has always been evident and strongly affirmed by Beccaria that a punishment implemented with an excessive distance of time from when the act was committed is ineffective, counterproductive, and ultimately unjust: Cesare Beccaria, *Dei delitti e delle pene* (first published 1764, Mediobanca 1984) 70–72. This sentiment also finds its basis in the statute of limitations. Among the studies dedicated to the statute of limitations, in relation to the procedural dimension see, eg, in addition to the sources listed at n 56, Fausto Giunta and Dario Micheletti, Tempori cedere. *Prescrizione del reato e funzioni della pena nello scenario della ragionevole durata* (Giappichelli 2003).

[47] See, C Cost (ord) 23 May 1991, 298; C Cost 28 June 1995, 281; C Cost 22 October 1996, 354; C Cost (ord) 4 February 2003, 33; C Cost (ord) 28 May 2004, 157; C Cost (ord) 29 March 2007, 112; C Cost (ord) 4 November 2011, 289 (which concerns also CPP Art 150).

[48] See in particular, C Cost 28 June 1995, 281.

[49] As is highlighted by Dei-Cas, 'Illegittima la disciplina riservata agli "eterni giudicabili"' (n 39) 2560, this need results from Art 28 of the Law 11 March 1953 no 87. This law also regulates the functioning of the Constitutional Court. In addition, it is important to note that this article provides that the Court cannot conduct, as part of judgments on constitutional legitimacy, any assessment of a political nature and any examination of the use of Parliament's discretion.

are constitutionally imposed), the Court has traditionally refrained from intervening in this matter.

A similar attitude has been taken by the Constitutional Court in a significant ruling that represents an important step in reaching the solution adopted a few years later.[50] In fact, the decision (C Cost no 23/2013) contains a constitutional ruling in terms of certain profiles of the rules resulting from the combined provisions of CPP Arts 71 and 72 and Penal Code Art 159, para 1. The Court found that this is a regulation that represents a 'real anomaly',[51] which is inconsistent both with the *rationale* of the statute of limitations and the grounds which are the basis of the suspension of the trial.[52] However, it stated that it could not resolve the matter, because of the plurality of reasonable possible solutions. In fact, this choice is up to the legislature.[53] The Court addressed a warning to the legislature, noting that legislative inaction regarding a similar problem is intolerable.[54] As anticipated, this decision by the Constitutional Court represented a kind of prelude to a subsequent intervention that, in this case, resulted in a declaration of partial unconstitutionality in the decision C Cost no 45/2015. This decision, which is analysed in the following section, constitutes the final step in the series of constitutional rulings given on the issues of '*eterni giudicabili*'.[55]

b) *The Judgment C Cost 25 March 2015, 45 and the perspectives for a legislative reform*

The analysis of this decision can be carried out, on the one hand, by briefly illustrating its general scope and, on the other hand, by highlighting certain distinctive features.

[50] See, in this chapter, section 3(b).

[51] C Cost 14 February 2013, 23, in particular para 3.1.

[52] According to Laura Scomparin, 'Prescrizione del reato e capacità di partecipare coscientemente al processo: nuovamente sub iudice la disciplina degli "eterni giudicabili"' [2013] Cassazione penale 1828–29, the reasoning of the Constitutional Court focuses particularly on the aspect of the reasonable duration of the trial. The conclusion follows from the connection (upheld by the ruling) between this right and the spirit and purpose of the statute of limitations. On this aspect, see Vittorio Grevi, 'Il principio della "ragionevole durata" come garanzia oggettiva del "giusto processo" penale' [2003] Cassazione penale 3204; Domenico Pulitanò, 'Tempi del processo e diritto penale sostanziale' [2005] Rivista italiana di diritto e procedura penale 522–30; Marta Bargis, 'La prescrizione del reato e i "tempi" della giustizia' [2005] Rivista italiana di diritto e procedura penale 1402.

[53] C Cost 14 February 2013, 23 para 3.2.

[54] C Cost 14 February 2013, 23 para 4. The category of monitory judgments, however, is otherwise determined by the Italian doctrine. For different points of view, see Franco Modugno, 'La funzione legislativa complementare della Corte costituzionale' [1981] Giurisprudenza costituzionale 1646; Maria Cristina Grisolia, 'Alcune osservazioni sulle «sentenze comandamento» ovvero sul «potere monitorio» della Corte costituzionale' [1982] Giurisprudenza costituzionale 826; Gustavo Zagrebelsky, *La giustizia costituzionale* (new edn, il Mulino 1988) 305–11; Roberto Pinardi, *L'*horror vacui *nel giudizio sulle leggi. Prassi e tecniche decisionali utilizzate dalla Corte costituzionale allo scopo di ovviare all'inerzia del legislatore* (Giuffrè 2007) 132–39. See also Franco Modugno, 'Corte costituzionale e potere legislativo' in Paolo Barile et al (eds), *Corte costituzionale e sviluppo della forma di governo in Italia* (il Mulino 1982) 19. On the scarce bearing of the monitory judgments on subsequent legislative action, see Lucio Pegoraro, *La Corte e il Parlamento: sentenze-indirizzo e attività legislativa* (CEDAM 1984); Roberto Bin and Chiara Bergonzini, 'La Corte costituzionale in Parlamento' in Roberto Bin et al (eds), *'Effettività' e 'seguito' delle tecniche decisorie della Corte costituzionale* (Edizioni Scientifiche Italiane 2006) 215.

[55] C Cost 25 March 2015, 45.

First of all, it should be noted that, in the present case, the issues of constitutionality brought to the attention of the Constitutional Court concerned CPP Art 159, para 1, previously mentioned, and were raised by two lower courts.[56] The Constitutional Court, however, found one of these issues inadmissible. It is therefore appropriate to summarise what was considered admissible.

The Court was called upon to conduct a constitutional examination with reference to Arts 3, 24, 27, para 3, and 111 of the Constitution. With regard to the equality principle set out under Art 3, the order finds that it is unreasonable that the mechanism of suspension of the statute of limitations applies in the same way to those who are permanently and temporarily incapable to participate consciously in the trial. The hypothesis regarding the violation of Art 24 of the Constitution suggests that, in the remote possibility of a person recovering those faculties necessary to exercise the right of defence, the faculties would remain, de facto, frustrated by the fact that a large span of time has elapsed from when the act was committed: it is obvious that this would adversely affect the ability to prepare an effective defence strategy. Similarly, the chronological distance to the committed fact seems in contrast with the rehabilitative function of punishment, laid down in Art 27, para 3 of the Constitution. Finally, as regards the violation of Art 111 of the Constitution, the excessive duration of the trial constitutes a violation of the due process requirement for reasonable trial duration.[57] In addition, such a principle finds an important legal basis in Art 6 of the European Convention on Human Rights, which establishes the right to a fair trial.[58]

The Constitutional Court, as stated earlier, found worthy of consideration the issue brought to its attention. In particular, the judges noted that the question raised by the applicant was similar—apart from the reference to Art 27, para 3—to that aspect of the judgment no 23/2013. By recalling important parts of this ruling, in the judgment subject to this analysis, the Court identified a violation of the equality

[56] Trib Milano (1) (ord) 21 March 2013; Giud Pace Gaeta (ord) 17 March 2014.

[57] With regard to 'due process' and 'reasonable duration of the process', see Giulio Ubertis, 'Giusto processo (dir. proc. pen.)' in *Enciclopedia del diritto. Annali II.I* (2008) in particular 425–26. Notably, on the 'reasonable duration', see Silvia Buzzelli, 'Processo penale (ragionevole durata del)' in *Enciclopedia del diritto. Annali III* (2010) 1017, 1020–21. On this issue, see also Vittorio Grevi, *Alla ricerca di un processo penale giusto: itinerari e prospettive* (Giuffrè 2000); Ennio Amodio, 'Ragionevole durata del processo, abuse of process e nuove esigenze di tutela dell'imputato' [2003] Diritto penale e processo 797; Paolo Ferrua, *Il giusto processo* (3rd edn, Zanichelli 2012). On the *speed trial*, also in relation to the Constitution, see Marafioti, *La separazione dei giudizi penali* (Giuffrè 1990) 3–82.

[58] 1. In the determination of his civil rights and obligations or of any criminal charge against him, everyone is entitled to a fair and public hearing within a reasonable time by an independent and impartial tribunal established by law. Judgment shall be pronounced publicly but the press and public may be excluded from all or part of the trial in the interests of morals, public order or national security in a democratic society, where the interests of juveniles or the protection of the private life of the parties so require, or to the extent strictly necessary in the opinion of the court in special circumstances where publicity would prejudice the interests of justice. 2. Everyone charged with a criminal offence shall be presumed innocent until proved guilty according to law. 3. Everyone charged with a criminal offence has the following minimum rights: (a) to be informed promptly, in a language which he understands and in detail, of the nature and cause of the accusation against him; (b) to have adequate time and facilities for the preparation of his defence; (c) to defend himself in person or through legal assistance of his own choosing or, if he has not sufficient means to pay for legal assistance, to be given it free when the interests of justice so require; (d) to examine or have examined witnesses against him and to obtain the attendance

principle.[59] On the one hand, this judgment referred to a passage of the previous decision, in so far as it maintains that a suspension of the trial for an indefinitely prolonged period is unreasonable, given the conflict that exists both with the *rationale* of the statute of limitations and with that of the suspension. On the other hand, the Court added further observations to those already made in the previous decision. The Court stated that the suspension should be treated as a parenthesis, which, by its nature, must have a beginning and an end: otherwise, it changes its nature and, consequently, that of the provision to which it applies. Therefore, it observed that an unlimited suspension of the statute of limitations implies a situation of unreasonable disparities—except, of course, in relation to indefeasible offences—between who is irreversibly incapable of consciously participating in the trial and all the other accused, including those who only temporarily are unable to exercise the right of defence. Moreover, the Constitutional Court observed that certain recent legislative changes give evidence in the sense of incompatibility between the suspension of the statute of limitations and a duration that can be prolonged indefinitely in time: this shows that the legislature also welcomes such an approach.[60] According to the Court, the provision on the suspension of the statute of limitation (CPP Art 159, para 1) is inconsistent with the equality principle (Art 3 of the Constitution) to the extent that it does not exclude the suspension of the statute of limitations when the process is suspended because of the irreversible incapacity of the accused to participate consciously in the trial.[61] In this way, there has been a limited elimination of '*eterno giudicabile*'. In fact, by virtue of the decision of the Constitutional Court summarised above, if the insanity of the accused adversely affects the faculties for the exercise of the right of defence, which are necessary to protect him or her interests, and this insanity is irreversible, the statute of limitation will be not suspended[62] and, consequently, at a judicial level, there will be a judgment of non-prosecution.

Nevertheless, the judgment did not solve every problem. The Court itself was aware of this. In fact, in its ruling, it acknowledged the insufficiency of its approach with respect to situations in which the limitation period is particularly long or, *a fortiori*, when the offence is indefeasible. In respect of the first category of case, the need (with

and examination of witnesses on his behalf under the same conditions as witnesses against him; (e) to have the free assistance of an interpreter if he cannot understand or speak the language used in court.

On this aspect, see Silvia Buzzelli et al, 'Art. 6. Diritto a un equo processo' in Giulio Ubertis and Francesco Viganò (eds), *Corte di Strasburgo e giustizia penale* (Giappichelli 2016) 128. It has been also pointed out that from a self-defence point of view, the provision of the European Convention requires not only the physical participation in hearings of the accused person, but also that he takes part in an appropriate psycho-physical condition, in order to be able to understand and follow the progress of the trial (ibid 194–95).

[59] C Cost 25 March 2015, 45, para 6.3.

[60] In particular, the Court refers to the example of the new para 4 of CPP Art 159 (Art 12, para 2, 128 April 2014, no 67). According to this new disposition, if the proceedings are suspended for the absent accused (CPP Art 420 *quater*), the suspension of the statute of limitations should also have limited duration.

[61] The issues raised in relation to other articles of the Constitution are included in this.

[62] Among the various hypothesis held in C Cost 14 February 2013, 23, the doctrine adopted this solution, eg, Mazza, 'L'irragionevole limbo processuale degli imputati "eterni giudicabili"' (n 37) 385–88.

very few exceptions) to carry out periodic assessments, which are substantially useless, in order to take account of the continuing inability of the accused person remains.[63] In the second category of cases, in addition, the accused is subject to the jurisdiction, permanently, until his or her death.

Moreover, there has been doctrinal criticism of this ruling. Some have pointed out that the choice of the Court to go against the *self-restraint*[64] previously adopted, represents a significant issue of methodology. It has been seen, in fact, that in the last-mentioned ruling the Court identified there are a number of possible solutions. Consequently, the choice on the way forward to solve the problem of '*eterni giudicabili*' is a decision for the legislature. It is worth noting that the Court warned the legislature, by stressing that the situation was intolerable. On the other hand, though, some have identified a fundamental inconsistency in the attitude of the constitutional judges. This is because in 2013 these judges claimed not to be able to declare the (partial) unconstitutionality of the provision in CPP Art 159, para 1, although they substantially recognised it, as it would not have been the only option to solve the problem and, accordingly, it was necessary to respect the margins of intervention of the legislature. The different approach adopted two years later, based on the inertia of the legislature, hardly appears compatible with those premises.[65]

Significantly, a bill currently before Parliament envisages a different solution from that resulting from the decision of partial unconstitutionality of the provision on the statute of limitations. In fact, the Government submitted to the Chamber of Deputies, in December 2014, a proposal which aims to introduce into the CPP a new Art 72 *bis*, as well as the amendment of Art 71, para 1.[66] Under this bill, the second provision would contain specific reference to the fact that the suspension may be ordered by the judge only when the incapacity of the accused person is reversible, while, the new Art 72 *bis*, following suggestions already put forward in the literature,[67] aims to introduce a ruling not to proceed in cases of irreversible incapacity of the accused unless a security measure, different from forfeiture, can be applied.[68]

[63] According to many, a remedy, even if only marginal, could be made by the provision of a reduction of periodic assessments in relation to the passage of time: see Marcello Daniele, 'Il proscioglimento per prescrizione dei non più "eterni giudicabili". La sorte degli imputati affetti da incapacità processuale irreversibile dopo la sentenza 45/2015 della Corte costituzionale' (2015) Diritto penale contemporaneo, available at: http://www.penalecontemporaneo.it/d/3850-il-proscioglimento-per-prescrizione-dei-non-piu--eterni-giudicabili.

[64] With reference to the constitutional jurisprudence, before 2015, the Italian literature usually refers to '*self-restraint*', Mazza, 'L'irragionevole limbo processuale degli imputati «eterni giudicabili»' (n 37) 385, with specific reference to the judgment no 23/2013; in general, Dei-Cas, 'Illegittima la disciplina riservata agli "eterni giudicabili"' (n 39) 2559.

[65] Marcello Daniele, 'Il proscioglimento per prescrizione dei non più "eterni giudicabili"' (n 63).

[66] It is the ddl C 2798, approved by the Chamber of Deputies on 23 September 2015 and under examination in Senate (ddl S 2067). Originally, the above-mentioned amendments to the CPP were contained in Art 9, which became Art 10.

[67] Laura Scomparin, 'Sospensione del processo per incapacità irreversibile dell'imputato: una normativa suscettibile di perfezionamenti, nuovamente "salvata" dalla Corte costituzionale' [2012] Cassazione penale 953.

[68] In this sense, para 2 of CPP Art 72 *bis*.

According to the Constitutional Court itself, such a solution could solve the above-mentioned profiles of inadequacy of the regulation, resulting from the declaration of partial unconstitutionality of CPP Art 159, para 1. However, it must be mentioned that part of the doctrine has raised some concerns in relation to the Bill. There are potential flaws in terms of balance between the punitive role of the state, the interests of the accused person, and procedural efficiency.[69]

4. The Concept of 'Insanity' Relevant to Consciously Participating in the Trial

The second issue that needs to be addressed concerns the distinction between the concept of 'insanity' adopted by the regulation regarding the capacity to participate consciously in the trial and the concept which is the basis of the rules governing the *vizio di mente*.

It has been pointed out[70] that, contrary to the rules provided by 1930 Code of Criminal Procedure, the new provisions that regulate the capacity to participate consciously in the trial have not been created on the same basis of the *vizio di mente*. Moreover, it has been argued that the stance adopted by the legislature has entailed important consequences in terms of constitutional compatibility of CPP Art 70, para 1. Indeed, the fact that the concepts cannot overlap led the Constitutional Court to recognise the contrast of the distinction between original and supervening insanity within Art 24, para 2, of the Constitution.

Therefore, it is necessary to understand what is meant by 'insanity' likely to cause an incapacity to participate consciously in the trial. In doing so, however, it should be pointed out that, as a whole, the Italian literature—legal, forensic psychiatric, and forensic psychopathological—has not focused on this issue. Similarly, it is noteworthy that the jurisprudence did not focus on the analysis of the interpretative issues raised by this concept, which presents some serious problems.

In any case, it is possible to develop some ideas, and, despite the absence of relevant authorities, some observations can be offered. A useful leitmotif can probably be found to that effect in the attempt to highlight the similarities and differences between the ascertainment of the capacity to participate consciously in the process and that of *vizio di mente*.

The divergence between the two concepts is based, first of all, not only on a different legal connotation, but also on different naturalistic preconditions. The doctrine has long been influenced by the fact that the two aspects—legal and ontological—should, as far as possible, go hand in hand. The observation, which has

[69] Marcello Daniele, 'Il proscioglimento per prescrizione dei non più "eterni giudicabili"' (n 63). It must be noted that the solution adopted by the Constitutional Court results in lower margins of application of security measures than for those irreversibly unable to participate consciously in the trial. In addition, the lack of mandatory inspections might preclude the possibility of regaining such capacity and, therefore, of re-starting the trial.

[70] See, in this chapter, section 2.

been authoritatively confirmed by reference to the substantive criminal law,[71] seems to apply also at a procedural level. Therefore, it appears that the nature of the situation underlying the *vizio di mente* and the incapacity to participate consciously in the trial are different. If both consist of insanity, it is equally true that the two effects occur in different situations. The *vizio di mente* exists when the insanity affects the capacity of discernment at the time of the fact; that is, simplifying the ability to weigh up the social value, positive or negative, of their conduct, and to inhibit their impulses[72] while the incapacity to participate consciously in the trial exists when the insanity prevents the accused from exercising the right to defend his or her interests.[73]

The awareness of this structural difference is also well known to those who apply the law. In the most used Italian work on forensic psychiatry,[74] for example, it has been indicated very clearly that the two concepts, although they can overlap to a certain extent, should be kept distinct. For this reason, it has been claimed that the 'insanity' placed at the basis of capacity to participate consciously in the trial should be understood in a much broader sense than the capacity that is at the basis of the *vizio di mente*. In fact, if the latter undermines the capacity of discernment, the absence of specific regulatory parameters to identify the former leads to the belief that the 'insanity' relevant for the purposes of CPP Arts 70 ff. is any pathological condition that can adversely affect the capacity of the accused to put in place an adequate and conscious defence.[75] This is a conclusion that is consistent with the need to promote the right to defence in the context of a criminal trial.

That said, it must be emphasised that—similar to what should happen in the investigation of *vizio di mente*,[76] bearing in mind the above-mentioned differences—the ascertainment cannot be limited to the diagnostic moment, but it also contemplates an unavoidable moment of functional evaluation.[77] In particular,

[71] Franco Bricola, *Fatto del non imputabile e pericolosità* (Giuffrè 1961) 4–7.

[72] See Mario Romano and Giovanni Grasso, *Commentario sistematico del codice penale*, Volume II, Art 85-149 (4th edn, Giuffrè 2012) 14–15; Stefano Canestrari et al, *Manuale di diritto penale. Parte generale* (il Mulino 2007) 602; Alberto Cadoppi and Paolo Veneziani, *Elementi di diritto penale. Parte generale* (6th edn, Wolters Kluwer-CEDAM 2015) 407.

[73] Aimonetto, *L'incapacità dell'imputato per infermità di mente* (n 10) 107, 283–84. See also Maria Teresa Sturla, 'Commento *sub* artt. 70-73 c.p.p.' in Ennio Amodio and Oreste Dominioni (eds), *Commentario del nuovo codice di procedura penale* vol I (Giuffrè 1989) 421; Roberto E Kostoris, 'Commento *sub* art. 70 c.p.p.' in Mario Chiavario (coordinator), *Commento al codice di procedura penale* (2nd edn, UTET 1993) 53.

[74] Ugo Fornari, *Trattato di psichiatria forense* (6th edn, UTET Giuridica 2015) 133–45.

[75] ibid 142. See also Alberto Manacorda, *La perizia psichiatrica nel processo penale* (CIC Edizioni Internazionali 2003).

[76] This view has been prevalent in the psychiatric forensic literature, and (in part) in the Italian criminal law literature, as well as being authoritatively validated by Cass (SU) 8 March 2005, 9163. See Marta Bertolino, *L'imputabilità e il vizio di mente nel sistema penale* (Giuffrè 1990) 393–403, 429; Fornari, *Trattato di psichiatria forense* (n 74) 42–56; see also Mattia Celva, ' "The Ghost in the Machine". Il vizio di mente tra vecchi e nuovi paradigmi: il rilievo attuale del nesso eziologico tra disturbo e condotta' [2014] L'Indice penale 440–45, 452–62.

[77] Fornari, *Trattato di psichiatria forense* (n 74) 142–45; Isabella Merzagora Betsos, 'Imputabilità, pericolosità sociale, capacità di partecipare coscientemente al procedimento' in Giusto Giusti (director), *Trattato di medicina legale e scienze affini*, Volume IV, *Genetica. Psichiatria forense e criminologia. Medicina criminologica* (2nd edn, CEDAM 2009) 204.

whereas the concept of 'consciousness' is difficult to define, the insanity eventually recognised must involve an 'incapacity'.[78] This is required by the provisions of the CPP.[79] It must be noted that this second analysis aims to verify how the insanity affects a number of faculties of the person examined. The Italian literature lists a large number of these faculties, so that it is possible to say that the capacity to participate consciously in the trial is a heterogeneous category. In principle, it is possible to identify its content by observing that, in its dimension at the same time psychopathological and legal, it involves a plurality of levels. For instance the following capacities should be mentioned: to understand the meaning, the content, and reasons for the investigation; to prepare and formulate the defence; to apply for admission of favourable evidence and to participate; not to provide unfavourable evidence; to appoint a defence counsel; to support the cross-examination; to decide not to answer to the questions of the Prosecutor; to assess whether or not to attend the hearing; to provide statements; to submit applications, statements, and written questions.[80]

To conclude, it must be pointed out that, by seeking tools that can be useful for the investigation of the capacity to participate consciously in the trial, the Italian literature tends to look with interest at the experience of the United States. In particular, the limited studies dedicated to this aspect seem to pay much attention to the medical–legal doctrine and to the US assessments, as well as to the criteria developed by the case law of the United States Supreme Court.[81]

[78] Fornari, *Trattato di psichiatria forense* (n 74) 144.

[79] By way of example, it must be noted that the heading of CPP Art 71 contains an explicit mention of 'the incapacity of the accused' and provides that the trial can be suspended when insanity impedes the conscious participation of the accused person in the trial.

[80] Fornari, *Trattato di psichiatria forense* (n 74) 135.

It seems useful to recall an empirical survey, conducted on the practice of assessing the capacity to consciously participate in the trial in Italian courtrooms (P Farinoni et al, 'La capacità di partecipare coscientemente al processo: quadro giuridico, soluzioni forensi, suggerimenti operativi' [2004] Rivista italiana di medicina legale 1051). The case law examined takes into consideration twenty-two cases. Some observations deserve special mention. First, although there are still some grey areas, the collected data accepts the discrepancy between the capacity to participate consciously in the trial and the *vizio di mente*. Secondly, among the cases examined, nine led to the suspension of the process. Seven of these cases related to neurological or neuropsychiatric disorders arising from physical diseases, one involved a chronic intoxication from alcohol, and only one concerned psychiatric disorders. This suggests that the parameters taken into account for the purposes of CPP Arts 70 ff. concerned more the practical-operational area that the creative and strong-willed area. In addition, it has been noted that the orders given by the courts have proven to fully comply with the experts' conclusions.

[81] This view has been adopted by Gabriele Rocca and J Richard Ciccone, 'Il contributo psichiatrico-forense in tema di "capacità di partecipare consapevolmente al processo" evoluzione dei criteri valutativi statunitensi e prospettive applicative nella realtà italiana' [2011] Rassegna italiana di criminologia 54. Scholars pay attention to the *Dusky* criteria and the subsequent jurisprudence on such criteria.

In general, on the scientific evidence in the Italian context, see Oreste Dominioni, *La prova penale scientifica. Gli strumenti scientifico-tecnici nuovi o controversi e di elevata specializzazione* (Giuffrè 2005); Giulio Ubertis, 'La prova scientifica e la nottola di Minerva' in Luisella de Cataldo Neuburger (ed), *La prova scientifica nel processo penale* (Atti di Convegno, CEDAM 2007) 83; Francesco Caprioli, 'La scienza "cattiva maestra": le insidie della prova scientifica nel processo penale' [2008] Cassazione penale 3525; Pier Paolo Rivello, *La prova scientifica* (Giuffrè 2014). More recently, Giulio Garofalo, 'Le prove atipiche fra "apertura" e "limite" al potere giudiziale di conoscere' in Luca Marafioti and Giovanni Paolozzi (eds), *'Incontri ravvicinati' con la prova penale* (Giappichelli 2014) 133–37.

5. Conclusion

This chapter aims to provide the reader with the essential tools to understand a general framework of the rules on the capacity to participate consciously in the trial in the Italian legal system. However, the issues related to this topic, as well as the concept of 'insanity' itself have been investigated to only a limited extent.

It is evident that, if compared with other jurisdictions, the recent Italian experience shows major gaps when it comes to dealing with the effects of mental disorders. Both from a substantial point of view—in relation to the *vizio di mente*—and a procedural one, there are rules which are problematic in relation to their content. It is evident that 'empty containers' cannot be filled with everything: indeed, there are elements that have to be considered important points of reference. However, it must be noted that serious uncertainties remain and, as a consequence, a degree of unpredictability in terms of application.

This is undoubtedly determined by the difficulty in finding, even extrajudicially, precise and stable references. Nevertheless, while in the past in Italy the analysis of the relationship between mental disorders and the criminal justice system was regarded as important,[82] nowadays the focus on these issues has faded, at least in part. This means that often it must be acknowledged that there is difficulty in investigating in depth certain concepts which are necessary to give effect to some rules. By way of example are those related to the capacity to participate consciously in the trial, governing the implementation of very important rights, such as the rights to defend oneself.

In this respect, it is to be hoped that interest in these issues will increase. Indeed, it is desirable that Italian theoretical analysis and judicial practice will be able to draw on the heritage that psychiatric research and modern neuroscience can make available, in order to clarify certain concepts that are still too opaque. In fact, if the suggestions emanating from these areas are examined with a critical eye—especially in a context like the Italian one—it is also true that certain inputs can offer important insights for an in-depth study.[83] It is hoped that Italian scholars, following the example of those from other countries, will seize this opportunity in order to ensure full implementation of the rules and categories which are designed to protect the unfit to stand trial.

[82] It is enough to recall the extensive debate on free will that, between the nineteenth and twentieth centuries was the subject of comparison and division between the classical school and the position of criminal law. On this issue, see Mario Sbriccoli, 'Il diritto penale sociale' [1974–75] 3–4 Quaderni fiorentini per la storia del pensiero giuridico moderno 557; Mario Sbriccoli, 'Il diritto penale liberale. La "Rivista penale" di Luigi Lucchini' [1987] 16 Quaderni fiorentini per la storia del pensiero giuridico moderno 105; Ettore Dezza, 'Imputabilità e infermità mentale: la genesi dell'articolo 46 del Codice Zanardelli' [1991] 21 Materiali per una storia della cultura giuridica 131; Ugo Spirito, *Storia del diritto penale italiano. Da Cesare Beccaria ai nostri giorni* (3rd edn, Sansoni 1974); and Alberto Cadoppi, *Tra storia e comparazione. Studi di diritto penale comparato* (Wolters Kluwer-CEDAM 2014) 35–38, 42–44.

[83] See Marta Bertolino and Giulio Ubertis (eds), *Prova scientifica ragionamento probatorio e decisione giudiziale* (Atti di Convegno, Jovene 2015); Ciro Grandi, *Neuroscienze e responsabilità penale. Nuove soluzioni per problemi antichi?* (Giappichelli 2016).

13

Fitness to Stand Trial under International Criminal Law

Ian Freckelton and Magda Karagiannakis

Introduction

This chapter considers international criminal law on the issue of fitness to stand trial.[1] It examines the mental and physical disorders that have been asserted in international criminal proceedings for defendants accused of genocide, crimes against humanity, and war crimes. It reviews the processes by which fitness is determined, distils the legal standards that international courts have utilised and probes the consequences of findings of unfitness by international courts. The chapter suggests the introduction of more nuanced and psychiatrically informed criteria for fitness determinations. It also proposes the introduction of adequately resourced secure facilities for the confinement of persons found unfit to stand trial in order to reduce the incentives for the assertion of unmeritorious claims of unfitness. Finally, it considers the possibility of introducing special hearings determining whether defendants found unfit have engaged in the acts alleged in order to advance the overall aims of international criminal justice.

Jurisprudential Responses to Fitness to Stand Trial in International Criminal Law

As in national jurisdictions, under international criminal law an accused person's mental state has the potential to form a ground to exclude criminal responsibility, as well as for mitigation of sentence.[2] It may also form the basis of a claim that the

[1] Parts of this chapter have been published previously by the authors in previous journal articles that are referenced herein.

[2] *Prosecutor v Delalić et al*, Judgment, Case No IT-96-21-A, App Ch, 20 February 2001. See I Freckelton and M Karagiannakis, 'Mental State Defences before the International Criminal Court for the Former Yugoslavia' (2005) 12 Psychiatry, Psychology and Law 249, and see generally: A Cassese, *International Criminal Law* (3rd edn, Oxford University Press 2013) 224–27; R Cryer et al, *An Introduction to International Criminal Law and Procedure* (3rd edn, Cambridge University Press 2014) 401–02; P Krug, 'The Emerging Mental Incapacity Defense in International Criminal Law: Some

Fitness to Plead: International and Comparative Perspectives. First Edition. Edited by Ronnie Mackay and Warren Brookbanks. Chapter 13 © Ian Freckelton and Magda Karagiannakis 2018. Published 2018 by Oxford University Press.

person is unfit to stand trial. Decision-making about fitness to stand trial and the consequences of a finding of unfitness are fundamental to the integrity of any criminal justice system.[3] International criminal law grapples with many of the same issues that are confronted in national jurisdictions.

The mental health of the defendant is usually the main issue in the threshold question of whether an accused is fit to stand trial,[4] or even to be interviewed or interrogated.[5] A mental disorder[6] prior to or during trial may give rise to impairment such that the trial should not continue because the defendant cannot adequately understand or participate meaningfully in the proceedings.[7] Similarly but less often, accused persons with somatic disorders have been found to be unfit to stand trial. In a number of cases defendants have suffered from both physical and mental conditions which have rendered them unfit.

The International Criminal Tribunal for the Former Yugoslavia (ICTY),[8] the International Criminal Tribunal for Rwanda (ICTR),[9] the Special Court for Sierra

Initial Questions of Implementation' (2000) 96 American Journal of International Law 317; TB Smith, 'Mental Abnormality and Responsibility in International Criminal Law' (1951) 37 Transactions of the Grotius Society, Problems of Public and Private International Law, Transactions for the Year 1951 99; M Scaliotti, 'Defences before the International Criminal Court: Substantive Grounds for Excluding Criminal Responsibility—Part 2' (2002) 2 International Criminal Law Review 1, 18–28; S Janssen, 'Mental Condition Defences in Supranational Criminal Law' (2004) 4 International Criminal Law Review 83.

[3] See ML Perlin, P Champine, HA Dlugacz, M Connell et al, *Competence in the Law: From Legal Theory to Clinical Application* (John Wiley & Sons 2008); GH Morris, AM Haroum, and D Naimark, 'Competency to Stand Trial on Trial' (2004) 4 Houston Journal of Health Law and Policy 193; J La Fond, 'Health Law in the Criminal Justice System' (2004) 4 Houston Journal of Health Law and Policy 181; Victorian Law Reform Commission, *Report on Crimes (Mental Impairment and Unfitness to be Tried) Act 1997* (VLRC 2014).

[4] Unfitness to stand trial is referred to in a number of different ways in decisions and in the legal literature—fitness to plead, fitness to stand trial, competence to stand trial, and capacity to stand trial. In this chapter we have opted to use the more modern term of 'fitness to stand trial' as it most accurately reflects the issues: See D Paull, *Fitness to Stand Trial* (Charles C Thomas 1993).

[5] See P Weiner, 'Fitness Hearings in War Crimes Cases: From Nuremberg to The Hague' (2007) 30 Boston College International and Comparative Law Review 190.

[6] Utilising the terminology of the American Psychiatric Association (APA), *Diagnostic and Statistical Manual of Mental Disorders* (5th edn, APA 2013).

[7] At common law, the justifications for not permitting a person to stand trial when they are unfit to do so are: to avoid inaccurate verdicts; maintain the 'moral dignity' of the trial process; ensure that the defendant is able to form a link between the alleged crime and the trial or punishment; and be accountable for his or her actions and avoid unfairness. See Victorian Law Reform Commission, *Review of the Crimes (Mental Impairment and Unfitness to Be Tried) Act 1997*, Consultation Paper (VLRC 2013) 52.

[8] Judgment, *Prosecutor v Strugar*, IT-01-42-A, Appeals Chamber, 17 July 2008 ('*Strugar Appeal Judgment*'), *Prosecutor v Kovačević*, IT-01-42/2-I, Trial Chamber, Public Version of the Decision on Accused's Fitness to Enter a Plea and Stand Trial, 12 April 2006 ('*Kovačević Fitness Decision*'); *Prosecutor v Goran Hadžić*, Case No IT-04-75-T, Trial Chamber, Consolidated Decision on the Continuation of the Proceedings, 26 October 2015 ('*Hadzic Decision*'), *Prosecutor v Goran Hadžić*, Case No IT-04-75-T, Trial Chamber, Public Redacted Version of 24 March 2016, Decision on Remand on the Continuation of Proceedings, 5 April 2016 ('*Hadzic Final Decision*').

[9] Only to a limited extent, see *Prosecutor v Nsengiyumva*, ICTR-98-41-T, Trial Chamber 1, Decision on Nsengiyumva Motions to Call Doctors and Recall Eight Witnesses, 19 April 2007; *Prosecutor v Nahimana et al*, Judgement and Sentence, ICTR-99-52-T, Trial Chamber, 3 December 2003; and *Prosecutor v Karemera et al*, ICTR-98-44-T, Trial Chamber Decision on Remand Regarding Continuation of Trial, 10 September 2009.

Leone (SCSL),[10] the Special Panels of the Dili District Court (East Timor Panel),[11] the War Crimes Chamber in the Court of Bosnia and Herzegovina (Bosnian Chambers),[12] the Extraordinary Chambers in the Courts of Cambodia (ECCC),[13] and the International Criminal Court (ICC)[14] have all dealt with the issue of fitness to stand trial with respect to assertions of mental and physical impairment by accused persons. Defendants have raised the question of their fitness for trials based on illnesses including dementia, psychosis, post-traumatic stress disorder (PTSD), stroke, cardiovascular disease, hypertension, and cancer.

Dementia, Alzheimer's, and Amnesia

The distinctions between psychiatric disorders and physical disorders that can have an effect on mental functioning are not straightforward. Examples are neurodegenerative conditions such as Huntington's disease,[15] which have the potential to erode rationality and inhibit lucid understanding of proceedings. More conventional difficulties arise as a result of dementia and memory loss caused by conditions such as Alzheimer's disease, which have founded claims of unfitness to stand trial. This is unsurprising given the advanced age of some of those who have become defendants, and is a particularly pronounced problem associated with international criminal justice. The jurisprudence indicates that the memory loss from dementia must be at an advanced stage before a defendant will be considered unfit. This is so notwithstanding the usually very poor prognosis for dementia.

Gustav Krupp—dementia

Gustav Krupp von Bohlen und Halbach[16] was a major Nazi industrialist[17] who was indicted at Nuremberg for engaging in a conspiracy to wage aggressive war and

[10] See Ruling on Motion on a Stay of Proceeding Filed by the Applicant, *Sankoh* (SCSL–03-02-PT), Trial Chamber, 22 July 2003; *Registrar Announces the Death of Foday Sankoh*, SCSL Press Release, 30 July 2003.

[11] See, eg, Findings and Order on Defendant Nahak's Competence to Stand Trial, *Deputy General Prosecutor for Serious Crimes v Josep Nahak* (01A/2004), Democratic Republic of East Timor Dili District Court Special Panels for Serious Crimes, 1 March 2005 ('*Nahak Decision*'); I Freckelton and M Karagiannakis, 'Fitness to Stand Trial under International Criminal Law: The Ramifications of a Landmark East Timor Decision' (2014) 21 Psychiatry, Psychology and Law 321.

[12] See, eg, Appellate Verdict, *Prosecutor's Office of BiH v Zrinko Pinčić* (X-KRZ-08/502), 2 December 2009.

[13] See I Freckelton and M Karagiannakis, 'Unfitness to Stand Trial Decision-making in the Extraordinary Chambers in the Courts of Cambodia' (2014) 21 Journal of Law and Medicine 813.

[14] See, eg, *Prosecutor v Laurent Gbagbo*, Decision on the Fitness of Laurent Gbagbo to Take Part in the Proceedings before the ICC (ICC-02/11-01/11), Pre-Trial Chamber I, 2 November 2012 ('*First Gbagbo Decision*') and *Prosecutor v Laurent Gbagbo*, Decision on the Fitness of Laurent Gbagbo to Stand Trial (ICC-02/11-01/15), Trial Chamber I, 25 November 2015 ('*Second Gbagbo Decision*').

[15] See, eg, I Freckelton, 'Huntington's Disease and Fitness to Stand Trial' (2017) 24(1) Psychiatry, Psychology and Law 1.

[16] I Freckelton and M Karagiannakis, 'Fitness to Stand Trial under International Criminal Law: The Historical Background' (2014) 21 Journal of Law and Medicine 748.

[17] *Trial of the Major War Criminals before the International Military Tribunal* (1947) Volume 1, Indictment, ('IMT Trial') 75.

to commit war crimes and crimes against humanity.[18] Throughout the months of preparation of the prosecution cases for the Nuremberg trial, Krupp was bedridden at his Austrian villa, in an advanced state of senile dementia, inarticulate, incontinent, and wholly incapable of being interrogated or standing trial.[19]

Krupp's defence counsel sought a deferral of proceedings either temporarily (until he recovered) or permanently.[20] The Tribunal appointed a committee of four medical officers to assess the defendant. It concluded unanimously that he was senile and incapable of understanding court procedure, and of understanding or co-operating in interrogation. They believed unanimously that he would never become fit, mentally or physically, to appear before the International Military Tribunal (IMT).[21]

As a result, the IMT granted the defence application for a postponement of Krupp's trial but ordered the charges in the indictment against him to be retained on the docket for trial if the physical and mental condition of the defendant permitted the conduct of a trial. No reasoning was provided for the conditional nature of the order. Despite the fact that Krupp did not stand trial, and so was unable to mount any form of defence on his own behalf, the IMT proceeded to make adverse factual findings against him,[22] in a way that is analogous to what occurs in a 'special hearing' in Australia.[23] Krupp's condition did not improve and he was never formally tried. He remained in Austria until his death in 1950.[24]

The Krupp case is notable because the unanimous opinions of all the medical experts from the service of his indictment onwards were that he was completely physically and mentally incapacitated, with no potential for improvement. Despite this, the court kept the case against Krupp alive while Krupp himself was clearly dying. It did so by postponing the trial until such time as his health improved, instead of permanently adjourning or dismissing it. The conditional nature of its order raises the real possibility that the court took this course on an unarticulated and pragmatic basis: namely, it did not wish to be seen as effectively excusing a senior industrialist by permanently postponing or dismissing his case.[25]

[18] ibid, Volume 1, Indictment, 29–35.

[19] T Taylor, *The Anatomy of the Nuremberg Trials: A Personal Memoir* (Little, Brown & Co 1992) 93. IMT Trial (n 17) Volume 1, Certificate of Service on Defendant Gustav Krupp and Attachments (Medical Reports), 116–23; DA Sprecher, *Inside the Nuremberg Trial: A Prosecutor's Comprehensive Account*, Volume 1 (University Press of America 1999) 135; A Tusa and J Tusa, *The Nuremberg Trial* (McGraw-Hill 1985) 138.

[20] IMT Trial (n 17) Volume 1, Motion on Behalf of Defendant Gustav Krupp von Bohlen for Postponement of Trial as to Him, 124–25; ibid, Volume II, Preliminary Hearing, Wednesday 14 November 1945, 1.

[21] ibid, Volume 1, Report of the Medical Commission Appointed to Examine Defendant Gustav Krupp von Bohlen, 127. ibid, Volume 1, Order of the Tribunal Granting Postponement of Proceedings against Gustav Krupp von Bohlen, 143.

[22] ibid, Volume 1, Judgment, 183–84.

[23] See Ian Freckelton, chapter 8 'Fitness to Stand Trial under Australian Law'.

[24] See H James, *Krupp: A History of the Legendary German Firm* (Princeton University Press 2012).

[25] Freckelton and Karagiannakis, 'Fitness to Stand Trial under International Criminal Law: The Historical Background' (n 16).

Rudolf Hess—amnesia

The second defendant to seek a postponement of the proceedings against him at Nuremberg on the basis of an alleged psychiatric disorder was Rudolf Hess.[26] He was Hitler's close personal confidant[27] and had been one of his senior deputies.[28] Shortly before the scheduled commencement of his trial, Hess's defence counsel made a motion requesting that medical experts be appointed to determine whether Hess was mentally competent and fit to be tried due to his apparent complete memory loss. [31] As in the Krupp case, the IMT appointed a commission consisting of physicians from each of the four countries of the IMT to examine Hess.[32]

The commission submitted three reports.[29] The Russian and French physicians agreed that Hess had a psychopathic personality and was at times paranoid and suicidal. In addition, they found he had hysterical tendencies which caused a primary symptom of amnesia. They found that Hess was sane and could understand proceedings to a sufficient extent but his ability to defend himself was impaired by his amnesia.[30] The case involved a combination of what today would be classified as pathology and personality disorders.[31] Because not all the reports were received before the commencement of the trial, Hess took his seat in the dock.[32] The remaining two medical reports by members of the commission largely conformed with the initial conclusions.[33] There was no suggestion that Hess was feigning amnesia, but the United States doctors suggested that he consciously exaggerated his loss of memory in order to protect himself against examination.[34]

The hearing on the motion on behalf of Hess was held on the ninth day of trial.[35] Defence counsel advised the IMT at the outset that Hess considered himself fit to plead.[36] Contrary to his client's instructions, defence counsel proceeded to argue that Hess was unfit and that proceedings should be suspended. He did so because he considered it his duty on the basis of the expert opinions[37] and his own observations that Hess was incapable of grasping the charges and neither remembered events from the past nor the persons with whom he had associated during the period relevant to the charges.[38]

The prosecutors opposed the motion. The United Kingdom prosecutor argued that the test for mental fitness was whether at the moment of plea and at trial the defendant understood the charges and the evidence against him, not whether he had

[26] JR Rees (ed), *The Case of Rudolf Hess: A Problem in Diagnosis and Forensic Psychiatry* (WW Norton 1948); Freckelton and Karagiannakis, 'Fitness to Stand Trial under International Criminal Law: The Historical Background' (n 16).

[27] See S McGinty and Z Camp, *The Secret Life of Rudolf Hess* (MacMillan 2011).

[28] IMT Trial (n 17) Volume 1, Judgment, 282–84.

[29] ibid, Volume 1, Report of the Commission to Examine Defendant Hess, 159–65.

[30] ibid 159–60. In relation to amnesia and unfitness to stand trial, see generally *R v Podola* [1960] 1 QB 325.

[31] See EF Torrey, 'Rudolph Hess's Mental Illness' (1987) 151 British Journal of Psychiatry 858; W Sargant 'Hess's Mental State' (1962) 2 British Medical Journal 1036.

[32] Taylor, *The Anatomy of the Nuremberg Trials: A Personal Memoir* (n 19) 151.

[33] IMT Trial (n 17) Volume 1, Report of the Commission to Examine Defendant Hess, 163–65.

[34] ibid 164.

[35] ibid, Volume II, Ninth Day, Friday 30 November 1945, 478–96.

[36] ibid 479.

[37] ibid 481–82.

[38] ibid 482.

a memory as to what happened at the time.[39] The United States prosecutor added that since Hess had refused all treatment for the conditions causing his amnesia he could not assert that he was unfit and therefore postpone his trial—he argued that Hess was 'in the volunteer class with his amnesia'.[40]

At the end of the hearing of arguments on his fitness, Hess made an extraordinary and dramatic statement to the tribunal. In order to forestall the possibility that he would be found unfit to be tried he admitted to simulating his memory loss for tactical reasons and promised that 'Henceforth my memory will again respond to the outside world.'[41] The statement was met by 'dead silence, then a ripple of laughter and then an outward rush of the press'.[42] The session was adjourned. The following morning the IMT ruled that in light of this statement and all the evidence Hess was fit to stand trial.[43]

This resolved the motion but it did not resolve the issues of whether, in fact, Hess had periodic amnesia and whether this actually affected his ability to give instructions to his lawyer and to give his account of the events of which he was accused. Subsequent medical opinions indicated that he did suffer from amnesia, which seriously impeded his ability to participate in his defence. The prison psychiatrist opined that the statement that Hess made in court was a typically hysterical gesture, which confirmed that he had indeed been suffering from amnesia rooted in hysteria.[44] A later report by the prison psychologist stated that during the trial Hess's memory loss became progressively worse, reaching a state of virtually complete amnesia where his memory span was about a half a day.[45]

In its final judgment, the IMT acknowledged that Hess acted in an abnormal manner, suffered from memory loss, and had mentally deteriorated during the trial. However, it concluded that there was:

> nothing to show that he does not realize the nature of the charges against him, or is incapable of defending himself. He was ably represented at the Trial by counsel, appointed for that purpose by the Tribunal. There is no suggestion that Hess was not completely sane when the acts charged against him were committed.[46]

Hess was found guilty of conspiracy and crimes against peace.[47] He was sentenced to life imprisonment and in 1987 died in Spandau Prison, after serving more than four decades of imprisonment.

With this finding, the IMT seemed to accept implicitly that all that was required for a finding of fitness was that the accused understood the charges (and the evidence). However, the defendant did not need to remember the pertinent events that gave rise to those charges or evidence, or the evidence given in court. The IMT's

[39] ibid 489. [40] ibid 493. [41] ibid 496.

[42] Taylor, *The Anatomy of the Nuremberg Trials: A Personal Memoir* (n 19) 179.

[43] IMT Trial (n 17) Volume III, Tenth Day, Saturday 1 December 1945, 1.

[44] Taylor, *The Anatomy of the Nuremberg Trials: A Personal Memoir* (n 19) 179.

[45] IMT Trial (n 17) Volume 1, Report of Prison Psychologist on Mental Competence of Defendant Hess, 166.

[46] IMT Trial (n 17) Volume 1, Judgment, 284. See also D Pick, *The Pursuit of the Nazi Mind: Hitler, Hess and the Analysts* (OUP 2012).

[47] IMT Trial (n 17) Volume 1, Judgment, 284–85.

acknowledgement of Hess's deteriorating state of mental health during the trial sits uncomfortably with its finding that there was not adequate proof that he was 'incapable of defending himself'. Furthermore, the IMT's reference to able legal representation as a remedial factor in its consideration of Hess's fitness lacks conceptual justification;[48] the adequacy of legal representation on factual issues is severely hampered if counsel were not able to obtain instructions from their clients as to why and how the testimony against them is incorrect. If defendants cannot recall the testimony of witnesses speaking against them and instruct their counsel as to the accuracy of evidence adverse to their interests, then vital information will not be conveyed to legal representatives for the purpose of confronting witnesses.[49]

Several other issues are raised by Hess's case. It highlights the difficulty for a court assessing protestations by a defendant about their mental state, an evaluative exercise which is complex for even independent mental health experts. Rather than relying on generalist psychiatrists and psychologists for assessments, objective psychometric testing, such as by forensic neuropsychologists, may have a useful role to play.

The *Hess* case also accentuates the importance of the role of counsel in arguing that a client is unfit in spite of their instructions—in Hess's case that he had been feigning his amnesia. His counsel's position on the issue was prescient given his client's subsequent mental decline. This highlights the duty of the counsel and the court to be constantly vigilant on the issue of fitness based on objective medical assessments and their own observations, rather than the words or conduct of the accused alone. In the opinion of a leading United States prosecutor at Nuremberg, Telford Taylor, Hess's statement made him think of Joseph Heller's *Catch-22*, one theme of which was that 'if he says he's sane, he must be crazy'.[50] Taylor concluded that it did not appear fair to put Hess on trial and his behaviour in the dock did not comport with the dignity of the proceedings.[51]

Pavle Strugar—dementia

Pavle Strugar[52] was a Lieutenant-General of the Yugoslav People's Army. He was charged with six counts of war crimes arising out of artillery and mortar shelling of the old town of Dubrovnik by forces under his command commencing on 6 December 1991. At the time he was brought to trial he was retired and seventy years of age.[53]

[48] The availability of legal representation was later to be held inadequate to remedy a cognitive deficiency which rendered a person unable to give adequate instructions: *Nahak Decision* (n 11) [131]; Freckelton and Karagiannakis, 'Fitness to Stand Trial under International Criminal Law' (n 11).

[49] Freckelton and Karagiannakis, 'Fitness to Stand Trial under International Criminal Law: The Historical Background' (n 16).

[50] Taylor, *The Anatomy of the Nuremberg Trials: A Personal Memoir* (n 19) 179. [51] ibid.

[52] See I Freckelton and M Karagiannakis, 'Fitness to Stand Trial under International Criminal Law: Current Challenges for Law and Policy' (2014) 12 Journal of International Criminal Justice 708–11; I Freckelton and M Karagiannakis, 'Unfitness to Stand Trial under International Criminal Law: The Influential Decision of the International Criminal Tribunal of the Former Yugoslavia in relation to Pavle Strugar and its Ramifications' (2014) 21 Psychiatry, Psychology and Law 445.

[53] *Prosecutor v Strugar*, IT-01-42-T, Trial Chamber Decision Re the Defence Motion to Terminate Proceedings, 26 May 2004 ('*Strugar Trial Decision*'), s 2.

The issue of Strugar's fitness to stand trial was first raised by his defence counsel at a late juncture—the day before trial commenced.[54] Ultimately the prosecution relied on the joint report of three experienced psychiatric experts, who concluded that Strugar suffered from uncomplicated vascular dementia and had mildly decreased memory and occasional word-finding difficulty. They did not agree that he suffered from post-traumatic stress disorder (PTSD) or major depressive disorder, contrary to a diagnosis of these illnesses by the defence expert.[55] Importantly, they found no evidence of a significant impairment in Strugar's ability to recall pertinent information or to focus his attention for extended periods of time.[56] They concluded that Strugar's cognitive impairments were too mild to prevent him from understanding the proceedings and assisting in his defence.[57]

About six months into the trial, the Trial Chamber accepted the evidence of the prosecution experts and found Strugar fit to stand trial. The finding was based on expert evidence and the judges' own observations during trial that the accused appeared to be 'collected, relevant, well structured and comprehensive'.[58] The court found Strugar guilty of two counts of war crimes for attacks on civilians and destruction of cultural property on the basis of command responsibility over the forces that shelled Dubrovnik. He was sentenced to eight years' imprisonment and appealed.[59] The Appeals Chamber upheld the Trial Chamber's judgment but, in consideration of the Strugar's deteriorating health since the judgment in 2005, it imposed a reduced sentence of seven-and-a-half years' imprisonment.[60] On 16 January 2009, Strugar was granted early release, effective the next month, for reasons which included his deteriorating health.[61]

In its decision the Appeals Chamber recognised that the issue of fitness is one which has the potential to affect the fair and expeditious conduct of the trial.[62] After examining national and international authorities comprehensively,[63] the Appeals Chamber affirmed the approach of the Trial Chamber[64] in concluding that the issue of fitness is not confined to the question of whether a particular condition is present but is better approached by determining whether the defendant is able to exercise his or her rights effectively.[65]

It found that a non-exhaustive list of the capacities to be evaluated when assessing an accused person's fitness to stand trial includes the capacity to plead; understand the nature of the charges; understand the course of the proceedings; understand the details of the evidence; instruct counsel; understand the consequences of the proceedings; and testify.[66] The Appeals Chamber explained that 'the applicable standard is that of meaningful participation which allows the accused to exercise his fair trial rights to such a degree that he is able to participate effectively in his trial, and has an understanding of the essentials of the proceedings'.[67] It held that the ability of the

[54] ibid, s 3. [55] ibid, ss 12–14. [56] ibid, s 16. [57] ibid, ss 16, 30.
[58] ibid, ss 50–51. [59] *Strugar Appeal Judgement* (n 8) s 25. [60] ibid, ss 391–93.
[61] *Prosecutor v Strugar*, Case No IT-01-42-ES, Presidency Decision of the President on the Application for Pardon or Commutation of Sentence of Pavle Strugar, 16 January 2009, s 15.
[62] ibid, s 34. [63] ibid, ss 45–54. [64] *Strugar Appeal Judgement* (n 8), ss 41–55.
[65] ibid, ss 41, 55. [66] ibid.
[67] ibid, s 55. It applied the decision in *Prosecutor v Nahimana et al*, Judgment and Sentence (n 9).

accused to participate in his or her trial should be assessed by looking at whether the person's capacities, viewed overall and in a reasonable and common sense manner, are at such a level that it is possible for him or her to participate in the proceedings and sufficiently exercise their rights.[68] It also found that when an accused person asserts he or she is unfit to stand trial, it is incumbent upon him or her to prove the contention on the balance of probabilities.[69]

The Appeals Chamber did not adopt the United States approach, applied in the *Nahak* decision discussed below, to require that the accused be able to make rational evaluations and to provide rational, reasonable, or lucid instructions and accounts to his or her legal representatives and the court.[70] It rejected the proposition that the test should require the accused person 'to fully comprehend the course of the proceedings in the trial, so as to make a proper defense'. Instead, it required a lower level of capacity to participate meaningfully in the trial[71] without setting out clear reference points for when this will be satisfied. It declined to disturb the Trial Chamber's findings that led to it determining Strugar to be fit to stand trial. What is uncertain in the aftermath of the *Strugar* decision is when phenomena such as irrationality, impoverished memory, or paranoia will overturn an accused person's capacity to participate in the trial process.[72]

Ieng Thirith—dementia caused by Alzheimer's

The ECCC issued a series of decisions with respect to Ieng Thirith's fitness to be tried and importantly, the issue of what actions should be taken in respect of an accused who is apparently permanently unfit to be tried.[73] The accused, who was born in 1932, was the Minister of Social Action of Democratic Kampuchea. She was accused of crimes against humanity: murder, extermination, imprisonment, persecution, and other inhumane acts committed under the Pol Pot Regime. Prior to her trial, and at the request of the defence,[74] Ieng Thirith was assessed by court-appointed experts, including a geriatrician and four psychiatrists, all of whom agreed that she suffered from a dementing illness, probably caused by Alzheimer's disease at stage five (of seven), namely 'early dementia moderately severe cognitive decline'.

The Trial Chamber accepted psychiatric evidence that the accused retained some capacity to enter a plea, to understand the charges and the details of the evidence against her, and to testify.[75] However, importantly, it found that the impairment of

[68] *Strugar Appeal Judgment* (n 8), s 55. [69] ibid, s 56.

[70] ibid, ss 51, 52 fn 139, 55 fn 152. See also W Brookbanks, 'Fitness to Plead—Best Interests Versus Autonomy: Does a defendant's paranoia matter?' (2013) 20 Psychiatry, Psychology and Law 1.

[71] *Strugar Appeal Judgment* (n 8), s 60.

[72] Freckelton and Karagiannakis, 'Fitness to Stand Trial under International Criminal Law: Current Challenges for Law and Policy' (n 52).

[73] ibid; see also Freckelton and Karagiannakis, 'Unfitness to Stand Trial Decision-making in the Extraordinary Chambers in the Courts of Cambodia' (n 13).

[74] Freckelton and Karagiannakis, 'Fitness to Stand Trial under International Criminal Law' (n 72); Freckelton and Karagiannakis, 'Unfitness to Stand Trial Decision-making in the Extraordinary Chambers in the Courts of Cambodia' (n 13).

[75] ibid, s 56.

her memory would be likely to impact upon her ability to recall events accurately and that this would affect her credibility if she were to testify.[76] It applied the *Strugar* test and found that she would not be able to follow the testimony in the trial sufficiently well to be able to provide information to counsel relevant to her defence.[77] Accordingly, it declared her unfit to stand trial. However, this left the difficult decision as to what should be done thereafter with the accused. The Trial Chamber split on whether it should order the accused to seek medical treatment or to release her without conditions.[78]

The Supreme Court Chamber resolved this on appeal by finding that the court is obliged to exercise jurisdiction in order to undertake 'remedial action in the light of a possibility, even slight, of meaningful improvement'.[79] In doing so it emphasised the 'strong public interest' in prosecuting the accused, including the interests of victims.[80] In an attempt to improve Thirith's mental health, the Chamber, Judge Jayasinghe dissenting, ordered the continued detention of Thirith in a hospital or comparable facility such as a modified ECCC detention facility. This allowed for the administration of the recommended treatment in a professional, court-controlled environment, as well as the protection of the rights of the accused.[81] It ordered the Trial Chamber to review the medical condition of Thirith within six months.[82]

However, Thirith's condition deteriorated.[83] All treatment options had been exhausted and her cognitive impairment worsened and was regarded as irreversible.[84] The Trial Chamber indefinitely stayed proceedings and released her from detention[85] without condition.[86]

However, the Supreme Court Chamber again overturned the Trial Chamber on appeal and decided that the ECCC could and should exercise jurisdiction.[87] It acknowledged that the issue of an accused who may never be fit for trial 'creates a tension between the fundamental rights of the accused on the one hand (eg, to be presumed innocent and to be tried within a reasonable time, as well as their rights to liberty and privacy) and the interests of justice on the other hand (eg, in prosecuting the accused for serious crimes), including the interests of the victims to have the truth ascertained and pursue their civil claims'.[88]

[76] ibid, s 57. [77] ibid, ss 58–59.

[78] ibid, ss 63, 65, 74, 77–81. In his follow-up report, the geriatrician had recommended a trial of Donepezil, an Alzheimer's drug found effective in some patients (s 37); the report by the psychiatrists also suggested a number of other measures which they concluded may be of benefit to the accused, including a structured cognitive stimulation programme (s 64).

[79] Decision on Immediate Appeal against the Trial Chamber's Order to Release the Accused Ieng Thirith, Dossier No 002//19-09-2007-ECCC-TC/SC(09), Supreme Court Chamber, 13 December 2011, ss 29.

[80] ibid, ss 28. [81] ibid, s 42. [82] ibid, s 49.

[83] She could not be treated with Donepezil because she was intolerant to it. Decision on Immediate Appeal against the Trial Chamber's Order to Unconditionally Release the Accused Ieng Thirith, Dossier No 002/19-09-2007 ECCC-TC/SC(16), Supreme Court Chamber, 14 December 2012 ('*Ieng Thirith Second Appellate Decision*') s 59.

[84] Decision on Reassessment of Accused Ieng Thirith's Fitness to Stand Trial following Supreme Court Chamber Decision of 13 December 2011, Dossier No 002/19-09-2007/ECCC/TC, Trial Chamber, 13 September 2012, ss 24, 26–28.

[85] ibid, ss 29–31. [86] ibid, ss 28, 32–39.

[87] *Ieng Thirith Second Appellate Decision* (n 83) ss 52–53. [88] ibid, s 40.

From its review of international and comparative national criminal laws the Chamber identified three potential approaches to the issue: (i) to suspend the proceedings without terminating them, with an option to employ measures aimed at facilitating their resumption; (ii) to bring the proceedings to a conclusion by deciding whether the accused committed the act with which she had been charged (special verdict) with an option to impose a range of measures aimed at protecting the accused and the public; and (iii) to terminate the criminal proceedings with the possibility of further action under mental health provisions.[89] It noted that the solution of suspending or temporarily staying proceedings and continuing to exercise jurisdiction even when proceedings are unlikely ever to resume was adopted at Nuremberg, and by the ICTY and the East Timor Panel.[90] Furthermore, while Rule 35 of the International Criminal Court Rules of Procedure and Evidence (ICC RPE), provides for regular review of a defendant initially found to be unfit, it does not contemplate a special solution in the event of a permanently unfit person.[91]

The Chamber found that the mere fact that proceedings remain pending against unfit accused persons charged with serious crimes, even if permanently unfit, is generally not considered a disproportionate infringement upon the accused's fundamental rights, in particular, the right to be tried within a reasonable time.[92] Accordingly, courts maintain jurisdictional control over the accused found unfit to stand trial. The key question in these circumstances is 'what measures, if any, are necessary and proportionate when the accused faces little prospect of ever being tried'.[93]

The Chamber decided that measures monitoring the condition of the accused were necessary. However, it decided to take only those measures which would have a minimal practical impact on the accused's rights against the arbitrary restriction of movement and to privacy, and therefore could be considered proportionate in the circumstances.[94] Accordingly, it decided to suspend proceedings and release Thirith from detention to live with her daughter under a regime of judicial supervision and six-monthly medical examinations by court-appointed experts.[95] Given the poor medical prognoses, no ongoing therapeutic treatment was ordered. Thirith died in August 2015 at the age of eighty-three, without facing trial.[96]

The Supreme Court Chamber decision in relation to Ieng Thirith is significant because of its finding that international courts retain jurisdiction over temporarily and potentially permanently mentally unfit persons after the suspension of criminal proceedings. The discretion to exercise this jurisdiction is wide and can be exercised to impose any coercive measures that are practically available. These could arguably include a wide range of initiatives from the highly restrictive, such as continued detention with or without medical treatment, but to more relaxed options such as release with minimal reporting conditions and restrictions on movement. However, the jurisdiction is not unfettered: the coercive measures must be necessary

[89] ibid. [90] ibid, ss 46–47. [91] ibid, s 48. [92] ibid, s 52. [93] ibid.
[94] ibid, ss 58–60. [95] ibid, ss 62–81.
[96] See T Fuller, 'Ieng Thirith, Khmer Rouge Minister in Cambodia, Dies at 83', 22 August 2015, *New York Times*, available at: https://www.nytimes.com/2015/08/23/world/asia/ieng-thirith-khmer-rouge-minister-in-cambodia-dies-at-83.html?_r=0.

and proportionate. This means balancing the rights of the accused with the interests of justice by applying measures which will have as small a practical impact on the accused's rights as possible whilst maintaining at least the notional possibility of prosecution for serious crimes should medical circumstances permit.[97]

Psychosis

Defendants in international trials have been remitted for medical assessment after displaying bizarre behaviours. Those who have been found to be suffering from illnesses inducing psychotic symptoms have been held by international tribunals to be unfit to stand trial. This in turn has resulted in the permanent suspension of a number of trials. However, the few cases where this has been the situation raise the issues of the extent to which symptoms can be faked, exaggerated, or effectively treated. In the case of Okawa, the elaborate delusions of the accused subsided after the termination of proceedings against him. In the case of Kovačević,, the accused man's condition was apparently controlled to the extent that he could be treated as an outpatient and yet he was not put subsequently on trial, preferring to return to the hospital as an inpatient for treatment for his on-going mental illness. Proceedings against him were later terminated. It is apparent that accused persons who present with psychotic symptoms need to be assessed by experienced forensic experts in order to minimise the possibility of faked or overstated symptoms. Further, accused persons need to be treated in adequately resourced facilities overseen by courts, so that there is as good a chance of successful treatment as possible and as good a prospect as can be secured for there to be a criminal trial when abatement of symptomatology permits.

Shumei Okawa—psychosis caused by syphilis

The International Military Tribunal for the Far East (the Tokyo Tribunal) dealt with the issue of fitness to stand trial in respect of one accused: Shumei Okawa.[98] Okawa had written numerous books, articles, and speeches advocating aggressive war for the expulsion of the white races from Asia.[99] In a trial against multiple persons, Okawa was alleged to be a propagandist who participated in a conspiracy with others to wage wars of aggression.[100]

In May 1946, the accused were arraigned and all but Okawa pleaded not guilty. Due to his behaviour in the courtroom, Okawa was excluded from the court and ordered to undergo a psychiatric evaluation.[101] His bizarre behaviour included unbuttoning his shirt in an apparent attempt to undress, putting his hands together

[97] Freckelton and Karagiannakis, 'Fitness to Stand Trial under International Criminal Law: Current Challenges for Law and Policy' (n 52).

[98] Freckelton and Karagiannakis, 'Fitness to Stand Trial under International Criminal Law: The Historical Background' (n 16).

[99] R Boister and R Cryer, *The Tokyo International Military Tribunal: A Reappraisal* (OUP 2008) 58.

[100] R Minear, *Victor's Justice: The Tokyo War Crimes Trial* (Princeton University Press 1971) 201 and 193 *et seq* (for judgment and findings on the Indictment).

[101] ibid 25.

in a strange gesture of prayer and slapping former Japanese Prime Minister Tojo in the back of the head while seated behind him in the dock.[102]

After the 'slapping incident' Okawa was removed from the trial, hospitalised, and treated with malaria fever therapy.[103] Treatment resulted in a gradual improvement in his condition and he was examined on the issue of his fitness.[104] The reports found that Okawa was suffering from syphilis, leading to 'meningoencephalitis (general paresis) manifested by overactivity, emotional lability, euphoria, grandiose delusions, visual hallucinations, defective judgement, and impairment of retention, recent memory, abstract thinking, and insight'.[105] Two United States neuropsychiatrists found that Okawa was fit to stand trial because he was able to understand the nature of the proceedings and to differentiate between right and wrong.[106] However, the Japanese psychiatrist found him lacking in the various faculties that are needed to stand trial, such as the power to discriminate between right and wrong.[107]

The tribunal ordered that no further proceedings be taken against Okawa because it was not satisfied that he had recovered the intellectual capacity and judgement to make him capable of standing trial and conducting his defence and because he had not pleaded to the charges and had not been able to instruct his counsel effectively during the proceedings. It ordered that Okawa be kept in custody subject to any order issued by the Supreme Commander for the Allied Powers. It also expressly stated that its order would not prevent the trial of the accused at a later date.[108]

Okawa was never brought to trial. However, he continued to be detained in Matsuzawa Hospital in Tokyo, where he translated the Koran into Japanese and wrote a biography of the Prophet Muhammed.[109] During this time he reportedly told both the US and Japanese psychiatrists that he was visited by the souls of many people, including King Edward VII, President Wilson, and the Prophet

[102] RJC Butow, *Tojo and the Coming of the War* (Princeton University Press 1961) 485; T Yamazaki and VD Morris, *Two Homelands* (University of Hawaii Press 2008); EB Fischel, *Defending the Enemy: Justice for the WWII Japanese War Criminals* (Hillcrest Publishing 2010), available at: http://pds15.egloos.com/pds/200909/08/60/a0015760_4aa5eabfe5858.gif. Also see Report of Dr Yusihi Uchimura, Professor at the Department of Psychiatry, Faculty of Medicine, Tokyo Imperial University and Head of Tokyo Municipal Hospital at Matsuwaza (23 February 1947), Northcroft Archive, Macmillan Brown Library, University of Canterbury, MB 1549, Box 200, 4, cited in Boister and Cryer, *The Tokyo International Military Tribunal: A Reappraisal* (n 99) n 270.

[103] See CJ Tsay, 'Julius Wagner-Jauregg and the Legacy of Malarial Therapy for the Treatment of General Paresis of the Insane' (2013) 86(2) Yale J Biol Med 245; JV Kragh, 'Malaria Fever Therapy for General Paralysis of the Insane in Denmark' (2010) 21(4) History of Psychiatry 471.

[104] Butow, *Tojo and the Coming of the War* (n 102) 486.

[105] Report of Herbert Posin, Ist Lieutenant MC, Neuropsychiatrist and William G Scweikert, Ist Lieutenant MC, Neuropsychiatrist, Neuropsychiatric Service, 361st Station Hospital, APO 1055, WWFF/vv (13 March 1947), Macmillan Brown Archives, MB 1549, Box 200, 1, cited in Boister and Cryer, *The Tokyo International Military Tribunal: A Reappraisal* (n 99) n 271.

[106] ibid 4: Butow, *Tojo and the Coming of the War* (n 102) 486.

[107] Report of Dr Yusihi Uchimura (n 102) 12, n 273.

[108] *The Tokyo Major War Crimes Trial: The Records of the International Military Tribunal for the Far East* (1998) Vol 42, Transcript, 28 April 1947, 19,637–19,638.

[109] See A Usuki, 'A Japanese Asianist's View of Islam: A Case Study of Okawa Shumei' (2012) 28(2) Annals of Japan Association for Middle East Studies 58, available at: http://www.academia.edu/3010300/A_Japanese_Asianists_View_of_Islam_A_Case_Study_of_Okawa_Shumei.

Mohammed.[110] After the Tokyo Tribunal closed, Okawa is reported as having recovered 'miraculously'.[111] He went on to write a number of books giving rise to the allegation that the tribunal had been duped.[112] Okawa was released in 1948 after being treated with penicillin for syphilis. He died in December 1957.[113]

Josep Nahak—schizophrenia

In 2005, the East Timor Panel ruled upon a complex case involving the contention that Josep Nahak, who was charged with crimes against humanity in the form of murder, attempted murder, and persecution committed in 1999, was unfit to stand trial.[114] In doing so, it drew upon the approach of the Trial Chamber of the ICTY in the *Strugar* case before the appellate decision in that case was issued.

The issue of Nahak's mental state was raised initially by the prosecutor on the basis that Nahak was 'behaving in a very peculiar manner' which appeared 'to a lay person ... to be abnormal'.[115]

In his judgment assessing Nahak's fitness to stand trial, Judge Rapoza applied the observation in the *Strugar* Trial Chamber decision that as it is necessary that a trial not take place in the absence of a defendant, a person must be able to be mentally present in court by reason of being able to defend himself or herself.[116]

Drawing on United States law on the subject,[117] Judge Rapoza found that a defendant is competent if he has a *rational* as well as a factual understanding of the nature and object of the proceedings against him; and a present ability to consult with his lawyer and to assist in the preparation of his defence with *a reasonable degree of rational understanding*.[118] Applying the *Strugar* Trial Chamber decision, he determined the standard of proof to be on the 'balance of probabilities' and decided not to depend on any onus of proof, simply addressing whether the evidence demonstrated that it was more probable than not that the defendant was fit to stand trial.

Judge Rapoza took into account expert evidence that Nahak was suffering from chronic schizophrenia of moderate severity, characterised by auditory hallucinations,

[110] Butow, *Tojo and the Coming of the War* (n 102) 486–87, citing the expert medical reports.

[111] RL Pritchard, 'The International Military Tribunal for the Far East and its Contemporary Resonances' (1995) 149 Military Law Review 25.

[112] Boister and Cryer, *The Tokyo International Military Tribunal: A Reappraisal* (n 99) 241.

[113] See E Jaffe, *A Curious Madness: An American Psychiatrist, A Japanese War Crimes Suspect and an* Unsolved *Mystery from World War II* (Scribner 2014).

[114] *Nahak Decision* (n 11). See Freckelton and Karagiannakis, 'Unfitness to Stand Trial under International Criminal Law: The Influential Decision of the International Criminal Tribunal of the Former Yugoslavia in relation to Pavle Strugar and its Ramifications' (n 52) 711–14; Freckelton and Karagiannakis, 'Fitness to Stand Trial under International Criminal Law' (n 11).

[115] *Nahak Decision* (n 11) s 1.

[116] ibid, ss 46–47. It compared the decision of the court in Judgment, *Prosecutor v Tacaqui*, Case No 20/2001, Democratic Republic of East Timor Dili District Court Special Panels, 12 December 2004, where it was held that a defendant had to be present not just physically but also 'in mind'. This was met where a defendant elected to be mute throughout proceedings.

[117] See, eg, *Dusky v United States*, 362 US 402 (1960); *Drope v Missouri*, 420 US 162 (1975); *Godinez v Martin*, 113 S Ct 2680 (1993).

[118] *Nahak Decision* (n 11) s 54 (emphasis added).

fatuous affect, and formal thought disorder and also factored into his decision his observations of Nahak in court.[119] He concluded that it was 'highly doubtful' that Nahak understood the basic elements of the charges against him or the nature and object of the proceedings against him.[120] He rejected the proposition that it was necessary for Nahak to be found to be suffering from a mental disorder in order for him to be found unfit for trial—'it is sufficient to conclude that the evidence demonstrates that the Defendant suffers from a form of mental disturbance that not only interferes with his routine functioning, but which also prevents him from having a rational as well as a factual understanding of both the charges against him, as well as the nature and object of these proceedings'.[121] He classified the ability of a defendant to consult with his or her lawyer and to assist in the preparation of a defence as 'perhaps the most significant element of the test of competence'.[122] He concluded that it was improbable that Nahak understood the role of the lawyer who had been appointed to represent him.

Judge Rapoza specifically adverted to the possibility that Nahak was feigning illness and commented that he was either a severely limited person whose mental issues rendered him incompetent to stand trial, or he was a particularly cunning individual who for years had calculated his actions to produce the impression of incompetence to avoid accountability. He concluded that the weight of the evidence was in favour of the conclusion that Nahak was severely limited rather than cunning.[123] This resulted in a ruling that Nahak was not fit for trial and an adjournment of the proceedings *sine die*, with permission extended to the Prosecutor to request the court to review and reconsider Nahak's competence should there be a change in his condition.

Judge Rapoza noted that many national jurisdictions provide for the hospitalisation of defendants determined not fit for trial in a way comparable to the situation of those found not guilty by reason of insanity, especially if they constitute a continuing danger to themselves or others. However, he observed that in East Timor there were no such local provisions, nor any mental health legislation, nor any inpatient mental health facilities that could receive Nahak if the Court were to require it. Thus, Nahak was released until further order, subject to the restrictive measures that were ordered for his initial provisional release pending trial.[124]

Vladimir Kovačević—paranoid psychosis

Vladimir Kovačević[125] was indicted by the ICTY prosecutor, along with Pavle Strugar and Admiral Miodrag Jokić, for the 1991 attacks on Dubrovnik. After Kovačević's arrest and transfer to the Hague in 2003 his mental state was significantly impaired to such an extent that the Trial Chamber did not allow him to enter

[119] ibid, s 109. [120] ibid, s 142. [121] ibid, s 146. [122] ibid, s 147.
[123] ibid, s 150. [124] ibid, ss 4, 162.
[125] Freckelton and Karagiannakis, 'Unfitness to Stand Trial under International Criminal Law: The Influential Decision of the International Criminal Tribunal of the Former Yugoslavia in relation to Pavle Strugar and its Ramifications' (n 52) 714–16.

a plea but ordered him to undergo medical examinations. These examinations concluded that Kovačević suffered from a serious mental illness subsequently revealed to be a paranoid psychosis,[126] which rendered him unable to plead and stand trial. They also recommended that he be offered urgent medical treatment in a Serbian-speaking facility.[127]

Kovačević was granted provisional release and ordered to be treated as an inpatient at the Belgrade Military Academy for an initial period of six months to ascertain whether he would regain his fitness to stand trial. He was ordered not to leave the hospital unless this was part of his treatment and only after receiving the consent of the Chamber.[128] At the end of the initial six-month period and after receiving further medical reports, the Chamber extended Kovačević's provisional release indefinitely. However, the court continued to monitor his condition by ordering periodic medical reports.[129]

On 12 April 2006, the Trial Chamber found that Kovačević was not fit to stand trial, without prejudice to any future criminal proceedings against him should his mental health condition change.[130] The Chamber explicitly applied the *Strugar* Trial test for fitness.[131] All of the experts concluded that Kovačević did not have the ability to meet the required criteria for fitness. The prosecution's expert found that the accused was able to meet some of the criteria but also found that 'it is highly probable that the subject does not have the capacity to cooperate with his Defence Counsel'.[132]

In November 2006 the case was transferred from The Hague to a Serbian national war crimes court for trial in the event that his mental health improved.[133] In the meantime Kovačević remained on the premises of the Belgrade Military Medical Academy subject to the terms of his initial provisional release order.[134] The indictment against Kovačević in Serbia was subsequently dismissed and six days later Kovačević was discharged from the Belgrade Military Medical Academy.[135] Thus, at that stage Kovačević resumed his status of being a free man without having stood trial in The Hague or in Serbia.

When the ICTY Prosecutor was informed of Kovačević's release and freedom, he advised the court and sought more information from the Serbian War Crimes prosecutor, who advised that his office had not known of the accused's release from hospital because his office had continued to receive reports from the hospital during 2008 that Kovačević's condition remained unchanged. The hospital based its

[126] *Prosecutor v Kovačević*, IT-01-42/2-AR11*bis*.1, Appeals Chamber, Decision on Appeal against Decision on Referral Under Rule 11*bis*, 28 March 2007, s 24.

[127] *Prosecutor v Kovačević*, IT-01-42/2-I, Trial Chamber, Decision on Provisional Release, 2 June 2004, 1.

[128] ibid 3. [129] *Kovačević Fitness Decision* (n 8), ss 18–20.

[130] ibid, s 50 Disposition. [131] ibid, ss 30–43, 47, 49–50. [132] ibid, s 47.

[133] *Prosecutor v Kovačević*, IT-01-42/2-I, Trial Chamber, Decision on Referral of Case Pursuant to Rule 11*bis* with Confidential and Ex Parte Annexes, 17 November 2006, ss 92–93.

[134] *Prosecutor v Kovačević*, IT-01-42/2-I, Trial Chamber, Prosecutor's Second Progress Report, 5 September 2007, s 10.

[135] *Prosecutor v Kovačević*, IT-01-42/2-I, Trial Chamber, Prosecutor's Interim Progress Report Public Redacted Version of 10 March 2009, 8 April 2009, s 2.

assessment on monthly outpatient examinations but apparently had not informed the Prosecutor's Office that Kovačević had been discharged.[136] In the meantime, between the ICTY prosecutor asking for additional information and the prosecutor providing this information, Kovačević was readmitted to the Belgrade Military Medical Academy pursuant to court order and pending further orders.[137]

The *Kovačević* case is an example of the difficulties that international courts may experience in monitoring the ongoing condition of an accused person who has been declared unfit to stand trial and is ordered to remain in medical detention in a national psychiatric institution. In such a scenario, the potential exists for national authorities to exercise significant latitude to facilitate the person's release without their standing trial, potentially quite contrary to international court orders.

PTSD

Post-traumatic stress disorder (PTSD) has been pleaded before international criminal courts as a basis for mitigation of sentence[138] and as a basis for a claim of unfitness. In the example of Erdemović the claim succeeded, but in the Gbagbo case it failed because the symptoms were not severe enough to preclude the defendant's meaningful participation in the trial process. In both cases the nature of the condition meant that it was treated successfully and the accused men were able to continue as defendants in the criminal proceedings.

Dražen Erdemović

Dražen Erdemović was a soldier in a firing squad that murdered an estimated 1,200 Bosnian Muslim men and boys in July 1995 as part of the Srebrenica genocide. He believed he had killed about seventy people. He stated that he did so because he had been threatened with death if he did not participate in the executions. He was charged with war crimes, pleaded guilty, and was eventually sentenced to five years' imprisonment taking into account mitigating factors including duress. Prior to his sentencing hearing, psychiatric expert reports observed that he was suffering from PTSD, the severity of which rendered him unfit to stand trial. The court postponed the sentencing hearing for a number of months until his condition improved.[139]

The decision was significant because it established that severe PTSD could render a defendant unfit to stand trial (for a time) and recognised that such a condition could be improved by treatment in detention to the extent that the accused could again become fit for trial.

[136] ibid, s 3. [137] ibid.

[138] These have not been successful; see, eg, *Prosecutor v Sikirica et al*, Sentencing Judgment, Trial Chamber, Case No IT-95-8-S, 13 November 2001, ss 198–99.

[139] *Prosecutor v Erdemović* (IT-96-22-T), Trial Chamber, 29 November 1996, ss 3–8.

Laurent Gbagbo

The issue of fitness was addressed by the ICC for the first time in the case of Laurent Gbagbo,[140] the former President of Côte d'Ivoire who had been charged with crimes against humanity allegedly committed in the context of post-electoral violence in Côte d'Ivoire between December 2010 and 12 April 2011. His fitness was assessed in the pre-trial and trial phases of his proceedings. On both occasions, the ICC chambers found him to be fit. They applied the meaningful participation test for fitness enunciated in the *Strugar* decision and followed in that involving Ieng Thirith.[141] Notably, the Pre-Trial Chamber did not utilise considerations of rationality, as Judge Rapoza did in the *Nahak* decision.

At the pre-trial stage the experts agreed that Gbagbo suffered from PTSD and 'hospitalisation syndrome', a form of institutionalisation or habituation to his environment, but they disagreed as to the extent that such syndromes affected his cognitive and communication abilities and, most importantly, his ability to participate meaningfully in the proceedings. In assessing the opinions before it, the Pre-Trial Chamber placed minimal weight upon a general practitioner's conclusions of mental incapacity.[142] Similarly it placed little weight upon the psychologist's diagnosis that the suspect had an intellectual deficit. It held that the question 'was not whether Mr Gbagbo is at present in full possession of the higher or better faculties he may have had in the past but whether his current capacities are sufficient for him to take part in proceedings against him'.[143] This finding is significant for previously high-functioning accused persons in international trials who have held high political or military office. The fact that such a person 'is the mere shadow of his former self'[144] does not properly address the legal question to be determined.

The Chamber based its conclusions of Gbagbo's fitness on the written report and testimony of the psychiatrist that the hospitalisation syndrome and PTSD suffered by Gbagbo were not serious—he possessed the capacity to understand the charges against him, as well as the conduct and the possible consequences of proceedings against him, and was capable of giving instructions to counsel, as well as of making a statement.[145] Accordingly, the Chamber found that Gbagbo was fit for his 'confirmation hearing' subject to practical measures being taken to alleviate his conditions.[146] He was found fit to be tried a second time by the Trial Chamber based on expert opinions that Gbagbo was no longer suffering from clinical PTSD or hospitalisation syndrome; he had recovered practically all of his intellectual functions.[147]

[140] Freckelton and Karagiannakis, 'Fitness to Stand Trial under International Criminal Law: Current Challenges for Law and Policy' (n 52) 722–24; I Freckelton and M Karagiannakis, 'Post-traumatic Stress Disorder and Hospitalisation Syndrome as Potential Aetiologies of Unfitness to Stand Trial: The *Gbagbo* Decision' (2014) 21 Psychiatry, Psychology and Law 645.

[141] *First Gbagbo Decision* (n 14) ss 49–50, *Second Gbagbo Decision* (n 14) ss 34–36.

[142] *First Gbagbo Decision* (n 14) ss 72–76. [143] ibid, ss 85–86. [144] ibid, s 85.

[145] ibid, ss 87–99. [146] ibid, ss 101–04. [147] *Second Gbagbo Decision* (n 14) s 42.

Physical illnesses

The physical health of a defendant may also impact upon the question of fitness, especially in so far as it affects mental capacity to appreciate the nature of the proceedings or the accused's ability to withstand the physical requirements of lengthy and complex international trial lasting months or years. Often defendants who may be elderly when appearing before international courts are far from the peak of health. Transient physical conditions may result in short periods when the accused is unfit for trial.[148] However, physical illnesses or conditions will usually have to be chronic and quite severe if they are to render an accused unfit for a period of time that would significantly disrupt or lead to the termination of an international criminal trial. Even if the defendant has such a condition, international courts are unlikely to terminate proceedings and therefore permanently (or at least long-term) relinquish jurisdiction over accused persons. Some chronic physical disorders or illnesses may mean the defendant is weakened but nonetheless fit for trial. In these circumstances, these somatic conditions may be dealt with by specified treatment regimens and modified hearing schedules allowing for shorter sitting hours and more adjournments in order to permit the trial to proceed.[149]

Slobodan Milošević—hypertension and heart disease

An example of the adoption of such accommodations occurred in the case of the self-represented accused Slobodan Milošević, the former President of Yugoslavia and then Serbia and Montenegro. He was on trial for genocide, crimes against humanity, and war crimes for atrocities committed in Croatia, Bosnia, and Kosovo.[150] He had two chronic cardiovascular conditions: severe essential hypertension and hypertrophic heart disease. Medical reports revealed that the stress of the trial had so badly exacerbated the conditions that careful monitoring by a cardiologist was necessary such that once his blood pressure elevated to unacceptable levels, an adjournment would be necessary until his condition returned to normal. This resulted in a substantial adjournment and significantly affected trial schedules.[151]

Despite treatment and monitoring by numerous medical experts and a modified and responsive trial schedule, the health conditions of Milošević were not stabilised and he continued to have hypertensive episodes and other complaints.[152] It was possible that this was attributable at least in part to the actions of Milošević. Throughout his detention, Milošević failed to act on medical advice, refused to

[148] *Prosecutor v Théoneste Bagasora et al*, Case No ICTR-98-41-T, Trial Chamber Decision on Nsengiyumva Motions to Call Doctors and to Recall Eight Witnesses, 19 April 2007.

[149] See, eg, *Prosecutor v Karemera et al* (n 9) ss 7–8, 17–19.

[150] See generally G Boas, *The* Milošević *Trial: Lessons for the Conduct of Complex International Criminal Proceedings* (CUP 2006).

[151] *Prosecutor v Slobodan Milošević*, Case No IT-02-54-AR73.7, Appeals Chamber, Decision on the Interlocutory Appeal of the Trial Chamber's Decision on the Assignment of Defence Counsel, 1 November 2004, s 4.

[152] Report to the President on the Death of Slobodan Milošević, Vic-President Parker, 30 May 2006 ('*Milošević Report*') ss 46–53, 57, 63, 65, 67.

undergo recommended tests, and declined to take prescribed medications or varied the dosage.[153] Importantly, blood tests undertaken by a toxicologist and the treating cardiologist revealed that he was administering an unprescribed drug, rifampicin,[154] to himself. This was a form of medication that could significantly counteract the effectiveness of medications prescribed to lower his blood pressure.[155] Rifampicin was not prescribed by his treating physicians but apparently smuggled into prison for him. In sum, Milošević was manipulating the effectiveness of his prescribed treatment. The defendant then used his poor health to allege that he was being deliberately mistreated in The Hague,[156] and made an application to the court to be released so that he could undergo treatment in Moscow. This request was refused by the Trial Chamber, which determined to impose counsel upon him in the interests of avoiding undue delay. Its decision was pending appeal[157] when, two months prior to the scheduled conclusion of the defence evidence, Milošević died of natural causes in prison as a result of a heart attack.[158]

By contrast to cases of feigned or exaggerated mental illness symptoms such as those alleged in *Hess* and *Okawa*, serious physical illnesses are much less susceptible to manipulation because their symptoms can more readily be diagnosed by pathological, haematological, and radiological testing. The *Milošević* case shows that physical illnesses can nonetheless be manipulated through the alteration of medications in order to attempt to stop a trial proceeding. It is therefore imperative that independent expert opinions, testing, and close prison monitoring be utilised in order to forestall such cases, maintain the health of the accused, and permit trials to proceed.

Foday Sankoh—stroke

Even if the defendant's prognosis is bleak, proceedings are unlikely to be stayed even temporarily pending medical assessment. One such example arose in the case of Foday Sankoh, who was the leader of a major rebel group in Sierra Leone and had been charged with war crimes and crimes against humanity in relation to murders, rapes, sexual slavery, and amputations committed by his rebel group.[159] In his initial appearance he was extremely frail and suffering major health problems following a stroke. He was unresponsive, wheelchair bound, incontinent, and unable to sit up or feed himself. His defence counsel sought a stay of proceedings pending further medical investigations and reporting.

The court declined but continued a previously ordered adjournment of proceedings while the accused remained in custody in hospital under twenty-four-hour care and treatment pending medical evaluation regarding the prospects of resuming

[153] See *Prosecution v Milošević*, 'Reasons for Decision on Assignment of Defence Counsel', Case No IT-02-54-T, 22 September 2004.

[154] See Drugbank, 'Rifamicin', available at: https://www.drugbank.ca/drugs/DB01045.

[155] *Milošević Report* (n 152), s 111. See too J Armatta, *Twilight of Impunity: The War Crimes Trial of Slobodan Milošević* (Duke University Press 2012) 427.

[156] *Milošević Report* (n 152), ss 181. [157] ibid, ss 194. [158] ibid, ss 39.

[159] See *Prosecutor v Sankoh* (n 10); *Registrar Announces the Death of Foday Sankoh* (n 10).

proceedings.[160] Less than a week later, on 29 July 2003, Sankoh died and the court subsequently endorsed the prosecutor's withdrawal of the indictment.[161]

Goran Hadžić—cancer

Even if the prognosis of an accused person is very poor or they have a terminal condition, international courts are unlikely to terminate proceedings and therefore relinquish jurisdiction until the accused's death. This is consistent with the consequences which have followed mentally unfit accused such as Thirith. The *Hadžić* case is an example of this approach as applied to defendants with a terminal physical illness.

Goran Hadžić was the president of a self-proclaimed autonomous region in Croatia, Krajina.[162] He was charged with crimes against humanity and war crimes for ethnically cleansing the non-Serbian population of that area. The defence case was well advanced and close to conclusion when the accused collapsed in the detention facility. He was diagnosed with a malignant brain tumour, *glioblastoma multiforme*, with an estimated median survival period of twelve months. While still in the detention centre he began palliative treatment and chemotherapy and radiotherapy. From this time, the trial was suspended because of Hadžić's treatment rendering him unfit to attend trial and his refusal to waive his right to be present.[163] Hadžić was then granted provisional release to Serbia and his family on humanitarian grounds, where he continued to be treated, pending a decision on his fitness for trial.[164]

The Trial Chamber subsequently found Hadžić was not unfit to stand trial.[165] It applied the legal standard of fitness set out in *Strugar*—meaningful participation that requires defendants to have a broad understanding of trial process as defined by their capacities rather than their condition.[166] Neuropsychological and neuro-oncological expert opinions found that the Hadžić's cognitive processing speed was severely impaired and that he would have trouble remembering testimony or processing events in real time.[167] However, the language and executive function areas of his brain were preserved.[168] He was found to understand the essentials of the proceedings and to have the ability to communicate with and instruct counsel.[169]

It was also clear that the Hadžić's condition was inoperable, incurable, and rapidly deteriorating; it was unlikely that he would live to see the trial to its end.[170] Therefore the interests of his inherent right to dignity and the presumption of innocence outweighed the advanced stage of the proceedings, the gravity of the crimes charged, and the interests of victims and witnesses.[171] This led the chamber to stay

[160] See *Prosecutor v Sankoh* (n 10); *Registrar Announces the Death of Foday Sankoh* (n 10).

[161] *Prosecutor v Sankoh*, SCSL–03-02-PT, Trial Chamber, Withdrawal of Indictment, 8 December 2003.

[162] See Bartrop PR (ed), *Bosnian Genocide: The Essential Reference Guide* (ABC-CLIO 2016).

[163] *Hadzic Decision* (n 8) s 7.

[164] *Prosecutor v Goran Hadžić*, Case No IT-04-75-AR65.1, Appeals Chamber, Decision on Urgent Interlocutory Appeal from Decision Denying Provisional Release,13 April 2015; Prosecutor *v Goran Hadžić*, Case No IT-04-75-T, Trial Chamber, Decision on Urgent Motion for Provisional Release Filed on 28 April 2015, 21 May 2015.

[165] *Hadzic Decision* (n 8) s 55. [166] ibid, ss 39–40. [167] ibid, ss 54.

[168] ibid, ss 64. [169] ibid, ss 54. [170] ibid, s 64. [171] ibid, s 65.

the proceedings for three months and order further medical assessments.[172] This decision was appealed successfully. The matter was remitted for reassessment of the fitness and consideration of the possibilities of continuing with hearings on the basis of updated medical reports.[173] The latest reports described a recent and marked deterioration in Hadžić's ability to communicate[174] He was therefore found to be unfit because his medical condition prevented him from communicating with and instructing counsel.[175]

The finding that he was unfit did not lead to the conclusion that proceedings must be terminated. The court recalled that it was not the practice of the ICTY to terminate proceedings due to an indefinite suspension of hearings because of a defendant's ill health. This practice was consistent with the obligation of the Chamber to protect the interests of alleged victims. The Chamber ordered a stay of proceedings in the interests of justice.[176] A few months later Hadzic died and proceedings were formally terminated.

Challenges

Assessing fitness of the accused

The ICTY's decision in *Strugar* developed the jurisprudence from the WWII tribunals and set out what is now the authoritative test for fitness to stand trial under international criminal law. Fitness, although connected with the physical and mental condition of an accused person, is primarily concerned with the person's capacities. The essence of the test is the capacity for meaningful participation. Defendants must be able to exercise their fair trial rights so that they can participate effectively in their trial, and understand the essentials of the proceedings. An evaluation of such matters is made viewing the capacities in a reasonable and commonsense manner.

This test for fitness falls short of articulating qualifications or modifications on the indicia of fitness/unfitness. This is in contrast to the rationality threshold set out in *Nahak*. Thus, the *Strugar* standard gives rise to practical uncertainties in relation to the level of capacity required for a person to be determined to be fit for trial. This has created latitude for decision-making that risks being affected by consequentialism and other unarticulated factors. Some level of qualification and modification, such as 'substantial understanding', 'reasonable capacity', or 'rational ability', may therefore need to be imported into this standard in order to avoid uncertainties.

Assessments of fitness by international courts have been challenging for a number of reasons: the episodic nature of many medical conditions, the fact that some levels of competence may be retained while others, such as memory, may be unacceptably low, the cultural differences in the expressions of mental illness, and the possibility that symptoms may be faked, exaggerated, or manipulated. These challenges can be met by high-quality forensic assessments that are culturally informed and, where

172 ibid, s 66.
173 *Hadzic Final Decision* (n 8) s 8.
174 ibid, s 23.
175 ibid, s 29.
176 *Hadzic Decision* (n 8) s 66; *Hadzic Final Decision* (n 8) s 30.

appropriate, made utilising well-regarded psychometric instruments,[177] rather than being the product of mere clinical impression. In addition, more consideration needs to be given to obtaining neuropsychological assessments, including whether claimed deficits are being feigned. Such assessments have the capacity to generate hard data and to be able to guard against impressionistic diagnoses and prognoses.[178]

Treatment and detention of unfit accused

International courts retain jurisdiction over temporarily and potentially permanently unfit persons after the suspension of criminal proceedings. The discretion of these courts is wide and they are empowered to take those measures that are reasonably open to them to attempt to return accused persons to a condition in which they are fit to participate in proceedings, such as by making orders for on-going treatment and assessment. The interests of justice and of victims in having justice done goes a long way towards establishing a justification for the detention of such persons for a reasonable period of time for the purpose of facilitating their becoming fit for trial. However, to protect the rights of persons found unfit to stand trial, such detention must not be indefinite or punitive.[179] It should be fettered by the principles of necessity and proportionality.

Court-imposed measures may be custodial or non-custodial. However, the reality is that specialised treatments do not exist in all countries, as was highlighted in the East Timor case of *Nahak* and the Cambodian case of *Ieng Thirith*. Even if such domestic facilities do exist, the *Kovačević* decision has demonstrated that international courts may experience problems in effectively monitoring the detention and treatment of persons found for the time being unfit to stand trial and thus in ensuring compliance with both the substance and spirit of their orders.[180]

Thus, decision making about how to deal with unfit accused persons will not only depend upon the legal framework criteria and the factual circumstances of the case, but also upon the actual availability of adequate and secure court-administered medical facilities. In the absence of such facilities, courts may release an accused person from detention, or order that he or she be treated and monitored in an unsecured treatment facility or as an outpatient. This raises the potential for the accused to avoid conviction and sentence without necessarily being confined to secure facilities pending a return to fitness.[181] Such an option is problematic because it provides

[177] See I Freckelton and H Selby, *Expert Evidence: Law, Practice, Procedure and Advocacy* (6th edn, Thomson Reuters 2018).

[178] See P Kirkish and S Sreenivasan, 'Neuropsychological Assessment of Competency to Stand Trial Evaluations: A Practical Conceptual Model' (1999) 27(1) Journal of the American Academy of Psychiatry and Law 101.

[179] See the decision of *Noble v Australia* by the United Nations Committee on the Rights of Persons with Disabilities, 2 September 2016, available at: https://www.ag.gov.au/RightsAndProtections/HumanRights/Documents/Noble-v-Australia-Views-of-2-September-2016.PDF; I Freckelton and P Keyzer, 'Fitness to Stand Trial and Disability Discrimination: An International Critique of Australia' (2017) 24 Psychiatry, Psychology and Law 770–83.

[180] ibid. [181] ibid.

an incentive for accused persons to assert unfitness and thus increases the potential for fabrication, or at least embellishment of symptomatology.

If, as in the *Hadžić* and *Thirith* cases, the preponderance of medical opinion indicates that an accused person's fitness is not likely to improve, proceedings should be suspended indefinitely and the accused released to be treated in a secure, neutral, and adequately resourced treatment facility, generally as an inpatient but at the very least as an outpatient. In this way, the on-going medically appropriate and humane treatment of the accused person could be ensured, their fitness could be continuously monitored, and the incentive to feign illness would be reduced because the accused person would continue to be subject to meaningful restrictions.[182]

Possibility of special hearings for unfit accused

In the *Ieng Thirith* decision in the course of its reasoning about the broad discretions that courts exercise over unfit persons, the appellate court referred to the practice of special hearings and verdicts for persons found unfit to be tried that has been adopted by some national courts,[183] such as in a number of Australian jurisdictions.[184] There is much to be said for the incorporation of special verdicts in the international criminal law process. Such a verdict does not subject an accused to conviction when they are unfit to be tried, thereby preserving their fundamental rights. However, it enables formal findings to be made as to what occurred in respect of very serious alleged crimes. This is important from the perspective of victims and also for the historical record.

The creation of the option for special hearings could play a constructive role in serving the interests of justice, and in particular the needs of victims because it would permit a court to make factual findings about the commission of crimes which in turn could ground a basis for victims' reparation claims. In this regard Ieng Thirith was one of a number of co-accused; the subsequent judgment against her co-accused had the potential to serve those aims without the necessity for a lengthy and costly special hearing for a mass atrocity. However, in other cases, where the unfit accused is being accused of crimes which do not involve other co-accused persons or where there are no other trials which address the same underlying crimes, it may well be constructive in the interests of justice for a court to be permitted to undertake a special hearing, as to whether the acts alleged took place, even though the verdict will not have an outcome in respect of determination of criminal guilt.

This is particularly important if a claim for reparation for victims can only be considered if grounded in findings made by a trial chamber about the commission of a crime under international criminal law. At the ICC, while it may be unsatisfactory to victims, compensation for harm suffered as a result of crimes can only be awarded if such crimes have been found to have taken place and the person standing trial has been found guilty.[185] Special hearings could act as a formal acknowledgement of

[182] ibid. [183] *Ieng Thirith Second Appellate Decision* (n 83) s 40.49.

[184] See Ian Freckelton, chapter 8 'Fitness to Stand Trial under Australian Law'.

[185] *Prosecutor v William Samoei Ruto and Joshua Arap Sang*, ICC-01/09-01/11, Pre-Trial Chamber V(A), Decision on the Requests regarding Reparations, 1 July 2016, 5.

the harm done to victims by a permanently unfit accused person and the first step to reparation. Such a reform would require an amendment to the documentation that establishes international criminal courts to give them the discretion to conduct special hearings in the interests of justice so that any findings of such hearings could be used for the purpose of ordering reparation.

Conclusion

As a result of the *Strugar* decision, the settled standard for assessing an accused person's fitness to be tried in international criminal justice involves a capacity-based assessment rather than one wholly based on the diagnosis of a particular medical condition. The most important evidentiary aspect of such assessments is the expert opinions from suitable professionals. Therefore, it is important that these opinions be based on methodologies that are rigorous, evidence-based, and culturally informed. A more vexed question is faced by courts in deciding how to exercise their considerable discretion as to how to treat accused persons who are fit, yet impaired, or persons who are unfit to stand trial and suffering from conditions with poor prognoses. Decisions with respect to the latter category of accused persons are particularly complex. They create a tension between the fundamental rights of accused persons such as the presumption of innocence, the right to liberty, the right to privacy, and that basic right to be treated humanely on the one hand, and the interests of justice and victims who wish to have the truth legally declared and to pursue claims for reparation on the other.[186] In this chapter we have argued in favour of the incorporation of special hearings into international criminal law and the use of broader forms of expert insight into the issues, including assessments undertaken by professionals such as neuropsychologists.

[186] *Ieng Thirith Second Appellate Decision* (n 83) s 40.

14
Conclusion

Ronnie Mackay and Warren Brookbanks

For readers of this book our aim has been to both inform and to stimulate interest in an area of growing importance in criminal jurisprudence. Our focus has been on providing an international and comparative perspective on the doctrine of unfitness to stand trial. We hope that readers will have gained some insights into the complexities—ethical, clinical, and legal—that inhabit this area of law and practice. Although the relevant rules, at least in the common law jurisdictions surveyed in this book, are of ancient lineage and well attested in both case law and legislation, it is clear that there is scope for further revision and reform. The minimalist prescription of the *Pritchard* test, which has undergirded the fitness rules in most common law countries for over 150 years, may no longer be fit for purpose in a legal and social climate that is much more attuned to the subtleties of mental impairment and its impact on decision-making capacity.

While the book aims to provide an account of the way unfitness to plead is managed within the legal systems of the jurisdictions surveyed, the particular perspective is that of clinicians, lawyers, and policy makers, but not that of the consumers who are the subjects of unfitness-to-stand-trial investigations. While their interests may overlap with some of the themes explored here, they are also distinctive and warrant a much fuller investigation. Furthermore, whereas the book endeavours to describe generic processes and procedures applicable to all offenders, it does not address how such processes might impact particular minorities whose disability, ethnic background, or social circumstances might make them more susceptible to the type of state intervention to which unfitness to stand trial gives rise. In addition, to the extent that the book does address issues of human rights arising in the unfitness-to-stand-trial context, these tend to be in collateral discussions but not as a matter of direct and fundamental concern. Yet these are legitimate concerns which deserve further investigation and which we flag as areas justifying future research and reflection.

In most jurisdictions based on the English common law, but including Scotland, there are three principal strands in determining fitness to stand trial. First, the criteria in establishing unfitness; secondly, the procedure used in establishing unfitness and; thirdly, the disposal options available once unfitness has been established. While there is agreement that these are the three pillars of any fitness inquiry, it is

Fitness to Plead: International and Comparative Perspectives. First Edition. Edited by Ronnie Mackay and Warren Brookbanks. Chapter 14 © Ronnie Mackay and Warren Brookbanks 2018. Published 2018 by Oxford University Press.

also now clear that there is scope for divergence as to the substance of the law governing each domain. Indeed, one of the themes that emerges early in the book is the variability, or as one author describes it the 'disuniformity',[1] of the statutory provisions for determining unfitness that exist across the jurisdictions. While in most of the countries surveyed the determination of unfitness involves the application of statutory rules together with common law reflection, England is unique in that there is still no statutory definition of unfitness to plead as a core concept. This has forced English courts to rely on common law rulings relating to decision-making capacity based on a narrow cognitive model which, at least according to a growing academic consensus, no longer reflects the more sophisticated demands of modern fitness enquiries, and may no longer be fit for purpose. Indeed, as discussion in a number of chapters has highlighted, it is increasingly difficult to maintain that an offender with, for example, active delusions which may, at any point, impact his decision making, may nonetheless be capable of having a fair trial. Yet existing tests for trial competence in a number of jurisdictions, based on a 'low' threshold of competence, still permit severely mentally disturbed and delusional defendants to go to trial where they are judged to possess basic trial capacities.

Further 'disuniformity' may also be evident in the fact that while in some jurisdictions to be unfit an offender must demonstrate a recognised mental disability as the source of the unfitness, in other countries, and under the English common law tradition, certain physical impairments may also warrant an unfitness ruling. Yet it is doubtful whether in New Zealand, for example, an offender whose incapacity was sourced solely in a profound hearing and speech impairment could be assessed as unfit to stand trial according to the statutory test. In New Zealand, a determination of unfitness to stand trial is based exclusively on a finding of 'mental impairment'. There is also the fact that while many modern jurisdictions only provide procedures for determinations of fitness to be made until the stage that all the evidence at trial has been concluded, the common law clearly contemplated that unfitness could be tested at any stage of the proceedings, up until the execution of judgment.

In the first substantive chapter (Chapter two) Professor Mackay outlines the current status of the unfitness-to stand-trial laws in England and Wales, drawing particular attention to the growing disaffection with the current common law test derived from *R v Pritchard* and the indivisibility of the current test for unfitness. Under current rules of practice if an offender fails any one of the current specified competencies, he or she will be found unfit, whether or not he is competent in other respects. Related to this is a concern, expressed in other contexts throughout the book, that an indivisible test of unfitness fails to allow for an appropriate distinction to be made between fitness to undergo a trial and fitness to plead guilty. The more nuanced approach being taken by appellate courts in many common law jurisdictions is now leading to assessments based on the ability to participate 'effectively' or 'meaningfully' in the trial process, not simply by the demonstration of rudimentary trial capacities. In this chapter Mackay also discusses the introduction of 'decisional competence' as part of a new test of unfitness to plead introduced in the law of the

[1] See Freckleton in his conclusion to Chapter 8 'Fitness to Stand Trial under Australian Law'.

island of Jersey, and summarises his empirical research into unfitness to plead in England and Wales. He concludes that the relatively small number of findings of unfitness to plead will not increase until there is meaningful reform of the *Pritchard* criteria.

In chapter 3 Rudi Fortson examines unfitness to plead in England and Wales from the perspective of a practitioner. The discussion highlights the variety of reasons why a person might be found unfit and the challenges associated with accurately identifying unfitness and determining appropriate dispositions. He demonstrates how the combined impacts of statutory intervention, judicial action, and contributions from different experts and organisations have led to the modification of the legal rules and practices affecting vulnerable defendants, in particular those adjudged unfit to stand trial. Different tactical motivations may impel a practitioner to raise the issue of fitness, including an invitation to the prosecution to offer no evidence, seeking adjournment pending recovery of competence, seeking the assistance of an intermediary, or seeking a ruling that certain evidence be excluded. While applications for proceedings to be stayed as an abuse of process, on the grounds of an accused unfitness are not unknown, they are seldom successful.

Fortson notes that failure to protect a mentally impaired or learning-disabled person from going to prison may not reflect simply a failure of the unfitness-to-plead rules, but may result from any one of a host of system-related failures, including current sentencing principles and deficiencies in the penal system, or the risk that an excessively high threshold for incapacity may disenfranchise an offender from seeking an unfitness finding. But because the meaning of 'under disability' has not, in England and Wales, been defined by Parliament, there is scope for courts to elaborate on the test for unfitness. However, Fortson does not consider that matching a defendant's relevant capacities for being found fit with decision-making capacity under the Mental Capacity Act 2005 (UK) necessarily implies the need for a finding of a mental impairment or disturbance, since tests and concepts applicable in a civil context are not always appropriate in criminal proceedings. This is relevant to the discussion in other chapters as to whether unfitness should be based exclusively on a psychiatric diagnosis, or extend also to other physical impairments.

Fortson's chapter also identifies the dilemmas that may be faced by lawyers acting for unfit defendants. There is the risk of unsafe convictions arising from a failure to identify a defendant's lack of capacity and how to accommodate a defendant's lack of desire to raise fitness in anticipation of a negotiated plea to a lesser charge. But perhaps the greater risk is counsel failing to investigate a condition an offender is known or suspected of suffering, and failing to pursue a plea of unfitness to plead, thus exceeding the boundaries of professional discretion and leading to a possible miscarriage of justice.

Fortson's conclusion that the judiciary should receive training to better understand and identify participation and communication difficulties apposite to vulnerable defendants, in order to give proper expression to effective participation warrants careful consideration. The practice implications of unfitness-to-plead investigations, expertly surveyed in this chapter, are increasingly complex and demand the input of highly trained legal and clinical professionals.

The theme of effective participation is also picked up in the fourth chapter by Miranda Bevan and Professor Ormerod. Here the focus is specifically on reform of unfitness to plead in England and Wales, arising from an emerging concern about the treatment of vulnerable witnesses generally. However, as the authors note, the treatment of vulnerable defendants in particular lags behind the priority given to vulnerable witnesses, especially regarding special measures available in the criminal trial process. Building on Professor Mackay's observations, Bevan and Ormerod build a strong case for a radical overhaul of the law around unfitness in England and Wales. While, as the authors observe, the introduction in 1991 of a 'trial-of-the-facts' procedure allowed defendants an opportunity to test the allegation and establish their innocence, the on-going jurisprudence around whether the trial of the facts could only consider the 'external' elements of an offence as opposed to the '*mens rea*' elements, has generated a fair degree of confusion and uncertainty. It is anticipated that these will be resolved when recommendations for reform made by the English Law Commission are ultimately enacted. It is anticipated that these will do at least three things: (i) bring the common law *Pritchard* test for fitness into conformity with modern psychiatric understanding by focusing, amongst other things, on a defendant's capacity as opposed to their understanding; (ii) align the fitness rules with the jurisprudence of the European Court on Human Rights; and (iii) allow for fair procedures at a reconstituted 'trial-of-the-facts' hearing.

Scots law on unfitness to stand trial (in that jurisdiction now known as 'unfitness for trial') differs in some important respects to its English counterpart. In chapter 5 Professor Maher has outlined the independent development of Scots law in this area, noting its focus on the trial process as a whole rather than the particular stage of pleading. In early Scots law the test for unfitness was regularly compounded with insanity as a substantive defence, with the obvious potential for confusion that represented. However, this has proven to be a relatively insignificant concern, granted the infrequency in which the plea in bar of trial was raised in Scotland. Even as late as 1995 Scottish lawyers were arguing whether the test for legal insanity was the same as the test for insanity in bar of trial, an issue that has seldom worried the English common law jurisdictions, but now resolved in favour of the view that insanity and unfitness are distinct concepts. Curiously, initially Scottish courts were resistant to looking at other jurisdictions for guidance that might have assisted the development of Scottish law in this domain. This attitude is changing and Scots law is now more willing to look at law and practice in other jurisdictions in the development of its law on fitness.

Canadian jurisprudence, surveyed in chapter 6 by Professor Ferguson, also prefers the expression 'unfit to stand trial', acknowledging, however, that the law of fitness is concerned with more than 'fitness at trial', but applies to all stages of the criminal process from first appearance to sentencing. From a very early period Canadian fitness jurisprudence assessed whether a defendant had the capacity to consider trial decisions analytically and rationally, particularly where the defendant suffered from delusions. Interestingly, in this regard case-law authority established that an accused was unfit if he would be unable to accurately describe or testify to the motivation behind his actions. Although jurisprudence prior to 1992 left open the question whether an offender could be found unfit where he or she was incapable of acting in his or her own best interests, legislative amendments in 1992 incorporated a new definition of 'unfit to stand trial'. This was a truncated version of the *Pritchard* test, and, according to Professor Ferguson, was insufficiently comprehensive to fully describe the necessary elements of a 'fitness' definition. In particular, subsequent case law limited the new definition to a 'limited cognitive capacity' analysis, rather than an 'analytical or rational capacity' test, indicating a low threshold for a finding of fitness and an indifference to whether an accused makes decisions contrary to his or her best interests, or whether he or she could participate meaningfully in a trial.

For these reasons, it is suggested that Canada is also in need of a comprehensive study, similar to those undertaken in England, and the Australian States of Victoria and New South Wales, to examine the tests for fitness that Canadian lower courts are actually using and the particular extra-legal factors that may be affecting fitness determinations. Professor Ferguson argues that an analysis of what would constitute the 'best' fitness test should include an examination of:

(i) the objectives of the fitness doctrine;
(ii) whether a 'rational capacity' or 'limited cognitive capacity' test best meets those objectives;
(iii) the difference between *capacity to make* and *actually making* rational choices;
(iv) the possible adoption of a functional, contextual test; and
(v) the desirability of a decision-making test similar to that proposed by the English Law Commission.

This recommendation fits well into areas of the need for reform in other jurisdictions, acknowledged in other chapters in this book. It is clear that rational capacity and decision-making *capacity,* in particular, have become highly contested issues in the developing fitness jurisprudence in many jurisdictions and at international law, and stand out as areas where a uniform approach would be highly desirable.

Unfitness to stand trial, in most jurisdictions, has acquired a ubiquitous character, as the issue is tested with increasing frequency by the courts. However, this has not always been the case. In New Zealand, for example, as discussed in chapter seven, the fitness doctrine was largely quiescent throughout most of the twentieth century, and seldom confronted by criminal courts. Major changes to mental health legislation in the 1990s and the enactment of dedicated legislation in the early 2000s targeting mentally impaired and intellectually disabled offenders, and led to the emergence of a more 'capacity-aware' legal culture. This has encouraged investigations of trial competence, especially involving juvenile, and intellectually disabled offenders. A burgeoning case law on unfitness to stand trial, and judicial grappling with concepts like 'evidential sufficiency' in the context of special hearings, decisional competence, and effective participation, has defined the parameters for future discourse on mentally impaired offenders within the jurisdiction. Developments in the other jurisdictions surveyed in this book will, no doubt, assist in informing the future development of the doctrine within New Zealand.

The Australian jurisdictions, discussed by Ian Freckelton in chapter 8 undoubtedly have a more developed jurisprudence around unfitness to stand trial. While the developing doctrine has common law roots in common with other comparable jurisdictions, the principal developments have been since 1958 and the *Presser*[2] decision. *Presser* has informed the development of the fitness rules in Australian jurisprudence and has been incorporated into legislation into a number of states. It has also been adopted as a common law extension of the fitness rules in New Zealand. However, as Professor Freckelton notes, the absence of any language qualifying the level or quality of required understanding in determining fitness under *Presser* has meant that the requirements for bringing a person to trial are low, requiring only an ability to take a 'sufficient' part in proceedings for trial to proceed. In addition, rationality, lucidity and reasonableness, play no part in a test which assesses capacity for comprehension and communication. However, in two major Australian jurisdictions reform of the legislation governing unfitness to stand trial has been a focus of official concern. While the New South Wales Law Reform Commission has focussed on updating the fitness provisions and maximising opportunities for mentally impaired defendant's to contest their involvement in a crime, the Victorian Commission has been more focussed on considerations of decision-making capacity and effective participation.

An increasingly important focus in fitness to plead jurisprudence is upon the values served by the fitness doctrine. These have been identified by Professor Bonnie in chapter 9 as dignity, accuracy (reliability), and autonomy. The dignity interest preserves the moral integrity of the criminal process, while reliability counters the dangers of false convictions and the risk of proceedings against defendants who are no more than mere bystanders to the proceedings. Autonomy engages the defendant's capacity for decision making and, in particular, the controversial notion of 'decisional competence'. This recognises the capacity of a defendant to make specific defence decisions as the court process unfolds. Controversy lies in whether the construct necessarily implies capacity to act in one's best interests, which most English common law jurisdictions have rejected as an element of unfitness to stand trial.

However, what decisional competence does do is recognise the multi-layered nature of decision making in the course of a trial and the variable capacities required for different kinds of decision. Most jurisdictions have moved well beyond a monolithic, one-time-only assessment of trial competence, recognising that the issue may arise more than once in the course of a trial, and engage different degrees of cognitive capacity. The question for future discussion is the place which evaluative constructs like decisional competence have in re-invigorating local tests of fitness to plead, and the extent to which values like dignity, accuracy, and autonomy are actually constitutive of practice in this domain.

Questions of dignity, accuracy, and autonomy are at the heart of the debate as to whether the state has the right forcibly to medicate an incompetent defendant to restore competence, discussed in detail by Professor Morse in chapter 10. As he notes, although in most jurisdictions this is primarily addressed as a mental health

[2] [1958] VR 45.

issue, in the United States it is an important criminal law question which has troubled the courts for a considerable time. The chapter lays bare the tension between the right of an incompetent individual not to be the subject of forcible medication with the state's interest in adjudicating guilt or innocence and in completing the consequences of guilt, such as sentencing and punishment. Although the case is made that what Professor Morse terms the state's interest in 'finality' in criminal proceedings should, if used appropriately after proper procedures to restore competence, sometimes justify the forcible medication of a refusing incompetent defendant, this remains a vexed issue that is not capable of easy resolution. Importantly, however, what this chapter does is to expose readers to a pressing problem which is rarely, if ever, addressed in other jurisdictions. Certainly, as far as English law is concerned those who are restored to competence after a finding of unfitness to plead will often have been medicated under the provisions of the Mental Health Act 1983 without any consideration being given as to the types of argument presented by Professor Morse in his chapter. It remains to be seen, therefore, if and when this important issue will begin to trouble the courts in England and in other jurisdictions.

We have seen that unfitness to stand trial is a cross-jurisdictional issue that is not confined to English common law jurisdictions. In the Netherlands, the jurisprudence of the European Court of Human Rights (ECtHR) and the rights preserved by the European Convention of Human Rights (ECHR) are determinative of how vulnerable defendants, including those found unfit to stand trial, are to be managed. An increase in adversarialism in the Netherlands, in a context previously viewed as primarily inquisitorial, has forced greater obligations on both defence lawyers and defendants in ensuring the fairness and veracity of criminal proceedings. This, as Professor van Kempen notes in chapter 11, requires a defendant who is a 'fully fledged participant' in the proceedings. While reinforcement of the rights and responsibilities of the defence may constitute an efficiency boost to criminal justice, where an offender is not capable of exercising his rights effectively this may result in a loss of quality, fairness, and efficiency.

Professor van Kempen also notes that the capacities for effective participation required by the ECtHR include an offender's physical condition, mental state, hearing, language competence, and intellectual abilities, in addition to a defendant's age, immaturity, and social background. When the possibility of effective participation is in doubt it becomes the state's responsibility to determine how such capacity is to be ensured. This suggests an affirmative obligation resting on statutory authorities to take positive steps to ensure effective participation. Within the Dutch system this may involve both remedial and compensatory measures, including, where appropriate, pain-suppressing medication, interpreters, additional explanations to defendants, and other prophylactic measures to facilitate trial participation.

The jurisprudence on unfitness to stand trial has developed differently in Italy, discussed in chapter 12 by Professor Cadoppi and Dr Celva, where it is described as 'capacity to participate consciously in the trial'. The issue is regulated by the Code of Criminal Procedure, but with reference to particular provisions of the Italian Constitution. What is described is a complex legislative process, which bears little similarity to common law approaches to determining unfitness to stand trial.

The two principal elements of the Italian fitness rules comprise the notion of *eterni giudicabili*—an expression which refers to people who are judged to be permanently non-justiciable—and the concept of 'capacity to participate consciously in the trial'. Within the Italian system, the principal concern is the protection of those, who by reason of 'insanity', are unable to assess the procedural events of which they become the main actors. Within this model a lack of capacity to participate consciously in the trial does not affect the capacity to be part of the trial as the accused; rather, it affects the ability to participate in the trial itself. This is a difficult distinction, which is not easy to grasp and, unsurprisingly, has given rise to litigation in the Constitutional Court. The authors acknowledge that recent Italian experience in this domain has exposed many gaps in dealing with the effects of mental disorder as a trial issue. These are both substantive and procedural, and have resulted in a measure of unpredictability in the application of the relevant provisions. There has also been an acknowledged diminishment in the official focus on the relationship between mental disorders and the criminal justice system, including the issue of unfitness to stand trial. Clearly, there is some scope for Italian legislators and policy makers to learn from the now extensive experience of many other jurisdictions in crafting laws and procedures better able to address the needs of mentally impaired offenders while addressing public safety concerns.

The final substantive chapter, chapter 13, by Ian Freckelton and Magda Karagiannakis considers fitness to stand trial as having a wider significance than the application of statutory and common law tests in particular national jurisdictions. Unsurprisingly, the increasing importance of international criminal law has given rise to acute questions of trial competence affecting a diverse cohort of accused persons being tried in international criminal proceedings for crimes of genocide and other crimes against humanity. At this stage of the development of international criminal law it is fair to say that the jurisprudence of unfitness to stand trial is inchoate, despite court challenges to the competence of defendants at least as early as 1945, with the trials of Gustav Krupp and Rudolf Hess. Early determinations of fitness tended to emphasise the accused's ability to understand the charges and the evidence, apparently regardless of the impact that amnesia might play in the accused's ability to remember events giving rise to charges against him. The trial of Hess was a reminder of the need for counsel and the court to be vigilant in relying on objective medical assessments and personal observations, as opposed to the accused's words or conduct.

It is significant that the decision of the Appeals Chamber in the trial of Pavle Strugar recognised the potential of the fitness issue to affect the fair and expeditious conduct of the trial, in particular the conclusion that fitness is not limited to the question of whether a particular condition is present, but the ability of a defendant to exercise his or her rights 'effectively'. In this regard, the recommendation arising from international jurisprudence to introduce a special hearing procedure into international criminal law processes makes good sense. It would enable formal findings to be made as to what occurred in respect of serious alleged crimes, thereby helping victims gain a measure of closure, while preserving the fundamental rights of those found unfit to be tried. Jurisprudence on unfitness to stand trial in international fora is now well established and as this chapter has demonstrated, offers another context for reflective judicial commentary on matters of great personal and constitutional significance. With this in mind it seems more than likely that litigation will continue in this important area of international criminal law.

As this survey has demonstrated, unfitness to stand trial has become an issue of theoretical and practical importance in both national and international jurisdictions. The various contributions to this book have demonstrated how unfitness to stand trial engages policy makers, and ultimately the courts themselves, in difficult questions of how to balance the rights of impaired defendants not to undergo trial when a relevant impairment prevents them from doing so, with the need to protect the public and ensure that offenders are held accountable. While individual jurisdictions have crafted their own solutions to questions of definition, procedure, and disposition, a range of specific issues have come to the fore requiring further analysis and resolution. These include the permissibility or otherwise of compulsorily medicating incapacitated defendants to restore competence, the desirability of disaggregating the unitary test for fitness, the movement from cognition to decision-making capacity as the focus of unfitness, the utility of the decisional competence construct, and the parameters of effective participation. These, and other concerns relating to the procedure for determining unfitness, present trans-jurisdictional challenges, many of which have been addressed in this book.

Yet despite the complexity of some of these theoretical concerns, the fundamental questions at the heart of a fitness enquiry remain the same. How do we know if someone is capable of conducting his or her defence? Does a person have the mental capacity to instruct his counsel? Can he understand advice given by his/her counsel? Can he explain his or her view of the facts to his legal counsel? Does it matter that he/she may make decisions which are against his/her best interests? Can he or she adequately understand or participate meaningfully in the proceedings? These and a host of other questions define the parameters of the fitness doctrine. In the final analysis, however, it is not a question of simply accumulating a set of functional skills which might together mark the person as competent to endure a trial but, rather, to ask whether there is an autonomous and capacitated adversary who is a fit object of proceedings brought against him or her by the state. Only when this question is answered in the affirmative can we say that a person is fit to plead and stand trial.

Finally, this book has brought together in one volume a range of contributions from different jurisdictions on how those who are unable to participate effectively in the criminal trial process should be treated. While no single jurisdiction offers an entirely satisfactory way of dealing with the unfit to plead, what the differing approaches show is how important it is to recognise that we should endeavour to find solutions to the problems which have long bedevilled the law and procedure in this complex area so that we can adapt, change, and improve the lot of a small group of alleged offenders who are vulnerable and deserve better and improved protection from the rigours of the criminal trial process. If this book, in any small way, achieves this, then it will have fulfilled its purpose.

Index

Tables are indicated by an italic *t* following the page number.